THE MIDDLE ENGLISH *PEARL*

THE
MIDDLE ENGLISH
PEARL
Critical Essays

EDITED BY

John Conley

UNIVERSITY OF NOTRE DAME PRESS

Notre Dame   London

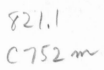

To
My Parents
and
My Wife

PREFACE

THE ANONYMOUS POEM KNOWN TO US AS *Pearl* OR *The Pearl*
was described several centuries ago by Sir Robert Cotton's
librarian, Richard James, in the following uncontroversial terms:
"An old English poem in which, under the fiction of a dream,
many things concerning religion and morals are explained
*(Vetus poema Anglicanum, in quo sub insomnii figmento, multa
ad religionem et mores spectantia explicantur)*. But in the present century *Pearl* became a controversial poem. The notorious
controversy over whether it is an elegy or an allegory was
initiated by William Henry Schofield in an essay entitled "The
Nature and Fabric of *The Pearl*," published in 1904 and reinforced, in 1909, by a revision, "Symbolism, Allegory, and Autobiography in *The Pearl*." Another matter of controversy, one
that has elicited various answers, is the theme. Still another
such matter has been the orthodoxy of *Pearl;* for many years,
in fact, its teaching concerning the equality of heavenly rewards
was said to be heretical. One consequence of all the controversy over *Pearl* is that no "Middle English poem, with the
exception of *Piers Plowman*, has been subjected to more elaborate allegorical or symbolical criticism" (Robert W. Ackerman,
"The Pearl Maiden and the Penny").

In general the selections in this anthology have been restricted not only to essays originally published in periodicals
but to ones published since the 1940's, which are a divide for
medieval studies as for much else. Within these limits I have
tried to ensure that various critical methods and persuasions
have been as fairly represented as possible.

One hitherto unpublished essay has been included, "Some Consolatory Strategies in *Pearl*" by Richard Tristman. The essay by Herbert Pilch on the relation of *Pearl* to the *Roman de la Rose* appears in translation for the first time. Several essays contain some new material, notably the essay by Norman Davis. Only a few of the selections—there are twenty in all—have been previously reprinted, and a number were published in periodicals that are not always to be found even in rather good college or university libraries. Translations or glosses accompany passages or words in Middle English or in a foreign language. Where it seemed worthwhile, cross references have also been added to page references. Further, it is hoped that, thanks in large part to the respective authors as well as to the editor of the University of Notre Dame Press, the *errata* in the essays as originally published have been corrected, just as it is hoped that no new errors have slipped by.

The absence of Marie Padgett Hamilton's well-known essay on "The Meaning of the Middle English *Pearl*" is owing, I should perhaps explain, to a reluctant editorial decision connected with restrictions of copyright. The essay is available, however, in two anthologies, *Middle English Survey,* ed. Edward Vasta (University of Notre Dame Press, 1965), and *Sir Gawain and Pearl,* ed. Robert J. Blanch (Indiana University Press, 1966).

The contents have been divided into three parts. Part one, which is introductory, consists of the temperately elegiac account of *Pearl* by its first editor, Richard Morris; part two, of essays on the general interpretation of the poem; part three, of essays or notes on special topics or cruces. In part two the arrangement is according to date of publication, for such an arrangement allows the reader to follow historically the controversy over the nature of *Pearl*. The arrangement of part three is topical; the first essay in this section, "The 'Heresy' of *The Pearl*" by D. W. Robertson, Jr., provides a transition.

Special acknowledgment is due Robert J. Blanch and the

Indiana University Press for their permission to reprint the essays by A. C. Spearing and C. A. Luttrell, which are included in one of the two anthologies already mentioned, *Sir Gawain and Pearl*. Special acknowledgment is also due Sister Hildegarde Marie Mahoney, President of the College of Saint Elizabeth, New Jersey, for permission to quote extensively from the translation of *Pearl* by the late Sister Mary Vincent Hillman (*The Pearl, Mediaeval Text with a Literal Translation and Interpretation,* University of Notre Dame Press, 1967).

For criticism of a tentative table of contents I am much indebted to a number of scholars of medieval English, namely, Morton W. Bloomfield, Alfred L. Kellogg, Francis Lee Utley, Robert W. Ackerman, Edward Vasta, Siegfried Wenzel, Marie Padgett Hamilton, William Matthews, Helaine Newstead, Robert R. Raymo, Albert C. Friend, E. G. Stanley, Arnold Williams, Charles R. Blyth, and J. Burke Severs. Certain revisions of the contents, all of which have greatly strengthened the anthology, are owing to Professors Wenzel, Vasta, Blyth, Hamilton, Newstead, and Utley.

Among other debts that should be acknowledged is one of a general kind that I owe to J. V. Cunningham. To Charles R. Blyth I owe knowledge of the essay by Richard Tristman; to Fr. Edwin A. Quain, S.J., knowledge of the essay by Bro. Louis Blenkner, O.S.B., while it was still in press. And for knowledge of a privately circulated bibliography of the so-called *Pearl*- or *Gawain*-Poet, I am indebted to the compilers, Francis Lee Utley and Richard Schrader. For the translation of Professor Pilch's essay I am indebted to Heide Hyprath. For supplying translations of material quoted in their essays I am indebted to various contributors; specific acknowledgment is made elsewhere. For assistance with the translation of certain Latin passages I am indebted to Maurice P. Cunningham and Carol C. Esler. For assistance with certain passages of Old French I am indebted to David E. Campbell. In connection with the translation of Professor Pilch's essay I am indebted to his assistant, Joachim Thurow. To my wife, Erma, I am indebted for advice and editorial assistance. To the editor of the University of Notre Dame Press, John Ehmann, I am indebted for saving me from numerous oversights.

Above all, I am indebted to the contributors and publishers for permissions and also for other courtesies.

University of Illinois at Chicago Circle
July, 1969

CONTENTS

xi

PART III

Contents

CONTRIBUTORS

Robert W. Ackerman, Professor of English, Stanford University.

Bro. Louis Blenkner, O.S.B., Assistant Professor of English, Saint John's University, Collegeville, Minnesota.

John Conley, Professor of English, University of Illinois at Chicago Circle.

Norman Davis, Merton Professor, Oxford University.

Sister Mary Vincent Hillman, until her death, Professor of English, College of Saint Elizabeth, New Jersey.

Stanton Hoffman, Associate Professor of English, Sir George Williams University, Montreal.

Wendell Stacy Johnson, Professor of English, Hunter College, City University of New York.

Alfred L. Kellogg, Professor of English, Rutgers University.

C. A. Luttrell, Senior Lecturer, Department of English, University of Leicester.

O. D. Macrae-Gibson, Lecturer in English, University of Aberdeen.

Charles Moorman, Graduate Dean, University of Southern Mississippi.

Herbert Pilch, Professor, English Seminar, University of Fribourg in Breisgau.

D. W. Robertson, Jr., Professor of English, Princeton University.

A. C. Spearing, Fellow of Queens' College, Cambridge, and University Lecturer in English.

Milton R. Stern, Professor of English, University of Connecticut.

Richard Tristman, Member of the Faculty in Literature, Bennington College.

Edward Vasta, Professor of English, University of Notre Dame.
F. T. Visser, Professor Emeritus, University of Nijmegen.

———————————

Richard Morris, first editor of *Pearl.*

———————————

PART I

ON *THE PEARL*, AN EXCERPT

Richard Morris

THE POEMS IN THE PRESENT VOLUME, THREE IN NUMBER [*The Pearl, Cleanness,* and *Patience*] seem to have been written for the purpose of enforcing, by line upon line and precept upon precept, Resignation to the will of God; Purity of life as manifested in thought, word, and deed; Obedience to the Divine command; and Patience under affliction.

In the first poem, entitled by me *"The Pearl,"* the author evidently gives expression to his own sorrow for the loss of his infant child, a girl of two years old, whom he describes as a

> Perle plesaunte to prynces paye
> *Pearl pleasant to princes' pleasure,*
> To clanly clos in golde so clere
> *Most neatly set in gold so clear.*   (1–2)

Of her death he says:

> Allas! I leste hyr in on erbere
> *Alas! I lost her in an arbour,*
> Þurȝ gresse to grounde hit fro me yot
> *Through grass to ground it from me got.*   (9–10)

The writer then represents himself as visiting his child's grave

Reprinted, by permission of the Early English Text Society, from Richard Morris, ed., *Early English Alliterative Poems in the West-Midland Dialect of the Fourteenth Century*, 2nd ed., rev., (London, 1869).

(or arbour) in the "high season of August," and giving way to his grief. He falls asleep, and in a dream is carried toward a forest, where he saw rich rocks gleaming gloriously, hillsides decked with crystal cliffs, and trees the leaves of which were as burnished silver. The gravel under his feet was "precious pearls of orient," and birds "of flaming hues" flew about in company, whose notes were far sweeter than those of the cytole or gittern (guitar). The dreamer arrives at the bank of a stream, which flows over stones (shining like stars in the welkin on a winter's night) and pebbles of emeralds, sapphires, or other precious gems, so

> Þat all the loȝe lemed of lyȝt
> *That all the deep gleamed of light,*
> So dere watȝ hit adubbement
> *So dear was its adornment.* (119–120)

Following the course of the stream, he perceives on the opposite side a crystal cliff, from which was reflected many a "royal ray."

> At þe fote þer-of þer sete a faunt
> *At the foot thereof there sat a child,*
> A mayden of menske, ful debonere
> *A maiden of honour, full debonnair;*
> Blysnande whyt watȝ hyr bleaunt
> *Glistening white was her robe,*
> (I knew hyr wel, I hade sen hyr ere)
> *(I knew her well, I had seen her before)*
> At glysnande golde þat man con schore
> *As shining gold that man did purify,*
> So schon þat schene an-vnder schore
> *So shone that sheen (bright one) on the opposite shore;*
> On lenghe I loked to hyr þere
> *Long I looked to her there,*
> Þe lenger I knew hyr more & more
> *The longer I knew her, more and more.* (161–168)

The maiden rises, and, proceeding along the bank of the stream, approaches him. He tells her that he has done nothing but mourn for the loss of his Pearl, and has been indeed a "joyless jeweller." However, now that he has found his Pearl, he declares that he is no longer sorrowful, but would be a "joyful jeweller" were he allowed to cross the stream. The maiden blames her father for his rash speech, tells him that his Pearl is not lost, and that he cannot pass the stream till after death. The dreamer is in great grief; he does not, he says, care what may happen if he is again to lose his Pearl. The maiden advises him to bear his loss patiently, and to abide God's doom. She describes to him her blissful state in heaven, where she reigns as a queen. She explains to him that Mary is the Empress of Heaven, and all others kings and queens. The parable of the labourers in the vineyard[1] is then rehearsed at length, to prove that "innocents" are admitted to the same privileges as are enjoyed by those who have lived longer upon the earth. The maiden then speaks to her father of Christ and his one hundred and forty thousand brides [i.e., according to the MS.], and describes their blissful state. She points out to him the heavenly Jerusalem, which was "all of bright burnished gold, gleaming like glass." Then the dreamer beholds a procession of virgins going to salute the Lamb, among whom he perceives his "little queen." On attempting to cross the stream to follow her, he is aroused from his dream, laments his rash curiosity in seeking to know so much of God's mysteries, and declares that man ever desires more happiness than he has any right to expect.

[1] Matthew 20.

PART II

2

SOME DEBATABLE WORDS IN
PEARL AND ITS THEME

Sister Mary Vincent Hillman

STANZA 5 OF *Pearl* WOULD SEEM TO INDICATE QUITE DEFInitely the homiletic character of the poem:

> Bifore þat spot my honde I spennd
> For care ful colde þat to me caȝt;
> A deuely dele in my hert denned
> Þaȝ resoun sette myseluen saȝt.
> I playned my perle þat þer waȝt spenned
> Wyth fyrte skylleȝ þat faste faȝt;
> Þaȝ kynde of Kryst me comfort kenned.
> My wreched wylle in wo ay wraȝte.
> I felle vpon þat flory flaȝt!
> Suche odor to my herneȝ schot
> I slode vpon a slepyng-slaȝte
> On þat prec[i]os perle wythouten spot.   (49–60)

> [Before that spot my hands I wrung
> For the care full cold that seized on me;
> A *deuely* grief lodged in my heart
> Though understanding would have brought me peace.
> I mourned my pearl which there was locked
> With violence which swiftly reasonings fought,
> Though the nature of Christ would have taught me comfort.
> My wretched will in woe aye tossed;

Reprinted, by permission of The Johns Hopkins Press, from *Modern Language Notes,* LX (1945), 241–248. All translations from *Pearl* are by the author.

> I fell upon that flowery sward.
> Such fragrance to my senses shot,
> I fell upon a deathlike sleep
> O'er that precious pearl without a spot.]

Deuely (51), which like many other words in *Pearl* has puzzled editors and translators,[1] is probably OE. *deoflic,* "devilish," "wicked." The line reads then—

> A wicked grief lodged in my heart.

The grief of the jeweler was wicked because it was contrary to reason (52) and to Christian teaching (55), and because it was deliberately indulged (56). And it is the jeweler himself who comments thus upon his own culpability. He was guilty of one of the "seven deadly sins," *covetyse,* inordinate love of earthly goods. Walter Hilton, the *Pearl* author's contemporary, writes of this sin as follows:

Covetousness also is slain in a soul by the working of love, for it maketh the soul so covetous of spiritual good and so influenced to heavenly riches that it setteth right nought by all earthly things. It hath no more joy in the having of a precious stone than a chalk stone . . . It setteth all things that must perish at one price . . . for he knows well that all these earthly things which worldly men set so great price by and love so dearly must pass away and turn to nothing both the thing itself and the love of it. And therefore he worketh his thoughts betimes into that judgment and esteem of them which they must come to hereafter, and so accounteth them as nought.[2]

This passage from Hilton might well furnish a key to the theme of the poem. A jeweler, having lost a pearl which he particularly (*in synglure,* 8)[3] prized—prized above his very spirit-

---

[1] Richard Morris and Israel Gollancz (ed. 1891) read the MS, *denely*; C. G. Osgood, Jr. (ed. 1906), emends *de[r]uely*, glossing, adv. as adj., "sudden"; G. G. Coulton (trans. 1906) ignores the difficulty, translating the line, "Dinned in my brain a doleful song."

[2] Walter Hilton, *The Scale of Perfection* (reprint of Cressy's text, 1901), Bk. III, ch. 9, 267 ff.

[3] The MS. *synglure* may stand, since in the poem *-er* and *-ur* words of French origin are not distinguished. Cf. *gyngure,* 43, and probably *lere,*

ual welfare and to such a degree as to make nought of his sins (*devoyde my wrange,* 15)[4]—is gradually won to a conviction of the nothingness (*nozt,* 274) of earthly riches in comparison with the value, the beauty, and the bliss of the immortal soul. This doctrine—held of paramount importance and in origin divine by spiritual teachers down the centuries since Our Lord's utterance of it in the words: "What doth it profit a man if he gain the whole world and lose his soul?"—was a doctrine which the *Pearl* author—if he is also the author of *Patience* and *Purity*—had much in mind. Cf. *Patience* (ed. Bateson), 13-14:

> Thay ar happen þat han in hert pouerte,
> For hores is þe heuen-ryche to holde for euer.

> [They are happy that have poverty in heart,
> for theirs is the kingdom of heaven to hold for ever.]

Purity (ed. Menner) 177-181 lists covetousness or the absence of this poverty of spirit among the faults which may so obliterate the thought of eternal happiness as to endanger a man's ultimate vision of God:

> For fele fauteʒ may a freke forfete his blysse,
> Þat he þe Soverayn ne se—þen for sloþe one,
> As for bobaunce and bost, and bolnande pryde,
> Þroly into þe develeʒ þrote man þryngeʒ bylyve;
> For covetyse, and colwarde and croked dedeʒ . . .

> [For many faults may a man forfeit his bliss,
> so that he may not see the Sovereign—for sloth,
> for boasting and swelling pride,
> violently into the Devil's throat one rushes at once;
> for covetousness and treacherous and crooked deeds . . .]

---

616. (See n. *infra*). The form is found elsewhere, as, e.g., "Synglure persone I doo none name," *Religious Lyrics of the Fifteenth Century* (ed. C. Brown), No. 173. Gollancz (ed. 1891) emends *synglere;* Osgood (ed. 1906), syng[u]l[e]re; Gollancz (ed. 1921) accepts Osgood's emendation.

[4] *Wrange* here as in *Patience* (ed. Bateson) 376: *þat þat penaunce plesed him þat playnes on her wronge* [that the penance would please Him [God] who complains of their wrongdoing].

The word *perle* throughout the poem (*Pearl*) stands some-times for the material gem (1, 12, 24, 36, 48, 60, 1173), some-times for the soul, the pearl of great price (258, 1182, 1192), sometimes for the kingdom of Heaven itself or the bliss thereof (732, 733–739). The jeweler at the beginning of his dream-vision identifies *perle,* the soul, with his material jewel—a natu-ral error, as dreams go, since immediately prior to the *slepyng-slaȝte* (59), he had been absorbed in grief over his loss.

The concluding stanzas of the poem emphasize the theme. Stanza 99 is particularly relevant:

> Me payed ful ille to be outfleme
> So sodenly of þat fayre regioun—
> Fro alle þo syȝteȝ so quyke & queme.
> A longeyng heuy me strok in swone.
> & rewfully þenne I con to reme.
> 'O perle,' quod I, 'of rych renoun,
> So watȝ hit me dere þat þou con deme
> In þys veray avysyoun.
> If hit be ueray & soth sermoun
> Þat þou so stykeȝ in garlande gay,
> So wel is me in þys doel-doungoun
> Þat þou art to þat Prynseȝ paye.'   (1177–1188)

> [Full ill it pleased me to be expelled
> So suddenly from that region fair,
> From all those visions so vivid and dear.
> An oppressive longing struck me into a swoon,
> And afterward, repentantly, I cried aloud:
> *'O perle,' quod I, 'of rych renoun,*
> *So watȝ hit me dere þat þou con deme*
> *In þys verray avysyoun!*
> If it be teaching real and true
> That thou are thus set in garland gay,
> Then happy am I in this prison of sorrow
> That thou art to that Prince's pleasure.']

For 1182–1184, I suggest the translation:

> "O pearl," quoth I, "of rich renown,
> So [i.e., to a like degree] was *it* precious to me
>   which thou didst appraise
> In this true vision."

Hit (1183) refers to the material pearl, which had been deemed of highest value by its owner until the vision-maiden (*of rych renoun*) had explained its nothingness. Lines 1185–1188 may be paraphrased as follows: "If I am to believe that you (the soul) will be thus set in a bright garland (the heavenly procession in which she had appeared to him), then my sufferings upon this earth are right—provided that you (the soul) please God."

The MS. *stykeȝ* (1186),[5] OE. *stician,* may be retained, with its ordinary meaning. The present may be used as future—a not uncommon use in ME., and occurring elsewhere in *Pearl,* e.g., *schyneȝ* (28)—though the verb may be read as present without impairing the sense. Parallels to *garlande,*[6] as I have translated it, appear in Dante. Cf. *Paradiso* X, 91–93, of the souls encircling Beatrice:

> Tu vuoi saper di quai piante s'infiora
> questa ghirlanda, che intorno vagheggia
> la bella donna ch'al ciel t'avvalora.

> [You would know what plants adorn with flowers
> this garland, which surrounds with delight
> the beautiful lady who strengthens you for heaven.]

Paradiso XII, 19–20, repeats the figure:

> Così di quelle sempiterne rose
> volgeansi circa noi le due ghirlande . . .

> [Thus of those eternal roses
> the two garlands circled around us . . .]

Souls are described as "precious stones," *lapilli, Paradiso* XX, 16, and specifically as "pearls," *margarite,* in XXII, 29. Having also the appearance of rubies—*Parea ciascuna rubinetto,* XIX,

---

[5] Gollancz and Osgood emend, *st[r]ykeȝ;* yet Osgood, *op cit.,* n. 735–736, quotes from the hymn of St. Ephrem, "Like pearls in a diadem, children are inserted in the kingdom."

[6] *garlande,* according to Gollancz, Osgood, and G. G. Coulton, is the crown worn by the maiden (205).

4—souls are addressed by Dante as "everlasting flowers"—
perpetui fiori, XIX, 22.

The last stanza of *Pearl* lends weight to the argument in
regard to the author's homiletic intention:

> To pay þe Prince oþer sete saȝte,
> Hit is ful eþe to þe god Krystyin;
> For I haf founden Hym boþe day & naȝte
> A God, a Lorde, a Frende ful fyin.
> Ouer þis hyiil þis lote I laȝte,
> For pyty of my perle enclyin,
> & syþen to God I hit bytaȝte
> In Krysteȝ dere blessyng & myn,[7]
> Þat, in the forme of bred & wyn,
> Þe preste vus scheweȝ vch a daye.
> He gef vus to be Hys homly hyne
> Ande precious perleȝ vnto His pay.   (1201–1212)

I offer a literal translation:

> To please the Prince or be reconciled,
> It is quite easy for the good Christian;
> For I have found Him both day and night
> A God, a Lord, a Friend full fine,
> Upon this hill this destiny I grasped,
> Prostrate in sorrow for my pearl;
> And thereupon to God I gave it up,
> Through Christ's dear grace and love,
> Whom, in the form of bread and wine,
> The priest to us shows every day.
> *He* granted us to be His household servants
> And precious pearls unto His pleasure.

þis lote (1205) looks back to 1201–1204, the lot or destiny of
a Christian being service of God and friendship with Him—a
truth comprehended (*laȝte,* 1205) by the jeweler through the
vision-maiden's teaching. The impediment to this service and

---

[7] For *in,* "by," "through," cf. *in Godeȝ grace,* 63. The usual translation of *in* is "in" or "into." *Myn* is usually translated as the pronoun,
with, I think, an unsatisfactory sense. Imperfect rhyme, here occasioned
by *myn,* "love," is not exceptional in *Pearl.*

friendship—inordinate attachment to the lost pearl—is by the grace of God removed (1207).

Gef[8] is no doubt the preterite indicative as in 174, 270, 734, 765, stating the fact of the Redemption, with which the poem is so largely concerned. It was Our Lord, the jeweler says, Who brought it about that we are not outcasts—as we were after the sin of our first parents (639 ff.)—but are truly His household servants and precious pearls pleasing to Him. The phrasing is recognizable as an echo of St. Paul, Ephesians 2:18–19: "For by him we have access both in one Spirit to the Father. Now, therefore, you are no more strangers and foreigners; but you are fellow citizens with the saints, and domestics of God."

The theory—for many years accepted without question—that *Pearl* is subjective, its author's lament over the death of his two-year-old daughter, receives its strongest support from line 483,

> þou lyfed not two ȝer in oure þede.

If it is remembered, however, that the jeweler's pearl was not of the inferior type found in British waters,[9] but a peerless jewel imported from the Orient, this line and those following it take on a meaning consonant with the interpretation of the poem offered in the present article. "You are an Oriental," the jeweler says to the maiden of the dream vision, still mistaking her for that pearl which had glittered away (*aglyȝte,* 245)[10] from him into the grass. "You lived not two years in our country—not long enough to learn even the ordinary Christian

---

[8] *Gef* here is pronounced a present subjunctive by Gollancz and by Carleton Brown, *MLN,* XXXIV (1919), 42–45, both expecting the conventional mediaeval prayer at the end of the poem. Osgood, also expecting the prayer, calls *gef* (pret.) a "probable error for *gyue* (pres. subj.)."

[9] Osgood, *op. cit.,* p. 54, n. 3, and Gollancz (ed. 1921), p. 115, n. 3 emphasize the fact that the best pearls came from the Orient.

[10] *aglyȝte* (cf. *glyȝt,* 114), derived by both Gollancz and Osgood from ON. *glia,* "shine, glitter"—a meaning particularly applicable to a jewel—is forced by both into the meaning "slip away," as if from *agliden.*

prayers, the Our Father and the Creed. How, therefore, could you possibly be made queen immediately upon your arrival in Paradise?"

The vision-maiden replies to the jeweler's question not directly, but with a discourse upon the vocation of every soul to that high estate (*lere,* 616)[11] which was hers, with a discussion of the sacraments of Baptism and Penance, of God's grace and of rewards.

But why did she not instantly correct the jeweler's error regarding her identity? Why did the poet represent her as almost encouraging the jeweler in his obsession? Why but because the poet wished his poem to go on? As a whole, the poem surely attests the diligence of the author in gathering an abundance of material from Holy Scripture for the edification of his readers. That material would have been completely wasted had he permitted his imagined jeweler to understand immediately the truth about the vision-maiden. If he, the jeweler, had at once recognized her as the soul, all the appealing narrative of the Laborers in the Vineyard, all the pageantry of the subject matter appropriated from the Apocalypse would have been lost to the poet's readers. There would have been no further opportunity for the exercise of that joy of medieval writers, the debate. The theme itself would have lacked the persuasive force lent to it by an incomparable artistry.

For, inspired by objective truth, a maker of beauty out of material already at hand, the author was, in the medieval sense, a true artist. He was, in addition, a theologian conversant with that branch of the sacred science known as mystical theology, and, therefore, clear on the mystical status of his fictional jeweler. The latter is depicted as in what might be called the primary grade of mysticism, the primer class. In the course of the

---

[11] The MS. *lere*, emended [*h*]*ere*, "hire, wage," by Gollancz and Osgood may possibly be the same as *lure* with the meaning "estate." Cf. E. Fenimore, "A Monetary Question in *Gautier D'Aupais?*" *MLN*, LV (1940), 338–342. For *-er* and *-ur* in words of French origin, v. *supra*, n. 3, *synglure*.

vision-experience he was instructed in the *A, B, C* of the mystical life, renunciation. It was through his rash attempt to reach Paradise—where the highest state, the unitive, is enjoyed by the soul—that he incurred expulsion from the vision-land. His act of contrition and of humility followed promptly (1189–1194): "Had I always bent to that Prince's Will, and yearned for no more than was granted to me, and kept myself there [i.e., on the hither side of the dividing stream] as the pearl that was so blessed [i.e., the vision-soul] exhorted me, thus disposed,[12] drawn to God's Presence, to more of His mysteries I should have been led."

Man is wont, he continues, to grasp at more than justly belongs to him (1195–1196). There is such a thing as covetousness even in spiritualities. For this fault he, the jeweler, was cast out from regions that last forever. Thus Heaven is not to be secured by presumption or by opposition to God's Will (1199–1200) but by cooperation. This cooperation is evidenced by those who reject the thraldom, the love-dominion (*luf-daungere,* 11)[13] of earthly goods, purchasing by renunciation of such inordinate attachment to them, that flawless pearl (743–744), eternal happiness. This teaching, as has been already said, belongs to the centuries—even to the twentieth.[14]

---

[12] MS. *helde,* pp. of *helden,* defined in *Prompt. Parv.* "inclino," may repeat the idea of *bente* (1189) or express a common meaning even of classical Latin, "favorably disposed." The form *helde* is the regular preterite. The final *-d,* even if the participle required it, could be dropped here in accordance with the usage of NWM dialect, especially in this poem. Cf. *hope,* 185. Gollancz glosses *helde* as the adv., "likely," Lancas. dialect, though, as he says, it is not found in ME. Osgood emends held[r]. "rather."

[13] *luf-daungere,* Gollancz (ed. 1921) unjustifiably translates "Severing Love," which, he says (*op. cit.,* n. 11) means "God's Will." Thus he quite reverses the sense of the line, and, at the very outset, blurs the theme of the poem.

[14] Cf. Dom Gaspar Lefebvre, O.S.B., *Saint Andrew Missal* (St. Paul, Minn., 1937), p. 1511: "The Duke (St. Hedwig's husband) having died, Hedwig, like the merchant mentioned in the Gospel, gave away all her riches to acquire the precious pearl of eternal life."

3

THE PEARL AS A SYMBOL

D. W. Robertson, Jr.

IN DISCUSSIONS OF *The Pearl* IT HAS NOT BEEN POSSIBLE TO formulate consistent symbolic value for the central figure in the poem which would meet with more than temporary or qualified acceptance. A reexamination of some of the relevant Scriptural commentary may yield a satisfactory value. Usually when commentaries are consulted, the result is a confusing list of possible symbols, none of which seems entirely consistent with the poem.[1] J. B. Fletcher made the Pearl a symbol of innocence, the possessor of innocence, or the means and reward of salvation.[2] More recently, Sister Mary Hillman has said that the Pearl stands for a gem, the soul, or the kingdom of Heaven.[3] It may be shown, I believe, that both of these interpretations are in a sense fundamentally correct. It is stated clearly in the

Reprinted, by permission of the author and of The Johns Hopkins Press, from *Modern Language Notes*, LXV (1950), 155–161. Translations of the Latin passages are chiefly by the author and Maurice P. Cunningham. Translations of indented passages from *Pearl* are by Sister Mary Vincent Hillman, *The Pearl, Mediaeval Text with a Literal Translation and Interpretation* (University of Notre Dame Press, 1967).

[1] Such a list may be found in Professor Osgood's note to lines 735–742, on pp. 82–83 of his edition.

[2] "The Allegory of *The Pearl*," *JEGP*, XX (1921), 1–21, esp. pp. 2, 12, 14.

[3] "Some Debatable Words in *Pearl* and Its Theme," *MLN*, LX (1945), 243 [page 12 above].

poem that the Pearl is among the hundred and forty-four thousand brides of the Lamb in the Celestial Jerusalem.[4] Her symbolic value should therefore be consistent with that of these brides.

In the set of homilies on the Apocalypse attributed to St. Augustine, the virgin brides are said to represent all members of the Church of pure faith, regardless of sex. It is explained on the authority of St. Paul that all good Christians should be chaste virgins prepared to marry Christ; that is, they should keep themselves free of the pollutions of heresy and worldly cupidity:

Hi sunt qui se cum mulieribus non coinquinaverunt, etc. (Apoc. 14:4). virgines hoc loco non solum corpore castos intelligamus, sed maxime omnem Ecclesiam, quae fidem puram tenet, sicut dicit Apostolus, *Sponsavi enim vos uni viro, virginem castam exhibere Christo* (II Cor. 11:2): nulla adulterina haereticorum commixtione pollutam, nec in male blandis et mortiferis hujus mundi voluptatibus usque ad exitum vitae suae absque remedio poenitentiae infelici perseverantia colligatam.[5]

[*These are they who did not defile themselves with women* . . . (Apoc. 14:4). By *virgins* in this passage we should understand not only those who are chaste in body but especially the whole Church, which keeps a pure faith, as the Apostle says, *For I have espoused you to one husband, to present you as a chaste virgin to Christ* (II Cor. 11:2), unsullied by any adulterous commingling with heretics nor bound by an unhappy perseverance in the evil blandishments and deadly pleasures of the world without the remedy of penance to the end of her life.]

It is explained further that through baptism and penance one may attain the purity necessary to a bride of Christ:

Addit post hoc dicens: *Et in ore ipsorum non est inventum mendacium* (v. 5). Non dixit, non fuit; sed, *non est inventum.* Qualem enim invenit Dominus cum hinc evocat, talem et judicat: nam aut per Baptismum, aut

---

[4] Stanzas 66, 73; Apoc. 14:1. The "inaccuracy" of the number in stanza 66 represents, I believe, a sort of poetic license. It was possible to suggest a familiar Scriptural passage or devotional text merely by hinting at it, or by quoting it incompletely. The technique is familiar in sermons.

[5] *PL*, 35, 2437.

per poenitentiam possumus in interiori homine et virgines effici et sine mendacio.[6]

[He adds after this, saying, *And in their mouth was not found a lie* (v. 5). He did not say "was not" but "was not found." As the Lord finds a man when He calls him hence, so He judges him. For either through baptism or through penance we can in our inner man be made both virgins and without a lie.]

Assuming that this interpretation is relevant, we may conclude that the Pearl represents those who are free of heresy and sin and are thus suitable brides of Christ. The validity of our assumption depends upon whether or not it is consistent with the poem. It is obvious at once that the interpretation elucidates the last stanza of the poem, where it is urged that all readers become "precious perleȝ" of Christ. The poet wishes all of his audience to become suitable brides of the Lamb, or, in other words, to prepare themselves for residence in the Celestial City.[7] But it is also obvious that the Pearl is something more than simply a good Christian.

A commentary on the Apocalypse by Bruno Astensis furnishes a means of classifying the various brides in the Celestial procession. Together they are said to represent "omnem Ecclesiae multitudinem" [the whole multitude of the Church]. Their number, however, is symbolic, so that the various parts of the number indicate a division among the virgins:

Merito ergo beatus Joannes centum quadraginta quatuor millia cum Agno stantes vidisse describitur, ut per centum summam virginum perfectionem, per quadraginta vero, omnes peccatores ad veram poenitentiam conversos: per quatuor autem cunctos Evangeliorum observatores, qui quasi quadrati lapides, semper firmi et stabiles in fide perstiterunt.[8]

[Rightly therefore blessed John is described as having seen 144,000 with the Lamb, that by *hundred* might be understood the supreme perfection

---

[6] *Loc. cit.* Note that "lying" is used figuratively.

[7] There is nothing "mystical" about this desire, or about the process of becoming a bride of Christ. To the medieval mind, one becomes either a bride of Christ or a servant of Satan; there is no alternative.

[8] *PL*, 165, 680.

of virgins; by *forty* all sinners converted to true penance; by *four* all keepers of the Gospels, who, like squared stones, have remained firm and stable in the faith.]

Some of the brides have never sinned and are in the highest state of virginal perfection; some are reformed sinners; and some are those who have been stable in the faith. Since the Pearl embraced the faith in infancy at the eleventh hour,[9] she must be placed in the first of these classifications. Other baptized Christians may be "pearls" too, as the last stanza of the poem indicates, but only if through penance they can approach the unspotted condition of the Pearl.

In the course of the poem it is emphasized that the Pearl is "wythouten spot," or, as it is phrased in the language of the Vulgate, *sine macula*. It is significant that all of the brides of the Lamb in the Apocalypse are said to be *sine macula* (Apoc. 14:5). More positively, the condition of being *sine macula* is a necessary prerequisite to a place in the Celestial City. The doctrine is expressed positively in Psalm 14:

> *Domine, quis habitabit in tabernaculo tuo,*
> *aut quis requiescat in monte sancto tuo?*
> *Qui ingreditur sine macula. . . .*
>
> [*Lord, who shall dwell in Thy tabernacle,*
> *or who shall find rest in Thy holy mountain?*
> *He who walketh without blemish. . . .*]

The sacred mountain represents eternal life, or, as St. Augustine put it, "supereminentiam charitatis Christi in vita aeterna" [the towering mountain of the charity of Christ in eternal life].[10] Quoting earlier authorities, Lombard glosses *sine macula* as "innocens."[11] In other words, a state of innocence, or freedom from spiritual blemish, is necessary to salvation.

As an infant who died shortly after baptism, the Pearl may

---

[9] See "The 'Heresy' of *The Pearl*," *MLN*, LXV (1950), 152–155.
[10] *PL*, 36, 143.
[11] *PL*, 191, 168.

be thought of as the archetype of innocence. That is, she represents the most clearly definable extreme of a condition which it is necessary for all Christians (in the medieval sense) to attain before salvation is possible. In general, as Dante observed:

> Fede ed innocenza son reperte
>   solo nei parvoletti; poi ciascuna
>   pria fugge che le guance sien coperte.[12]

> [Faith and innocence are found
> only in little children; then both
> are put to flight before their cheeks are covered.]

In adults, this childlike innocence must be restored, so that the soul is *sine macula*. The *Pearl* poet puts it, "þe innocent is ay saf by ryȝt," a theme which he elaborates in stanza 61:

> Jesus con calle to hym hys mylde,
> & sayde hys ryche no wyȝ myȝt wynne
> Bot he com þyder ryȝt as a chylde,
> Oþer elleȝ neuer more com þerinne.
> Harmleȝ, trwe, & vndefylde,
> Wythouten mote oþer mascle of sulpande synne—
> Quen such þer cnoken on þe bylde,
> Tyt schal hem men þe ȝate vnpynne.
> Þer is þe blys þat con not blynne
> Þat þe jueler soȝte þurȝ perre pres,
> & solde alle hys goud, boþe wolen & lynne,
> To bye hym a perle watȝ mascelleȝ.   (721–732)

> [Jesus called to Him His tender ones,
> And said His kingdom no man might win
> Unless he came thither just as a child,
> Else never more might he come therein.
> Sinless, true, and undefiled,
> Without speck or spot of polluting sin,
> When such knock there at the dwelling,
> Quickly for them shall men unbolt the gate.
> There is the bliss which doth not cease,
> Which the jeweler sought through a mass of gems,

[12] *Paradiso*, 27, 127–129.

And sold all his goods, both woolen and linen,
To buy him a pearl that was spotless.]

The "jueler" referred to is the *negotiator* [merchant] of Matt.
13:45–46, who sold all of his jewels for a pearl of great price.
In the next stanza, this Scriptural text is interpreted, and it is
said in effect that the pearl of great price is the life in the
Celestial City, for the sake of which we are advised to forsake
the "worlde wode" [mad world], or cupidity for temporalia.
The Pearl herself possesses such a pearl which she wears as a
token on her breast:

This maskelleȝ perle, þat boȝt is dere,
Þe joueler gef fore alle hys god,
Is lyke þe reme of heuenesse clere;
So sayde þe Fader of folde & flode;
For hit is wemleȝ, clene, & clere,
& endeleȝ rounde, & blyþe of mode,
& commune to alle þat ryȝtwys were.
Lo, euen in myddeȝ my breste hit stode!
My Lorde þe Lombe, þat schede hys blode,
He pyȝt hit þere in token of pes.
I rede þe forsake þe worlde wode,
& porchace þy perle maskelles.   (733–744)

[This peerless pearl, which is dearly bought—
The jeweler gave all his goods for it—
Is like the Kingdom of Heaven's brightness:
So said the Father of earth and sea,
For it is spotless, pure, and clear,
And round without end and bright of tone,
And common to all who righteous were.
Lo, exactly in the center of my breast its place!
My Lord the Lamb, Who shed His blood,
Firmly He fixed it there in token of peace.
I counsel thee to renounce the foolish world,
And purchase thy pearl spotless.]

It should be observed that lines 733–735 do not represent a
quotation or paraphrase of the Scriptural text, where the Kingdom of God is compared with the merchant. The lines state a

conclusion or *sentence* based on the text. A similar interpretation is given by Bruno Astensis:

Simile est igitur regnum coelorum, id est sancta Ecclesia, homini negotiatori, quoniam sicut ille unius margaritae desiderio omnia vendidit, et eam emit; ita et ista pro amore patriae coelestis et aeternae felicitatis, non solum ea quae habuit vendidit, verum etiam se ipsum servituti subjugavit, ut eam emere et possidere valeat.

[The Kingdom of Heaven, therefore, that is Holy Church is like the merchant, because, just as he out of desire for a single pearl sold everything and bought it, so she also, through love for her heavenly country and eternal happiness, not only sold what she had but even reduced herself to slavery that she might be able to buy and possess it.]

The members of the earthly church, that is, renounce what they have in this world in order to obtain the pearl "aeternae felicitatis." Basically, this is a traditional interpretation of the parable.[13]

The Pearl, who, as we have seen, may be considered to represent the archetype of innocence, wears on her breast the symbol of eternal life which was placed there by Christ. The appropriateness of this arrangement is obvious when we reflect that only through the Redemption may those who are *sine macula* attain the pearl of eternal felicity. The relation between the Pearl and the jeweller's pearl is clearly expressed in the opening lines of Psalm 14 already quoted. These lines say, in terms of the poem, that only those who are pearls (*sine macula*) will obtain the pearl of the celestial life. The Pearl thus not only typifies innocence; she typifies those who dwell in the Celestial City, or, since such folk determine the character of eternal life, she typifies that life also. We arrive at the conclusion, then, that the Pearl typifies both the characteristics necessary to life in the New Jerusalem and that life. The pearl of

---

[13] Cf. Bede, *PL*, 92, 69, where the pearl is the celestial life; Rabanus, who quotes St. Gregory, *PL*, 107, 953. The authority of Gregory, Bede, and Rabanus is certainly sufficient to establish a tradition. Of the passages cited by Professor Osgood, pp. 82–83, not all refer to this parable.

the parable and the Pearl of the poem are two aspects of one symbol.

Perhaps this conclusion may be clarified by applying it to the poem as a whole. At the beginning of the poem, the dreamer is described as one who has lost a pearl. The meaning of this situation is clear if we consider the dreamer to be not the poet but any typical adult. What he has lost is the innocence or spotlessness of childhood,[14] and concomitantly eternal life in the Celestial City. His vision of the Pearl is a device by means of which the poet may impress upon his audience, the members of which are in much the same situation as the dreamer, the necessity for regaining and maintaining a life of innocence. To this end he stresses what is for him the captivating beauty of innocence and of the Celestial City. The love of innocence and that of eternal life are corollary to the first precept of charity, which is a matter of the heart. Only when the will is turned toward charity is the individual capable of a state of grace. The beauty of the poem, which was intended to move the hearts of its audience toward charity, thus rests on a sound theological basis. To most medieval thinkers, it is necessary for the reason to grasp a concept before the will can desire what that concept represents. This fact accounts for the elaborate doctrinal exposition in the poem. The poet wished his audience to understand the concept of innocence and that of the *denarius* [penny] awarded those who realize innocence. He also wished his audience to desire these things.

The symbol of the Pearl may be thought of on four levels. Literally, the Pearl is a gem. Allegorically, as the maiden of the poem, it represents those members of the Church who will be among the "hundred" in the celestial procession, the perfectly innocent. Tropologically, the Pearl is a symbol of the soul that attains innocence through true penance and all that such penance implies. Anagogically, it is the life of innocence in the

---

[14] It should be stressed that this lost innocence is not necessarily sexual.

Celestial City. The allegorical value presents a clear picture of the type of innocence; the tropological value shows how such innocence may be obtained; and the anagogical value explains the reward for innocence. To these meanings the literal value serves as a unifying focal point in which the other values are implied to one who reads the book of God's Work on the level of the *sentence*. The homiletic purpose of the poem to which Sister Mary Vincent Hillman has called attention results from the poet's emphasis on the tropological level. The author wished the members of his audience to learn how to become through Christ's Redemption "precious perleʒ vnto his pay" [precious pearls unto His pleasure].

4

THE IMAGERY AND DICTION OF
THE PEARL: TOWARD AN INTERPRETATION

Wendell Stacy Johnson

I

SINCE ITS FIRST PUBLICATION IN 1864 THE FOURTEENTH-
century poem *The Pearl* has been the subject of considerable
research, theorizing, and dispute: problems of textual emendation, of origin, sources, and above all of symbolic interpretation
have engaged and sometimes vexed scholars for these many
years, not always with clearly positive results. A record of such
engagements and vexations is given by René Wellek in his study
of the poem, and Professor Wellek concludes:

All these debates, we feel, about dialect, authorship, elegy versus allegory, theology, symbolism, etc., though they have been almost the only
occupation of scholarship, say very little about the Pearl as a work of
art. We may grant that a rigid conception of the poem has cleared the
way for an artistic appreciation, but the actual study of the artistic
value of the poem is still in its beginnings.[1]

The difficulty of this, we are tempted to reply, is that there is in
fact no "rigid conception" yet, as Professor Wellek's own survey

---

Reprinted, by permission of the author and of The Johns Hopkins
Press, from *ELH,* XX (1953), 161–180. Translations have been supplied
by the author.
[1] "The Pearl: An Interpretation of the Middle English Poem," in
Studies in English (Prague: Charles University, 1933), IV, 28.

of scholarship indicates. But the intention of these remarks is certainly a good one, and it may be that they do point in the right direction. For it proves almost impossible to investigate the artistic value of the poem without turning back to the subject of meaning. What, after all, is the poetic art other than meaning— pure sound or visual "decoration" or an inconceivable manner without matter? And the very investigation of what might be called "artistic" elements in the poem leads, perhaps on a new and better path, to the central problem of symbolism and sense, the problem of interpretation.

Interpretations previously made can be summed up briefly. Such early scholars as Sir Israel Gollancz, Carleton Brown, and C. G. Osgood agree in seeing the poem as primarily, if not entirely, elegiac, but this idea is attacked by W. H. Schofield, who, in two articles, insists upon its allegorical nature.[2] The Schofield position is maintained by most subsequent writers on the subject, and the fantastic and wholly unwarranted biographies of the poet built up by Gollancz and others to explain his relationship with the pearl-maiden are repudiated at the same time that new and sometimes equally unwarranted readings of the allegory are evolved and published. W. H. Garrett takes the poem to be an allegorical representation of the Eucharist;[3] Jefferson B. Fletcher sees the pearl as a symbol of innocence and of the Virgin Mary, but considers it possible for the poem to be at once an allegory and an elegy;[4] and according to Sister Mary Madaleva the pearl is the poet's own soul, and the poet is a mystic writing his own spiritual autobiography.[5] There are other

[2] See I. Gollancz ed. (London, 1891); Carleton Brown, "The Author of the Pearl . . . ," *PMLA,* XIX (1904), 115–153; C. G. Osgood ed. (Boston, 1906); and W. H. Schofield, "The Nature and Fabric of the Pearl," *PMLA,* XIX (1904), 154–215.

[3] *The Pearl: An Interpretation,* University of Washington Publications in English, IV, 1 (Seattle, 1918).

[4] *JEGP,* XX (1921), 1–21.

[5] *Pearl: A Study in Spiritual Dryness* (New York: Appleton, 1925).

points of view: W. K. Greene believes that the parable of the vineyard workers represents the poet's major theme and that the pearl-maiden is simply a poetic device.[6] René Wellek suggests that the poem's symbolism is subtle and shifting, the pearl coming to represent not only a single pure maiden but the whole realm of heaven.[7] Not inconsistent with this, there is the moderate view expressed by J. P. Oakden, who holds that the poem is about a real child who gains heaven "by innocence through the rite of baptism," and that this innocence is the pearl of great price which she advises the poet to buy: as *Purity,* probably by the same author, has it, "through shrift and penance [the sinner] may become a pearl, [that is, he may] regain his former innocence."[8] Finally, a recent note by D. W. Robertson, Jr., discusses the symbolism of the pearl on four levels, taking it to represent both innocence and the kingdom of heaven.[9] These last three views seem most reasonable, if only on the grounds of the close reading of text which Professor Wellek urges.

This paper, while largely in agreement with the expressed views of Professors Wellek, Oakden, and Robertson, attempts to go further in the examination of specific details than their remarks do, and at the same time to avoid forcing the details into a too esoteric allegory. The result is an emphasis upon a ubiquitous sense of contrast between the nature of heaven and the nature of earth, the revelation of which seems, for our present reading, to be the poem's main purpose. This new emphasis —not a complete interpretation, but the basis for one—depends primarily upon internal evidence, upon a significant imagery and a closely related form and plot.

---

[6] "The Pearl: A New Interpretation," *PMLA,* XL (1925), 814–827.

[7] In *Studies in English,* IV, 17–28.

[8] *Alliterative Poetry in Middle English: A Survey of the Traditions* (Manchester: Manchester University Press, 1935), p. 75.

[9] "The 'Heresy' of *The Pearl,*" *MLN,* LXV (1950), 152–154. Robertson points out that the parable of the vineyard is not heretically misinterpreted, defending the *Pearl* poet's consistent orthodoxy.

II

The plot situation of *The Pearl* is a perfectly familiar one, for the poem is basically a dream or vision allegory in the popular medieval tradition. We are introduced to our poet's subject in the opening stanza, an apostrophe to the pearl which he has lost "in an *erbere*," in a garden;[10] and the next two stanzas elaborate on this obviously symbolic gem's virtues, as well as the poet's pain in his loss. Then the story begins: on a certain festal day in August, on the very spot where the pearl was lost, our narrator falls into a sleep as he is complaining of his bereavement. Quickly his spirit "sprang in space" (IV): and so we enter the second and central part of the poem. The poet wanders in a paradise of crystal and jewels, refreshed by the beauty of this magical realm in which he finds himself, until he comes to a stream, its banks paved with precious stones. It appears that even in paradise there is discontent, for the dreamer longs to cross over to the other side of the water, where the land is even more bright and fair. At this point his desire is only increased by the discovery of a maiden standing on the other side, a pure maiden all in white, crowned and decked with pearls, whom he identifies as his real pearl, the very subject of his plaint. Now at least one level of allegory is clarified, whether the pearly maiden is only a literal person or another symbol. The pearl recognizes the poet (as her "jeweler"), but she chides him for his sorrow: if he loved her, he would rejoice in her present state, although they are parted. She counsels him, if he wishes to join her in that place across the river, to wait patiently, with faith—which he avows, faith in Christ, Mary, and John, now, rather than in the maiden, as "grounde of alle my blysse." The maiden expounds the blissfulness of her present state, calling herself bride of the Lamb, and Queen. At this the dreamer is surprised. Is not Mary the Queen of Heaven? Yes, replies the maiden, she is Queen of

---

[10] The text used is that of C. G. Osgood. Quotations from it are identified simply by line numbers in parentheses.

Courtesy; but there are many Queens here where all are noble. And if this seems strange, it is because the standards of eternity are not those of the temporal world: there is no quarrel between more or less in heaven. St. Matthew's story of the workmen in the vineyard illustrates this contrast between the judgments of heaven and those of earth, the difference between God's grace (manifest in the sacrifice of Christ) and man's justice. Jesus called the children, the pure and spotless, to him; and so this childlike maiden is one of his band of brides in the New Jerusalem. The new city is itself a pure and divinely perfect structure, and it contrasts with the old Jerusalem as God's eternal grace does with man's temporal standards, and as the pearl in her present state does with the mortal "rose" which she was (on earth). The dreamer is fascinated by all that he is told, and particularly by the idea of the new city, the abode of the Lamb, which he longs to see. He is allowed to gaze upon it briefly, then, from across the river; and he describes this Jerusalem in the imagery of St. John's Apocalypse, as a city of precious jewels, with a throng of virgins proceeding toward the throne of the Lamb Himself, the throne surrounded by Angels and Elders singing His praises. This ecstatic and genuinely moving descriptive passage, the climax of the vision, is broken off as the poet returns to the mound where he has fallen asleep. Then, still under the effect of his experience, he declares his fealty to the God "Þat, in þe forme of bred & wyn,/ Þe preste vus scheweʒ vch a daye" [that, in the form of bread and wine, the priest shows us every day] (1209–1210).

This synopsis suggests the threefold division of the poem into a very brief introduction, in the garden (five stanzas); a major section, the vision (some eighteen times as long); and a (five-stanza) conclusion. The consistent use of the same word to end five (in one case six) consecutive stanzas, along with the linking device of *concatenatio,* or the repetition, in each stanza's first line, of this last word from the preceeding stanza, provides a tightly constructed form of twenty five–stanza-groups.[11] The stanzas are unified, as well as distinguished, by this form, which is complementary to a threefold division of the matter. In discussing the imagery and diction of *The Pearl* we will often have a need to allude to both the work's formal structure and its thematic structure in an effort to show how all these elements unite to make a whole. For this is a poem whose nature is at least largely revealed by itself: it is not so much a *secret* allegory as a work of art in which art and meaning are one.

As the following paragraphs are intended to show, the imagery of the poem can in the main be divided into two groups: on the one hand, images out of the world of growing things, images of the garden and the vineyard which are associated with the dust of the earth; on the other, images of light and of brilliant, light-reflecting, gems, free of any spot (dust) and associated with whiteness and with emblems of royalty. These two groups are directly and explicitly opposed to each other, sometimes in the manner of an obvious symbolism and sometimes only in implied contrasts. In either case the opposition is significant both for the sake of meaning and for its aesthetic effect, which contributes to the meaning.

The first five stanzas, which constitute the first stanza group and the first "plot" division, in the *erbere*, deserve a good deal of attention because they introduce the work's basic imagery and because they offer certain significant verbal problems. We begin with the description of the pearl "plesaunte to prynces paye" [pleasing to a prince's pleasure] (this phrase will be echoed and will take on great importance at the end): it is small, round, smooth, and *reken,* noble or radiant. Here, as throughout the poem, there is conscious ambiguity, for ideas of both radiance and nobility are to be attached to the gem. The first eight lines of this opening stanza, describing the unique and precious object, are in dramatic contrast with the final four lines (the

---

[11] See Osgood on stanza construction, in the introduction to his edition.

final four lines are indented, as in all stanzas, by Gollancz), which tell of the pearl's falling into the common earth. The speaker pines for the loss of "þat pryuy perle wythouten spot" [that special pearl without a spot]; and the idea of purity ("wythouten spot" = without blemish) is strikingly opposed to that of the pearl's being now in the (pearl-blemishing) ground. The possibility of an ambiguous reading, again, associates the gem's disappearance with its purity: "wythouten spot" could also mean without location or place. *Spot* in the rest of this stanza group has only this meaning. The phrase is an important one, since *spot* is the key word for this first part of the poem, occurring in the first and last line of the next four stanzas; further, it represents the major and recurrent theme of unearthly purity and brilliance. But it gives some difficulty: the poet, in III, speaks of *þat spot* where the gem was lost, where spices and brilliant flowers must bloom, "Þer such rycheȝ to rot is runne" [where such richness to decay is gone] (26); and if one accepts the reading "wythouten spot" = without place, then it is paradoxical that the pearl's decay should enrich *this spot.* However, the paradox becomes a quite meaningful one for us if we consider that the poet's phrase is intended to signify what the poet *as a dramatic figure* could not know before the vision, and that the very opposition of these two ideas, the expressed one of the pearl's decay in the earth and the implied one of its being without worldly location, is a first aspect of the contrast upon which the poem's construction and meaning depend.

To elaborate upon the imagery of the first several stanzas: we have first the clear contrast of a perfect gem with the ground of a garden, the unique and individual with the common, the pure and shining with the literally earthly. The pearl's "color" is "clad in clot" [clothed in clay]: "O moul, þou marreȝ a myry iuele" [O mould, you mar a bright jewel] (22–23); and so mould and clay stain the jewel's bright beauty. The products of this earth are, themselves, beautiful: in this harvest season ("Quen corne is coruen wyth crokeȝ kene" [when corn is cut down with sharp scythes]—40) the garden spot is covered with lovely flowers giving off a fair fragrance. Yet, even in the midst of this beauty, the poet is not comforted, but longs for the precious jewel he has lost. Earth at its best—an earth which that jewel's decay must, as the bereft man supposes, enrich—offers no loveliness to take the place of the pearl. The images of vegetable life—flowers and fruits and herbs, all growing things—pale beside the image of perfectly pure and simple sphere, the gem *wythouten spot*. For the symbols of life are also those of death: the garden mound is like a grave, the pearl's grave. "Vch gresse mot grow of graynez dede" [all grass has to grow from dead grains (graynez also = pearls)] (31). And the minor fact that this is harvest season adds to a sense of the life-death cycle in this place.

So, using these images of unearthly purity and of earthly nature, the poet must imagine that his spotless gem is mortal, that it returns to the common earth, and he grieves for its destruction in spite of Christian teaching, "Þaȝ kynde of Kryst me comfort kenned" [though *kynde* of Christ showed me comfort] (55) (another ambiguity: *kynde* = both nature and kindness, or mercy). While faith points beyond, the poet's understanding, in this first part, is limited to the spot, to earth which is a grave. The rest of the poem is an extending of this vision (through *a* vision) toward its outer limits, to include and reconcile this world and another world.

Falling into a deep slumber, the poet remains on the flower-covered grave, but his spirit springs forth *from the spot* into space. The region where, by God's grace, he finds himself— "I ne wyste *in þis worlde* quere þat hit wace" [I did not know *in this world* where it was]—is fantastically bright and gorgeous, a wonderland which is much more intriguing to all the senses than the beautiful *erbere* where he has been. The key word in the second stanza-group is *dubbement, splendor*, with the participial form meaning *arrayed*, and the imagery presents transfigured phenomena, the world arrayed in a strange glory: all is shining, shimmering, gleaming, glowing, flaming, bright; the colors have an incredible brilliance; and the very gravel on the ground is pearl. The effect which the poet describes is that of supremely intense light cast upon all natural objects, the basic image being one of *reflected* brilliance. The dreamer sees the *array,* the clothing of that very world he has left, the world of "Þe playn, þe plontteȝ, þe spyse, þe pereȝ/ & raweȝ & randeȝ" [the plain, the plants, the spices, the pear trees, and rows and river banks] (104–105), by supernal light. Compared with this, natural light is dim: "Þe sunnebemeȝ bot blo & blynde/ In respecte of þat adubbement" [the sunbeams are dull and dim compared to that splendor] (83–84). At last, when the wandering dreamer approaches a river, the passage reaches a climax: "I wan to a water by schore þat schereȝ;/ Lorde, dere watȝ hit adubbement!" [I got to a river by a shore that it shears; Lord, precious was its splendor] (107–108). Certainly the river is extraordinary enough. It flows with a kind of music, and it is paved with glowing jewels. According to Howard Rollin Patch, this "river barrier suggests something of the Latin visions [of the other world], and the jewels in the stream and the fragrant fruit remind one of the Garden of Eden. . . ."[12] The land on this side of the river, that is, bears a considerable resemblance to the Earthly Paradise of the medieval accounts. And the stream as a barrier *and* a way to heaven is a familiar means of separating the earthly and the celestial lands. But, as both C. G. Osgood and Professor Patch point out, the *Pearl* poet's treatment of these motifs is not entirely a stock treatment; it is original in several details as well as in omissions of traditional accessories to the vision of paradise.[13] Water could properly be associated with the natural world, with its fertility and its cyclical nature; but this river, shining bright and paved with gems, is obviously allied, too, with the other images, those of spotless brilliance.

---

[12] *The Other World* (Cambridge: Harvard University Press, 1950), p. 190.

[13] See Patch's chapter on Allegory, pp. 175–229.

The river of gems is a common part of the literary vision, but it fits significantly into the scheme of this uncommonly subtle poem.

On this side of the stream is a natural land of fruits and plants and hedgerows, of wonderful birds: a land in which nature is transformed by light, but in which the source of light does not appear. On the other side is the even more wonderful realm of light itself. The more he follows the stream, the more is the dreamer's joy, and yet the more he longs to pass over to the other side. *More* is repeated until the word has an almost hypnotic effect in establishing the intensity of the desire. To live on this side of the water is to experience this ever-increasing desire to cross into greater beauty, greater brightness: the feeling is, in fact, the mystic's wish for union with the perfect, the desire to attain to a state of perfection. That highest state is conceived of aesthetically as pure light; psychologically as *royal:*

> I seȝ byȝonde þat myry mere
> A crystal clyffe ful relusaunt;
> Mony ryal ray con fro hit rere.   (158–160)

> [I saw beyond that glorious river
> A crystal cliff all aglow;
> Many royal rays rose from it.]

In these, the grandest terms he can command, the poet describes the apparently perfect place.

Beneath these "royal rays" sits a bright maiden, like ivory and dressed in pure white, glowing as a light, and "as glysnande golde" [glistening gold]. This maiden, whom the dreamer quickly recognizes, is explicitly identified as his pearl, and she is appropriately adorned with pearls. In the section which describes her, the fourth, *pyȝt* (adorned) is the key word; and the adornment is plainly significant. The ideas of whiteness, purity, and light are associated with her nature, as with the pearls. Now *perle* has taken on several senses: the appropriate decoration, the person, and the "wonder perle wythouten wemme / In myddeʒ her breste" [wonderful pearl without blemish in the middle of her breast] (221–222), obviously a symbol, to be associated with all the lesser pearls and with the pearl-maiden. The poem has passed from the vision of nature arrayed in (reflecting) light to one of a land and a person set in gems and adorned by an "inner" brightness, of which gem and crown are radiant symbols.

When he speaks to her, the bereaved man repeats the theme of his opening lines: he has lost this very pearl, and is now a "joyleʒ juelere" [joyless jeweler]. The maiden replies that he is mistaken, and she proceeds to explain why. Here, in her contrast between the earth-flower and vision-jewel sets of images, we come to a crucial point in the poem's symbolism. The pearl calls this *cofer,* in which she now dwells, a "gardyn gracios gaye" [gracious gay garden] (260); and the symbolic contrast between earthly garden and (heavenly) jewel seems to break down with this fusion. But the similarity between *erbere* and *gardyn* is consciously utilized here. The emphasis is to be put upon *this* garden (as opposed to the first one in the poem) which is a *coffer,* and hardly gardenlike in any literal sense: not an earthly flower—or fruit—garden but a place of gems (*cofer* = jewel case or strongbox) quite unlike the normal kind. It may seem to be forcing a point to declare for a mild irony in the word, but the descriptions of the land across the river, as well as the conjunction of *cofer* and *gardyn,* indicate at least that there is an important distinction to be made between the garden of flowers and the garden of jewels. The maiden's declaration that she was on earth *not* a pearl, but a perishable flower, only strengthens and clarifies the distinction. It is through the poet's imagination that the mortal maiden has seemed to be a gem: the true pearl could not, did not, decay; but the rose, part of the garden-grave world, did. What the poet commenced by imagining—the perfection of his loved one—comes, in the vision, to be true. And so we see that the *erbere* world is one where perfection is an appearance only, while this vision-land, according to the maiden, is the perfect gem's rightful home.

If the earth-heaven contrast is imagined here in the images of the flower and the pearl, it is also implied in the closely associated imagery of natural or reflected light and the brilliance of this land. Only through the nature of that *kyste* or coffer did the rose become more than a reflection of light—become a part of the realm of light, a pearl. Earth's flowering, through *kynde* (both the heavenly *nature* and *kindness*), is proved ("put in pref") a "perle of prys" [pearl of great price] (272). (Again in the same stanza, *kynde* is used to mean both *grateful* or *loving* and *natural:* if you complain about your own pearl's being proved truly a pearl, says the maiden, then "þou art no kynde jueler" [you are no *kynde* jeweler]). Thus the distinction between the *erbere* and the land of light and of brilliant gems is made explicit, with some implied transition from one to the other. Plainly, the antithesis is one between mundane and spiritual realms. The spiritual is infinitely brighter and better. And the jeweler who can rightly judge the nature and the value of a gem (as the poet has failed to do) will see this, not literally but by faith.

Further carrying out the contrast, the poem now makes clear a difference between the earthly body and the soul in that realm across the river:

> Þou wylneʒ ouer þys water to weue;
> Er moste þou ceuer to oþer counsayl;
> Þy corse in clot mot calder keue;
> For hit watʒ forgarte at paradys greue. (318–321)

> [You wish to pass over this water;
> First you must come to another course;
> Your corpse must colder pass into clay;
> For it was ruined in the woods of paradise.]

The significance of "this water" is intensified by its association with the water imagery of later sections. Now, however, the emphasis is upon the two lands, and the idea is extended in the seventh stanza-group, where the key word is *blysse,* and the repeated phrase (in the last line of each stanza) *grounde of alle my blysse.* The earthly maiden (the pearl or rose) has been the ground of the poet's bliss; now her heavenly estate is this *ground.* So, as they can help him to be with her in this estate, are the mercy of Christ, of the Virgin, and of St. John. And, on a higher plane, she espouses "My Lorde þe Lamb" as the unearthly "rote [root] and grounde of alle my blysse" (420). *Blysse* here suggests not only joy but also blessedness. The mortal and divine *grounds* represent the two realms, the one of *stok* and *ston* [stump and stone] in which man is "bot mol," only dust (and where joy's grounds are mortal), and the one in which the (transfigured) maiden, whose blessedness is grounded in Christ, can be made the Bride of the Lamb and be crowned a queen.

The pearl can be crowned because of divine *cortayse,* graciousness (or simply grace, theologically speaking), of which quality the blessed Virgin is the epitome. This is appropriate, this and the association of *cortayse* with the crown and symbols of royalty pertaining to the pearl, in view of the word's origin and connotation: it describes the virtue of the court, of royalty (here, in conferring royalty). And so the images of this (eighth) part are those of nobility and rank; an importance of all the body's parts in the unity of the body (Christ) makes each part noble. The psychological effect of the idea of royalty must be a great one for the medieval poet. Royalty is consistently associated with his images of light and jewelry, and we recall the natural association in the opening phrase "Perle plesaunte to Prynces paye" [pearl pleasing to a prince's pleasure], as we come to think of Christ as a Prince.

The image-structure thus far represents a progression toward the fuller understanding of this symbolic picture: the contrasting impressions of earth and of another place associated with jewelry, brightness, royalty. Now a new aspect of the contrast between these image groups is introduced with Matthew's parable of the vineyard workers. In this, the ninth group of stanzas, bodily labor is opposed to royal reward, and earthly time to divine timelessness. *Date* is used in the senses of *position, limit* ("þer is no date of hys goodnesse" [there is no *date* to his goodness]—493), *season, goal, time.* In God's mercy there is no limit, time, or season (the rich ambiguity of the word here is exploited by the whole passage), while human judgment is based upon these earthly limits. In the vineyard, a place of vegetation comparable with the garden-grave, the sense of *more* is possible (the desire for more reward or for more bliss and beauty, as in the land just this side of the river), but in the divine sense the *more* is freely given: not limited by the standard of time, but demanded by the quality of mercy, which is infinite. So

> Queþersoeuer he dele nesch oþer harde,
> He lauez hys gyftez as water of dyche,
> Oþer gotez of golf þat neuer charde.　　(606–608)

> [Whether he deals soft or harsh
> He pours out his gifts like the water from a dike
> Or gushes from a gulf that is never exhausted.]

God's mercy must always be enough.

Innoghe is the key word in the eleventh stanza-group. The water imagery, picturing divine grace as a never-exhausted fountain, is reinforced with the traditional symbols of the water and the blood: grace given in the form of baptism and of the saving sacrifice. Through baptism the maiden has attained grace:

> Innoghe of grace hatz innocent;
> As sone as þay arn borne, by lyne
> In þe water of baptem þay dyssente;
> Þen arne þay borozt into þe vyne.　　(625–628)

> [Enough of grace have the innocent;
> As soon as they are born, one by one
> They descend into the water of baptism;
> Then they are brought into the vine.]

For

> Innoghe þer wax out of þat welle,
> Blod & water of brode wounde:

Þe blod vus boȝt fro bale of helle,
& delyuered vus of þe deth secounde;
Þe water is baptem, þe soþe to telle,
Þat folȝed þe glayue so grymly grounde,
Þat wascheȝ away þe gylteȝ felle
Þat Adam wythinne deth vus dround. (649–656)

[Enough there waxes from that well,
Blood and water from broad wounds:
The blood bought us from the horrors of Hell,
And delivered us from the second death;
The water is baptism, truth to tell,
That followed the spear so grimly ground,
That washes away the deadly sins
That Adam drowned us with in death.]

When we consider the emphasis upon baptism in this passage, a possible symbolic importance of the water flowing before the crystal cliff comes to mind; the river may be associated with the baptismal water, and thus not only mark the boundary between the land of *reflected* light (the Earthly Paradise) and heaven, but also represent, in a sense, the means of passing even into the realm of light. This river, we see later, is apparently identified with the river of the water of life which flows from the Lamb's throne. And of course the water of life is represented by the water of baptism. Further, there is some precedent for this interpretation. While the river barrier between earth and heaven is a familiar motif in medieval and classical lore, the application of Hebrew symbolism to the Styx is neither rare nor surprising: for one example, in the *Pelerinage de Vie Humaine,* Guillaume de Guileville, using the dream framework, sees the very heavenly Jerusalem which our dreamer is to see, and on his way toward it he must be plunged into the "River of Baptism."[14] Finally, the water as a symbol for baptism is perfectly consistent with later details and with the whole sense of the poem, and, according to this reading, would be the appropriate passage from an earthly to a heavenly state.

[14] Patch, p. 188.

By the means of grace—Christ's sacrifice and the subsequent salvation of the baptized—all is made right, and men are justified. *Ryȝt* is used in both the sense of *privilege* and *justice* in the twelfth group: compare "Þe innosent is ay saue by ryȝte" [the innocent is always saved by ryȝt] (684) and "By innocens & not by ryȝt" [by innocence and not by ryȝt] (696). The state of perfection symbolized by the pearl of great price could be attained either by simple baptism of the child or by the virtue of the man who is faithful in confession and in receiving communion. The water and blood are closely associated, then, with baptism and Eucharist. But *perfection* is a loose term as used here. Professor Oakden speaks of a sinner's regaining *innocence* when he calls attention to the significant first and second stanzas of the thirteenth group, where the maiden first says that no one can come to Christ who is not as morally spotless as a child, and then identifies her own childlike spotlessness—or innocence— as the biblical pearl of great price.[15] But neither word is entirely satisfactory, because of a shift in the symbolism in these stanzas. Because of this shift and because these are crucial lines for interpretation, the only lines which specifically provide meaning for the symbol of the pearl, we may as well look at them a little more carefully. The maiden reminds us that Jesus would have us childlike, "Harmleȝ, trwe, & vndefylde, / Wythouten mote oþer mascle of sulpande synne" [harmless, true, and undefiled, / Without blemish or bit of sullying sin (724–725). To the person with these qualities (or negatives!) the gate of heaven is unbarred; and there, in heaven, is the *blys* which the biblical jeweler sought when he sold all his goods to purchase a spotless pearl: for heaven is like that pearl,

> Wemleȝ, clene, & clere
> & endeleȝ rounde, & blyþe of mode,
> & commune to alle þat ryȝtwys were.   (737–739)

[15] Oakden, *Alliterative Poetry* . . . , p. 75.

[spotless, pure, and clear
And perfectly round, and blithe of temper,
And belonging to all who were righteous.]

And, the maiden continues, the Lamb set it, this pearl, in her breast. Depending on whether the antecedent of *hit* [it] (in lines 737, 740, and 742) is the symbolic pearl of great price or literally the realm of heaven—and it could be either—the large pearl is symbolically or actually heaven itself. So, when she bids the "jewler" to "porchase þy perle maskelles" [purchase your matchless pearl] (744), the pearl-maiden is telling him to buy heaven, the pearl of great price. If she has heaven set in her own breast, it is because a part of heaven is *heavenliness*.[16] Obviously, this purity, perfection, innocence, whatever else the quality can be called, is available to a grown man as well as to the baptized innocent, although it is equated, since the pearl herself seems to be a child, with the spotlessness of childhood. It is common to all who are *ryȝtwys,* righteous, or set right, including both the innocent, who are baptized, and shriven sinners. The pearl means, then, both heaven and the personal freedom from sin which is salvation and heaven within and which reflects the heavenly nature. Both child and adult are saved by *ryȝt,* one by *privilege* and the other by *righteousness;* and the two senses are included in *ryȝtwys,* so that the pearl of heavenliness belongs to both.

The objection that, from an earthly point of view, there must be only one bride and queen, brings about a final and climactic reiteration of the earth-heaven contrast. When the poet calls her *makeleȝ* as well as *maskelleȝ,* the maiden takes the word to mean *mateless* rather than *matchless,* and she replies that she is not without mate: she is one of the brides of the Lamb, described by St. John's Apocalypse, in the New Jerusalem.

[16] According to Robertson ("The Pearl As A Symbol," *MLN,* LXV [1950], 155–161), the pearl may represent both the soul that attains innocence, or the freedom from sin, and life in the Celestial City.

Then she speaks of the crucifixion of her Lamb in the language of courtly romance ("in Jerusalem watʒ my Lemman slayn" [In Jerusalem was my lover slain]) (805), describing Him "as trwe as ston" [as true as stone] (822), a phrase which recalls the symbolic overtones of jewel-stone imagery in the poem. And she compares this old Jerusalem, in which the most exalted was humbled, to the new Jerusalem, where all, like the Lamb, are spotless white, where there can be no such thing as negative, and no strife, all being "in honour more & neuer þe lesse" [in honor more and never less] (852). In the new city of God there is no sense of lesser degree, and this is emphasized by the repetition of the word *less* (in the fifteenth stanza-group).

> "Lasse of blysse may non vus bryng
> Þat beren þys perle vpon oure bereste,
> For þay of mote couþe neuer mynge,
> Of spotless perleʒ þat beren þe creste." (853–856)[17]

> [None may bring less of bliss to us
> Who wear this pearl upon our breast,
> For they could never display a fault
> Who bear the crest of spotless pearls.]

The city, of course, is the heaven we have been told about before, the city symbolized by the pearl. In it everyone has the qualities of the gem: all the maidens in the train of the Lamb are like him in hue (white), are individual pearls (as contrasted with the clay of their earthly corpses), and "Vchoneʒ blysse is breme and beste,/ & neuer oneʒ honour ʒet neuer þe les" [Each one's bliss is full and best,/ And not one's honor is yet ever less] (863–864). In a psychological sense, theirs is a new world. So, externally, the flawless Jerusalem is not a physical city like the old one.

The dreamer can hardly understand what is meant by Jerusalem, and, still confused, asks about the difference between this abode of the Lamb and the old Jerusalem of the Jews. "I

---

[17] Note that Osgood believes this passage to be an interpolation. See his edition, p. xlvi.

am bot mokke & mul among,/ & þou so ryche a reken rose"
[I am amid only muck and dirt,/ And you so rich a radiant
rose]. (905–906). The distinction between his own earthbound
nature and her *reken* one is the reason for his obtuseness, for it
is hardly easy to ascend at once from an earthly to a clearer
understanding. Although he calls her *rose* here, he refers to all
the brides in this place a few lines later as "so cumly a pakke of
joly jueleȝ" [so comely a group of beautiful jewels] (929) who
must have a wonderful dwelling. And this dwelling, fit for such
jewels, the maiden describes: it is a *mote* (city on a hill) both
without *mote* (blemish) and without *moote* (moat) (948),
a city unlike the earthly place symbolized by old Jerusalem; and
the contrast between the two is expressed in imagery throughout
this passage. The antithesis is between crowned and pearl-
decked maidens and earth-stained bodies; the radiant gems and
"mokke and mul," white shining objects and dirt. The heavenly
city, according to St. John, is a place of ineffable brilliance.
Going toward the water's source, the poet sees this city, across
the river from him: it is described as being constructed of gems;
the supreme source of light is here; and all details bear out the
idea of whiteness and brilliance. From the eighty-third through
the eighty-seventh stanzas there is a parable devoted to the
enumeration and description of the precious stones of which
the city is built, all suggested by the Apocalypse. Section
eighteen, repeating the comparison of divine with natural light,
shows the moon itself as *spotty* [spotted] and *grym* [repellent]
beside the stream flowing from God's throne, presumably the
stream which the poet has followed.[18] All beneath the moon is

---

[18] The ninetieth stanza describes the twelve trees which bear the fruit
of life, or time, growing "aboute þat water" (1077). These trees are to be
associated with the earthly and mortal world of the garden rather than
with the city of gems, and they might seem to be out of place here. But
"aboute þat water" is a vague phrase, and the trees probably are intended
to stand on the stream's edge but not in the heavenly city. The idea that
the life of earth proceeds from this stream is perfectly fitting, particularly
if one remembers the association of baptismal water with fertility myth.

blemished; all in Jerusalem is pure. The climax of this, and of the poem, is the ecstatically described procession of virgins, headed by the Lamb Himself, the divine Person, described as a *Lantern,* the source of light. This emotional climax is epitomized in the repeated word *delyt.* And in delight the vision ends.

III

The contrast between heaven and earth is made explicitly, as well as through the sets of images which can be traced through the poem, for it is not only a physical and symbolical one. The repetition of the words *more* and *less,* for instance, and the maiden's insistence that earthly ideas of degree are not valid for heaven, all point to this distinction. In fact, the concepts of degree and judgment are the specific ones in which the poem's intellectual content centers. The idea that there is degree in heaven only in that there is *greater* blessedness is of course illogical: the maiden seems to be saying that the least one in this realm has enough grace that there *may* be superiority but *can* be no inferiority; that perfection, heavenliness, admits of increase and yet that no one can have *less* of it than another. This appears to be perfectly meaningless unless we suppose that the maiden is representing the feelings and attitudes of the blessed, the pearl-like: unlike the person who is aware of inferiority in earthly society, the pearl could have no sense that another's blessedness detracts from her own. In any case, this heavenly negation of negation is difficult if not impossible to understand, and the poet is quite conscious of presenting a paradox when he makes the divine ideas of degree only positive; the paradox is beyond our limited and human understanding.

In the same way divine and human judgment differ. In the beginning of the sixth stanza the maiden condemns, as false and blind, the man who believes only what he sees: God's word, she says, conveys a larger and truer vision than what man's unaided sense reveals. The idea of a vision beyond earth is emphasized in these lines, contrasting the good judgment of an ordinary man with the judgment of God and of the true jeweler. Man judges only on the basis of his erroneous impressions, but God judges men perfectly, with complete knowledge. Thus the two senses of *deme* are played upon, *to deem* and *to judge* or *doom*.

So, in symbol and also in stated contrasts, the natures of the heavenly and the earthly are probed. If we consider the poet's probable intention, to justify a position of blessedness for a person whose loss grieves him, for a soul departed from earth before it could labor long in the vineyard, we find the poem's development perfectly natural. The vineyard is the earth (as the mound or grave is); and according to the understanding of men who remain at work in it, remain on earth, the innocent infant could hardly deserve a place with saints and martyrs or even with those who lived and suffered long: her position must be inferior. But the biblical parable of the vineyard itself refutes this belief, and the poet turns to that parable to justify his faith that heaven does not discriminate against the infant. And how can the idea of what heaven *is* like for the innocent maiden be communicated graphically, poetically? The vineyard parable presents no actual vision of reward, but only the application of divine judgment to earth and to men. Because he needs a positive means of symbolizing the celestial life, the poet uses the most vivid one accessible, the one found in the Apocalypse. And from these two biblical passages—the parable of the vineyard and the Apocalyptic description of the heavenly city—the poem draws its imagery and substance.

Thus the basic image-scheme of *The Pearl:* the vineyard with its vegetation, its cyclical nature, its beauty and fertility purchased only by toil and by death, symbolizes the earthly nature; the city, with its jewels, its perfect hardness and constancy, its brilliance and purity—the very opposite of dust—all associated with royalty and with light, symbolizes the heavenly. But there is a third set of images which becomes increasingly important near the end of the poem: that which includes water and blood.

In the water and blood, liturgical symbols which are, again, drawn from the Bible, the poet imagines the connection between heaven and earth. The link is the saving blood of Christ symbolized in the water of baptism and the wine of Eucharist.[19] It was the baptismal water which brought the maiden to salvation, and this water is shown as the boundary between earthly and heavenly realms; it is the blood of Christ which saves all men, and which, in the form of wine, must be accepted by them as a way to heaven: and so, appropriately, the poem ends with an allusion to the Lord "Þat, in þe forme of bred & wyn,/ Þe prests vus schewe vch a daye" [that, in the form of bread and wine, the priest shows us every day] (1209–1210).

The central symbol in the poem, the pearl itself, can best be understood as a part of this whole scheme. It may stand for a righteous person, for the perfect or *potentially* perfect soul (the poet pledges his own pearl to the Lord), or, in its largest sense, for the kingdom of heaven. Further scholarship in the background for this symbolism may augment these levels of meaning

---

[19] Garrett suggests that the Eucharist is the basis for the allegory of the poem, but a more convincing starting point' for its symbolism, and one which has never been much emphasized, is the rite of baptism. Whiteness and purity have always been associated with this rite; and the poem's specific concern with the fate of a baptized child, as well as its specific mention of the baptismal water which flows from the dying Christ, are tied up with these ideas. The poet's use of both white and shining garments and light for symbols of purity could be derived in part from the use of both symbols in the ancient Catholic rite: the baptizing priest gives the infant a veil, saying "Receive this white garment, which mayest thou carry without stain before the judgment seat of Our Lord Jesus Christ, that thou mayest have eternal life"; and a candle, saying "Receive this burning light, and keep thy baptism so as to be without blame." See "Baptism," in *The Catholic Encyclopedia* (New York, 1907), II, 273. Furthermore, the pearl's allusion to Christ's words, "Of such is the kingdom of heaven," is appropriate to the baptism service; the passage quoted from Mark (10:13–16) is used in the Anglican baptism, and may well have been so used in the fourteenth century. Finally, the poet's naming of John (along with Christ and Mary) as ground of his future bliss might intend John the Baptist rather than Saint John the Divine (in spite of his use of the latter's Apocalyptic City): in a very early sixteenth

and supply a full interpretation—answering the problems of the pearl's possible use to represent the poet's own soul, or the Virgin Mary, or particular qualities—but it must take into account the complete scope of the imagery, of gem, earth, and water images, which makes *The Pearl* a picture of two worlds and the means of transition between them, a vision embracing heaven and earth.

---

century *Ritus Baptizandi,* part of the York manual, the passage John 1:1–14, is prominent, and this passage is full of light imagery connected with John and with the idea of baptism: "And the light shineth in darkness; and the darkness comprehend it not. There was a man sent from God, whose name was John. The same came for a witness, to bear witness of the Light, that all men through him might believe" (1611 version). See *Manuale et Processionale ad Usum Insignis Ecclesiae Eboracensis,* in the Publications of the Surtees Society, LXIII (Durham, 1875). The use of these verses might well extend back to the fourteenth century in various parts of England. In any case, all these associations make plausible the notion of the poet's starting to justify the salvation and high estate of a child saved by baptism with the use of imagery suggested by this rite: the water of life, the brilliant Light as divine symbol, and so on. Then he may have been led naturally into the parabolic and Apocalyptic use of appropriate and allied imagery.

5

PEARL AND A LOST TRADITION

John Conley

> *Felix qui potuit boni*
> *fontem visere lucidum,*
> *felix qui potuit gravis*
> *terrae solvere vincula.*
>
> [Happy is he who has managed to view
> the clear spring of good;
> happy is he who has managed to free himself
> from the heavy chains of earth.]
>
> —Boethius, *De Consolatione*
> *Philosophiae*, III, m. xii

I

THE DISPUTE OVER *Pearl* DEMONSTRATES, GENERALLY SPEAK-ing, that even to scholars the Christian tradition is a lost tradition.

The presumed and belabored issue of *Pearl*—whether the mourned loss is fictitious or real—is, in fact, secondary, as surely will become obvious in the course of this interpretation. The Realists, who from the beginning have been the party in power, generally assume that *Pearl* can be saved as poetry only if the

Reprinted, by permission of the University of Illinois Press, from the *Journal of English and Germanic Philology*, LIV (1955), 332–347, with minor revisions. Translations have been supplied by the author except as indicated.

virtues of spontaneity, concreteness, and pathos be imputed to it. For the *Zeitgeist* has long since revealed that didacticism and abstractness are unaesthetic and that reality is to be identified with naturalism. Thus Israel Gollancz, an early editor of *Pearl,* asserts (*The Encyclopaedia Britannica,* 11th ed.): "Those who hold" the nonautobiographical "view surely ignore or fail to recognize the subtle personal touches whereby the poem transcends all its theological interests and makes its simple and direct appeal to the human heart." G. G. Coulton tells the readers of his translation of *Pearl:*

... it is mainly as literature that I bring this poem before the general public; as the sincere cry of a father's heart at the grave of his infant girl. There are few more powerful pictures in any language of sorrow and love, despair and reconciliation. His child has died before the end of her second year. Mourning one day in the "arbour" under which her little bones are laid, he falls asleep, and sees in his dreams the glorified spirit of his little daughter.[1]

And the readers of *A Literary History of England* (1948), edited by Albert C. Baugh, are told:

There is symbolism, to be sure, in incidental ways in the poem, and the problems of divine grace and the equality of heavenly rewards constitute the major theme for discussion, but there are too many features which are meaningless on any other assumption than that the poet mourns the loss of a real child ...

Viewed as a personal elegy the *Pearl* is a poem of deep feeling, the poet's grief yielding gradually to resignation and spiritual reconciliation.[2]

---

[1] *Pearl Rendered into Modern English* (London, 1906), pp. vii–viii. Coulton's essay "In Defence of *The Pearl,*" *MLR,* II (1906), 39–43, is said by Albert C. Baugh (*A Literary History of England* [New York, 1948], p. 234, footnote) to have disposed of W. H. Schofield's "objections to an autobiographical interpretation."

[2] P. 235. The latest editor of *Pearl,* E. V. Gordon, essays a compromise (*Pearl* [Oxford, 1953], pp. xviii–xix). Additional realists of the elegiac persuasion are R. Morris, the original editor of *Pearl;* B. ten Brink, C. G. Osgood (another editor of *Pearl*), J. E. Wells, A. S. Cook, K. Sisam, O. Cargill, M. Schlauch, J. P. Oakden, and H. H. Glunz (see also the list provided by Schofield, "The Nature and Fabric of *The Pearl,*" *PMLA,* XIX [1904], 154–155).

The realist interpretation even appears in the studies of *Pearl* by René Wellek, Sister M. Madeleva, and W. K. Greene. Although Wellek denies that *Pearl* is an elegy, its purpose being, he asserts, to demonstrate the (quite orthodox) doctrine of the beatification of baptized infants, he believes that a real child is being mourned.[3] In *Pearl: a Study in Spiritual Dryness* (New York and London, 1925), Sister M. Madeleva constructs, despite an animadversion on hypothetical biographies,[4] the autobiography of an anonymous monk. Greene's "parabolical" interpretation assumes that the narrator and the author are identical.[5] Further (*ibid.*):

. . . I am unwilling to reject all reality by denying the emotion of the poet and thus reducing him to the level of an architect, who coldly and mechanically constructs an amazingly symbolical structure without shedding a tear—or, what is worse, sheds tears over a pure abstraction, which has no relation to his personal experience.

To date, the symbolic interpretation[6] has also been weakly argued. No wonder the privilege of private interpretation was granted, not long ago, by a Continental scholar, to all readers of *Pearl*.[7] The father of the symbolic interpretation, W. H. Schofield, knew where the looking should be done—in the Christian tradition—but unfortunately he failed to correlate the obvious.[8]

To my knowledge, only one general interpretation of *Pearl*

[3] "*The Pearl:* An Interpretation of the Middle English Poem," *Studies in English,* IV, Charles University (Prague, 1933), 5–33.

[4] See p. 2 of her study.

[5] "*The Pearl*—a New Interpretation," *PMLA,* XL (1925), 826.

[6] Perhaps one should note that the symbolic interpretation does not necessarily deny to *Pearl* a realistic occasion.

[7] Fernand Mossé, *A Handbook of Middle English,* tr. James A. Walker (Baltimore, 1952), p. 248: "each reader is at liberty to give" *Pearl* "the interpretation which corresponds with his own temper[a]ment." The original French edition was published in 1949.

[8] Schofield's interpretation is to be found in two long essays, published in 1904 and 1909 ("The Nature and Fabric of *The Pearl*," *PMLA,* XIX, 154–215, and "Symbolism, Allegory, and Autobiography in *The Pearl*," *ibid.,* XXIV, 585–675). Out of *pietas* I should have liked to dedicate this essay to the memory of Professor Schofield.

approximates correctness, Sister Mary Vincent Hillman's, published in *Modern Language Notes* (April, 1945), under the title "Some Debatable Words in *Pearl* and Its Theme."[9] Sister Vincent sees *Pearl* as a wholly symbolic poem dealing with the "*A, B, C of* of the mystical life, renunciation":[10]

An [imaginary] jeweler, having lost a pearl which he particularly . . . prized—prized above his very spiritual welfare and to such a degree as to make nought of his sins . . . is gradually won to a conviction of the nothingness . . . of earthly riches in comparison with the value, the beauty, and the bliss of the immortal soul.[11]

The jeweler "was guilty of one of the 'seven deadly sins,' *covetyse,* inordinate love of earthly goods."[12] One merit of Sister Vincent's interpretation is that a crucial datum of *Pearl* is at least partially explained. This datum is the presentation of the

[9] LX, 241–248. Shortly after my interpretation was written, Wendell S. Johnson's appeared: "The Imagery and Diction of *The Pearl:* Toward an Interpretation," *ELH,* XX, 3 (Sept., 1953), 161–180. Mr. Johnson's concern is with "a ubiquitous sense of contrast between the nature of heaven and the nature of earth, the revelation of which seems, for our present reading, to be the poem's main purpose" (p. 163) [page 29 above]. Unfortunately, the details of Johnson's interpretation are largely unsatisfactory. Concerning, for example, the symbolism of the pearl, we are left with a rather unhelpful conclusion: the pearl "may stand for a righteous person, for the perfect or *potentially* perfect soul (the poet pledges his own pearl to the Lord), or, in its largest sense, for the kingdom of heaven" (p. 179) [page 48 above]. Earlier (p. 171) [page 39 above] Johnson observes, correctly in part: the "earthly maiden (the pearl or rose) has been the ground of the poet's bliss; now her heavenly estate is this *ground.*" Seemingly, the "poem's main purpose" is not identical with "the poet's probable intention, to justify a position of blessedness for a person whose loss grieves him, for a soul departed from earth before it could labor long in the vineyard . . ." (p. 178) [page 47 above]. Johnson is receptive to a baptismal interpretation; we are told, for example, in a footnote: "Garrett suggests that the Eucharist is the basis for the allegory of the poem, but a more convincing starting point for its symbolism, and one which has never been much emphasized, is the rite of baptism" (p. 179) [page 48 above]. Johnson's analysis of key words is a welcome affirmation, at times wayward, of *Pearl's* subtlety.

[10] *Ibid.,* p. 247 [page 17 above]. I have adapted this quotation.

[11] *Ibid.,* pp. 242–243 [pages 10–11 above].

[12] *Ibid.,* p. 242 [page 10 above].

narrator's grief as reprehensible. In the words of the narrator's preceptress:[13]

> 'Bot, jueler gente if þou schal lose
> Þy ioy for a gemme þat þe watȝ lef,
> Me þynk þe put in a mad porpose,
> And busyeȝ þe aboute a raysoun bref;
> For þat þou lesteȝ watȝ bot a rose
> Þat flowred and fayled as kynde hyt gef.'   (265–270)

[But, courteous jeweler, if you would lose
your joy for a gem that was dear to you,
it seems to me that you are bent on madness
and busy yourself about a passing matter,
for what you lost was only a rose
that flowered and withered in accordance with nature.]

Regrettably, Sister Vincent's interpretation succumbs to a kind of fundamentalism. The lost pearl, despite the consequences, is taken literally; thus the appearance of the beatified virgin, the narrator's preceptress, becomes a factitious crux, one that Sister Vincent would explain by resorting to a so-called "vision-soul," a concept that seems to derive from Sister Madeleva's study.[14] By forcing the meaning of "deuoyde my wrange" (15), Sister Vincent apparently turns the narrator into a hardened sinner ("and to such a degree as to make nought of his sins").[15] Renunciation, as perhaps should be remarked, seems to be thought of as theology's private property. Finally, the virgin's failure to correct "instantly the jeweler's [alleged] error regarding her identity" is explained, as is much else, at the

---

[13] The text of *Pearl* used throughout this essay is that of E. V. Gordon's edition.

[14] See *Pearl*, p. 192. The concept of the "vision-soul" is a kind of inverted parody of the hypostatic union.

[15] Of course, in a general sense, mortal sin may certainly be said to imply hardening of the heart. I do not believe that Sister Vincent is concerned with this sort of distinction, however. Sister Vincent also forces "deuely" (51) to mean " 'devilish,' 'wicked' " ("Some Debatable Words," p. 242) [page 10 above].

expense of the poem and of the poet (*ibid.*, p. 247) [page 16 above]:

As a whole, the poem surely attests the diligence of the author in gathering an abundance of material from Holy Scripture for the edification of his readers. That material would have been completely wasted had he permitted his imagined jeweler to understand immediately the truth about the vision-maiden. If he, the jeweler, had at once recognized her as the soul, all the appealing narrative of the Laborers in the Vineyard, all the pageantry of the subject matter appropriated from the *Apocalypse* would have been lost to the poet's readers. There would have been no further opportunity for the exercise of that joy of mediaeval writers, the debate. The theme itself would have lacked the persuasive force lent to it by an incomparable artistry.

II

A desideratum in the dispute over *Pearl* is a rule book, so to speak. Such a book should contain at least these principles; inevitably, they flow into each other.

First, the principle of coherence. Strictly speaking, no general interpretation of *Pearl* hitherto proposed is coherent, for even the one that allows this principle something like its due,[16] Greene's, does not account for all the essential data. His interpretation of the lost pearl, for example, is meliorative: "divine grace . . . gloriously manifested in the personified Pearl."[17] The incoherence of Schofield's interpretation has already been demonstrated by others, notably by Coulton and Greene;[18] and there seems little need to fashion a series of waxworks.

Second, the principle of probability. Naturalistic interpreta-

---

[16] Gordon's comments on this principle are markedly ineffectual (*Pearl*, especially p. xii). In "*The Pearl* as a Symbol" D. W. Robertson, Jr., asserts that what the narrator "has lost is the innocence or spotlessness of childhood and concomitantly eternal life in the Celestial City" (*MLN*, LXV, 3 [March, 1950], 160) [page 25 above].

[17] "New Interpretation," p. 826.

[18] "In Defence of *The Pearl*," p. 42 especially, and "New Interpretation," pp. 824–825 especially.

tions of *Pearl* are suspect before this principle.[19] The radical anachronism to which *Pearl* has been subjected is the premise, part of the marrow of latter-day Western man, that human love cannot be other than laudable: the Unpardonable Sin is defined for us at the foot of Graylock, in "Ethan Brand." The narrator of *Pearl,* not without some ineptness on the part of the author,[20] is accordingly thought to exemplify a model father who, in decorous self-abandon, is selflessly concerned about the welfare of his daughter. He is granted assurance in either of two forms: (1) his daughter is not dead after all; (2) though too young to have gained any merit, she is nevertheless gloriously saved (and, some would add, heretically rewarded[21]). One witness is E. V. Gordon, in his edition of *Pearl* (1953):

The final consolation of the father was not to be found in the recovery of a beloved daughter, as if death had not after all occurred or had no significance, but in the knowledge that she was redeemed and saved and had become a queen in Heaven. Only by resignation to the will of God, and through death, could he rejoin her.[22]

A second anachronism, scarcely any less radical than the first, is the premise that the lost pearl must symbolize primarily some sort of sinlessness: scholarly discipline is routed by provincialism and sentimentality. Schofield is thus able to assert: "our analysis shows that the symbolism of the poem centres on the fundamental conception of the pearl as 'immaculate.'"[23] In the

---

[19] Of pertinence here is Étienne Gilson's "Le moyen âge et le naturalisme antique," *Héloïse et Abelard* (Paris, 1938), pp. 183–224.

[20] See, for example, Stanley P. Chase, *The Pearl* (New York, 1932), p. lvi, and E. V. Gordon, *Pearl,* p. xli.

[21] The charge of heresy against *Pearl* is another scholarly aberration, by now moribund (in my opinion, James Sledd gave the *coup de grâce* in "Three Textual Notes on Fourteenth-Century Poetry," *MLN,* LV [1940], 381). Let us hope that this charge will lie in an unmarked grave.

[22] P. xviii.

[23] "Symbolism," p. 623. E. V. Gordon (*Pearl,* p. xxviii) provides this gloss: "The poet of *Pearl* uses the pearl symbol variously, but always with traditional significations, and to express the attributes of purity and preciousness. The poem begins with praise of the poet's *precios perle*

Christian tradition *pearl* has a number of symbolic meanings, as both Osgood[24] and Schofield[25] have shown. In the instance of *Pearl* beauty and preciousness are primarily ascribed to the lost pearl; he has lost, the narrator tells us in the opening stanza, a matchless pearl:

> Perle, plesaunte to prynces paye
> To clanly clos in golde so clere,
> Oute of oryent, I hardyly saye,
> Ne proued I neuer her precios pere.
> So rounde, so reken in vche araye,
> So smal, so smoþe her sydeʒ were,
> Quere-so-euer I jugged gemmeʒ gaye,
> I sette hyr sengeley in synglere.
> Allas! I leste hyr in on erbere;
> Þurʒ gresse to grounde hit fro me yot.
> I dewyne fordolked of luf-daungere
> Of þat pryuy perle wythouten spot.   (1–12)

> [Pearl, pleasing to a prince
> and fit to be set in gold so bright:
> in all the East, I affirm,
> I never found her precious equal.
> So round, so elegant in every setting—
> so fine, so smooth her sides were—
> that wheresoever I judged bright gems
> I accounted her unique.
> Alas, I lost her in a garden;
> through grass to earth it went from me.
> Stricken by love's power, I languish
> for my own pearl without a blemish.

Unless we interpret the introduction postpositively, according to data transposed from the vision, we surely must acknowledge

---

wythouten spotte, which as the symbolism of the poem unfolds is the pure and spotless maiden who has died, his precious child. When she is found again in Heaven, the pearl becomes more definitely a symbol of her immaculate spirit and the blessedness of her heavenly state."

[24] *The Pearl* (Boston and London, 1906), pp. xxxii and 82–83.
[25] "Symbolism," pp. 634–636.

that the imagery of this crucial stanza has neither an ethical nor a theological tinge and is, in fact, markedly secular. In the first two stanzas the lost pearl is mourned in courtly terms that should remind one of those employed by Chaucer's man in black, who declares, in the midst of his eulogy:

> '. . . certes, y trowe that evermor
> Nas seyn so blysful a tresor.'[26]

> [. . . indeed, I believe that never again
> was seen such a blessed treasure.]

In short, what the narrator of *Pearl* has lost is not, except subsequently and secondarily, a symbol of innocence but a beloved treasure of matchless beauty.

Subsumed under the principle of probability is the principle of aesthetic convention. Schofield is applying this principle when he asserts:

And anyone then [in the fourteenth century] who wrote or read a poem entitled *The Pearl* would *expect* the treatment to be allegorical. He would not, however, expect the author of a poem to include a list of all previous or possible interpretations of the word, but only such as the poet chose to emphasize at that particular time for a particular purpose.[27]

Third, the principle of authorial competence. This might also be called the principle of critical humility, with the proviso that what is pride in one man may be humility in another. In general, no principle is more frequently contravened by scholars of medieval literature than this one. The source of apparent deficiencies in what, to the modern and even Catholic reader, is the largely distasteful literature of the Middle Ages can be only the author and his times. Courthope concludes that the author of *Pearl* probably

did not know how to reach the heart by those exquisite touches that lend such pathos to the parallel situation in Dante's *Vita Nuova*. Nor does the

---

[26] *The Book of the Duchess* (*The Works of Geoffry Chaucer*, ed. F. N. Robinson, 2nd ed. [Boston, 1957], p. 275, ll. 853–854).

[27] "Symbolism," p. 638.

allegory itself appear to be very happily conceived: no great powers of invention are required to feign that one has lost a pearl, and afterwards indicate that what has been really lost is a daughter or sister.[28]

Stanley P. Chase is convinced that like "so many other allegorical compositions . . . *The Pearl* attains its wider meaning at some sacrifice of coherence and consistency."[29] Osgood, in the introduction to his edition of *Pearl,* asserts:

If the poem is allegorical [the term is loosely meant], then, contrary to the rule of mediaeval allegory, the interpretation is nowhere given, or even suggested, by the poet. On the other hand, it is obscured by many details whose symbolism is imperceptible, or whose allegorical interpretation is impossible.[30]

Fourth, the principle of economy (the law of parsimony or " 'Occam's' razor"). The elegiac interpretation of *Pearl* violates this principle grieviously, requiring maximal postulates that in general take the form of *petitio principii.* Such representative assertions as the following belong not to literary criticism but to the history of error: "there are too many features which are meaningless on any other assumption than that the poet mourns the loss of a real child"[31]; or without "the elegiac basis and the sense of great personal loss which pervades it, *Pearl* would indeed be the mere theological treatise on a special point, which some critics have called it."[32] All special postulates, then, including the one that the lost pearl is primarily a symbol of what interpreters vaguely call purity, are to be rejected.

Fifth, the principle of aesthetic determinism. The terms *unity* and *coherence* are too wide and *inevitability* is too narrow; the

---

[28] *A History of English Poetry* (New York and London, 1895), I, 350–351.

[29] *The Pearl,* p. lvi.

[30] *The Pearl,* p. xxxiv.

[31] Baugh, *Literary History,* p. 235.

[32] Gordon, *Pearl,* p. xviii. The dominion of the realist fallacy has long been apparent in studies of *Piers Plowman* and of Chaucer (a specific is J. V. Cunningham's magisterial essay "The Literary Form of the Prologue to the *Canterbury Tales," MP,* XLIX [1952], 172–181).

term needed is one that fixes the general element of causality within a literary work. Had this deterministic principle been observed in the dispute over *Pearl,* the error of the Undistributed Middle, to give it a name, might well have been avoided. Thus Greene might never have concluded that "the poem as a whole was designed to illustrate the doctrine of Divine Grace."[33] The middle, as well as the end, of the poem might have been seen, in other words, to be implicit in the beginning.

Finally, the principle of subtlety. In art, subtlety is one of treatment, generally, rather than of idea. In medieval *belles-lettres* only the anachronistic reader need be on guard against what may seem to be special learning or arbitrary symbolism. We must count not only on subtlety of definition, however, as in the great hymns of St. Thomas Aquinas, but also on subtlety of aspect, especially in the forms of irony, of word play, and of metaphor.[34] *Pearl* is deeply ironic, much in the fashion of the "Knight's Tale" and *Troilus and Criseyde* except for a certain general austerity, an austerity that does not preclude humor, however.[35] The irony of Christian paradox is manifested early in *Pearl,* in the lines

> For vch gresse mot grow of grayneȝ dede;
> No whete were elleȝ to woneȝ wonne.[36]   (31–32)
>
> [For all grass must come from dead grains;
> otherwise no wheat would be brought to bins.]

As in Boethius's *Consolation of Philosophy,* the concept of bad fortune is also ironic. And there is the radical irony, as we shall see, of folly. Concerning the ingenuity with which the term *pearl*

---

[33] "New Interpretation," p. 815.

[34] "Wit and Mystery: a Revaluation in Mediaeval Latin Hymnody," by Walter J. Ong, S.J. (*Speculum,* XXII [1947], 310–341), is to be recommended, though with reservations.

[35] Though apparently unremarked by critics of *Pearl,* the narrator's outburst in ll. 482 ff. is plainly humorous.

[36] This is of course an allusion to John 12:24–25. Of 25 Cornelius à Lapide has commented: "*Haec ergo Christi sententia est axioma, basis, fundamentum et compendium vitae Christinae*" [This saying of Christ is the rule, base, foundation, and epitome of Christian life] (*Commentarii in scripturam sacram,* VIII [Lyons and Paris, 1875], 1056).

is handled,[37] we will not be at a loss if we already have done some reading in a biblical commentary. The discovery awaits us that the lost pearl is not, despite Courthope, a banal artifice, and that the symbolism of this poem is not incoherent, much less partly unintelligible: rather, *Pearl* is a structure of extraordinary allusiveness, seriousness, and power.[38]

III

As the educated person of the Middle Ages would surely have been expected to perceive, *Pearl* is, in brief, a Christian *consolatio*.[39] Although the specific coloring of each is not

---

[37] The symbolic meanings of *pearl* in *Pearl* are in need of a comprehensive gloss, despite the recent scrutiny of Johnson, "The Imagery and Diction of *The Pearl*," pp. 175 and 179 [pages 43 f. and 48 above]. The gloss provided by Sister M. Hillman, "Some Debatable Words," p. 243 [page 12 above] is exceedingly inaccurate. Coolidge O. Chapman's *An Index of Names in Pearl, Purity, Patience and Gawain* (Ithaca, 1951) is of rather little help here. Perhaps one should note that although *pearl* as a common noun is included, this index does not contain the two occurrences of *pearl* in *Sir Gawain and the Green Knight* (954 and 2364).

[38] The association of *pearl* with *peril* is not to be found in *Pearl*, and perhaps would not be made by a Middle English audience. This pun occurs, however, in a gloss of Chaucer's *Boece*, in a passage relevant to *Pearl*: "He dalf up precious periles, (*That is to seyn, that he that hem first up dalf, he dalf up a precious peril; for-why for the preciousness of switch thyng hath many man ben in peril*)" (Robinson p. 393)..

[39] In his "Boethius the Scholastic" (*Founders of the Middle Ages* [Cambridge, 1941], p. 136) E. K. Rand remarks: "Once on a time, Boethius's *Consolation of Philosophy* was one of the hundred best books—one of those books that no educated man left unread. . . . As Morris puts it in the preface of his edition of Chaucer's translation of Boethius, 'No philosopher was so bone of the bone and flesh of the flesh of Middle-Age writers as Boethius. Take up what writer you will, and you find not only the sentiments, but the very words of the distinguished old Roman.'" Howard R. Patch's *The Tradition of Boethius* (New York, 1935) is a jejune treatment of a rich subject.— The *consolatio* seems badly to need study. Some help is provided by Sister Mary E. Fern, *The Latin Consolatio as a Literary Type* (St. Louis, 1941) and by Benjamin Boyce, "The Stoic *Consolatio* and Shakespeare," *PMLA*, LXIV (1949), 771–780. I have not yet seen

identical,[40] in theme, situation, roles, and treatment *Pearl* is analogous to Boethius's then-revered *Consolation of Philosophy*.[41]

Whether, in the conventional sense, *Pearl,* like *The Consolation,* is semiautobiographical, we shall apparently never know nor, as was implied earlier in this essay, need we ever know.[42] In fact, probability compels the conclusion that the secular age of the virgin is to be accounted for parabolically rather than realistically:[43] as a datum that allows the author of *Pearl* to

---

Constant Martha, "Les Consolations dans l'Antiquité," *Études Morales sur l'Antiquité* (Paris, 1893), to which Boyce refers in footnote 3.

[40] After the introduction the coloring of *Pearl* tends to be that of theology rather than that of moral philosophy, whereas the coloring of *The Consolation* is largely that of moral philosophy.

[41] Schofield perceived that in general *Pearl* and *The Consolation* are much alike, and he even correctly identifies the blindness ascribed to Boethius. Schofield did not understand, however, that he had come upon the lost treasure, so to speak, and continues his search through medieval literature. His conclusion concerning the resemblance is more impressive out of context than in ("Nature and Fabric," p. 179): "Hardly, I think, can one compare the parallel accounts of these scenes in *The Pearl* without coming to the conclusion that the author of the former was indebted to Boethius for definite suggestions in the treatment of his theme, even for details of phraseology." The route of my interpretation, incidentally, was by the way of *Troilus and Criseyde*.

[42] To be sure, medieval man did not scruple to write autobiography, and he has left us various accounts of bereavement. An especially pertinent example for an understanding of much of the thought in *Pearl* is the lament, by that remarkable English monk Ailred of Rievaulx (1100–1167), for a fellow monk named Simon, in *Speculum caritatis* (*Patrologiae Latinae cursus completus* . . . [Paris, 1844–1864], CXCV, cols. 505–620). A neglected part of Boccaccio's *Olympia,* the influence of which on *Pearl* Schofield accepted, is perhaps the line: "*Non sum quae fueram dum tecum parvula vixi . . .*" [I am not as I was while as a child I lived with you] (as printed in Israel Gollancz, *Pearl* [London, 1921], p. 272, l. 141).

[43] The virgin is represented (483) as being less than two at death. A child of two or thereabout in the pre-Wordsworthian era with which we are dealing, besides being a symbol of innocence, was also, as even now, a symbol of irrationality. In *The Romaunt of the Rose* we find (Robinson, p. 668, ll. 400–402): "She [Elde] had nothing hirsilf to lede, / Ne wit ne pithe in hir hold / More than a child of two year old."

enforce maximally a point concerning salvation, a point of which the typical sinner always needs to be reminded—that ultimately salvation depends on God.[44]

The theme of *Pearl*, as of *The Consolation*, might be called the sovereign theme of the Christian tradition, as of life itself: the nature of happiness, specifically false and true happiness. Like the Boethius of *The Consolation*, as well as like St. Augustine of *The Confessions* and Troilus of *Troilus and Criseyde*, the narrator of *Pearl* had mistaken false for true happiness. In losing his pearl,

'Þat er watȝ grounde of alle my blysse . . .'   (372)

[That once was the ground of all my happiness . . .]

he had lost his happiness. When the virgin informs him, in a beautiful superimposed metaphor, that what he has lost "was but a rose"

'Þat flowred and fayled as kynde [nature] hyt gef,'   (270)

[That flowered and withered in accordance with nature]

the lost pearl is plainly identified as a transient, therefore, in the language of *The Consolation*, as an imperfect good.[45] In

[44] St. Thomas Aquinas comments: "*Ostensum est autem . . . quod beatitudo est quoddam bonum excedens naturam creatam. Unde impossibile est quod per actionem alicujus creaturae conferatur; sed homo beatus fit solo Deo agente, si loquamur de beatitudine perfecta*" [But it has been shown that happiness is a certain good transcending created nature. Accordingly it is impossible that it be conferred through the action of any creature; but man is made happy through God alone, if we speak of perfect happiness] *S.T.*, I-II, q. 5, a. 6. All citations to St. Thomas in the original are from the New York reprint of the Parma edition (1948–1950).

[45] *Quoniam igitur, quae sit imperfecti, quae etiam perfecti boni forma, vidisti, nunc demonstrandum reor, quonam haec felicitatis perfectio constituta sit.*" *Philosophiae consolationis libri quinque*, ed. Karl Büchner (Heidelberg, 1947), III, pr. 10. All citations to the original are from this edition. ("Since then you have seen the form both of the imperfect and the perfect good, I think I should now show you where lies this perfection of happiness." *The Consolation of Philosophy* [New York, 1943], p. 60.)

Boethian symbolism, which is also to say, in medieval symbolism, the lost pearl is another lost Eurydice (*De Consolatione,* III, m. xii):

> *Heu noctis prope terminos*
> *Orpheus Eurydicen suam*
> *vidit, perdidit, occidit.*
> *Vos haec fabula respicit,*
> *quicumque in superum diem*
> *mentem ducere quaeritis.*
> *Nam qui Tartareum in specus*
> *victus lumina flexerit,*
> *quicquid praecipuum trahit,*
> *perdit, dum videt inferos.*[46]

Chaucer's translation provides us with a gloss drawn, apparently, from two famous commentaries, Trivet's and Pseudo-Aquinas's:

This fable apertenith to yow alle, whosoevere desireth or seketh to lede his thought into the sovereyn day (*that is to seyn, into cleernesse of sovereyn good*). For whoso that evere be so overcomen that he ficche his eien into the put of helle (*that is to seyn, whoso sette his thoughtes in erthly thinges*), al that evere he hath drawen of the noble good celestial he lesith it, whanne he looketh the helles (*that is to seyn, into lowe thinges of the erthe*).[47]

---

[46] Translation of the first three lines: "Alas! at the very bounds of darkness Orpheus looked upon his Eurydice; looked, and lost her, and was lost himself" (*The Consolation of Philosophy*, p. 73).

[47] Robinson, p. 358. Pseudo-Aquinas comments on this passage (*Commentum super lib. Boetii de consolatu philosophico, Sancti Thomae Aquinatis . . . Opera Omnia.* [New York, 1950], XXIV, 83): "*Nota quod quia intellectus et ratio impediuntur et obscurantur per affectionem et desiderium terrenorum, quia corpus quod corrumpitur aggravat animam quando corpori est subjecta, ideo philosophia petit fugar nebulas terrenae molis*" [Note that because the intellect and reason are impeded and darkened by affection for and desire of earthly things, because the body, which is corrupted, oppresses the soul when it is subject to the body, therefore Philosophy seeks to put to flight the clouds of earthly weight]. Trivet comments (as given in *The Poems of Robert Henryson*, ed. G. Gregory Smith, I, STS [Edinburgh and London, 1914], lv): "*applicando fabulam hanc ad propositionem hortatur uitare illud quod contemplacionem summi boni impedit . . . flexerit lumina scilicet rationem et intellectum a celesti*

[This story pertains to all of you who wish or seek to bring your minds into sovereign day, that is, into the brightness of the supreme good. For whoever is so worsted that he turns his eyes to the pit of hell—that is to say, whoever sets his thoughts on earthly things—all of heavenly good that he has won he loses when he looks on hell, that is to say, on the low things of the earth.]

Plainly, if Eurydice is to be viewed as one of the "lowe thinges of the erthe," then immunity should not be imputed to an infant.

The reprehension of natural love is profoundly Christian, as anyone knows who has read the *New Testament,* which is full of sayings harsh to carnal ears:

If any man come to me, and hate not his father, and mother, and wife, and children, and brethren, and sisters, yea and his own life also, he cannot be my disciple.[48]

If we turn to St. Thomas we find:

Now the aspect under which our neighbor is to be loved, is God, since what we ought to love in our neighbor is that he may be in God. . . . In like manner it would be wrong if a man loved his neighbor as though he were his last end. . . .[49]

Correlatively, the narrator's past identity, which is involved with the identity of the lost pearl, is now plain: he was natural

---

bono . . . perdit dum uidit inferos id est dum est intentus istis terrenis et temporalibus que sunt infima" [by applying this fable to the proposition, she (Philosophy) urges us to avoid what impedes the contemplation of the highest good . . . whoever turns his eyes, that is, reason and intellect, from the heavenly good . . . loses while looking into hell (whatever good he has acquired), that is, while he is intent on those earthly and temporal things that are the lowest]. This is the commentary that Henryson follows in the "Moralitas" to his *Orpheus and Eurydice.* The allusion to Boethius in the "Moralitas" is not mentioned by Patch, *The Tradition of Boethius.*

[48] Luke 4:26. A softened version, in a no less stern whole, is Matthew's 10:37.

[49] The *"Summa Theologica" of St. Thomas Aquinas,* tr. Fathers of the English Dominican Province [London, 1917], pt. II, q. 25, a. I. All translations of the *Summa* will be from this edition. The last part of this quotation reads in the original ". . . *reprehensibile esset, si quis proximum diligeret tamquam principalem finem.* . . ."

man—variously termed, in the Christian tradition, *homo animalis, carnalis, or sensualis* [bestial, carnal, or sensual man]. *Homo animalis,* the intended audience of *The Consolation,* is addressed more than once: as *"o terrena animalia"* [earthly animals] (III, pr. iii), as *"caeci"* [blind] (III, m. viii); and, earlier (III, pr. ii), he is likened to a drunken man who does not know the way home.[50] The *locus classicus* is that of St. Paul, I Cor. 2:14: "But the sensual man perceiveth not these things that are of the Spirit of God; for it is foolishness to him, and he cannot understand, because it is spiritually examined."

Sin, we should remind ourselves at this point, may be said to consist of preferring the mutable (temporal, apparent, external, false) good to the immutable (perfect, or true) good, that is, the *summum bonum.* To cite St. Thomas: "Now every sin consists in the desire for some mutable good, for which man has an inordinate desire, and the possession of which gives him inordinate pleasure."[51] The narrator's sin, in terms of a traditional distinction,[52] is not carnal but spiritual—and *Pearl,* being free thereby of a certain grossness, gains much.

---

[50] *"Sed ad hominum studia revertor, quorum animus etsi caligante memoria tamen bonum suum repetit, sed velut ebrius, domum quo tramite revertatur, ignorat."* It is a pleasure to record that E. V. Gordon (*Pearl,* p. xviii) notes the "persistent earthliness of the father's [?] mind."

[51] *S.T.,* I-II, q. 72, a. 2: *"Omne autem peccatum consistit in appetitu alicujus commutabilis boni, quod inordinate appetitur; et per consequens in eo jam habito inordinate aliquis delectatur."* In St. Augustine one finds similar definitions of sin, as in *"De Libero Arbitrio, Augustini Opera Omnia,* I [Paris, 1865], col. 1240: "'Est ita ut dicis [*Augstine*], et assentior, omnia peccata hoc uno genere contineri, cum quisque avertitur a divinis vereque manentibus, et ad mutabilia atque incerta convertitur'" [It is as you say, (Augustine), and I agree, that all sins are comprised within this one kind, when anyone is deflected from what is divine and truly lasting and is drawn to what is mutable and uncertain].

[52] *"Sic igitur illa peccata quae perficiunter in delectatione spirituali, vocantur peccata spiritualia; illa vero quae perficiuntur in delectatione carnali, vocantur peccata carnalia. . . ."* *Ibid.* [Accordingly those sins which consist in spiritual pleasure are called spiritual sins, while those which consist in carnal pleasure are called carnal sins . . .]. St. Thomas (*ibid.*) cites delight *"in laude humana, vel in aliquo hujusmodi"* [in

According to one principle of classification,[53] the narrator's sin may indeed be defined as cupidity or avarice, that is, as St. Thomas tells us, an "inordinate desire" for a "temporal good."[54] A preferable—and correlative—classification is folly (*stultitia*), the antithesis of wisdom (*sapientia*).[55] St. Thomas defines folly in terms of a distinction between it and fatuity (*fatuitas*):

And folly differs from fatuity, according to the same authority [i.e., Gregory], in that folly implies apathy in the heart and dulness in the senses, while fatuity denotes entire privation of the spiritual sense. Therefore folly is fittingly opposed to wisdom.[56]

In fact, folly "denotes dulness of sense in judging, and chiefly as regards the highest cause, which is the last end and the sovereign good."[57] This dullness is of two sorts: the one which proceeds from a "natural indisposition" is of course not a sin; as for the other sort, however, which consists of a man's "plunging his sense into earthly things, whereby his sense is rendered inca-

---

human praise or the like] as illustrative of spiritual sin. This sort of delight St. Thomas also calls *animalis*; its character is defined in terms that illuminate *Pearl*: "*duplex est delectatio: una quidem animalis, quae consummatur in sola apprehensione alicujus rei ad votum habitae . . .*" (*ibid.*). ". . . pleasure is twofold. One belongs to the soul, and is consummated in the mere apprehension of a thing possessed in accordance with desire. . . ."

[53] In the Middle Ages the classification of sins was not the pigeon-holing affair that we like to think. Morton Bloomfield's admirable remark on the cardinal sins should perhaps be included here (*The Seven Deady Sins* [East Lansing, 1952], p. 107): "Medieval writers did not have the cardinal sins in mind every time they referred to sin, and to believe so does violence to a proper appreciation of medieval thought."

[54] See *S.T.*, I-II, q. 84, a. I.

[55] In contrast to its role in Christian thought generally, folly is scarcely given more than a few lines, apparently, in the medieval manuals of sin. St. Thomas classifies folly as a species (of luxury [*luxuria*] i.e., excess) rather than as a genus.

[56] *Ibid.*, II-II, q. 46, a. 1.

[57] *Ibid.*, a. 2. ". . . *stultitia . . . importat quemdam stuporem sensus in judicando, et praecipue circa altissimam causam, quae est finis ultimus, et summum bonum.*"

pable of perceiving Divine things, according to I Cor. 2:14
... suchlike folly is a sin."[58] It should be obvious now that the
sin of *stultitia,* the sin proper to *homo animalis,* is imputed to
the narrator of *Pearl.* In the end he repents his "mad porpose"
and embraces the counsel of the virgin, which is the counsel of
Christianity itself:

> 'I rede þe forsake þe worlde wode
> And porchace þy perle maskelles.'   (743–744)

> [I advise you to forsake the mad world
> and purchase your spotless pearl.]

The action of *Pearl* is implicit in these two lines. Through
grace the original and false "grounde" of "blisse"[59] is renounced
for the true "grounde"; the mutable (imperfect) good, for the
immutable (perfect) good or *summum bonum;* correlatively,
carnal or earthly love (ultimately self-love) is renounced for
spiritual or heavenly love. In the words of the conclusion of
Pearl, which are the words of the spiritual man who has put off
the carnal man:

> Ouer þis hyul þis lote I laȝte
> For pyty of my perle enclyin,
> And syþen to God I hit bytaȝte
> In Krysteȝ dere blessyng and myn,

---

[58] *Ibid.* Significantly, Philosophy tells Boethius that "the cause, or
the chief cause," of his "sickness" is that he has forgotten what he is
(*"quid ipse sis, nosse desisti,"* I, pr. vi).

[59] *Cf. De Consolatione,* III, pr. i. Boethius asks where Philosophy is
trying to lead him. Philosophy replies: "To the true happiness of which
your soul too dreams; but your sight is taken up in imaginary views
thereof, so that you cannot look upon itself." Pseudo-Aquinas comments:
*"Nota: sicut somnians putat phantasmata sibi occurrentia esse veras res
de quibus somniat, et tamen non sunt ipsae res, sic Boetius in istis temporalibus putavit esse veram felicitatem quae tamen non est"* [Note:
just as a dreamer thinks that the phantasms of which he dreams are
real and yet they are not, so Boethius among temporal things thought
that to be true happiness which nevertheless is not] (*Commentum*).
True happiness and the *summum bonum* are, as Philosophy· tells Boethius, identical (see *De Consolatione,* III, pr. x, next to last sentence).

Þat in þe forme of bred and wyn
Þe preste vus scheweʒ vch a daye.
He gef vus to be his homly hyne
And precious perleʒ vnto his pay.

[On this mound this lot befell me,
prostrate with sorrow for my pearl,
and afterwards I committed it to God
in Christ's precious blessings and my blessing—
Christ whom the priest shows us daily
in the form of bread and wine.
He allowed us to be His domestics
and precious pearls for His pleasure.]

Just as in *The Consolation*, however, the resolution is delayed so as to allow the author to demonstrate that the narrator's rebellion is also nothing but folly. The crux, which has been insufficiently appreciated, is, as in *The Consolation*, God's apparent injustice. The narrator complains:

'What wyrde hatʒ hyder my iuel vayned,
And don me in þys del and gret daunger?'   (249–250)

[What fate has brought my jewel hither
and caused me this grief and great distress?]

In her reply the virgin points out that in accusing his "wyrde," he has accused God:

'And þou hatʒ called þy wyrde a þef,
Þat oʒt of noʒt hatʒ mad þe cler . . .'   (273–274)

[And you have called your fate a thief,
that out of nothing has clearly made you . . .]

And just as Philosophy tells Boethius that bad fortune is good fortune,[60] the virgin tells the narrator that

'Þou blameʒ þe bote of þy meschef . . .'   (275)

[You blame the remedy for your misfortune . . .]

The narrator begs the virgin's pardon; then, shortly thereafter,

[60] See *De Consolatione*, II, pr. viii.

his rebelliousness again is inflamed at the news, which he of course misunderstands, that the virgin has been made a queen of Heaven:

> 'And quen mad on þe fyrst day!
> I may not traw, so God me spede,
> Þat God wolde wryþe so wrange away.
> Of countes, damysel, par ma fay,
> Wer fayr in heuen to holde asstate,
> Oþer elleʒ a lady of lasse aray;
> Bot a quene! Hit is to dere a date.'   (486–492)

> [And made queen on the first day!
> I cannot believe, God help me,
> that God would work so unjustly.
> It would be fair to hold in heaven
> the rank of countess, of miss, by my faith,
> or else of a lady of lesser degree,
> but a queen! That's going too far.]

God's justice is then defended in terms of His grace. At first the narrator rejects the virgin's argument, which is based, in keeping with tradition, on the parable of the workers in the vineyard. In an ironical reversal of roles, the narrator charges, in language that echoes the virgin's reply to his first charge:

> 'Me þynk þy tale vnresounable.
> Goddeʒ ryʒt is redy and euermore rert.
> Oþer Holy Wryt is bot a fable . . .   (590–592)
> Now he þat stod þe long day stable
> And þou to payment com hym byfore,
> Þenne þe lasse in werke to take more able,
> And euer þe lenger þe lasse, þe more.'   (597–600)

> [Your account seems to me unreasonable.
> God's justice is prompt and always awake.
> Otherwise Holy Writ is just a fiction . . .
> Now if you were paid ahead of him
> who stood steadfast the long day,
> then those who have done less work are able to earn more,
> and invariably the longer one works less,
> the more one will earn.]

70

The virgin patiently explains (1) that no one need fear being done out of his reward, for God "laueʒ hys gyfteʒ as water of dyche" (607), i.e., the beatific vision is infinite; (2) that if justice be the criterion of desert, then, innocents excepted, who has not forfeited salvation sometime? (3) that in justice God cannot very well deprive the baptized innocents of the penny even though they come into the vineyard at the eleventh hour.

The narrator's rebellion is now extinguished, and he listens contritely as the virgin comes to the climax of her argument: (1) every sinner is assured of grace if he be truly penitent; (2) it is time that he purchase his "perle maskelles," i.e., put off *homo animalis* and put on *homo spiritualis*. The narrator's folly is dwelt upon almost to the end of the poem and even provides the reason for the breaking off of the vision: the narrator tries to cross the stream that separates earth and Heaven.

The essential argument of this interpretation has now been stated; a summary follows. First: The dispute over *Pearl* demonstrates, generally speaking, that even to scholars the Christian tradition is a lost tradition. Second: The presumed and belabored issue of *Pearl*—whether the mourned loss is fictitious or real—is, in fact, secondary. Third: A desideratum in the dispute over *Pearl* is a rule book, so to speak; such a book should contain at least the principles listed. Fourth and last: As the educated person of the Middle Ages would surely have been expected to perceive, *Pearl* is, in brief, a Christian *consolatio,* analogous in theme, situation, roles, and treatment to Boethius's then-revered *Consolation of Philosophy.*

I believe *Pearl* to be better than, for example, *Sir Gawain and the Green Knight,* for all its brilliance. I should deny greatness to *Pearl,* however, according to the principle that all great art, somberly or smilingly, takes us into the depths of the dark wood, where dwell the Mysteries. *Pearl* takes us only part way in.[61] What is lacking in its vision is supplied us, not unexpectedly,

---

[61] No corresponding judgment of *The Consolation,* a sublime work, is to be inferred.

in the unblinking pages of St. Thomas Aquinas. In effect, the passage is both gloss and critique:

> . . . through God's mercy, temporary blindness [i.e. *folly*] is directed medicinally to the spiritual welfare of those who are blinded. This mercy, however, is not vouchsafed to all those who are blinded, but only to the predestined, to whom *all things work together unto good* (Rom. 8:28). Therefore, as regards some, blindness is directed to our healing; but as regards others, to their damnation, as Augustine says.[62]

[62] *S.T.*, I-II, q. 79, a. 4. In the original the concluding words read: *"ut August, dicit in lib. de QQ. evang. (loc. cit. in arg. 3)."* In E. Talbot Donaldson's "Chaucer the Pilgrim" (*PMLA*, LXIX [1954], 928–936), I have subsequently found independent corroboration for much in this paper. Professor Donaldson treats (p. 934) the "tradition of the fallible first person singular" and (*ibid.*) identifies "the protagonist of the *Pearl*" as "mankind whose heart is set on a transitory good that has been lost—who, for very natural reasons, confuses earthly with spiritual values."

6

AN APPROACH TO *THE PEARL*

Milton R. Stern

ALTHOUGH THERE ARE SOME BASIC AGREEMENTS ABOUT *The Pearl*, the area of critical accord is surprisingly small. Beyond a few trustworthy suppositions about the manuscript itself (MS. Cotton Nero A.x., British Museum), the record of the Pearl Poet and the historicity of the Pearl Maiden are lost in the fogs of time and conjecture. Since Schofield's attempt to lift the significance of the poem above the narrative level of elegy, there has been a heated, running controversy concerning *The Pearl* as an elegiac, allegorical, or symbolic construct.[1] Stemming from studies like J. B. Fletcher's, which points out that elegy and allegory are not mutually exclusive, there has been a growing critical unity in accepting the poem as something more than pure

Reprinted, by permission of the author and of the University of Illinois Press, from the *Journal of English and Germanic Philology*, LIV (1955), 684–692. Translations of *Pearl* are by Sister Mary Vincent Hillman, *The Pearl, Mediaeval Text with a Literal Translation and Interpretation* (University of Notre Dame Press, 1967).

[1] Three articles by W. H. Schofield form a convenient center for the growth of controversy about *The Pearl*. See "The Nature and Fabric of *The Pearl*," *PMLA*, XIX (1904), 154–203; "The Source of *The Pearl*," *PMLA*, XIX (1904), 203–215; and "Symbolism, Allegory and Autobiography in *The Pearl*," *PMLA*, XXIV (1909), 585–675. Factual and conjectural aspects are summarized in the introductory material of E. V. Gordon's edition of *The Pearl* (Oxford, 1953), which furnishes the text used for this study.

elegy.[2] But still, as a recent article concludes, "to date, the symbolic interpretation has . . . been weakly argued."[3]

Accordingly, students have had to "explain" the poem using the standards of medieval conventions as they are exposed within *The Pearl* itself. It is not within the scope of this brief study to evaluate the claims of rival approaches and exegeses, but rather to recall attention to two well-known conventions that can aid interpretation. One is a consideration of the multiple levels of meaning discovered in traditional scriptural exegesis according to the four senses,[4] and the second is a consideration of the gemological meanings found in the lapidary tradition. When the poem is explicated in the light of these traditions, specific details of meaning emerge which provide a basis for such analyses as those by John Conley, Sister Mary Vincent Hillman, and Wendell S. Johnson.[5]

Although the four senses and gemology cannot limit explication, they provide a set of directive suggestions apparent in the first few stanzas. (Some critics have noted that the structure and theme of *The Pearl* are implicit in the introduction, but there is still a paramount need for patterned examination of details.)

[2] "The Allegory of the Pearl," *JEGP*, XX (1921), 1 ff.

[3] John Conley, "*Pearl* and a Lost Tradition," *JEGP*, LIV (1955), 333 [page 52 above].

[4] The literal or historical, the allegorical, the moral, and the anagogical. The most convenient study of the four senses is by Walter J. Burghardt, S.J., "On Early Christian Exegesis," *Theological Studies*, XI (March, 1950). I am indebted to Dr. Arnold Williams for suggesting Burghardt's article and this double approach to *The Pearl*.

[5] Conley insists that *The Pearl* is primarily a Christian *consolatio*. "The theme of *Pearl* . . . might be called the sovereign theme of the Christian tradition . . .: the nature of happiness, specifically false and true happiness." ("*Pearl* and a Lost Tradition," *ibid.*, p. 341) [page 63 above]. Hillman views the poem as a symbolic statement about the need for renunciation ("Some Debatable Words in *Pearl* and Its Theme," *MLN*, LX [1945], 241–248). Johnson perceives that *The Pearl* is centered about "a ubiquitous sense of contrast between the nature of heaven and the nature of earth, the revelation of which seems . . . to be the poem's main purpose." ("The Imagery and Diction of *The Pearl*," *ELH*, XX [1953], 161–180.)

For instance, Pearl at once is associated with the noblest metal (gold), and with the Orient, which is the eastern direction literally representative of the most priceless gems and anagogically representative of sun, light, Christ, and Jerusalem.[6] Immediately the singularity and spotlessness of the Pearl remove it from the domains of earth. The narrator, however, loses his Pearl through the literal medium of grass and earth, and it becomes evident that the poem grows out of the medieval rage for order which struggled to create an orthodox Christian unity from the Platonic duality of world and ideal. The narrator's plaint,

> O moul, þou marreȝ a myry iuele,
> My priuy perle wythouten spotte.[7]

> [O earth, thou marrest a lovely jewel,
> My own pearl without a spot!]

discloses the tension within the unified duality: the narrator is unable to maintain his earthly existence in union with a Pearl-value which is the basis of Christian happiness. At the same time, life without that value is torment. Consequently, although the meaning of Pearl is not yet specified, apparently it will reside largely in the third or moral sense, because the narrator's loss of Pearl is synonymous with loss of happiness.[8] The fundamental

---

[6] Almost all the lapidaries agree in placing the greatest value in eastern gems. Orientality is specified as highly significant.

[7] *Pearl*, ll. 23–24.

[8] The narrator loses no time in establishing the relationship between himself and the Pearl:

> Syþen in þat spote hit fro me sprange,
> Ofte haf I wayted, wyschande þat wele,
> Þat wont watȝ whyle deuoyde my wrange
> And heuen my happe and al my hele.
> Þat dotȝ bot þrych my hert þrange,
> My breste in bale bot bolen and bele.   (13–18)

> [Since then, in that spot where it sprang from me,
> Oft have I watched, wishing for that wealth
> That was wont for a while to make nought of my sin,
> And exalt my fortune and my entire well-being—
> Which doth but crushingly afflict my heart,
> But swells and burns my breast with grief.]

tension becomes an opposition of the meanings of earth and Pearl, and discovery of those meanings is discovery of the significance of the poem as well as of a particular medieval mind.

The third, fourth, and fifth stanzas complete the introductory evaluations of Pearl. The gem, as symbol, creates fruitful and reproductive qualities without which earthly life would wither. The reader is introduced to the garden arbor of the Pearl's grave in "*hyƷ* [high] *sesoun*," in August, during the day of the Assumption of the Virgin on the fifteenth of that month—a fruitful time *"Quen corne is coruen wyth crokeƷ kene"*[9] [When corn is cut with sickles keen]. The moment of introduction to the Pearl in her arbor is charged with suggestions of the Virgin and consequently of the Virgin's qualities: faithful chastity, humility, holiness, and servitude as a submissive instrument of God's will—all qualities of the renunciation of earth and human will. The generative and cleansing powers of the ideal are then linked with the Virgin Marylike Virgin Pearl by the last few lines of stanza three, wherein the generality of "spices" is given concrete significance by the enumeration of certain spices in the garden arbor. The gilliflower was considered an aromatic and *healing* clove; the ginger an aromatic and *energizing anti-irritant;* the gromwell bears polished, white, stony nutlets very much like *pearls;* the peony is transmitted to medieval medicine from antiquity as the emblem of Παιάν, the Greek god of healing. The "spices" are earthly manifestations of heaven's beneficence, and the anagogy parallels the literal level, wherein the bodily decay of the earthly Pearl Maiden enriches the ground for new growth. Briefly, in implications that suggest the doctrine of works (which undercuts the *visio's* [vision's] argument for the doctrine of grace), the poem suggests that the proper Christian behavior must continue to result in peace and rejuvenation. Good must continue to come of good:

> Of goud vche goude is ay bygonne;
> So semly a sede moƷt fayly not,

---

[9] Charles Osgood, "Introduction," *The Pearl* (Boston, 1906), p. xvi.

Þat spryngande spyceȝ vp ne sponne
Of þat precios perle wythouten spotte.[10]

[From good every good thing is ever begun!
So lovely a seed could not come to nought
So that sprig and spice-blooms would not grow up
From that precious pearl without a spot.]

The Pearl, as equated with the ideal, is to be associated with that one foundation for all being, faith in the perfect, unified order of the divine creation.[11] The chaos resulting from rejection of all that the Virgin Pearl symbolizes is to be equated with Satanic evil as manifested in mankind by sin. The most direct key to the opposition of earth and Pearl appears in a determination of the Satanism exemplified by the narrator in his revelation of his own personality.

The Pearl-ideal is the purity of spotless faith, the unswerving devotion and submission to the will of God which results in perfect order and regeneration. But without any observations about good or bad, the narrator simply states that the fears and longings of his earthly mind almost overpower his faith in the ideal. His man's will attempts to question the nature of Christ and the will of God. Such a revealing statement would need no moralizing for the medieval reader or listener. The narrator's basic negative sin is lack of faith, accompanied by its positive consequence and Satanic counterpart, Pride—the first of the Seven Deadly Sins.

Bifore þat spot my honde I spenned
For care ful colde þat to me caȝt;

[10] *Pearl*, ll. 33–36. The poem can be treated fruitfully as a revelation of the tension (often unconscious) between the desire to follow a rationally founded order of behavior, which triumphed in the official acceptance of Thomism, and the more idealistic Pauline doctrine of greater renunciation and fideism. For instance, The Pearl is a valuable medieval art-document for a discussion of such doctrines as the nominalist heresy.

[11] Although the narrative-level image of stanza three is only that of putting grains in barns for storage, it is highly probable that a medieval poet would keep a sharp eye out for all tropological possibilities in interpretation. At least the image almost certainly would suggest Joseph and the Parable of the Tares.

> A deuely dele in my herte denned,
> Thaȝ resoun sette myseluen saȝte.
> I playned my perle þat þer watȝ spenned
> Wyth fyrce skylleȝ þat faste faȝt;
> Þaȝ kynde of Kryst me comfort kenned,
> My wreched wylle in wo ay wraȝte.[12]

> [Before that spot my hands I wrung
> For the care full cold that seized on me;
> A wicked grief lodged in my heart
> Though understanding would have brought me peace.
> I mourned my pearl which there was locked
> With violence which swiftly reasonings fought,
> Though the nature of Christ would have taught me comfort.
> My wretched will in woe aye tossed . . .]

The inability to accept God's will and grief over the loss of the historical Pearl have made the narrator lose the allegorical, moral, and anagogical Pearl as well. The narrator falls from the medieval ideal of the ignorant man who, with limited knowledge, has a faith more valuable than all the intellection in the world. And it is faith, symbolized by jasper, that is the first foundation for all the other fundaments of the Heavenly City, which the narrator is permitted to glimpse.[13] The narrator is unable to

---

[12] *Pearl*, ll. 49–56.

[13] The early fifteenth-century *London Lapidary of King Philip* comments: *"The veray bokes tellen us that the gode Iaspe is grene & of grete grenehed, & signifieth the trewe peple of man that ben of the lesse vunderstandyng in the ffader & the sonne & the holy gost; thei be lewde men, that yef a gode clerc opposed hem thei couth not answere hym, for thei ben bounden, and signifien Iaspe. Moyses seith that this stone is ful gode ayeins temptacion of fendes, of Iewes, & sarazins. Seint Iohn seith vs in the Appocalipce that [in] the fundament of the heuenly kyndgome of Ierusalem the Iaspe is first, and therefore hit signifieth thre vertues that shulde be in euery gode man. Iaspe is that stone that is cleped feith, the second hope, & the thridde charite, & he that grene Iaspe beholdeth ayeins day, of the feith of Ihesu Xrist he shoulde haue mynde"* [The very books tell us that the good jasper is green and of great greenness and signifies the true people of man that are of less understanding in the Father and the Son and the Holy Ghost; they are ignorant men, so that if a good cleric questioned them, they could not answer him, for they are serfs and signify jasper. Moses says that this

retain the one "spice," faith, which is the only effective medicine for his torment. Had he been able to say, "The Lord giveth and the Lord taketh away," and to add with complete acceptance, "Blessed be the name of the Lord," the poem never could have been written.[14]

As the association with the Virgin makes plain, purity is more than simple sexual chastity. It is the abstract spotlessness typified by faithful maidenhood.[15] The *visio's* debate about innocence versus righteousness emphasizes that heaven's decision, as stated by the Pearl, is decisively in favor of grace and God's sovereignty as opposed to the good works of a mortal will that cannot escape vitiation because of its postlapsarian condition. And so

---

stone is full good against temptation of fiends, of Jews, and Saracens. Saint John tells us in the Apocalypse that in the foundation of the heavenly kingdom jasper is first, and therefore it signifies three virtues that should be in every good man. Jasper is that stone that is called faith; secondly, hope, and third, charity, and he that green jasper views in daylight, of the faith of Jesus Christ he should have mind]. Reprinted in Evans and Serjeantson, *English Medieval Lapidaries* (1933), pp. 23–24.

[14] The fact that the poem *was* written (and was written in a manner that emphasizes the very faith the narrator could not accept) strongly suggests that the Pearl Poet's intention was the creation of extended *exemplum* rather than elegy, which was utilized as the vehicle and not the burden of the poem.

[15] Schofield calls attention to the Pearl Poet's exhortation to his maiden readers (*Clanesse,* 1110–1132) that they become spotless pearls in order that they may enter heaven. "To speak of maidens in this similitude was . . . no new thing. Long before our poet's time they had been so described. A notable instance is one that occurs in the famous tract of the English Saint Aldhelm, *De Laudibus Virginitatis* (written A.D. 706): at the end the author salutes the maidens whom he had particularly in mind as '*Margaritae Christi, Paradisi gemmae*' [pearls of Christ, gems of Paradise]. Maidenhood, moreover, was frequently written about in England as a 'gemstone' more precious than any other in God's esteem, which, if preserved clean, would insure participation in the highest bliss of paradise." Schofield also cites the *Love-Rune* of the thirteenth-century Franciscan, Thomas de Hales, who describes abstract purity of maidenhood as a gem of all-surpassing beauty which "shineth bright in heaven's bower . . ." (*Old English Miscellany,* ed. Morris, Early English Text Soc. [1872], 93 ff.) "The Nature and Fabric of *The Pearl*," *PMLA,* XIX (1904), 167.

in accordance with the general (albeit early) preference for the *vita contemplativa* [contemplative life], the poem insists that purity is born of unspoiled faith. Pure faith becomes the quintessential and innocent avoidance and ignorance of earth and its ways. Insofar as the simple, ignorant, or extremely young person is the purest, *The Pearl* is in agreement with medieval literature's general estimation of earth: Adam's fall made it inevitable that the best mind and will shall become corrupted in time. Argues the Pearl,

> Where wysteʒ þou euer any bourne abate,
> Euer so holy in hys prayere,
> Þat he ne forfeted by sumkyne gate
> Þe mede sumtyme of heueneʒ clere?
> And ay þe ofter, þe alder þay were,
> Þay laften ryʒt and wroʒten woghe. . . .[16]
> I rede þe forsake þe worlde wode,
> And porchace þy perle maskelles.[17]

> [Where knewest thou ever any man to lose zeal,
> However holy in his prayer,
> That he did not forfeit in some kind of way
> The reward sometime of Heaven's brightness?
> And ever the oftener the older such were
> They abandoned right and evil wrought . . .
> I counsel thee to renounce the foolish world,
> And purchase thy pearl spotless.]

The stains of faithlessness and pride ruin the purity of the mortal narrator. The no-longer *"maskelles"* mortal cannot enter the kingdom of heaven until the stains have been washed from the soul by faith and repentance. And in concurrence, there is a tremendous concentration on whiteness and spotlessness in the vision of heaven.

But the narrator persists in willful pride. He attempts to cross the water barrier and enter the Heavenly City by storm. The stream which separates the narrator from heaven is a traditional

[16] *Pearl*, ll. 617–624.
[17] *Pearl*, ll. 743–744.

death-and-rebirth water symbol, one of the mystical and conventional borderlines between the natural and supernatural worlds, in this case between earth and ideal.[18] In context, in the moral sense the stream represents the waters of absolution, purification by faith and repentance. More especially is this interpretation tenable when the jewels of the streambed are considered as gemstones of virtue. The jewels are "adubbement" [adornment] in all the connotations of the word: the soul must "walk" on virtue in crossing the barrier between earth and heaven. But the prideful narrator finds the barrier too deep and turbulent. In his urge to reclaim the Pearl, he is not permitted to enter heaven using as footing virtues which he cannot claim and has not earned.

Although the streambed is packed with various jewels, only three are specified. Beryl, described in the lapidaries as having the color of pure water, is an emblem of the entrance into heaven of the sum of all virtue—it is symbolic of the Resurrection. Emerald is symbolic of chastity, faith, and good works. Sapphire signifies hope and the saving of a good man by Jesus. The enumeration of only these three gems among all the others in the streambed would seem to indicate that the Pearl Poet quite consciously intended to make his poem one huge typological metaphor of orthodox Christian behavior. And as we have been led to expect from the relationship of the Pearl to the narrator, the theme of behavior is based upon the moral sense of the Pearl's significance. The meaning of the loss of Pearl on the historical level can be only an educated guess. But allegorically, loss of Pearl becomes loss of spiritual peace, perhaps loss of ability to receive spiritual sustenance from the church.[19] Morally,

---

[18] Howard R. Patch, *The Other World* (Cambridge, Mass., 1950), *passim*.

[19] Sister Madeleva suggests that the meaning of the poem exists on this level. But such restriction of meaning as well as the application of the pertinence of the poem to those in religious life seems too exclusive. See *The Pearl: A Study in Spiritual Dryness* (New York, 1925), *passim*.

loss of Pearl is loss of faith. And in the consequent anagogical sense, loss of Pearl is loss of heaven. The total loss of happiness is dependent upon the moral loss, and it is salient that when the narrator speaks of his former peace and joy in faith and submission, he speaks in terms almost identical to those used by the Pearl in describing her present state in heaven.

The resolution of the tension between earth and Pearl is a typification of Pauline doctrine. The best purification of will, the best exercise of will, and the best choice of moral conduct is the renunciation of will. Such renunciation is a consequence of submission to God and a withdrawal from earth. The withdrawal is retention of total purity and so becomes a retention or a regaining of Pearl in all the four senses.

It is not necessary to prove that the Pearl Poet consciously based his symbolism upon lapidary material. Gemology was so common in exegetical tradition that it is hardly possible that the poet did not take his jewel symbolism for granted. A curious parallel within the poem itself provides internal evidence that the poet blithely did use such material in a manner that, for a modern, would require deliberate effort in choice of materials. When the Pearl lectures the narrator, she lists attributes of the complete virtue which the narrator must regain in order to find peace. First, she emphasizes the doctrine that man must have *faith* in the grace and sovereignty of God.[20] Second, the statement is recast in terms of the resultant necessity for *hope*.[21] Third, the good that can be obtained by the loss of pride is demonstrated. Specifically, for the narrator, the proper acts to which will must be bent are the meekness and charity of speech and behavior which he so patently lacks. More inclusively, the third attribute of *charity* is the generality of *good works*.[22] Fourth, the youth, innocence, and purity of the Pearl are reintroduced, recalling again the *chastity* or *cleanliness* of the Virgin.[23] Fifth,

[20] Stanzas 25, 26.
[21] Stanzas 27–29.
[22] Stanza 34.
[23] Stanzas 36–40 (especially line 426).

there is a statement of the need for *repentance*.[24] Sixth, Jesus is suddenly introduced as the open gate through which innocents pass to eternal bliss. For human behavior, the necessary attribute is the *meekness and love of Jesus*.[25] Seventh, the miracles of Christ are recounted. The discussion of metamorphosis from sin to virtue, from stain to whiteness, and from grave to life focuses attention upon the miracles of the *holy gift* of redemption and the formative spirit of love, or *the Holy Ghost,* which is not named as such in the Pearl's *exhortatio* [exhortation].[26] Eighth, there is a reminder of the translation of the state of the Lamb in the historical Jerusalem to the state of the Lamb in the anagogical Jerusalem. The reminder is a statement to man about the rewards of virtue, *the Resurrection*.[27] Ninth, the narrator discovers that because he has not been purified by the travail of repentance, he cannot enter heaven. The final need of the narrator is patient *travail,* and indeed, because of his impatient pride he is forced back to earth to spend the rest of his days in the travail in which he was first introduced, when his *"breste in bale bot bolne and bele"*[28] [breast in grief swells and burns]. It is not until he reaches the purified state suggested by the tone of the last stanza that he can utter words of peaceful resignation.[29]

[24] Stanzas 51, 52.

[25] Stanzas 57, 58, 60, 61.

[26] Stanzas 63–71.

[27] Stanzas 68–75.

[28] Stanzas 79–100.

[29] The final statement of stanza 101 constitutes one of the poem's major flaws. The journey of the narrator extends from ignorance to enlightenment in methods of regaining the Pearl. The narrator's last action is a rebellion. His last speech (stanzas 99, 100) is a realization and acceptance. The expectation is fully developed that he will be cast back to earth to enter his period of enlightened travail. Stanza 101, however, has the narrator utter words which properly belong to the completion of that period. In fact, were it not for the mystagogical statement in lines 1209 and 1210, there would be no difficulty in believing that the narrator actually is now in heaven. His language and attitude are identical with that of the Pearl during the debate. At this point a statement of glory gained is unnecessary. The reader already has digested one hundred stanzas of such statement and implication, and our expectations for the narrator have been defined fully: either the narrator will continue in

The poem then builds rapidly to the crescendo of the beatific vision, and in immediate juxtaposition to the lessons the narrator has learned in the conventional debate, the fundaments of the Heavenly City are enumerated. The medieval and Renaissance lapidaries generally evaluate the fundament stones, in order, as follows: jasper is faith; sapphire is hope; chalcydon is good works; emerald is chastity; sardonyx is repentance; ruby is Jesus; chrysolite is the miracles of Christ, the holy gift, and the Holy Ghost; beryl is the Resurrection; topaz is the nine orders of angels; chrysoprase is travail; jacinth is safety in far places; and amethyst is Christ's robe.[30] The fact that the poet has not paral-

---

pride and be denied heaven, or, as stanzas 99 and 100 make more probable, he will embark upon a new life of purification. The purpose of the poem has been fulfilled. Its instruction and theme are complete. On the one hand the final stanza is not prepared for by any passage of earthly time in the poem—there is not even a transitional passage between stanzas 100 and 101 as there is between the introduction and the *visio*. On the other hand inclusion of a passage of earthly time would necessitate the writing of a new poem, perhaps much like the Book of Job thematically, in which it is shown *how* the narrator overcomes the obstacles of earth and time, and earns the right (morally as well as structurally) to make the statement of lines 1201 and 1202:

> To pay þe Prince oþer sete saȝte
> Hit is ful eþe to þe god Krystyin . . .
>
> [To please the Prince or be reconciled,
> It is quite easy for the good Christian . . .]

Appearing as it does, the 101st stanza of resolution and reconciliation is gratuitous and facile.

[30] The most important of the medieval lapidaries is the Latin Lapidary of Bishop Marbodus, with its many Latin and vernacular derivatives. Also noteworthy are the *Etymologiae* (Bk. XVI) of Isidore of Seville, the *Steinbuch* of Volamar, the Latin Lapidary of Albertus Magnus, the commentary on Aaron's breastplate by St. Epiphanius, the *Explanatio Apocalypsis* of Bede, the *Commentarium super Apocalypsim* by Primasius, the *De Expositione Veteris et Novi Testamenti* of St. Paterius, the *De Universo* of Rabanus Maurus, the *Summa de Exemplis* of St. John a St. Geminiano, and the collections of L. Pannier, *Les Lapidaires Francais*, and J. Evans and M. Serjeantson, *The English Medieval Lapidaries*. Among Renaissance lapidaries, some of the most important are the *Speculum* of Leonardus, *De Gemmis* of Ruet, *De Subtilitate* of Cardan, *Le Lapidaire* of Mandeville (pseudo), *Gemmarum et Lapidum Historia*

leled the plight of the narrator with the stones of the fundaments in the cases of topaz, jacinth, and amethyst indicates that the poet did not order the parallel consciously. But the extent of the parallelism that does exist makes it difficult to doubt that he was fully conscious of and immersed in the traditions with which he worked.

An approach to *The Pearl* governed by exegetical traditions may leave much to be desired in the quantity of material it explains. But it is an important approach, for, because of the lack of a demonstrable historical level, the student is faced with a necessity for not confusing the unknown intentions of an unknown poet with the discoverable intentions of a known poem. And the exegetical traditions demonstrate that no matter what degree of elegy obtains in *The Pearl,* the result is still a revelation of a medieval mind working out a moral instruction and a religious attitude.

---

of Boodt, *Trattato della Gemme* of Dolce, *Rerum Naturalium* of Scribonnius, *Universae Naturae Theatrum* of Bodin, *Magicae Naturalis* of Porta. Don Cameron Allen, who lists the foregoing Renaissance lapidaries, suggests that all the Renaissance works were in the medieval tradition except the seventeenth century Dolce and Boodt, who exhibit a scientific scepticism "coupled with a suggestion of seventeenth century rationalism." See "Drayton's Lapidaries," *MLN,* LIII (1938), 93.

7

THE *PEARL:* NOTES FOR
AN INTERPRETATION

Stanton Hoffman

I

THERE ARE THREE POSSIBILITIES IN ANY INTERPRETATION OF the *Pearl:* the poem is a total allegory, the poem is a personal elegy, or the poem is a combination of both allegory and elegy. I shall in this paper be concerned with the first, a possibility of interpretation which, as so far presented, opens itself to several important objections. It is also my intention to present for consideration four points ignored, either singly or wholly, by this type of interpretation, for it is my belief that these four points must be considered before any further allegorical interpretation of the poem can be made.

Allegory was first argued for by W. H. Schofield, who found, in medieval literature and thought, at least eighteen allegorical interpretations of the pearl symbol and stated that generally the pearl must be protean in its symbolism. Beyond this, he found it necessary to try to identify the pearl as the emblem of clean

Reprinted, by permission of the author and of The University of Chicago Press, from *Modern Philology*, LVIII (1960), 73–80. Copyright © 1960 by The University of Chicago Press. Translations have been supplied by the author, along with a correction of the last quotation.

maidenhood, or of immaculateness and purity,[1] but, by making his symbol so protean, he made it almost no symbol. When he related the pearl to clean maidenhood, he was unable to explain just how this purity, once lost, transferred itself to heaven and just what consolation such a transference would be to the narrator (especially if he were the one who had lost the pearl). Here Schofield neglected the individuality of the narrator. Furthermore, by stating that the poem progressed from the literal to the symbolic, from the material to the spiritual, from the actual to the figurative, he committed the error of his successors and worked from the assumption that the one pearl symbol becomes another pearl symbol as the poem progresses and that the pearl symbols throughout the poem are not kept distinct.

Sister Madeleva's more precise interpretation of the poem as an exposition of spiritual dryness or interior desolation, accompanied by subsequent questionings, hopes, and resignations,[2] and her relating the poem to the body of European and British mystical writings in terminology, imagery, and idea may also be open to objections. When she says of the spice garden of the third stanza that the flowers of the most substantial virtues grow from the graves of renunciation, self-conquest, and spiritual bereavement, the meaning is confused because she represents the pearl as the soul's state of interior sweetness and yet speaks of the pearl in this case as if it referred to fleshly love or love of life. She ignores also the possibility of the poet's originality when she argues that the poem cannot be a personal elegy because neither religious nor secular writing showed any general tendency to symbolize childhood or the individual child under the figure of the pearl. By arguing that the conclusion represents the poet's identification of humanity

[1] "Symbolism, Allegory, and Autobiography in 'The Pearl,' " *PMLA*, XXIV (1909), 638.

[2] Sister Mary Madeleva, *Pearl: A Study in Spiritual Dryness* (New York, 1925), p. 3.

with precious pearls, and by arguing that, if this poem were an elegy, these final five lines would be addressed to the daughter, she ignores the possibility that this final prayer might be the conventional address to the reader found throughout much medieval writing. Furthermore, she overlooks the presence in the poem of several specific references to physical decay and death, and she confuses the distinctly different pearl symbols in the poem, concluding somewhat absurdly that the pearl could not be the poet's dead daughter because the figure of the poet's grinding pearls upon the ground (81–82) would become a thing of "crude and utter roughness." When she goes on to claim that the pearl's image of the rose is what every spiritual director tells a person who laments a subtraction of spiritual consolation, she ignores the context and the commoner usage of this metaphor as the metaphor of mortality. Her interpretation of the line "She was nearer to me than aunt or niece" as expressing a nearness outside of and beyond the kinship of nature is somewhat farfetched. The poet would have been more likely in this case to say: "She was nearer to me than daughter or mother"—unless, of course, he happened to be a religious, in which case he would still have a mother. And, when she states that children are not mentioned in the pearl's heaven, Sister Madeleva is committing the narrator's error of applying earthly distinctions to heavenly unity. Finally, and most important, Sister Madeleva's entire method breaks down in her discussion of the vineyard parable. She states that the eleventh-hour worker cannot apply to a child, "whose happiness in heaven is a consequence of baptismal innocence and not the reward of a single hour's labor in God's vineyard." It is odd that she refuses to accept the word *labor* as metaphoric when she accepts all else as such.

The more recent arguments for total allegory are, in general, of two types. There are those which argue that the poem represents a clash of two worlds—the material and the spiritual—that the pearl represents things in both worlds, and that the meaning of the poem is to be gotten from the interplay of the two worlds. Stern with his reading of the poem as expressing the tension between the Platonic duality of world and idea,[3] Conley with his Christian *Consolatio* theory and his regarding the pearl in the opening of the poem as the pearl representing false happiness,[4] Sister Mary Hillman with her pearl as representing a material gem and material wealth,[5] and Wendell Johnson with his theory of the interaction of two sets of images—those of this world, and those of the next[6]—belong to this first group. On the other hand, there are those who see the poem as a minor biblical epic, a *Paradise Regained,* on the theme of the fallen soul and its salvation, with references to Eden and Golgotha. The interpretations of Marie P. Hamilton,[7] J. B. Fletcher,[8] and, to an extent, W. K. Greene[9] belong to this second group. And, of course, there are those interpretations which are of neither type: that of Robertson,[10] who argues for a pearl-innocence equation, and that of Garrett,[11] who sees the pearl as symbolizing the Holy Eucharist, the former ignoring the individuality of the narrator and the latter ignoring what is central to the poem, the sacrament of baptism.

These interpretations are based on two essential errors—

[3] Milton Stern, "An Approach to *The Pearl*," *JEPG*, LIV (1955), 684–692.

[4] John Conley, *"Pearl and a Lost Tradition,"* *JEPG*, LIV (1955), 332–347.

[5] Sister Mary B. Hillman, "Some Debatable Words in 'Pearl' and Its Themes," *MLN*, LX (1945), 241–248.

[6] "The Imagery and Diction of *The Pearl:* Toward an Interpretation," *ELH*, XX (1953), 161–180.

[7] "The Meaning of the Middle English *Pearl*," *PMLA*, LXX (1955), 805–824.

[8] "The Allegory of the *Pearl*," *JEGP*, XX (1921), 1–21.

[9] Walter K. Greene, "The 'Pearl'—A New Interpretation," *PMLA*, XL (1925), 814–827.

[10] D. W. Robertson, Jr. "The Pearl as a Symbol," *MLN*, LXV (1950), 155–161.

[11] R. M. Garrett, "The Pearl: An Interpretation" ("University of Washington Publications," Vol. IV, No. 1 [Seattle, 1918]).

either there is a failure to keep really distinct pearl symbols separate, or there is a failure to avoid making distinctions where there are none. For instance, it is difficult to consider the first pearl symbol as representing a material gem or material wealth and the falsely desired things of this world and not to ignore the context in which this symbol appears and such concrete statements as can be found in lines 259 and following. Likewise, it is hard to explain such lines as "O moul, þou marreʒ a myry iuele" [O Earth, you are destroying a merry jewel] and various other references to physical death and decay. Furthermore, such a generally astute criticism as that of Wendell Johnson, in attempting to work out this World-Spirit duality in terms of structure and imagery, makes the error of confusing levels of meaning in its attempt to see the basic image contrasts of the poem unified through the contrasting of the vineyard and heavenly city images. This is an attempt to force a unity and to seek a system of analogies which will give the poem its meaning; but it is unsuccessful, for the vineyard is still a parable and the heavenly city is still an actual.

Also, a representation of the pearl as man's fallen nature and his saved nature neglects the fact that the poem contains distinct pearl symbols and that the pearl symbol of the opening appears at the close. In fact, the narrator still laments his loss, the same loss, in the same tone, hardly the case with a *Consolatio.*

II

The confusion resulting from the plethora of interpretations given the *Pearl*—interpretations not mutually exclusive—can be reduced to order, I believe, by a consideration of the poem from four points.

An important part of the poem is the use of the pearl figure as a symbol for various things. The pearl seems to be used to signify that which is lost, a specific, first and unifying meaning; beyond this, in the course of the poem it is used to represent, respectively, the gravel of the ground, the costumes of all who are similar to the maiden in purity and innocence, the purified spirit itself which is salvation, Christ as the epitome of this, and the foundations of the New Jerusalem. Thus in addition to its first meaning, the pearl signifies spiritual purification and salvation; Christ is the epitome of this purity and also the means, end, and object of this salvation. The pearl of the crown, of the garment, and of the Pearl's breast is the symbol of the purity which is the object's. This leaves only the first use of the pearl as that which is lost and lamented to be explained, a use which has caused the poem's commentators the most difficulty, for it is believed rightly that, if one is to see the poem as a unified whole, he must consider this pearl in the context and the light of the other pearls. But to do this does not mean that this pearl becomes the later pearls, nor, on the other hand, does it mean that this pearl is exclusive of the others.

For example, one school of interpreters, as already indicated, has seen the first pearl figure as the things of this world or false happiness. Sister Hillman has gone so far as to accept this pearl as a real, material pearl which is to be transcended by the pearl of purity. Unfortunately, this is to ignore two things: context and the fact that the first meaning of the pearl is carried throughout the poem. In the last sections, specifically stanzas 98–101, the pearl is used as it has been used in the opening stanzas. There has been no modification of the sense of this symbol, except that it is now enriched by the other senses in which the pearl has been used—that is, to represent purity, salvation, and Christ. I believe that the pearl lost of stanza 1 is the same pearl of stanzas 24, 28, 32, 76, 98, 99, and 100. It is the pearl lost in human terms, in worldly and fleshly terms; that it has been found in a vision does not negate this first point that it has been lost on earth and in the grass of this arbor. This is to say that in the poem we find together several meanings of the pearl figure and that they are kept distinct. Critics such as Sister Hillman assume that the pearl of the first part of the poem cannot be the pearl of the vision, which, I think, is to ignore something fundamental—that the poet speaks to the pearl and about her at the beginning in a way which is *essentially* the same as that of the ending. When the poet says, "For pyty of my perle enclyin" (1206), or when he refers to the pearl's straying to the ground (1173), I fail to detect any shifting from one symbol to another, and the only change is the natural one that the pearl has become recognized in a new context and as the teacher of a vision. Furthermore, if the pearl of the opening represented false happiness, as Conley contends, and if the progress of the poem represented the narrator's learning the difference between false and true bliss, then it would seem that in the last few stanzas the narrator had unlearned this difference, something that he should have retained.

A second group of critics and commentators have made the pearl in its first meaning and usage refer to innocence, purity, or salvation. This interpretation causes, I believe, as many difficulties as the first; moreover, it has the difficulty of explaining exactly what consolation the poem's narrator would get, and it, as already mentioned, involves a complete ignoring of his specific personality. It would seem that these interpreters have gone to the other extreme. The first group made distinctions where there were none; this second group fails to see distinctions where they exist. To make the pearl a symbol of innocence is to assume that a second or third meaning of the symbol absorbs and changes a first meaning. Yet an analysis of a stanza such as 21 or 63 will indicate that the meanings of the symbol are kept distinct.[12] There are in the latter stanza

---

[12] In st. 21 the pearl of l. 241 is the pearl who is the speaker, who dwells in Paradise, but also in this line there are the pearls which adorn her garment. In l. 242 the pearl is the pearl which has been lost by the poet. In st. 63 there is the matchless pearl of l. 745, which is the same pearl of ll. 755 and 756, and there are the pure pearls of l. 745 and the pearl of price of l. 746.

three different pearls; the modification, if any, results from context and is one of extension, not one of nature or basic meaning.

A second point to consider is the use of the term and the concept of "innocence" and "the innocent" in the poem. There seem to be two uses of innocence here, one of which is actually an extension of the other; yet, it is in its first and basic use that the term becomes important. In this use, it is part of the term "the innocent," and "the innocent" refers specifically to little children, to infants. For example, the lines

> Bot innoghe of grace hatȝ innocent.
> As sone as þay arn borne, by lyne
> In þe water of babtem þay dyssente:
> Þen arne þay broȝt into þe vyne.
> Anon þe day, wyth derk endente,
> Þe nıȝt of deth dotȝ to enclyne　　　(625–630)

> [But enough of grace the innocent have
> As soon as they are born, by line
> In the waters of baptism they descend:
> Then are they brought into the vineyard.
> Anon the day, with dark inlaid,
> To the night of death does incline]

seem a specific reference to the innocent as little children, especially when one considers that a great deal of the debate is centered around baptism and its effect on salvation. Also in lines 743–744

> I rede þe forsake þe worlde wode
> And porchace þy perle maskelles

> [I advise thee forsake the mad world
> And purchase thy spotless pearl]

and in the earlier lines

> Where wysteȝ þou euer any bourne abate,
> Euer so holy in hys prayere,
> Þat he ne forfeted by sumkyn gate
> Þe mede sumtyme of heueneȝ clere?　　(617–620)

> [Where knew you ever any man endured
> Ever so holy in his prayer
> That he didn't forfeit by some way
> The reward sometimes of heaven clear?]

the poet seems to be suggesting that life itself by its nature must involve sin and loss of innocence. Thus several things seem to be related here: that the term "the innocent" refers to little children (remember the emphasis on the pearl's extreme youth), that a major part of the poem deals with the meaning and effects of baptism, and that there is a suggestion that life involves stain and the loss of innocence. Innocence in its basic sense is that which is possessed by infants and which gains them their salvation; on a broader level it can mean all which is pure and spotless.

The lines

> Bot resoun of ryȝt þat con noȝt raue
> Saueȝ evermore þe innossent;
> Hit is a dom þat neuer God gaue,
> Þat euer þe gyltleȝ schulde be schente   (665–668)
>
> [But reason of justice that cannot go astray
> Saves evermore the innocent,
> It is a judgment that God never gave
> That ever the guiltless should be discomfited]

seem more than just the pearl's answer to the narrator; they seem to express a fundamental meaning of the poem—and to present the pearl as the guiltless and innocent. If we consider that life consists of corruption and sin, and that the only way to escape stain is to escape the world (although this does not mean that one regains innocence, but rather that he gains salvation, for here the meaning of "spotless pearl" must be kept separate from its other meanings—it means primarily salvation), it would seem evident that Pearl cannot represent something which is part of the narrator, such as his soul or his happiness. For the pearl, by her answer and argument, is identified with absolute purity, and the man who has toiled long in God's vineyard may be righteous, but not innocent, for he cannot in the long run avoid sin and lapse. The pearl, itself, implies perpetual innocence and the absence of the corrupting world in all its conditions; it would be an innocence which could never refer to the narrator's spiritual sweetness and its loss due to the material world because it is something he should never be able to possess, for man's soul is corrupted by having existed in the body, by life. The poet may gain purity, but he can never be of the innocent. In this sense, because innocence is not a state of the narrator's life, and because references to it are placed in the context of references to the pearl's infancy, and the descent of grace at birth through Divine Grace, I believe it can only refer to the state which is truly the infant's. Any extension of its meaning must start from this point.

In the first stanza of the thirteenth stanza-group Jesus' statement must not be taken as an isolated statement or as a statement that the soul's state should be like that of a child. It is an argument for the innocent's (the child's) admission and reward. The poet is saying that, since Jesus said that all who come to him must come to him as a child, it follows that the child must of necessity be saved and blessed. Yet it would seem that most critics have approached this statement incorrectly. And one should remember that the narrator is forbidden to stretch in the street of heaven because he is not clean or without spot; life in his terms is greatly a "dungeon of sorrow." Thus, I consider three things important in any examination of what is meant by "innocence" in the poem. One, the central figure of the poem, the most important image of Christ, is the Christ of baptism, and baptism and the renewing blood are emphasized throughout. Two, the poet makes a distinction between innocence and righteousness and goes further to imply the impossibility of total innocence to one who has lived in this "dungeon of sorrow." And three, "the innocent" seems to refer directly to children; it must be seen in the light of statements about age made by the narrator and by the pearl and in the light of the reference to Christ's words as a proof that children must be saved, *not* as a direction to mankind on the means of salvation.

A third point of consideration is strangely enough ignored by most commentators upon the poem. Throughout the *Pearl* there are frequent references to physical death. For instance, such lines as

> Þat lelly hyȝte your lyf to rayse,
> Þaȝ fortune *dyd your flesch to dyȝe*   (305–306)

> [That faithfully promised your life to raise
> Though fortune *made your flesh to die*]

> Er moste þou ceuer to oþer counsayle:
> *Þy corse in clot mot colder keue.*
> For hit watȝ forgarte at Paradys greue;
> Oure ȝorefader hit con myssezeme   (319–322)

> [Before you must attain to other counsel
> *Your body in earth must colder sink.*
> For it was corrupted at Paradise grave
> Our forefather did it abuse]

> Alþaȝ *oure corses in clotteȝ clynge,*
> And ȝe remen for rauþe wythouten reste,
> We þurȝoutly hauen cnawyng;
> Of on dethe ful oure hope is drest   (857–860)

> [Although *our corpses in earth cling*
> And you cry out for grief without rest,
> We completely have knowing;
> For one death full our hope is drawn]

> Þat is þe borȝ þat we to pres
> Fro *þat oure flesh be layd to rote*   (957–958)

> [That is the town to which we hasten
> From that *our flesh be laid to decay*]

> For pyty of my perle enclyin   (1206)

> [For pity of my pearl lying prostrate]

emphasize the decaying and dying flesh and the act of physical dying. They speak of a literal death, not a figurative one. Line

858 represents the poet's case, his actual grief, and this is further accented by lines 345–348:

> For þoȝ þou daunce as any do,
> Braundysch and bray þy braþeȝ breme,
> When þou no fyrre may, to ne fro,
> Þou moste abyde þat he schal deme.

> [For though you leap in agony as any do,
> Toss about and bray thy agonies fierce,
> When you no further may in any direction,
> You must abide what He shall deem.]

Lines such as these cannot be explained by such interpretations
of the pearl as innocence or purity—abstractions; the grief
itself is real, and if the pearl represented lost innocence, false
happiness, the fallen state of the soul, the Eucharist, or the loss
of spiritual sweetness, what sense would the pearl's consoling
words to the narrator make?

> That juel þenne in gemmeȝ gente
> Vered vp her vyse wyth yȝen graye,
> Set on hyr coroun of perle orient,
> And soberly after þenne con ho say:
> 'Sir, ȝe haf your tale mysetente,
> To say your perle is al awaye,
> Þat is in cofer so comely clente
> As in þis gardyn gracios gaye,
> Hereinne to lenge for euer and play,
> Þer mys nee mornyng com never nere.'   (253–262)

> [That jewel then in gems fair
> Veered up her face with eyes gray
> Placed on her crown of orient pearl,
> And soberly after then did she say;
> 'Sir, you have your tale misrepresented
> To say your pearl is all away
> That is in coffer so comely fastened
> As in this gracious garden graciously gay,
> Herein to stay for ever and rejoice,
> Where sorrow nor mourning come never near.]

This would be a strange answer if the pearl on this level were
meant to represent mistaken desires on the narrator's part, for

why would these desires or this false happiness, or even this lost innocence, be comely fastened in a coffer in this garden, this specific garden which has a literal existence and is also analogous to the garden of paradise and the New Jerusalem? And when the poet very movingly breaks out into lament in lines 23–24:

> O moul, þou marreȝ a myry iuele,
> My priuy perle wythouten spotte.
>
> [Oh, Earth, you are destroying a merry jewel,
> My own pearl without spot.]

could he mean the earth is destroying its own children or what? I would suggest that, in relationship to the references to physical death and the pearl's answer, which is the first step in the consoling of the person who laments death, the earth is destroying a corpse, the flesh, and the physical person. The narrator is to learn that the person of the pearl, who is the innocent one, lives on. And in line 282, if we can accept E. V. Gordon's gloss of "don out of dawe," as a colloquial way of saying a person has died, we have something overlooked by everyone, that the literal statement of death has overcome the poet's figure—the allegorical or symbolic statement; for the figure, according to most critics, is a consistent one of loss, not of physical decay.

Finally, earlier, in criticizing Sister Madeleva's interpretation of the pearl's rose metaphor, I suggested that she was overlooking several important things: that this metaphor had more common traditional associations than those she ascribed to it and that it is used not once but six times in the poem, three times in a cluster early in the poem and three times in a near-cluster later in the poem. The first three appearances of this figure are in relationship to death, the lament; the second are in relationship to the New Jerusalem, the consolation. It is my belief that these metaphors are part of a broader identification used consistently throughout the poem and basic to the poem's

meaning—the constant identification of flower, fruit, and jewel.
Lines such as

> Quen þat frech as flor-de-lys
> Doun þe bonke con boȝe bydene   (195–196)
>
> [When that one fresh as the fleur de lys
> Down the bank did go straightway]
>
> Hiȝe pynakled of cler quyt perle,
> Wyth flurted flowreȝ perfet vpon   (207–208)
>
> [High pinnacled of clear white pearl
> With figured flowers perfect upon]
>
> For þat þou lesteȝ watȝ bot a rose
> Þat flowred and fayled as kynde hyt gef (269–270)
>
> [For what you lost was but a rose
> That flowered and failed as nature ordains]
>
> Þy colour passeȝ þe flour-de-lys   (753)
>
> [Thy color passes the fleur de lys]
>
> And þou so ryche a reken rose,
> And bydeȝ here by þys blysful bonc
> Þer lyueȝ lyste may neuer lose   (906–908)
>
> [And you so rich a fresh rose,
> And dwell here by this blissful bank
> Where life's joy may never be lost]
>
> 'Moteleȝ may so meke and mylde';
> Þen sayde I to þat lufly flor   (961–962)
>
> ['Spotless maiden so meek and mild'
> Then said I to that lovely flower]

create a flower, garden, jewel, maiden identification and are
related to an apparent motif in the poem, the death-and-resur-
rection motif, which has a further presentation in the two
Jerusalems and the figure of Christ. The first three flower-
jewel identifications appear in a context of lament and mortality, of fleshly death; the second three appear as the revelation
progresses, during the resurrection, so to speak, and suggest a

renewal which then has its unity and its analogue in the third stanza of the poem:

> Flor and fryte may not be fede
> Þer hit doun drof in moldeȝ dunne;
> For vch gresse mot grow of grayneȝ dede;
> No whete were elleȝ to woneȝ wonne.
> Of goud vche goude is ay bygonne;
> So semly a sede moȝt fayly not,
> Þat spryngande spyceȝ vp ne sponne. (29–35)

> [Flower and fruit may not be faded
> Where it fell down in earth's hill,
> For each grass must grow from dead grains;
> No wheat were else to dwelling place brought.
> From good, each good is ever begun;
> So seemly a seed must not fail
> That springing spices might not spring up.]

In lines 259 and following, the garden image is again presented and is identified with paradise, also becoming an analogue to it. That which is lost is safe and secure in this garden; this garden is the place of death and resurrection. The jewel symbol suggests permanence and stability; the flower image is a reminder of mortality and of the cycle of life translated into religious terms. The body dies and is resurrected, the spirit lives on in a New Jerusalem, and the rose which had once died because it was ordained by nature is born again as the pearl and the infant soul.

The poem is written during a "high season"; it is possibly related to the harvest. The soul is referred to in the language of renewal; we are

> As newe fryt to God ful due (894)

> [As new fruit to God full due],

and the flower-jewel identification is broadened into a fruit-flower-jewel identification. The picture of heaven itself contains an analogous statement of the entire motif:

> Aboute þat water arn tres ful schym,
> Þat twelue fryteȝ of lyf con fere ful sone;

Twelve syþeȝ on ȝer þay beren ful frym,
And renowleȝ nwe in vche a mone.   (1077–1080)

[About the waters are trees full bright
That twelve fruits of life did bear full soon;
Twelve times a year they bear full of rich growth
And renew newly every moon.]

III

Thus we have four points upon which to base an interpretation of the poem. The *Pearl* uses the symbol of the pearl in various ways which are kept distinct. The poem uses "the innocent" in terms of infants and their salvation, and the pearl, in being identified with total innocence, is most likely the symbol for infants or for a specific infant. The poem contains important references to physical death, and it makes use of the death and renewal motif of the spice garden, for life brings forth new life which is salvation. It is my belief that these points are all closely related. First, there is the first meaning of the pearl symbol, a meaning which appears throughout the poem. Second, this meaning is identified with "the innocent," which is used primarily to refer to infants and their salvation. Third, the poem is concerned with physical death; this is related to the pearl symbol and the questions of salvation which are posed. And fourth, the poem ends on a note of renewal, which is the renewal of life and the resurrection. Further, I believe this is a poem about death, about the death of the infant child (we cannot ignore the great lament of its opening). The pearl is something apart from the narrator, and he laments its death and is consoled by a resurrection and a renewal, all accented by the use of the death-resurrection motif in terms of the flower-jewel identification. The poem is basically an elegy; its concern is actual death, its meaning, and its resolution. This is not to deny allegorical meaning, for in a sense the application can be made broader—the final vision is not only a vision of a specific maiden in a procession but also a vision of the procession and of the New Jerusalem. But any allegorical interpretation must start, I believe, from the point of physical death, and it must be able to bring the poem into some kind of unity with that fact.

Related to all this is the theme which creates the poem's form and direction and provides another means of unity. As the narrator begins his vision, he states:

> My goste is gon in Godeȝ grace
> In auenture þer meruayleȝ meuen.   (63–64)

> [My spirit is gone in God's grace
> In adventures where marvels exist.]

This is the theme of spiritual adventure, the journey of the soul as it goes forth seeking truth. Faced with the fact of death, the poet grieves, and the poem is a seeking for a truth which will answer the where and the why of this specific death, the death of the infant child. The poet's spirit is instructed, and, if we learn something also of man's fate—something beyond the specific incident of the poem—it is, I think, a sign of the poet's success, for his poem answers not only for the child's death, but, in all its extended meanings, for our own deaths.

8

THE ROLE OF THE NARRATOR IN *PEARL*

Charles Moorman

IT IS DECIDEDLY *not* THE INTENTION OF THIS PAPER TO INTRO-
duce a radically new interpretation of the Middle English
Pearl, a poem which has already been done almost to death
by its interpreters. The criticism already devoted to the poem
contains judgments as to its meaning and purpose so varied
and, at times, so downright contradictory that *Pearl* is in
danger of becoming a scholarly free-for-all, another "Who
was Homer?" or "Why did Hamlet delay?" The disputed question in *Pearl* is, of course, "What is the pearl-maiden?" So far
it has been suggested that she is the poet's daughter,[1] clean
maidenhood,[2] the Eucharist,[3] innocence,[4] the lost sweetness of

Reprinted, by permission of the author and of The University of
Chicago Press, from *Modern Philology*, LIII (1955), 73–81, Copyright
© 1955 by The University of Chicago Press. Translations have been
supplied by the author.

[1] See the commentaries in the editions of the poem by R. Morris (London, 1864); I. Gollancz (London, 1891); and C. G. Osgood (Boston,
1906); and especially G. G. Coulton's defense of the autobiographical
basis of the poem in *MLR,* II (1906), 39–43.

[2] W. H. Schofield, "The Nature and Fabric of *The Pearl*," *PMLA*,
XIX (1904), 154–215, and "Symbolism, Allegory, and Autobiography in
The Pearl," *ibid.*, XXIV (1909), 585–675.

[3] R. M. Garrett, "*The Pearl*": *An Interpretation* ("University of Washington Publications in English," Vol. IV, No. 1 [Seattle, 1918]).

[4] See Jefferson B. Fletcher, "The Allegory of the *Pearl*," *JEGP*, XX
(1921), 1–21; and D. W. Robertson, "The 'Heresy' of *The Pearl*" and
"The Pearl as Symbol," *MLN*, LXV (1950), 152–161.

God,[5] the Blessed Virgin,[6] heaven itself,[7] and a literary fiction functioning only as an introduction to theological debate.[8] Such interest in the figure of the girl and in the peripheral aspects of source and imagery is understandable. A poem containing possible allusions to the *Roman de la rose,* Boccaccio, Chaucer, Dante, and the Vulgate and utilizing possibly heretical theology, the medieval dream-vision, the elegy, and the *débat* is a critic's land of heart's desire. However, such interpretive scholarship, while undeniably of great interest and value in opening up new avenues of critical insight, is nevertheless fragmentary, in that it is all too seldom directed, except in the most parenthetical manner, toward exploring the total meaning of the poem. We become easily lost in exploring the technicalities of the theology, the possible levels of symbolism in the maiden, and the details of the vision of the New Jerusalem and so are content to leave the center of the poem untouched or to murmur that its theme is obvious and pass on.

I would suggest that the quickest way to come to the heart of the poem would be to waive entirely all questions of allegory and symbolism and to concentrate not upon the figure of the girl but upon that of the narrator. For whatever else the poem may be—dream-vision, elegy, allegory, debate—it is, first of all, a fiction presented from a clearly defined and wholly consistent point of view; we accompany the "I" of the poem through his vision, and it is through his eyes that we see the magical landscapes and the girl. In the terms of Henry James, the narrator-poet is the "central intelligence" of the poem; in those of Brooks and Warren, the poem is the "narrator's story," in that we are never allowed to see and judge the experience

---

[5] Sister Mary Madeleva, *"Pearl": A Study in Spiritual Dryness* (New York, 1925).

[6] Fletcher.

[7] Sister Mary Hillman, "Some Debatable Words in *Pearl* and Its Theme," *MLN,* LX (1945), 241–248.

[8] W. K. Greene, *"The Pearl":* A New Interpretation," *PMLA,* XL (1925), 814–827.

presented by the poem objectively and for ourselves but are, instead, forced, by the point of view which the poet adopts, to accept the experience of the vision only in terms of its relationship to him. The mind of the narrator in *Pearl,* like the mind of Strether in *The Ambassadors* or, to come closer home, the mind of Dante the voyager, is the real subject under consideration. It is with the figure of the narrator alone in an "erbere" [arbor] that the poem begins and ends; it is he who controls the argument with the pearl-maiden by introducing the subjects for debate and by directing the path of the discussion with his questions; it is for his benefit that the maiden relates the parable of the vineyard and allows him to view the New Jerusalem.

The girl—to most critics the center of attraction simply because of her enigmatic and apparently shifting nature—is not introduced until line 161 and does not become actively engaged in the poem until line 241, when she is addressed by the narrator. She then disappears at line 976, to appear only once thereafter in a single reference within the vision of the New Jerusalem. In a poem of 1,212 lines, the girl herself is present on the scene for only 815 lines and can be said to participate in the action for only 735 lines, a little over half the length of the poem. Moreover, the pearl-maiden cannot be said to function, except peripherally, in the narrative movement of the poem. During that middle section of the poem which she seems to dominate by her presence, the poet never allows us to lose our sense of the narrator's presence. We know that he is there and listening carefully, interjecting questions and remarks from time to time. We are constantly aware of the fact that it is for his benefit that the girl talks and that it is his consciousness which is directly affected by her remarks. In short, the poet has so constructed the poem that it becomes obligatory that the reader judge the figure of the pearl-maiden not in isolation but entirely in terms of her relation to the narrator, the "I," the central intelligence of the poem.

The effect of this fact upon interpretation would seem to

be twofold. First, it forces the reader to regard the action of the poem within the implied dramatic framework which the poet provides, and, second, it requires the reader to fit into that framework all the details, however seemingly unrelated, which the poet introduces—most significantly, the parable of the vineyard, the debate over grace and merit and the ensuing description of the place of the innocent in the heavenly hierarchy, the girl's description of her life in the New Jerusalem, and the vision of the New Jerusalem which is given to the poet.

The poem begins with a direct statement by the poet-narrator that he has lost "in on erbere"[9] [in an arbor] a certain pearl of great value, one which is to him without peer in all the world. He is so terribly grieved by the loss of the pearl that he cannot forget his former delight in possessing the gem; he laments his loss, "wyschande þat wele, / Þat wont watȝ whyle deuoyde [his] wrange / And heuen [his] happe and al [his] hele" [wishing that happiness / That once (him) freed from care / And restored (his) hap and all (his) joy] (14–16). But his grief takes another form also: it brings into his mind a series of paradoxes concerning the relationship of beauty and death or, more specifically, of growth and death. He knows that he sang "neuer so swete a sange" [never so sweet a song] (19) as that which he sings now in his hour of deepest grief; he reflects that the pearl's presence in the earth of the arbor will cause "blomeȝ blayke and blwe and rede" [golden and blue and red blossoms] (27) to prosper over her grave; he knows that "vch gresse mot grow of grayneȝ dede" [each blade must grow from dead seed] (31). In short, the narrator's grief-stricken statements reflect more than personal sorrow over the loss of the pearl. In his grief he begins to consider the paradoxical nature of the universe in which he lives, a universe in which the decay of the body contributes directly

---

[9] *Pearl*, ed. E. V. Gordon (Oxford, 1953), l. 9. All line references in the text are to this edition.

to the beauty of nature, where "Flor and fryte may not be fede / Þer hit doun drof in moldeȝ dunne" [flowers and fruit may not fail where this pearl dropped down into dark earth] (29–30). Like Shelley in "Adonais," he wonders how

> The leprous corpse, touched by this spirit tender,
> Exhales itself in flowers of gentle breath;
> Like incarnations of the stars, when splendour
> Is changed to fragrance, they illumine death
> And mock the merry worm that wakes beneath.

Having established the narrator's grief and, more importantly, this questioning of the nature and justice of the universe which his grief inspires, the poet goes on to begin the dramatic movement of the poem. The narrator states that he has come to "þat spot" (49) where he lost the pearl; he has come there, moreover, in the very midst of August, when all growing things have blossomed, when the corn must be cut and the flowers— gillyflowers, ginger, gromwells, and peonies—are "schyre and schene" [bright and shining] (42). Here, in the midst of joy, his sorrow becomes even more acute, and in spite both of "resoun," which offers only the most temporary relief to his "deuely dele" [dreadful care] (51), and of the "kynde of Kryst," his "wreched wylle in wo ay wraȝte" [nature of Christ], [wretched will in woe was caught] (56). It is in this mood that the vision begins.

Thus in the first section of the poem we are introduced, even before we know that the poem is to take the form of a vision, to two facts about the situation of the narrator. First, we learn that he is overcome with inconsolable grief, and from the allusion to the "huyle" [mound] (41) we judge that the poet is grieving the death of a loved one. Second, we learn that his grief has taken the form of an awareness, almost of an indictment, of the mixed nature of the world. Standing amid the joyful flowers of August, he can think only of death and of the fact that the rotting body of his beloved child, "so clad in clot" [clothed in clay] (22), has produced this profusion

107

of color. The two are so connected in the mind of the narrator, moreover, that his last thoughts upon going to sleep are of his own "wreched wylle" and, paradoxically, of the fragrance which springs into his senses as he falls asleep. In short, the poet's immediate grief has developed at the very beginning of the poem into a pondering of universal problems of life and death.

This questioning of the nature of things introduced at the outset is to occupy the poet throughout the poem. In order to assuage his grief, the poet must thus accomplish a reconciliation of the apparently dual nature of heavenly justice. And it is precisely this struggle for understanding which gives the poem its permanence and its enduring appeal. We are seldom, if ever, satisfied with the purely occasional poem, and the elegy which records only a particular grief never becomes in any way meaningful to us. In the elegy, moreover, the poet's grief is made universal and thus meaningful by exactly the process we see at work here in *Pearl*. The reader's attention is directed by the elegiac poet not toward the figure of the deceased, but toward the poet's own struggle to accept his loss and, more importantly, toward his struggle to understand in universal terms the final meaning of death and the conditions under which death may be meaningful to him. In "Lycidas," we remember, we are not allowed to become interested in the figure of Edward King. Our attention instead is focused from the beginning upon the struggle of the young Milton, first, to accept the possibility of his own premature death and, second, to understand, in both personal and universal terms, the significance of King's death. Likewise, in "In Memoriam" the figure of Arthur Hallam moves out of our consciousness as Tennyson explores the terms upon which he can accept a traditional faith in a skeptical age. "Adonais" and "Thyrsis" are more concerned with the struggles of the living Shelley and the living Arnold than with the praises of the dead Keats and the dead Clough.

And so it is with *Pearl*. The first section of the poem introduces the poet's struggle to reconcile the apparent contradiction expressed for him in the contrast of the flowers and the corpse; stanzas 2–5 introduce the means whereby he can approach a resolution of that contradiction. From the side of the grave his "spyryt þer sprang in space" [spirit leapt through space] (61), and his body "on balke þer bod in sweuen" [remained in a dream on the mound] (62). He finds himself in a strange world, far removed from the familiar earthly garden where he fell asleep; he "ne wyste in þis worlde quere þat hit wace" [new not in this world where it was] (65). He sees about him the items of the natural world—cliffs, forests, trees; but here these familiar sights are transformed into strange shapes and materials: crystal cliffs, forests filled with "rych rokkeȝ" (68), silver leaves, and pearls scattered about as gravel. This is the Earthly Paradise, where the ordinary natural objects of earth are displayed within and altered by a supernatural context. As Wendell Stacy Johnson points out, the images of the garden here reflect a brightness and light coming from outside themselves.[10]

Yet even this vision is not the ultimate perfection. Across the stream by which he walks lies the Heavenly Paradise, the complete antithesis of earth. The images pass here from "the vision of nature arrayed in (reflecting) light to one of a land and a person [the pearl-maiden] set in gems and adorned by an 'inner' lightness."[11] Both gardens, however, have a recuperative effect upon the narrator; the first "Bylde in [him] blys, abated [his] baleȝ, / Fordidden [his] stresse, dystryed [his] payneȝ" [increased (his) joy, relieved (his) sorrow, / Allayed (his) distress, destroyed (his)pain] (123–124). But the second paradise, that which lies across the stream, seems even more wonderful to him; there, he feels, lies the answer to his dilemma:

[10] "The Imagery and Diction of *The Pearl:* Toward an Interpretation," *ELH*, XX (1953), 169 [page 37 above].
[11] *Ibid.*

> Forþy I þoȝt þat Paradyse
> Watȝ þer ouer gayn þo bonkeȝ brade.
> I hoped þe water were a deuyse
> Bytwene myrþeȝ by mereȝ made;
> Byȝonde þe broke, by slente oþer slade,
> I hoped þat mote merked wore.   (137–142)

> [Indeed I thought that Paradise
> Beyond broad banks lay there displayed.
> I thought the stream to be a ruse,
> Between two joys a boundary made;
> Beyond the stream, on slope, in dell,
> I thought to see the City laid.]

But the water is deep, and, in spite of his longing, the narrator cannot cross.

The narrator has now reached a position midway between earth, with its unsolvable riddles of life and death, and heaven, where all contradictories are united. In mythical terms, the narrator has arrived at a testing point; he is midway in the hero's mythical initiation cycle from earth to the strange land of adventure to earth again. Having accomplished the necessary journey to a strange land, having accepted the "call to adventure,"[12] he finds his mind "radically cut away from the attitudes, attachments, and life patterns of the stage left behind [his normal earthly life]."[13] In the more familiar terms of Arnold Toynbee, the narrator has accomplished a "withdrawal" from society which "makes it possible for the personality to realize powers within himself which might have remained dormant if he had not been released for the time being from his social toils and trammels."[14] Within the context of the poem, the narrator is at a point midway between problem (the apparently paradoxical nature of death) and solution (the resolving of

[12] Joseph Campbell, *The Hero with a Thousand Faces* (New York, 1949), pp. 49–59.

[13] *Ibid.*, p. 10.

[14] Arnold Toynbee, *A Study of History*, abridged by D. C. Somervell (Oxford, 1947), p. 217.

that paradox). His world has become neither earth nor heaven but a middle ground, where earth and heaven can, under certain conditions as in the dream-vision, meet. In the midst of his wonderment, just as he is about to attempt a crossing, he sees before him, on the other side of the stream, the lost pearl, and at this point the debate begins.

What I have just called the "debate," which is to say simply the conversation between the narrator and the pearl-maiden, falls conveniently, as I have implied, into four parts: (1) the parable of the vineyard, (2) the girl's discussion of the relative grounds of grace and merit as means of salvation and her ensuing explanation of the place of the innocent in the heavenly hierarchy, (3) her description of Our Lord's suffering in the Old Jerusalem and of her life with him in the New Jerusalem, and (4) the vision of the New Jerusalem. I would claim that these episodes in the discussion are not digressions used either for their own sakes or for purposes of general instruction but that they are well-defined and climactically arranged stages in the process by which the narrator is made to understand the meaning of the girl's death and so is freed from the burden of his grief. It is my general thesis here that the long debate between the narrator and the girl is the only means by which the narrator can resolve the paradox of beauty and decay, of growth and death, which has troubled him and, by that resolution, come to accept the death of his daughter. For it becomes quite clear in the course of the conversation between the living narrator-poet and the dead maiden that their differences are profound. He is a man, she an angel, and the nature of the stream that divides them and the function of the vision itself become clear within the context of those differences. Earth cannot receive her; he is not ready for heaven. The debate in which they engage thus becomes a contest between two points of view, the earthly and the heavenly, between a point of view which sees natural death only as an irreducible paradox of decay and growth and a point of view which can reconcile that paradox in terms of a higher unity. Thus the terms of the central episode of the debate—grace and merit—are of no great consequence in themselves but have meaning within the dramatic framework of the poem only as they relate to the attitudes which they serve to reveal in the course of the talk.

Wendell Stacy Johnson has already shown, by means of a careful study of the imagery of the poem, that *Pearl* involves "an emphasis upon a ubiquitous sense of contrast between the nature of heaven and the nature of earth, the revelation of which seems, for our [Johnson's] present reading, to be the poem's main purpose."[15] I would agree with Johnson's demonstration of the contrast between earthly values and heavenly values, but this contrast seems to me to constitute only the means used by the poet to attain a yet higher end. The poet's earthbound nature, which we, as readers, share and which causes him to balk and quibble at each of her explanations, is in reality the source of his discontent. The girl's purpose in the debate is thus not primarily to prove to him the theological validity of the saving doctrine of grace but to demonstrate to him a point of view which will allow him to accept the differences in their attitudes and, through this acceptance, to come to a realization of the meaning and purpose of her death. To show the successful resolution of the two points of view exhibited in the poem and, through this resolution, the concomitant acceptance by the narrator of the fact of death thus becomes the main purpose and theme of the poem.

It remains to chart briefly the progress of the argument. The narrator—who, we remember, is the central intelligence and thus, in a sense, the reader—begins with the most natural of questions, a question which stems from his own interrogation of the justness of God and from his earthbound point of view:

> "O perle," quod I, "in perleʒ pyʒt,
> Art þou my perle þat I haf playned,

---

[15] P. 163 [page 29 above].

Regretted by myn˙ one on nyȝte?
Much longenyg haf I for þe layned,
Syþen into gresse þou me aglyȝte.
Pensyf, payred, I am forpayned,
And þou in a lyf of lykyng lyȝte,
In Paradys erde, of stryf vnstrayned.
What wyrde hatȝ hyder my iuel vayned,
And don me in þys del and gret daunger?"

(241–250)

["O Pearl," I said, "in pearls bedight,
Are you the pearl that I have mourned
And grieved for by myself at night?
By grief for you have I been torn
Since into grass you slipped away.
Pensive and careworn, I have grieved,
While you enjoy a life of play
In Paradise from strife relieved.
What fate has there my jewel placed
And left to me this pain and care?"]

If both the tone and substance of his question reveal his earthly
point of view, both the tone and substance of the pearl-
maiden's answer reveal the gulf between them:

"Sir, ȝe haf your tale mysetente,
To say your perle is al awaye,
Þat is in cofer so comly clente
As in þis gardyn gracios gaye,
Hereinne to lenge for euer and play,
Þer mys nee mornyng com neuer nere.
Her were a forser for þe, in faye,
If þou were a gentyl iueler."   (257–264)

[Sir, you have your tale mistold,
To say your pearl was snatched away,
Since now she lies in royal state
In this fair garden sweet and gay,
Herein to dwell in constant joy
With loss and mourning never near.
Here might you see a treasured tomb
If you were a gentle jeweler.]

As E. V. Gordon has said, "In the manner of the maiden is

portrayed the effect upon a clear intelligence of the persistent earthliness of the father's mind: all is revealed to him, and he has eyes, yet he cannot see."[16] The narrator, as quick to be comforted here by the girl's answer as he was by his first glimpse of the earthly paradise, suggests that he join her by crossing the stream. She replies, as of course she must, that he is "madde" (290). The narrator, at this point, though professing to understand the blessed state of the girl, quite obviously can interpret their relationship only in the familiar terms of earth, a sort of relationship which to her can no longer exist. He is human, he has our sympathy, but he is still completely dominated by earthly standards. The pearl-maiden must thus rebuke him, reminding him of his status as a living man:

> "Deme now þyself if þou con dayly
> As man to God wordeʒ schulde heue.
> Þou saytʒ þou schal won in þis bayly;
> Me þynk þe burde fyrst aske leue,
> And ʒet of graunt þou myʒteʒ fayle." (313–317)

> [Judge now yourself if you have said
> Those words to God you daily ought.
> You think this land to be your own;
> I think permission should be sought
> Even though that gift might be denied.]

The first section of the argument, a sort of prelude to the debate proper, thus establishes the nature of the differences between the narrator and the maiden. He asks pity; she demands full understanding. Neither can grant the other's request or acknowledge the other's point of view.

Then the narrator, in the course of blaming the girl for her happiness at his expense ("In blysse I se þe bly þely blent, / And I a man al mornyf mate; / ʒe take þeron ful lyttel tente, / Þaʒ I hente ofte harmeʒ hate" [In joy I see you blithely blent, / And I a man by mourning dazed; / You take thereof full little heed / That I am oft by sorrow razed] [385–388]),

---

[16] *Pearl*, p. xviii.

questions her right to the high place which she holds in the heavenly hierarchy; if she is

> . . . quen þat watȝ so ȝonge.
> What more honour moȝte he acheue
> Þat hade endured in worlde stronge,
> And lyued in penaunce hys lyueȝ longe
> Wyth bodyly bale hym blysse to byye? (474-478)

> [. . . queen while yet so young,
> What greater honor might he achieve
> Who had endured this world's distress,
> And lived in penance all his life
> To buy by pain true happiness?]

She lived, he says, for only two years; she never learned how to pray, knew neither "Pater ne Crede" [the Our Father nor the Creed]. Her position is thus to the narrator "to dere a date" [too great a reward] (492). It is at this point in her explanation that the girl replies to the narrator's objections with the parable of the vineyard, in which first and last are paid alike, and she ends her telling of the story with an assertion which serves, significantly at this point, to emphasize the differences between the points of view which separate father and daughter:

> More haf I of ioye and blysse hereinne,
> Of ladyschyp gret and lyueȝ blom,
> Þen alle þe wyȝeȝ in þe worlde myȝt wynne
> By þe way of ryȝt to aske dome.   (577–580)

> [More have I of joy and bliss herein,
> Of ladyship true and honor's height
> Than all men in the world might win
> Who sought reward by way of right.]

But, at this stage of the poem, the narrator, relying wholly upon his earthly standard of value, cannot begin to accept such a departure from what he considers true justice, and he, matching her appeal to biblical authority with his own, tells her that her tale is "vnresounable" (590). Thus her first attempt at conversion fails, since the narrator refuses to acknowledge, or even to recognize, her point of view and instead continues to advance earthly standards in opposition to her.

The maiden, however, pursues her case by the only means left open to her, by explaining carefully and in detail the relationship between grace and merit and the place of the innocent, "saf by ryȝt" [safe by right] (684), in heaven in order to assert that the grace of God is "gret inoghe" (612) to overcome earthly difficulties and standards of justice based entirely upon merit and "gret inoghe" to allot to each a full share of heavenly grace. Moreover, toward the end of her description of the place of the innocent in heaven, which concludes the second main episode of the debate, the maiden sharply underlines her point in continuing the debate thus far. She says:

> Harmleȝ, trwe, and vndefylde,
> Wythouten mote oþer mascle of sulpande synne,
> Quen such þer cnoken on þe bylde,
> Tyt schal hem men þe ȝate vnpynne.
> Þer is þe blys þat con not blynne
> Þat þe jueler soȝte burȝ perré pres,
> And solde alle hys goud, boþe wolen and lynne,
> To bye hym a perle watȝ mascelleȝ.   (725–732)

> [The innocent, true, and undefiled
> By spot or stain of filthy sin,
> When these come knocking at the door
> The warders quick the gate unpin.
> Within is the joy that never fails,
> Which the jeweler thought in gems to catch
> And sold his goods, linens and wool,
> To buy him a pearl without a match.]

And she ends her speech by admonishing her father to forsake his earthly standards:

> I rede þe forsake þe worlde wode
> And porchace þy perle maskelles.   (743–744)

> [I bid you forsake this madding world
> And purchase this pearl without a match.]

The point of her remark, occurring as it does at the end of
her attempt to explain to him heavenly standards of justice, is
that the difference in standards between heaven and earth is
such that the achieving of the pearl (here plainly symbolizing
beatitude) demands a complete renunciation of wealth and
hence earthly standards of wealth. That the narrator is beginning to see the point of the girl's remarks is evident in that, for
the first time in the poem, he himself seems to perceive the
nature and width of the river which separates them:

> O maskeleȝ perle in perlez pure,
>
> . . . .
>
> Quo formed þe þy fayre fygure?
>
> . . . .
>
> Þy beauté com neuer of nature;
> Pymalyon paynted neuer þy vys,
> Ne Arystotel nawþer by his lettrure
> Of carped þe kynde þese propertéȝ.
> Þy colour passeȝ þe flour-de-lys;
> Þyn angel-hauyng so clene corteȝ.   (745–754)

> [O matchless Pearl arrayed in pearls
>
> . . . .
>
> Who framed for you your figure's grace?
>
> . . . .
>
> Your grace springs not from natural source
> Nor did Pygmalion paint your matchless face.
> Aristotle did not in all his works
> Include your gentle properties,
> Your color surpassing fleur-de-lis,
> Your heaven-sent pure courtesy.]

Gordon, in his edition of the poem, notes of these lines that
they are reminiscent of a passage in the *Roman de la rose*
"where it is argued that neither the 'philosopher' . . . nor the
artist, not even Pygmalion, can imitate successfully the works
of Nature."[17] But this is plainly not the function of the comparison in this context. The narrator here would seem to realize

[17] *Ibid.*, p. 72.

117

for the first time the fact that the maiden before him is no longer the girl he knew on earth as his daughter. Her beauty is a new, an unnatural, beauty; her face and color derive from supernatural sources and from a realm of experience which even Aristotle, who catalogued all the forms of natural things, left untouched. Thus the parable of the vineyard and the discussion of grace and merit and of the place of the innocent in heaven are by no means digressive in character; they are integral to the movement and purpose of the poem as the first steps in the process whereby the poet-narrator comes to understand, or if not to understand, at least to accept, the heavenly point of view which the pearl-maiden represents.

But in spite of this sudden revelation of the central meaning of the maiden's speech, the narrator cannot as yet apply to his own situation the lesson he has apparently learned. For at the maiden's statement that Christ has "pyȝt [her] in perleȝ maskelleȝ" [robed (her) in matchless pearls] (768), he reiterates his argument that she is unworthy to surpass those women who "For Kryst han lyued in much stryf" [lived for Christ in sore distress] (776) and so, in effect, reopens the discussion.

The maiden's third attempt to assuage the poet's grief by explaining to him the differences in attitude which separate them takes the form of a description of Christ's sufferings in the Old Jerusalem and of her life in the New Jerusalem. Again, her point is the same, that heavenly standards are not earthly standards, but this time she deals directly with the paradox which lies at the root of the narrator's difficulty:

> Alþaȝ oure corses in clotteȝ clynge,
> And ȝe remen for rauþe wythouten reste,
> We þourȝoutly hauen cnawyng;
> Of on dethe ful oure hope is drest.
> Þe Lombe vus gladeȝ, oure care is kest . . . .
>
> (857–861)

[Although our corpses lie in graves
And you in grief remain alive,
We still have knowledge sure enough
That from one death our hopes derive.
The Lamb us gladdens, our cares are gone . . . .]

Upon hearing this statement, the narrator comes closer than before to a true and lasting understanding of their differences:

I am bot mokke and mul among,
And þou so ryche a reken rose,
And bydeʒ here by þys blysful bonc
Þer lyueʒ lyste may neuer lose.   (905–908)

[I am but muck and mold indeed
And you a rich and noble rose,
Who on this blissful shore reside
And never may life's savor lose.]

He realizes, in short, that his world of "mokke and mul" is forever separate from the world "by þys blysful bonc." Yet, for one last time, he cannot resist asking a favor; he would see the New Jerusalem himself. The reasons for his asking such a question again stem from his earthly point of view. He has looked about on the other side of the stream and has seen no hint of "castel-walle, / Ne maner þer [the girl] may mete and won" [a castle wall, / Nor manor where (the girl) might dwell] (917–918). He has seen only "þyse holteʒ" [these groves] (921), and he knows with all the dogmatic surety of earth that Jerusalem is *really* "in Judee" (922). It is the most natural of questions for him. He has come, by now, largely to accept the girl's point; he realizes that out of "mokke and mul" may come a "reken rose" and that even though the mysteries of heaven are forever incomprehensible to man, yet death, even his daughter's death, has a place in the divine plan, however unknowable it may be. As yet, he is still a man, and seeing is, after all, believing. And so the vision follows.

The vision, the final step in the process by which the poet

comes to understand the meaning of death, involves, as did
the parable of the vineyard, the debate on grace and merit,
and the description of life in heaven, the distinction between
earthly and heavenly standards of value. Here, in the New
Jerusalem, the separation is complete; there is no need of
earthly light or even of earthly religious forms:

> Sunne ne mone schon neuer so swete
> As þat foysoun flode out of þat flet;
> Swyþe hit swange þurȝ vch a strete
> Wythouten fylþe oþer galle oþer glet.
> Kyrk þerinne watȝ non ȝete,
> Chapel ne temple þat euer watȝ set;
> Þe Almyȝty watȝ her mynster mete,
> Þe Lombe þe sakerfyse þer to refet. (1057–1064)

> [Sun nor moon shone never so sweet
> As that fair flood flowed from the throne;
> Swiftly it poured through every street,
> Unchecked by filth or scum or stone.
> No church was ever built therein,
> No crypt, no temple ever set;
> Almighty God was church enough,
> The Lamb their sacrifice complete.]

The climax of the vision, and of the poem, comes when the
poet perceives, with his own eyes, his "lyttel quene" (1147)
sitting among her peers, happy and again "wyth lyf" (1146),
though a different kind of life from that he had first wished
for her. And at this vision of an existence forever separate
from earth, all his doubts disappear. In an ecstasy, he wishes
to cross over to her but is awakened from his dream and finds
himself again in the garden, his head upon the grave.

It is significant that the narrator's first words upon awakening show his single-hearted devotion to Christ. "Now al be to
þat Prynceȝ paye" [Now all be to that Prince's joy] (1176),
he says, and we are to understand, I think, that all doubts, all
challenges, all questionings, have been removed from him. He
realizes his own unworthiness to enter as yet into the heavenly

life, his own incapacity to know finally the mysteries of the universe. But through a *rite de passage*, he has journeyed to the strange land and has returned, having been initiated into a new and more meaningful life. He will thus accept the standards of God, for the most part without understanding but also without questioning. It is enough for him; "wel is me," he says, "in þys doel-doungoun / Þat þou art to þat Prynseȝ paye" [well for me . . . in this dungeon of sorrow / since you are that Prince's joy.] (1187–1188). The poem thus ends with the narrator's lamenting, not, as before, the death of his daughter and the corruption of her body, but the corruptness of his own soul which has kept him from her and with his prayer that he may himself eventually be counted among the lowly servants and "precious perleȝ" of God.

The theme and the poetic method of *Pearl* are thus the theme and the poetic method of most elegies, the acceptance, through suffering and revelation, of death as a part of the universal plan. In *Pearl,* the parts of the dream-vision become the stages of redemption. The narrator here comes to learn, through a series of trials, to accept his place among the living. Like Milton's Adam, he can be said to say:

> Greatly instructed I shall hence depart,
> Greatly in peace of thought, and have my fill
> Of knowledge, what this vessel can contain;
> Beyond which was my folly to aspire.
> Henceforth I learn that to obey is best,
> And love with fear the only God.

9

SYMBOLIC AND DRAMATIC
DEVELOPMENT IN *PEARL*

A. C. Spearing

BOTH BEFORE AND SINCE THE BEGINNINGS OF THE CURRENT
controversy about the application of patristic exegesis to the
study of medieval literature, the poem *Pearl* has been subjected
to allegorical interpretations of various kinds, and these have
naturally been chiefly concerned with the poem's central symbol,
the pearl itself. Some commentators have claimed that the pearl
stands for the soul of the poem's narrator;[1] others, among them
one of the leading proponents of the exegetical approach in general, have asserted that it is to be understood according to the
standard "four levels" of scriptural exegesis;[2] and there have
been many other interpretations.[3] Although such attempts to find

Reprinted, by permission of the author, from *Modern Philology*, LX
(1962), 1–12; also by permission of the Indiana University Press and
Robert J. Blanch. Translations of *Pearl* are by Sr. M. Vincent Hillman,
*The Pearl, Mediaeval Text with a Literal Translation and Interpreta-
tion* (University of Notre Dame Press, 1967). In three places, however,
because crucial differences of interpretation are involved, alternate ren-
derings have been supplied.

[1] Sister Mary Madeleva, *"Pearl": A Study in Spiritual Dryness* (New
York, 1925); M. P. Hamilton, "The Meaning of the Middle English
Pearl," *PMLA*, LXX (1955), 805–824.

[2] D. W. Robertson, "The Pearl as a Symbol," *MLN*, LXV (1950),
155–161; M. R. Stern, "An Approach to *The Pearl*," *JEGP*, LIV (1956),
684–692.

[3] I do not catalogue them here, since they are summarized in most
recent articles on *Pearl*. There is a useful brief analysis in the article

some hidden layer of meaning in the poem seem to me misconceived, it is not my purpose here either to enter into the theoretical controversy about exegesis (to which so distinguished a contribution has recently been made in this journal by Professor Bloomfield[4]) or to offer any detailed criticism of the various existing interpretations of *Pearl.* I hope simply, by outlining an adequate nonallegorical reading of the pearl symbolism, to show that whether or not allegorical explication is desirable it is at least not necessary. I think, certainly, that one strong argument against supposing that the poem's readers need make some effort of allegorical interpretation is the fact that the poet seems to make the pearl-Maiden herself provide exegesis wherever exegesis is necessary. Thus, after the parable of the vineyard has been recounted, the Maiden does not rely on the Dreamer, and the poet does not rely on his reader, to interpret it out of his own knowledge of current exegesis. An explicit and careful interpretation is supplied in the poem:

> Bot innoghe of grace hatȝ innocent.
> As sone as þay arn borne, by lyne
> In þe water of babtem þay dyssente:
> Þen arne þay boroȝt into þe vyne.
> Anon þe day, wyth derk endente,
> Þe niyȝt of deth dotȝ to enclyne:
> Þat wroȝt neuer wrang er þenne þay wente,
> Þe gentyle Lorde þenne payeȝ hys hyne. (625–632)[5]

> [But enough of grace have the innocent;
> As soon as they are born, in order of birth
> Into the water of Baptism they descend;
> Then into the vineyard are they brought.
> Forthwith—that day with darkness marked—

in this journal by Stanton de Voren Hoffman, "*The Pearl*: Notes for an Interpretation," *MP*, LVIII (1960), 74–75 [pages 88–89 above].

[4] M. W. Bloomfield, "Symbolism in Medieval Literature," *MP*, LVI (1958), 73–81.

[5] This and all subsequent quotations from *Pearl* are taken from the edition of E. V. Gordon (Oxford, 1953).

> The might of death causes to bow low
> Those who never wrought evil ere thence they went.
> The noble Lord thereupon payeth His servants.]

The intended meaning of each element in the parable is expounded, in the manner of a medieval sermon—that is to say, of a work which *uses* allegorical exegesis, but is not itself allegorical. Again, after nine stanzas have been devoted to a description of Jerusalem, with constant references to John's vision in the Apocalypse—references which, if some effort of interpretation were expected, one would think sufficient to incite the audience to apply their knowledge of exegesis—the pearl-Maiden goes on to make at some length the elementary distinction between the Old Jerusalem, the city of God, and the New, the vision of peace.[6] Cases such as these seem to me to make it unlikely, on the ground of simple probability, that the poem or its central symbol has any *concealed* allegorical meaning.[7] But to say this is not to deny that the pearl symbol as it is presented in the poem is extremely rich in meaning, and rich in a way which, if like many scholars we are unfamiliar with the richness of meaning that belongs to poetry, we may be tempted to call allegorical rather than literal. And it seems likely enough that for an educated fourteenth-century reader the pearl concept would have been felt to be pregnant with symbolism per se, quite apart from the poem *Pearl*.[8] These two

[6] *Pearl*, ll. 937–960.

[7] And the case of the distinction between the two Jerusalems surely casts doubt on Hoffman's contention that "in the poem we find together several meanings of the pearl figure and . . . they are kept distinct" (*op. cit.*, p. 76) [page 91 above]. If the poet had wished to keep several meanings of the symbol distinct, would he not have distinguished among them explicitly, as he does between the Old Jerusalem and the New?

[8] Cf. W. H. Schofield, "Symbolism, Allegory, and Autobiography in *The Pearl*," *PMLA*, XXIV (1909), 585–675: "a learned man of the fourteenth century was so used to intepretations of the pearl that the word could hardly be mentioned without a great many rising to his memory instantly" (p. 639).

facts are certainly connected: the particular kind of success which the *Pearl* poet has achieved would hardly have been possible if he had not shared with his audience a common preexisting symbolism. But this must not lead us to suppose that there is no difference between the pearl symbol as it existed in the fourteenth-century consciousness and the pearl symbol as it exists in *Pearl,* so that in order to discover the meaning of the latter we have only to look up lapidaries, biblical commentaries, and so forth for evidence about the former. The *Pearl* poet is a poet; he *uses* the symbol provided for him by his age; and if we wish to understand his poem as a poem we must surely begin not by superimposing on it some system of allegorical significance drawn from external sources, but by examining carefully those symbolical meanings which are indicated by what the poet actually says. Within the religious verse of the Middle Ages, many short pieces, such as lyrics, and also the less successful of the longer works, tend to be parasitic upon the symbolic consciousness of their age: they depend upon it for what power they possess, and give nothing in return. To understand the appeal of such works, we have to try to reconstruct artificially the world of symbolism which lies behind them. But there are certain long poems which are successful as poems, which reconstruct current symbols within themselves, and in doing so give them a permanent and unique validity. The outstanding examples in Middle English are *Pearl* and *Piers Plowman*, and the way in which these poems reconstruct symbols is to incorporate them in an extended dramatic narrative, so that we do not have to apprehend their significance instantaneously, but can feel it being built up piece by piece over a period of time. In some ways it may be that we can better take *Pearl* as a guide to medieval symbolism than medieval symbolism as a guide to *Pearl*. If only for this reason, it seems worth while to attempt a detailed study of the treatment of the poem's central symbol. If this is done, it will be found that, as Schofield wrote over fifty

125

years ago, "The author's plan is to let the symbolism of his poem disclose itself slowly."[9] The pearl symbol is not static but dynamic: it develops in meaning as the poem extends itself in time, and this development in meaning is coordinated with the developing human drama of the relationship between the Dreamer and the Maiden.[10] The whole force and poignancy of the poem derives from its basic structure as an encounter involving human relationship; and it is through the synthesis of symbol with drama that the writer of *Pearl* conveys his meaning, and not, I believe, through any concealed layers of allegory.

The pearl symbol appears in the first word of the first line of the poem, and the similarity between this first line—"Perle, plesaunte to prynces paye" [Pearl, pleasing to the fancy of a prince]—and the last—"Ande precious perleʒ vnto his pay" [And unto His pleasure precious pearls]—has not escaped notice. The "his" of the last line refers to a prince, but to the Prince of Heaven, and this fact has led even so moderate a modern interpreter of the poem as Gordon to follow the earlier commentators cited by Schofield[11] and claim that the prince of the first line means "literally a prince of this world and symbolically Christ."[12] It is true of course that the parallel between the first and last lines is quite deliberate, and that on a second

---

[9] *Ibid.*, p. 588.

[10] Moorman seems to me right in insisting that within the drama of the poem the role of the narrator is at least as important as that of the Maiden (see Charles Moorman, "The Role of the Narrator in *Pearl*," *MP*, LIII [1955]), but I cannot agree with him when he remarks that "we are never allowed to see and judge the experience presented by the poem objectively and for ourselves but are, instead, forced, by the point of view which the poet adopts, to accept the experience of the vision only in terms of its relationship to him" (p. 74) [pages 104 f. a.]. Here and elsewhere in his article, though not consistently, Moorman fails to allow for any difference between the narrator and the poet: thus at one point he refers to "the poet's immediate grief" (p. 75) [page 108 above]. For evidence that the poet sometimes invites us to "judge," not merely to "accept," the narrator's experience, see below.

[11] *Op cit.*, pp. 589 ff.

[12] *Pearl*, note on ll. 1–4.

and subsequent readings of the poem the first line will recall the last. But this is not to say that it will *mean* the last, even symbolically; and we can hardly agree that it does mean the last without denying the nature of the poem as an object which, for its reader, is extended in time, and is therefore capable of discursive or dramatic development. And in this case we may miss the whole point of the first section of the poem. If we read the poem's first four lines:

> Perle, plesaunte to prynces paye
> To clanly clos in golde so clere,
> Oute of oryent, I hardyly saye,
> Ne proued I neuer her precios pere

> [Pearl, pleasing to the fancy of a prince!
> To set without flaw in gold so clear,
> Out of the Orient, confidently I say,
> I never tested her (Hillman: its) precious peer]

we shall see that, taken by themselves, they refer to the pearl as a lapidary might, as a literal precious stone, valued by literal earthly princes. This is the primary meaning of *perle* throughout the first group of five stanzas, but not the only meaning. For the symbol *is* being used in a secondary sense here—a sense which might be called "allegorical"—but this secondary sense is not one which is concealed now and only disclosed later in the poem, but one which is glanced at in the first stanza. In line 4, quoted above, the pearl is referred to as feminine, and the gender might be either natural or merely grammatical; but the next two lines develop the hint of natural femininity:

> So rounde, so reken in vche araye,
> So smal, so smoþe her sydeʒ were.   (5–6)

> [So round, so perfect in every array,
> So fine, so smooth her (Hillman: its) surfaces were.]

The first of these lines is appropriate mainly to a precious stone, but the second both to a precious stone and to a girl (with *sydeʒ* meaning "flanks"). We are therefore to understand, though the

equation is not explicit, that the narrator is using the image of
the loss of a precious stone to express the loss, presumably
through death, of a girl. The vagueness here—the fact that the
suggestiveness of the phrasing is not pinned down by any explicit
statement—no doubt belongs to poetry rather than theology; but
it is made clearer by the use of the language of courtly love in
the last two lines of the first stanza:

> I dewyne, fordolked of luf-daungere
> Of þat pryuy perle wythouten spot.   (11–12)

> [I pined away, sore-wounded by the love-dominion
> Of that pearl of mine without a spot.]

If the poem went no further, its implied allegorical structure
would be similar to that of the *Roman de la Rose.* After the first
stanza, which gives us the necessary hint of his human reference,
the narrator reverts to his metaphor, and speaks of his loss as
that of a "myry iuele" [lovely jewel] (23), which "trendeled
doun" [went rolling down] on a "huyle" [hillock] (41). This
continuing use of jewel terminology is important. It is clear that
what the narrator has lost is something intrinsically precious and
precious to him, but he is seeing its preciousness as that of a
beautiful and valuable stone—he thinks it appropriate to speak
of the girl's death as involving an irrevocable and total loss of
her preciousness. To this loss he reacts with an attitude of elegiac
melancholy, somewhat reminiscent of that of the "man in blak"
in *The Book of the Duchess.* In *Pearl,* even more than in Chaucer's poem, this melancholy is made attractive, framed as it is in
a scene which delights the senses with strange music and with the
brightness and fragrance of flowers and herbs. But our response
to the melancholy should not be one simply of surrender. The
locus amoenus [lovely place; park or pleasance] of the *Pearl*
garden is presented not on the conventional May morning but
in August, harvesttime, "Quen corne is coruen wyth crokeʒ
kene" [When corn is cut with sickles keen] (40); and this
unusual season may have symbolic associations of one sort or

another,[13] but it also has an inescapable poetic effect, an effect
in harmony with the landscape's noticeable lack of one essential
feature of the traditional *locus amoenus,* namely the stream or
river.[14] The landscape provides an objective correlative to the
emotions of the narrator: about both there is a hint of the over-
ripe, the unrefreshed, and, indeed, perhaps of the merely pas-
sive—the corn awaiting the scythe, the narrator surrendering
to his luxuriant emotion. He does not see things with May-
morning clarity; though he feels the pearl to be precious, by relying merely on feeling he undervalues its preciousness, seeing it
not, as at the end of the poem, as precious to the Prince of
Heaven, but as precious only to earthly princes. That we are
intended to adopt a critical attitude toward the narrator, even
while feeling fully the pathos of his situation, is suggested by his
reference to the flowers growing on the spot where his pearl
was lost:

> Blomeʒ blayke and blwe and rede
> Þer schyneʒ ful schyr agayn þe sunne.
> Flor and fryte may not be fede
> Þer hit doun drof in moldeʒ dunne;
> For vch gresse mot grow of grayneʒ dede;
> No whete were elleʒ to woneʒ wonne.   (27–32)

> [Blossoms pale and blue and red
> There will shine full bright against the sun.
> Flower and fruit can not be withered
> Where into dark molds it hurried down;
> For from dead grains each blade of grass must grow;
> No wheat would else be won for homes.]

The last two lines embody an allusion to John 12:24: "Verily,
verily, I say unto you, Except a corn of wheat fall into the

---

[13] Schofield, *op. cit.,* suggests some connection with the feast of the
Assumption of the Virgin, and with S. John's Great Reaper (p. 616,
n. 2).

[14] For the traditional elements of the *locus amoenus* motif, see E. R.
Curtius, *European Literature and the Latin Middle Ages,* trans. W. R.
Trask (New York, 1953), pp. 183–202.

ground and die, it abideth alone, but if it die, it bringeth forth much fruit." But it is clear that the narrator has misunderstood the scriptural text to which he alludes: he has taken the fruit which grows from the dead grain to be material, like the flowers on the grave, but it is in fact, as the next verse in John makes clear, the spiritual fruit of eternal life. By forgetting that the girl's soul is immortal, even though her body dies, the Dreamer has underestimated her absolute value. The nature of his under-estimation is partially hinted at in the last stanza of the poem's first section, where the earliest explicit Christian reference occurs:

> A deuely dele in my hert denned,
> Þaȝ resoun sette myseluen saȝt.
> I playned my perle þat þer watȝ spenned
> Wyth fyrce skylleȝ þat faste faȝt;
> Þaȝ kynde of Kryst me comfort kenned,
> My wreched wylle in wo ay wraȝte.   (51–56)

> [A desolating (Hillman: wicked) grief lodged in my heart
> Though understanding would have brought me peace.
> I mourned my pearl which there was locked
> With violence which swiftly reasonings fought,
> Though the nature of Christ would have taught me comfort.
> My wretched will in woe aye tossed.]

But this suggestion of a conflict between the narrator's actual feeling about his loss and an as yet undefined rational and Chris-tian attitude toward it is not developed here, for at this point the narrator falls asleep and becomes the Dreamer.

His body remains in the garden, but his spirit is transported to a new landscape, once again a version of the traditional *locus amoenus,* but this time a different version, shining with brilliant light and hard with metal and precious stones. It is towards the end of a description emphasizing these qualities of the dream landscape that the pearl symbol is next introduced:

> Dubbed wern alle þo downeȝ sydeȝ
> Wyth crystal klyffeȝ so cler of kynde.

Holtewodeʒ bryʒt aboute hem bydeʒ
Of bolleʒ as blwe as ble of Ynde;
As bornyst syluer þe lef on slydeʒ,
Þat þike con trylle on vch a tynde.
Quen glem of glodeʒ agaynʒ hem glydeʒ,
Wyth schymeryng schene ful schrylle þay schynde.
Þe grauayl þat on grounde con grynde
Wern precious perleʒ of oryente.   (73–82)

[Adorned were all the margins of the down
With crystal cliffs exceeding clear of kind;
Forests bright around them stand
With boles as blue as color of Ind;
Like burnished silver slip away the leaves
Which quiver thick on every branch.
When the gleam of the glades against them glides,
With a glittering glimmer full brilliantly they shone.
The gravel which underfoot did grind
Was precious pearls of the Orient . . .]

This particular context draws out two further aspects of the meaning latent in the symbol: the brilliance of the pearl and its hard permanence. Light, the effusion of God Himself, is the favorite medieval expression of beauty, and here the more human, though idealized, beauty which the pearl had at first in the narrator's memory—"So smal, so smoþe her sydeʒ were" [So fine, so smooth her sides were]—has begun, through emphasis on new aspects of the same symbol, to merge into a heavenly beauty, to become part of a landscape dazzling, overpowering in its brightness:

For vrþely herte myʒt not suffyse
To þe tenþe dole of þo gladneʒ glade.   (135–136)

[For earthly heart may not suffice
For the tenth part of that joyance glad.]

And the preciousness which was capable of death has in the same way begun to turn into a more permanent but harder preciousness. Thus although the pearl symbol has for the moment reverted to its original sense of a precious stone, it has done so

131

only in order to develop in other directions. We shall find that none of its separate senses is abandoned, but that any may momentarily become primary for the sake of a further development of associations.

This is the only mention of pearls in the second or third sections of the poem; but in the third section the Maiden appears for the first time. She is not at once identified with the lost pearl; by making use of the slow perception of his Dreamer, the poet is able to unfold his symbolism gradually, to hint before he states. And so at first the Dreamer sees in the Maiden only the whiteness and brilliance of the pearl:

> A mayden of menske, ful debonere;
> Blysnande whyt watʒ hyr bleaunt.
> I knew hyr wel, I hade sen hyr ere.   (162–164)

> [A maiden of dignity, of high estate,
> Gleaming white was her garment rich—
> I knew her well, I had seen her before.]

> On lenghe I loked to hyr þere;
> Þe lenger, I knew hyr more and more.   (167–168)

> [For an interval long I gazed toward her there—
> The longer, I recognized her more and more.]

In this slow process of recognition, the development of the symbolism is communicated to us in human terms: the growth of meaning is possible only through a growth in understanding on the Dreamer's part, and this is accompanied by a reluctant intellectual exertion which is sometimes comic in effect:

> Wyth yʒen open and mouth ful clos
> I stod as hende as hawk in halle.   (183–184)

> [With eyes open and mouth tight closed,
> I stood as alert as hawk in hall.]

As a sign that the recognition is complete, I think we may take the following lines, with their reminiscences of the poem's opening stanza:

Þat gracios gay wythouten galle,
So smoþe, so small, so seme slyȝt,
Ryseȝ vp in hir araye ryalle,
A precios pyece in perleȝ pyȝt.　　　(189–192)

[That beautiful bright one from blemish free,
So flawless, so graceful, so pleasingly slight,
Arises in her royal array,
A precious person adorned in pearls.]

"So smoþe, so smal" recalls line 6 ("So smal, so smoþe her sydeȝ were"); "hir araye ryalle" recalls the royal associations of line 1. In the stanzas which follow, the Maiden's "pearl" qualities are intensified by the normal medieval descriptive method, that of accumulation rather than selection of detail. Her garments are described one by one; each is covered with pearls, and we remember that in the fourteenth century pearls were highly prized as ornaments by the fashionable,[15] so that it is now apparent that the courtliness suggested by the earlier use of the language of courtly love has not been abandoned with the development of a Christian significance. This fact is emphasized by a recurrence of the ideas of royalty:

Perleȝ pyȝte of ryal prys
Þere moȝt mon by grace haf sene.　　　(193–194)

[Pearls of royal price set in place,
There by grace might one have seen . . .]

Her semblaunt sade for doc oþer erle.　　　(211)

[Her expression grave, like duke's or earl's . . .]

The culmination of this description of the Maiden's garments is reached with the single pearl on her breast:

Bot a wonder perle wythouten wemme
Inmyddeȝ hyr breste watȝ sette so sure;
A manneȝ dom moȝt dryȝly demme,
Er mynde moȝt malte in hit mesure.

---

[15] See Gordon, *op. cit.*, p. xxxiv and note on l. 228.

> I hope no tong moȝt endure
> No sauerly saghe say of þat syȝt,
> So watȝ hit clene and cler and pure,
> Þat precios perle þer hit watȝ pyȝt.   (221–228)

[But a wondrous pearl without a flaw
Securely in the center of her breast was set.
A man's judgment must in exhaustion stop
Before the mind dissolve in appraisal of it.
I suppose no tongue would be able to last
To utter an appreciative statement of that sight,
So flawless it was and clear and pure,
The precious pearl where it was set.]

To attempt to distinguish this one pearl in symbolic significance from the pearl-Maiden herself is, I believe, to misunderstand the poet's methods. Certainly, this pearl seems to have special associations with purity or virginity, in such phrases as "wythouten wemme," but these only recall and develop an idea which had been present from the first stanza group, with its use of "wythouten spot" as the refrain phrase. The order in which the poem's symbolism is unfolded is, as I am arguing, significant, but it is a single symbol, with a single though complex meaning, which is being evolved, and any attempt at such minute allegorical distinctions will only obscure the central achievement of the poem.

We may note that in the last passage quoted the idea of overpoweringness, hitherto applied generally to the whole landscape of the dream, is transferred to the Maiden's pearl:

> A manneȝ dom moȝt dryȝly demme,
> Er mynde moȝt malte in hit mesure.

There is a dramatic significance in the fact that the Dreamer should see this quality in the Maiden's chief decoration, for he sees that her appearance "exceeds our organs," but does not take the hint that her teaching too may now be beyond his earthly understanding. This gives a certain pathos to his earlier "So smoþe, so smal, so seme slyȝt," and to his first speech to her in the next section; and perhaps a similar intention, dramatic rather than doctrinal, may help to explain the controversial line, "Ho watᴣ me nerre þen aunte or nece" [She was nearer to me than aunt or niece] (233). The poet leaves the Dreamer's relationship with the Maiden undefined so as to be able to draw at once on the emotions of romantic love and of fatherly affection; and he makes the Dreamer use the phrase "aunte or nece"—slightly comic, slightly pathetic—in order to indicate that he is continuing to think of the relationship in naïvely familial terms, comically and pathetically unaware of their inadequacy for the visionary situation in which he is now placed. Similarly, in a line quoted above—"Her semblaunt sade for doc oþer erle" [Her expression grave, like duke's or earl's]—he expresses a naïvely earthly conception of the Maiden's regal qualities.

In the fifth section, after the Dreamer's touching speech of recognition has been met with an austere rebuke from the Maiden—"Sir, ᴣe haf your tale mysetente" ["Sir, you have ill considered your speech"] (257)—she does her best to make him understand that the situation is not as he has been seeing it, by explaining that what he has lost was not a pearl at all, but a rose "Þat flowred and fayled as kynde hyt gef" [Which, as nature granted, flowered and failed] (270): it belonged to the merely natural world of *amour courtois* represented by the garden and the elegiac tone of the beginning. And this rose has now become a "perle of prys" [pearl of price] (272). It must be observed that the courtly rose, subject to "kynde," is not the same as the pearl, nor is it something totally different, which must be rejected and replaced: it has "proved to be" the pearl, which is to say that, from the Dreamer's point of view, it has been *transformed* into the pearl:

> . . . þurᴣ kynde of þe kyste þat hyt con close
> To a perle of prys hit is put in pref.   (271–272)
>
> [. . . through the character of the chest which doth enclose it,
> As a pearl of price is put to the test.]

Between the earthly and heavenly worlds there exist at once difference and continuity, and this complex relationship is easily misunderstood: it is misunderstood by the Dreamer, who sees

only continuity, and expects the heavenly Maiden to be the same
as the earthly pearl he lost, and it is misunderstood by those
modern commentators such as Hoffman, who see only difference,[16] and wish to make a total distinction between the earthly
and heavenly pearls. But the combination of continuity and
difference is figured forth in the fact that the "erber grene" [gar-
den green] and the brilliant dream landscape are different versions of the same traditional *locus amoenus,* and it appears
centrally in the developing conception of the nature of the pearl's
preciousness. This is accompanied by the gradual disclosure of
a Christian courtliness including and transcending the worldly
courtliness which is limited by transience. The language of *amour
courtois* recurs throughout the poem from the beginning, where
we have already seen it applied to the earthly pearl, to the climactic point at which the Dreamer sees the heavenly pearl
among the Brides of the Lamb and exclaims that

> Þat syȝt me gart to þenk to wade
> For luf-longyng in gret delyt.   (1151–1152)

> [That sight caused me to think of crossing
> For love-longing in great delight.]

It is also applied, as in many devotional lyrics, to the relationship between Christ and the individual soul:

> In Jerusalem watȝ my lemman slayn
> And rent on rode wyth boyeȝ bolde.   (805–806)

> [In Jerusalem was my Beloved slain,
> And, with malefactors, rent on rood.]

A continuity is thus established in *Pearl* between earthly and
heavenly love, and this is a familiar motive in medieval literature, both secular and religious. It is for instance a fundamental
idea of Chaucer's *Troilus and Criseyde,* where earthly love is

---

[16] And see W. S. Johnson, "The Imagery and Diction of *The Pearl,*"
ELH, XX (1953). "The result is an emphasis upon a ubiquitous sense
of contrast between the nature of heaven and the nature of earth, the
revelation of which seems, for our present reading, to be the poem's main
purpose" (p. 163) [page 29 above].

first celebrated in religious terminology and then finally gives way to the love of Christ; while in *The Wooing of Our Lord* (to take a well-known example of devotional writing, and one which was still being read in the fourteenth century as part of *A Talking of the Love of God*) Christ, the heavenly lover, is shown successively to possess in the highest degree all those qualities which win love in the world. Thus the continuity found in *Pearl* between earthly and heavenly values, which makes possible a movement from the one to the other, is nothing new in medieval literature. But, as I have said, along with continuity we also find difference, and in this way the *Pearl* poet offers a considerable refinement of the attitudes displayed in *The Wooing* and in many other medieval devotional texts—works in which we often feel that by the use of erotic imagery heavenly love has simply been reduced to the level of earthly love. In *Pearl* earthly feelings and relationships are themselves conceived with a finer courtliness than other religious texts usually have to offer, and although these feelings and relationships have analogies in the heavenly world of the dream, it is precisely the inability of the Dreamer to realize the disparity between the two, the transcendent relation of the one to the other, which provides the poem's human and emotional interest.

To return to the text: the "perle of prys" in line 272 suggests, of course, the pearl of great price of Matt. 13:45–46, to purchase which the merchant sold all he had. This allusion, for which we have perhaps been prepared by the repeated references in the refrain line to the Dreamer as a *juelere* [jeweler], is reinforced by the following two lines, which continue the language of trade, of profit and loss:

> And þou hatȝ called þy wyrde a þef,
> Þat oȝt of noȝt hatȝ mad þe cler.   (273–274)[17]

---

[17] This seems to me a more plausible interpretation of the lines than A. L. Kellogg's suggestion (*Traditio*, XII [1956], 406–407) that the allusion is to the doctrine of *creatio ex nihilo*, a reading which does not seem to explain *þef* or *cler*.

> [And thou hast called thy fate a thief
> That something from nothing hath made thee clearly]

But these allusions are lost on the Dreamer. He has totally failed to understand the situation, and, seeing the Maiden's heavenly life simply as a kind of miraculous prolongation of her earthly life (seeing, that is, continuity but not difference), he assumes that he will now be free to join her, and that they will "live happily ever after"—

> I trawed my perle don out of daweȝ.
> Now haf I fonde hyt, I schal ma feste,
> And wony wyth hyt in schyr wod-schaweȝ,
> And loue my Lorde and al his laweȝ
> Þat hatȝ me broȝt þys blys ner.   (282–286)
>
> [I believed my pearl utterly gone;
> Now I have found it, I shall rejoice
> And dwell with it in bright woodlands,
> And praise my Lord and all His laws,
> Who has brought me near this happiness.]

This misunderstanding draws an even more stinging rebuke from the Maiden and a devastatingly complete analysis of his error. With this, the fifth section closes, and a complete change comes over the poem. By his failure to understand the Maiden's image of the transformation of the rose into a pearl, the Dreamer has shown himself unable to make any further progress through the development of symbolism. He is impossibly literal-minded and the method of symbolic development is therefore abandoned in favor of simpler, more explicit forms of exposition. For more than four hundred lines the pearl symbol undergoes no further development, and indeed the very word *perle* occurs only four times: twice in Section 6 as a name—"My precios perle dotȝ me gret pyne" [My precious pearl causes me anguish great] (330) and "When I am partleȝ of perle myne" [When I am deprived of my peerless one] (335)—and twice in Section 7 in the form of references to what has already occurred when the poem begins:

Fro þou watȝ wroken fro vch a woþe,
I wyste neuer quere my perle watȝ gon.　(375–376)

[From the time thou wast cut off from every search—
I never knew where my pearl was gone.]

Þow wost wel when þy perle con schede
I watȝ ful ȝong and tender of age.　(411–412)

[Thou knowest well, when thy pearl did fall
I was full young and tender of age.]

In Sections 8 to 12 the word *perle* does not occur at all. The Maiden's second rebuke has the effect intended: the Dreamer is startled out of his fool's paradise and is made to recognize that submission is the only attitude appropriate to his position:

For þoȝ þou daunce as any do,
Braundysch and bray þy braþeȝ breme,
When þou no fyrre may, to ne fro,
Þou moste abyde þat he schal deme.　(345–348)

[For though thou mayst prance like any doe,
Threaten and shout thy furies wild,
When thou canst no farther, to or fro,
Thou must await what He shall decree.]

He apologizes for his mistakes and displays a new humility:

Þaȝ cortaysly ȝe carp con,
I am bot mol and manereȝ mysse.　(381–382)

[Though you are able to speak with courteous wit,
I am but dust and great eloquence lack.]

The Maiden expresses her approval of this change:

"Now blysse, burne, mot þe bytyde,"
Þen sayde þat lufsoum of lyth and lere,
"And welcum here to walk and byde,
For now þy speche is to me dere."　(397–400)

["Now must blessedness befall thee, noble sir,"
Then said she, lovely in form and face,
"And welcome here to walk and bide,
For now thy speech is dear to me."]

The emotional readjustment makes possible further intellectual progress, and now direct doctrinal exposition replaces symbolic development as the mode in which meaning is communicated. The Maiden speaks discursively, making plain her position as a royal Bride of the Lamb, and employing the parable of the vineyard to explain the *cortaysye* of God by which she is granted this position. Against her the Dreamer quotes the authority of the Psalter (593ff.). She replies with a further theological explanation of grace and merit, plentifully supported with other scriptural confirmations and concluding, in the last lines of Section 12, with a reference to Matt. 19:14:

> Do way, let chylder vnto me tyȝt.
> To suche is heuenryche arayed.   (718–719)

> [Forbear! Suffer children to come unto Me;
> For such the Kingdom of Heaven is prepared.]

Since my chief concern is with the development of the pearl symbol, I shall not discuss any further this part of *Pearl* in which the symbolism is in abeyance and more straightforward homiletic methods of instruction are used,[18] except to mention that it contains further references to the ideas of royalty previously associated with the pearl—references which show to what extent the Dreamer remains confined by earthly notions. Thus he protests against the Maiden's claim to be a queen in heaven, saying,

> Of countes, damysel, par ma fay,
> Wer fayr in heuen to halde asstate,
> Oþer elleȝ a lady of lasse aray;
> Bot a quene! Hit is to dere a date.   (489–492)

> [As countess, damsel, by my faith,
> 'Twere fair in heaven to hold estate,

---

[18] It might be compared with the *Vita de Dowel* section of *Piers Plowman*, which consists largely of sermonlike speeches from various personified abstractions, and in which Piers himself appears in the B text not at all, and in the C text only once, and that briefly. There are many similarities between *Pearl* and *Piers Plowman*, despite their great difference in length (cf. n. 19 below).

> Or else a lady of lesser degree—
> But a queen! 'Tis a term too highly rated!]

and we are reminded of his earlier attempt to express her dignity: "Her semblaunt sade for doc oþer erle" (211). A countess is the wife of an earl: he is unable to conceive of hierarchy in any other than these familiar terms.

The way in which the pearl symbolism is taken up again after this long gap is of particular interest. The idea of "the kingdom of heaven," introduced by the reference to Matt. 19:14 with which Section 12 concludes, is used by the Maiden as a transition to Matt. 13:45–46, in which "the kingdom of heaven" is likened to a pearl of great price:

> Þer is þe blys þat con not blynne,
> Þat þe jueler soȝte þurȝ perré pres,
> And solde alle his goud, boþe wolen and lynne,
> To bye hym a perle watȝ mascelleȝ.   (729–732)

> [There is the bliss which doth not cease,
> Which the jeweler sought through a mass of gems,
> And sold all his goods, both woolen and linen,
> To buy him a pearl that was spotless.]

But the pearl of great price was an association which the symbol was given in line 272, immediately before the long homiletic interlude, and thus the pearl symbolism is taken up again in Section 13 at precisely the point in its development at which it was abandoned in Section 5. The *jueler* of lines 252 to 301, who was then the Dreamer, is reintroduced in line 730 as Matthew's merchant, and the scriptural reference which was before only implicit is now made explicit. We could hardly ask for a more striking indication that the meaning of the pearl symbol is developed step by step along with the poem's human drama, and that it is intended to be apprehended in this way rather than as totally present in allegorical simultaneity from the beginning. In the stanza which follows, the new extension of the pearl symbolism which associates it with the kingdom of heaven is further emphasized, and there seems to be an attempt to gather together some of the other associations previously accumulated by the symbol:

> This makelleȝ perle, þat boȝt is dere,
> Þe joueler gef fore alle hys god,
> Is lyke þe reme of heuenesse clere:
> So sayde þe Fader of folde and flode;
> For hit is wemleȝ, clene, and clere,
> And endeleȝ rounde, and blyþe of mode,
> And commune to alle þat ryȝtwys were.
> Lo, euen inmyddeȝ my breste hit stode.
> My Lorde þe Lombe, þat schede hys blode,
> He pyȝt hit þere in token of pes.
> I rede þe forsake þe worlde wode
> And porchace þy perle maskelles.   (733–744)

> [This peerless pearl, which is dearly bought—
> The jeweler gave all his goods for it—
> Is like the Kingdom of Heaven's brightness:
> So said the Father of earth and sea.
> For it is spotless, pure, and clear,
> And round without end and bright of tone,
> And common to all who righteous were.
> Lo, exactly in the center of my breast its place!
> My Lord the Lamb, Who shed His blood,
> Firmly He fixed it there in token of peace.
> I counsel thee to renounce the foolish world,
> And purchase thy pearl spotless.]

"Wemleȝ, clene, and clere" reminds us of such previous phrases as "wythouten wemme" [flawless] and "wythouten spot," and our attention is now again focused on the single pearl on the Maiden's breast, as it were the symbol of the symbol. But, once again, there would surely be no profit in trying to distinguish separate layers of meaning in the pearl, and to differentiate between the pearl as the Maiden and the pearl as the kingdom of heaven. These figurative senses are inextricably entangled, and any attempt to schematize them is only too likely to result in an impoverished perception of the richness of the symbolic whole.[19] The fusion of the various senses is recognized by the Dreamer in the very phrasing of the lines in which "he sums up the complex symbolism of the passage"[20] we have been discussing:

[19] Such an attempt would be rather similar to that of the Dreamer in *Piers Plowman* to distinguish the various "names" of Liberum-Arbitrium [Free Choice] and their "causes":

> "Ʒe ben as a bischop," quath ich · al bordynge that tyme,
> "For bischopes blessed · thei bereth meny names,
> *Presul* and *pontifex* · and *metropolitanus*,
> And other names an hepe · *episcopus* and *pastor*."
> "That is soth," he seide · "now ich seo thy wil
> How thow woldest know and conne · the cause of alle here names,
> And of myne, yf thow myghtest · me thynketh by thy speche!"
> "Ʒe, syre," ich seyde, "by so · that no man were a-greued.
> Alle the science vnder sonne · and alle sotile craftes
> Iche wolde ich knewe and couthe · kyndeliche in myn herte!"

> ["You are like a bishop," said I, quite in jest then,
> "For blessed bishops they bear many names;
> Bishop, Pontiff, and Metropolitan,
> And other names in great number—Diocesan and Pastor."
> "That is so," he said, "now I see thy will;
> How thou wouldst know and understand the cause of their names
> And of mine, if thou couldst, it seems to me by thy speech."
> "Yes, Sir," I said, "provided that no man were annoyed.
> All the knowledge under the sun and all subtle arts
> I wish I knew and understood thoroughly in my heart!"]

(Ed. W. W. Skeat, 2 vols [Oxford, 1886], C. XVII, ll. 202–211.) And the attempt would perhaps seem to the *Pearl* poet to deserve a rebuke similar to the one Langland's Dreamer receives:

> "Thanne art thow inparfyt," quath he · "and on of Prydes knyghtes;
> For such a luste and lykynge · Lucifer fel fro heuene:
> *Ponam pedem meum in aquilone, et ero similis altissimo*
> Hit were a-geyn kynde," quath he · "and alle kynne resoun.
> That eny creature sholde conne al · excepte Cryst one"

(*Ibid.*, ll. 212–215).

> ["Then art thou imperfect," said he, "one of Pride's knights;
> For such a desire and liking Lucifer fell from heaven:
> 'I shall set my foot in the north, and I shall be like the Most High.'
> It would be contrary to nature," said he, "and reason of every kind,
> That any creature should understand all except Christ alone."]

[20] Dorothy Everett, *Essays on Middle English Literature* (Oxford, 1955), p. 93.

> "O maskeleȝ perle in perleȝ pure,
> Þat bereȝ," quod I, "þe perle of prys. . . ."   (745–746)

> ["O spotless pearl in pearls pure,
> That wearest," said I, "the pearl of price. . . ."]

There is now a return to a question discussed previously: the Dreamer again asks how the Maiden can be a Bride of the Lamb to the exclusion of all others. But he has now become more reverent and patient in his enquiry than he was before:

> Why, maskelleȝ bryd þat bryȝt con flambe,
> Þat reiateȝ hatȝ so ryche and ryf,
> Quat kyn þyng may be þat Lambe
> Þat þe wolde wedde vnto hys vyf?   (769–772)

> [Why, spotless bride, who bright dost shine,
> Who hast marks of royalty so rich and rife,
> What sort of Being can that Lamb be
> Who thee would wed as His wife?]

> "Neuer þe les let be my þonc,"
> Quod I, "My perle, þaȝ I appose;
> I schulde not tempte þy wyt so wlonc,
> To Krysteȝ chambre þat art ichose."   (901–904)

> [Never the less let my pardon be,
> My pearl," said I, "though I questions pose.
> I should not test thy wit so fine
> Who to Christ's chamber art elect."]

This time, enlightenment is his reward. The Maiden, with frequent *confirmationes* [supporting texts] from the Apocalypse, explains to him about the 144,000 Brides, expounds the doctrine of Christ as the sacrificial Lamb of God, and goes on to describe the New Jerusalem. This last description includes a list of precious stones taken directly from John (Rev. 21:19–20), but there is no evidence that these are to be understood in any allegorical sense. It may be, of course, that the type of audience for which *Pearl* was written would be sufficiently familar with lapidaries and scriptural commentaries for the mere naming of the stones to evoke allegorical significances. Certainly, if we wish to recapture a fourteenth-century reading of the poem, we shall do well to find out what these significances were. But it must be remembered that the poem itself does not indicate any particular set of significances, so that as many interpretations would be possible as could be found in commentaries on the Apocalypse. This fact surely makes it clear that no such allegorical sense could be more than peripheral to the poem's meaning. The chief function of the catalogue of stones is decorative, which is to say, not that it is a meaningless ornament, but that it has a *poetic* function, to evoke by the normal medieval accumulative method the color and brightness of the New Jerusalem. Still following John, the Maiden adds that each of the city's twelve gates was made of "a margyrye, / A parfyt perle þat neuer fateȝ" [of one pearl / A perfect pearl which never fades] (1037–1038). And here, we may be sure, the pearl has precisely the value as a symbol which it has acquired in the poem so far.

During this long passage based on the Apocalypse there has been occurring a further, and final, development of the pearl symbol. In answering the Dreamer's question, "Quat kyn þyng may be þat Lambe?" [What sort of Being can that Lamb be?] the Maiden has referred to Christ as "My Lombe, my Lorde, my dere juelle" [My Lamb, my Lord, my dear Jewel] (795); *juelle* is a term which has previously been applied to the Maiden herself—"That juel þenne in gemmeȝ gente" [That jewel then in noble gems] (253)—in the section where the Dreamer is called a *jueler*. From this point onward there is a gradual movement toward the association of Christ himself with the pearl symbol. Thus as the Lamb of God he is given the pearl's whiteness and its spotlessness:

> Thys Jerusalem Lombe hade neuer pechche
> Of oþer huee bot quyt jolyf
> Þat mot ne masklle moȝt on streche,
> For wolle quyte so ronk and ryf.   (841–844)

[This Jerusalem Lamb had never a shred
Of other hue save beautiful white.

145

> Him neither spot nor speck could reach
> Because of the white wool so rich and rife.]

And when the Dreamer achieves his vision of the New Jerusalem, he sees the Brides of the Lamb, his own pearl among them—

> Depaynt in perleȝ and wedeȝ qwyte;
> In vchoneȝ brest watȝ bounden boun
> Þe blysful perle wyth gret delyt   (1102–1104)

> [Arrayed in pearls and raiment white;
> On each one's breast was fixed the destined,
> The blessèd pearl beyond delight.]

—and at their head the Lamb himself:

> Wyth horneȝ seuen of red golde cler;
> As praysed perleȝ his wedeȝ wasse.   (1111–1112)

> [With seven horns of clear red gold;
> Like prizèd pearl His garments were.]

The association of the pearl with the Lamb goes no further than this: there is never any identification of the two, and this inconclusiveness seems to me an essential element in the poem's doctrine and drama. The Dreamer has been brought to see an increasingly deeper meaning in the symbol which at the beginning of the poem appeared as a literal pearl. Its preciousness, at first thought to be transitory, has gradually been shown to transcend the merely human; but to see in the precious stone the ground of its own preciousness—to achieve the genuinely mystical experience of seeing God in a point—is denied to the Dreamer by the failure of his own patience. *Pearl* has connections with the great efflorescence of English devotional writing in the fourteenth century as much as with the tradition of secular dream poetry which goes back to the *Roman de la Rose,* but the experience of the poem does not represent a completed mystical experience. As the Dreamer rashly tries to cross the river and join the Maiden, he awakes from his dream, and his awakening returns him to the garden and pearl of the poem's opening:

> Þen wakned I in þat erber wlonk;
> My hede vpon þat hylle watȝ layde
> Þer as my perle to grounde strayd.   (1171–1173)

> [Then wakened I in that garden fair;
> My head upon that hill was laid
> Where my pearl to ground had strayed.]

He at once laments his lack of patience and its unfortunate results:

> To þat Prynceȝ paye hade I ay bente,
> And ȝerned no more þen watȝ me gyuen,
> And halden me þer in trwe entent,
> As þe perle me prayed þat watȝ so þryuen,
> As helde, drawen to Goddeȝ present,
> To mo of his mysterys I hade ben dryuen.   (1189–1194)

> [To that Prince's will had I always bowed,
> And craved no more than to me was given,
> And held me there in true intent
> As the pearl me urged, who was so blessed,
> Thus disposed, drawn to God's Presence,
> To more of His mysteries I would have been led.]

The *mysterys* which he has failed to attain are no doubt adumbrated in the incomplete movement toward an identification of the pearl and the Lamb. However, despite its incompleteness, the Dreamer's visionary experience has a significant effect on his life in the waking world. His loss of patience in the dream situation has deprived him of a deeper insight into God's *mysterys,* but his recognition of this fact brings to him a gain of patience in his real-life situation: submitting to God's will, he now accepts positively the loss of his pearl, as he was unable to do at the beginning of the poem. "Lorde," he exclaims, "mad hit arn þat agayn þe stryuen" [Lord, mad are they who strive against Thee] (1199), and he goes on, summing up his experience:

> Ouer þis hyul þis lote I laȝte,
> For pyty of my perle enclyin,
> And syþen to God I hit bytaȝte
> In Krysteȝ dere blessyng and myn.   (1205–1208)

147

> [Upon this hill this destiny I grasped,
> Prostrate in sorrow for my pearl.
> And afterward to God I gave it up
> In the dear blessing and memory of Christ.]

Though the Dreamer's visionary experience is incomplete, the dramatic possibilities of his initial situation have been brought to a satisfying conclusion. The body of the poem has taken the form of a dramatic process in which symbolic development has gone along with human development, and which we are able to act out imaginatively for ourselves as often as we read it. It is this process, and not merely the doctrine embodied in it, which gives *Pearl*—the poem and the symbol—its lasting value.[21]

[21] A fuller account of *Pearl*, incorporating some of the material of this article, is to appear in the author's *The Gawain-Poet: A Critical Study* (Cambridge University Press).

10

THE PEARL-MAIDEN AND THE PENNY

Robert W. Ackerman

CHRISTIAN ALLEGORY AS THE PRIMARY BASIS FOR INTERPRETING medieval literature, or at least the undiscriminating use of patristic commentary on the Bible, is currently under attack from several quarters.[1] As a result, one is tempted to veer to the opposite extreme and espouse what he considers a completely literal reading of the work in question. No Middle English poem, with the exception of *Piers Plowman,* has been subjected to more elaborate allegorical or symbolic criticism than *Pearl,*[2] though now an almost inevitable reaction has set in. As a recent writer puts it: "Perhaps we should take *Pearl* as a guide to medieval symbolism rather than medieval symbolism as a guide

© 1964 by the Regents of the University of California. Reprinted from *Romance Philology,* XVII, 615–623, by permission of the Regents and of the author. Translations havè been supplied by the author.

[1] On this matter, see M. W. Bloomfield, "Symbolism in Medieval Literature," *MP,* LVI (1958–1959), 73–81; and *Critical Approaches to Medieval Literature,* ed. Dorothy Bethurum (New York, 1960), esp. pp. 1–26.

[2] See, e.g., D. W. Robertson, Jr., "The Pearl as a Symbol," *MLN,* LXV (1950), 155–157. Perhaps the most extravagant treatment of *Pearl* in terms of the four levels of scriptural exegesis is the unpublished dissertation of B. P. Farragher, *Pearl and Scriptural Tradition* (Boston University, 1956). In *"Pearl* and a Lost Tradition," *JEGP,* LIV (1955), 333–347, J. Conley argues sensibly against certain symbolic interpretations.

to *Pearl*."[3] There is little doubt that a number of critics have imputed to the *Pearl*-poet, and *pari passu* to his first audience, an implausible degree of sophistication in scriptural exegesis. On the other hand, the Christian schooling of the fourteenth-century mind was all-enveloping. What would then have been at once recognized as a pregnant allusion may all too easily be passed over by a modern reader intent on finding the plain, "literal" sense.

The general purpose here is to point out that clues to important allusions and images are occasionally to be found in the popular treatises of medieval religious instruction—that mass of mainly subliterary writings of the thirteenth and fourteenth centuries which spell out, often in allegorical terms, the elements of the Christian faith as taught to and received by the people. It may properly be said that the community of belief to which the poets of the Middle Ages could appeal is defined in these vernacular works and also, but to a smaller extent, in contemporary sermons.[4] All the reflections of popular Christianity to be observed in *Pearl* may not be treated here. Instead, the present essay seeks to uncover the backgrounds in certain Old French and Middle English tracts of two significant motifs in the poem—first, the Pearl-Maiden as a divine instructress and, second, the penny of the Parable of the Vineyard—by way of indicating how they may well have been understood by the original audiences and further to consider what bearing this understanding has on our grasp of *Pearl* as a whole.

It is surprising that more attention has not been paid the relationship of the Pearl-Maiden to the long line of celestial teachers stemming from the "omnium magistra virtutum" [mistress of all virtues], Lady Philosophy, of Boethius's *De Consolatione Philosophiae*. The relevance of such a background was

---

[3] A. C. Spearing, "Symbolism and Dramatic Development in *Pearl*," *MP*, LX (1962–1963), 2–3 [page 125 above].

[4] On the vernacular treatises as an embodiment of popular Christian beliefs and practices, see my article, *"The Debate of the Body and the Soul* and Parochial Christianity," *Spec.*, XXXVII (1962), 545–549.

asserted by W. H. Schofield in a seminal article that long ago freed *Pearl* from an unrelieved autobiographical interpretation. Schofield calls Pearl

as purely an allegorical figure as the various other beautiful ladies who before our author's time had appeared in imagination to disconsolate poets for their counsel, comfort, and illumination—Philosophy, Nature, Reason, Holy Church, and their kind, the famous instructors of Boethius, Alain de l'Isle, the authors of the *Romance of the Rose,* Langland, and other didactic writers.[5]

But, in his *Tradition of Boethius,* H. R. Patch associates *Pearl* only with Thomas Usk's *Testament of Love.*[6] And in a far more recent study John Conley argues ably that *Pearl* is to be read as a Christian *consolatio,* yet he fails to examine the heavenly instructress herself.[7]

To the present writer, however, some characteristics of the teachers and their settings in the fully developed Boethian tradition are helpful in suggesting the viewpoint of the *Pearl*-poet and the expectations of his audience. Among the many successors to Lady Philosophy, Dame Grace Dieu in Guillaume Deguileville's trilogy, Part I, known as *Le Pèlerinage de vie humaine,* seems to combine the largest number of traits which also mark the Pearl-Maiden. Written in 1330–1332, then expanded some years later by the original author, *Le Pèlerinage* reached a very wide public, to judge from the "exceedingly large numbers" of surviving MSS. It was rather promptly turned into French prose and also appeared in Middle English versions, of which John Lydgate's translation (1426) of the later form is the best known.[8] That Deguileville's allegory was read in Eng-

---

[5] "The Nature and Fabric of *The Pearl,*" *PMLA,* XII (1904), 175.

[6] (New York, 1935), p. 105.

[7] "*Pearl* and a Lost Tradition," pp. 332–347.

[8] *Le Pelerinage de Vie Humaine,* ed. J. J. Stürzinger (London, 1893), pp. v–vi; *The Pilgrimage of the Life of Man, Englisht by John Lydgate,* ed. F. J. Furnivall, EETS, ES, LXXVII, LXXXIII, XCII (1899–1904), Introduction, pp. xii ff. See also Dorothy L. Owen, *Piers Plowman. A Comparison with Some Earlier and Contemporary French Allegories* (London, 1912), pp. 6–9, 154 ff.

land before 1370 is strongly suggested by Chaucer's poem, "An ABC," which translates a hymn to the Virgin incorporated in *Le Pèlerinage*.[9] There is no intention of holding here that the *Pearl*-poet knew and made use of Deguileville. It is sufficient to note that the heavenly teacher was a staple of the didactic allegories of the century and that the author of *Pearl* was drawing on the tradition to a greater extent than is commonly recognized.

Several of the most obvious perquisites of Pearl and Grace Dieu go back to Boethius' Lady Philosophy. The supernatural origin, the striking beauty, and the magnificent raiment of Lady Philosophy are bequeathed to her successors along with her teaching techniques and her patience in dealing with a sometimes obtuse pupil. The later instructresses are more nearly human, yet they retain a mystic aura. For example, their pupils come very slowly to recognize in them a long-familiar figure. Only after some moments of conversation does Boethius identify "nutricem meam" [my nurse];[10] the same slowly dawning recognition appears in *Pearl*.[11]

In *Le Pèlerinage*, the beauty of Grace Dieu ravishes the Dreamer-Pilgrim, and he observes appreciatively her regal bearing and array: the carbuncles at her waist, the green belt, and the crown, surrounded by a "grant foison d'estoiles luisans" [great abundance of shining stars] (231–245). The extended Old French version, represented by Lydgate's translation,[12] adds more details: the gown is white (like the linen robe of Lady Holy Church in *Piers Plowman*[13]), a luminous "nouche" [brooch or ornament] blazes on the divine creature's breast,

---

[9] *The Complete Works of Geoffrey Chaucer*, ed. W. W. Skeat (Oxford, 1899), I, 261–271.

[10] *De Consolatione Philosophiae*, eds. H. F. Stewart and E. K. Rand. Loeb Class. Libr. (Cambridge, Mass., 1918), Bk. I, Pr. iii, p. 138.

[11] Ed. E. V. Gordon (Oxford, 1953), ll. 169–252.

[12] Lydgate's Middle English poem is accepted here as a sufficiently close rendering of the later form of Deguileville's work. See the comparative analysis of the two in Lydgate, pp. xvii–xxxi.

[13] Ed. W. W. Skeat (Oxford, 1924), B-Text, Passus I, v. 3.

and a dove flies out of her bosom (679–706). The supernal beauty of Pearl and the splendor of her apparel are so well known as scarcely to require quotation. Her skin is "whyt as playn yuore" [white as clear ivory], her "hyȝe pynakled" [high pointed] crown is of pearl, the seams and hems of her elaborate dress are edged with margarites, and on her breast is "a wonder perle wythouten wemme" [a marvelous pearl without flaw]. Only her hair—"as schorne golde schyr her fax þenne schon" [her hair shone as bright as newly wrought gold]— contrasts with her shimmering, unearthly whiteness (178 ff.).

Grace Dieu and Pearl take their teaching duties as seriously as does their progenitor, Lady Philosophy, although their pupils are somewhat more recalcitrant and obstinate than Boethius admits to being. Boethius only once returns a flat "nihil" to his mentor, when she asks if he knows himself to be anything more than a mortal (Bk. I, Pr. vi, p. 166). But, especially in the longer form of *Le Pèlerinage,* the Pilgrim is most querulous when informed by Grace Dieu that he must submit to washing in the river. Fearful of drowning, he argues tenaciously that he could not be in need of a bath since he is very young and since his parents had once been cleansed of sin. He is persuaded to enter the stream only after considerable rebuke and instruction in baptismal doctrine (885–1294). In the same vein, but even more stubbornly, the Dreamer in *Pearl* voices objection after objection to his teacher's discourse. He tells Pearl that he can understand how she might be a countess in heaven but that she should be a queen is scarcely credible:

> "Bot a quene! Hit is to dere a date."　　　(492)
>
> [But a queen! That is too high a goal.]

Shortly thereafter, having listened to a sermon on the rewards of heaven in terms of the Parable of the Vineyard, the Jeweler is even more captious and abrupt:

> "Me þynk þy tale vnresounable.
> Goddeȝ ryȝt is redy and euermore rert,

153

Oþer Holy Wryt is bot a fable.
In Sauter is sayd a verce ouerte
Þat spekeʒ a poynt determynable:
'Þou quyteʒ vchon as hys desserte.
Þou hyʒe kyng ay pretermynable.' "   (590–596)

[It seems to me that your story is unreasonable.
God's justice is prompt and ever supreme,
Or else Holy Scripture is only a fable.
In the Psalter is said in a plainly understood verse,
Which expresses a definite point,
"You pay each one according to his deserts,
You High King, ever preordaining."]

Only after additional instruction and much forebearance on Pearl's part is he willing to accept her statement as to her celestial rank.

A prominent feature of the setting in which Grace Dieu appears to the Pilgrim is a body of water. When the Pilgrim reveals his great longing to enter the Holy City, which he has seen imaged in a glass, Grace Dieu explains that the journey is impossible without her aid and counsel. Furthermore, he must begin his pilgrimage from her abode. She then conducts him to a point from which her ancient, towered house ("xiii^c et xxx ans auoit" [it was 1330 years old]) may be seen suspended in the air, not unlike the Tower of Truth in *Piers Plowman*.[14] The Pilgrim observes the scene closely:

Celle maison volentiers vi
Et au veoir mout m'esbahi
Quar toute haut en l'air pendoit
Et entre terre et ciel estoit
Tout aussi com fust venue
La du ciel et descendue.   (401–406)

----

[14] As I bihelde in-to the est an heigh to the sonne
I seigh a toure on a toft trielich ymaked. (B-Text, Pro., ll. 13f.)

[As I looked eastward on high, toward the sun,
I saw a tower on a knoll, expertly made.]

[I was eager to see that house,
And it abashed me very much,
For it hung very high in the air
And was between earth and heaven
As if it had come
And descended there from the sky.]

Before the house extends a body of water, an unbridged river, which must somehow be traversed:

Mes ce mout me desconfortoit
Que une eaue devant avoit,
Et celle me failloit passer,
S'en la maison vouloie entrer.   (409–412)

[But it disturbed me much
That a river lay there
Which I was not able to cross,
If I wished to enter the house.]

His entrance into the water symbolizes his baptism. Thereafter in Grace Dieu's house, or the Church, the Pilgrim is presented with pageantlike expositions of the other six Sacraments by Grace Dieu's assistants, chiefly the horned Moses and Reason.

The jewel-paved, crystal stream in *Pearl* is a far more significant story element than the river before Grace Dieu's house, since it functions as an effective barrier between the temporarily released soul of the Dreamer and Paradise. It is the Dreamer's mad attempt to fling himself into the stream and join his Pearl that terminates his vision. By following the banks of "beryl bryʒt" the Dreamer had first come upon the Pearl-Maiden seated on the opposite shore. After his perplexities as to the rewards of the saved are resolved, the Dreamer asks to see Pearl's habitation, "þat myry mote" [that fair walled city]. Still remaining on his side of the water, he is conducted to a vantage point:

Tyl on a hyl þat I asspyed
And blusched on þe burghe, as I forth dreued,
Byʒonde þe brok fro me warde keued,
Þat schyrrer þen sunne wyth schafteʒ schon.

155

> In þe Apokalypce is þe fasoun preued,
> As deuyseʒ þe apostel John.
>
> As John þe apostel hit syʒ wyth syʒt,
> I syʒe þat cyty of gret renoun,
> Jerusalem so nwe and ryally dyʒt,
> As hit was lyʒt froþe heuen adoun.　　　(970–988)

> [Until I looked toward the hill
> And gazed on the city, as I pressed forward.
> Beyond the stream that lay low before me,
> It shone brighter than the sun with its rays;
> The nature of it set forth in Apocalypse,
> As the Apostle John describes it.
>
> As John the Apostle saw it with his eyes,
> I saw that city of wide renown,
> Jerusalem so new and regally adorned,
> For it had descended from the heavens.]

The dwellings of both Grace Dieu and Pearl are visible across a water; both seem to have come down from the skies.

In the face of these correspondences, it is difficult to deny that Deguileville and the *Pearl*-poet are adhering rather closely to a common tradition. The medieval audience in touch with this tradition would be far better prepared for a discourse from the heavenly teacher on the religious truths necessary for the salvation of the soul than for a sentimental reunion of the Dreamer with the spirit of a deceased child.

A second element of *Pearl* on which doctrinal treatises offer a potentially helpful commentary is the use made of the Parable of the Vineyard (493–708). In response to the Dreamer's peevish surprise at her statement that she, a mere child, is a member of the elect company following the Lamb, Pearl embarks on a lengthy exaltation of innocence. The parable (Matt. 20:1–16) serves as the scriptural basis of her demonstration that the reward of heaven is a free gift of grace, not to be earned by the merit of good works. Pearl is at pains to explain that she as an innocent has greater joy and honor in heaven than the righteous, those who had lived long in the world:

"More haf I of ioye and blysse hereinne,
Of ladyschyp gret and lyueʒ blom,
Þen alle þe wyʒeʒ in þe worlde myʒt wynne
By þe way of ryʒt to aske dome."   (577–580)

[Here I have more of joy and bliss,
More of great ladyship and bloom of life,
Than all the people of the world may attain
Who ask to be judged on their righteousness.]

Somewhat ruefully, she repeats the Dreamer's skeptical view—
he says "þat I my peny haf wrang tan here"—and then elucidates more carefully. Salvation in itself, she observes, is not
greater or less. All who are saved, the innocent and the righteous
alike, are paid the penny of everlasting life. But the baptized
innocents are in less need of mercy than the righteous, who
have sinned and atoned.[15]

Most students of *Pearl,* in commenting on the function of the
parable in the poem, dwell on the Maiden's admission that she
is a late-comer to the vine ("In euentyde into þe vyne I come"),
an emphasis encouraged by the common exegetical interpretations.[16] But a different note is struck in an allusion appearing
in a didactic treatise, *Le Somme des Vices et des Vertues* (c.
1279), written in part at least by Friar Lorens, confessor to
Phillip III of France. "One of the most popular books of its
kind,"[17] *Le Somme* was Englished under the title *Aʒenbite of
Inwyt* in about 1340, and again as *The Book of Vices and Virtues* about sixty years later. Chaucer utilized it to some extent
in his *Parson's Tale,* another prose treatment was written in
1440, and Caxton translated the work anew in his *Book Ryal.*

The allusion to the parable and specifically to the penny

---

[15] *The Pearl,* ed. Sister Mary Vincent Hillmann (Convent Station,
N. J., 1961), pp. vii–ix.

[16] See, e.g., Gordon's ed., pp. xix ff., esp. xxvi; also the *Glossa Ordinaria,* in *Patr. Lat.,* ed. Migne (Paris, 1879), CXIV, col. 150.

[17] W. A. Pantin, *The English Church in the Fourteenth Century* (Cambridge, Engl., 1955), p. 226.

occurs in Friar Lorens' exposition of the fourth petition of the *Pater Noster*:

Panem nostrum cotidianum da nobis hodie. Moult nous enseigne nostre dous mestres a parler humblement et sagement. . . . Cest pains est . . . le vray corps ihesucrist et lame. . . . Cest le dernier que il donne a ces ouvriers quant vient au vespre cest a la fin de la vie.[18]

[Give us this day our daily bread. Our sweet master teaches us to speak humbly and wisely. . . . This bread is . . . the very body and soul of Jesus Christ. . . . It is the penny he gives to his workers when they come in the evening, that is at the close of life.]

The association of the daily bread in the Lord's Prayer with the gift of salvation and also the Eucharist is standard in medieval scriptural commentary.[19] But Lorens further equates the daily bread—i.e., the consecrated Host—with the penny of the parable. The latter association seems by no means to be a commonplace among the exegetes, though Berchorius, in his mid-fourteenth-century *Dictionarium Morale,* comes close to saying the same thing when, after identifying the bread of the fourth petition with the *panis sacramentalis*, he refers to God as the *paterfamilias* who sends refreshment out into the field of the world to his farmers and workers.[20] Whether Lorens himself took the short step of calling the *paterfamilias* the owner of the vineyard in the parable from Matthew and then explicitly likening the food, the Host, with the penny or whether in so doing he followed the lead of an exegetical writer of his day is unimportant. The fact is that this particular passage in *Le Somme* was

[18] MS Brit. Mus. Royal 19. c 11 (MLA Rotograph No. 306), fols. 43*a* and 44*b*.

[19] *"Panem nostrum quotidianum: . . . panem,* id est Christum, sic agere debemus, ut eum quotidie possimus accipere ad remedium" [*Our daily bread . . . bread,* that is, Christ; thus we ought to act so that we may receive Him daily for our salvation] (*Glossa Ordinaria,* CXIV, col. 876). For other commentaries to the same effect, see *PL,* LII, col. 667; XXXVIII, col. 389.

[20] Petrus Berchorius, *Omnia Opera* (Moguntiae [Mainz], 1609), III, 1164, s.v. *panis.*

faithfully carried over into later, influential versions of the work. Thus, Dan Michel of Northgate translates as follows in his *Aʒenbite of Inwyt*:

Mochel ous tekþ oure guode mayster/ to spekene myldelyche/ and wysliche. . . . þet bred . . . is þe zoþe bodi of Iesu crist and þe zaule. . . . þet is þe peny þet he yefþ to his workmen/ huanne euen comþ. þet is þe ende of þe liue.[21]

[Our good master teaches us to speak very mildly and humbly. . . . This bread is . . . the very body and soul of Jesus Christ. . . . It is the penny he gives to his workers when they come in the evening, that is at the close of life.]

Thus the association of the penny of the parable with the Host found a place in vernacular treatises that achieved some currency in fourteenth-century England.

In the context of the 200-line passage of *Pearl* devoted to the parable, the penny figures as the gift of salvation. No direct statement in this section of the work encourages one to attach further significance to it. On the other hand, the final stanza, and, in particular, the Eucharistic scene with which the poem closes, is worth examining in a new light:

> To pay þe Prince oþer sete saʒte
> Hit is ful eþe to þe god Krystyin;
> For I haf founden hym, boþe day and naʒte,
> A God, a Lorde, a frend ful fyin.
> Ouer þis hyul þis lote I laʒte,
> For pyty of my perle enclyin,
> And syþen to God I hit bytaʒte
> In Krysteʒ dere blessyng and myn,
> Þat in þe forme of bred and wyn
> Þe prest vus scheweʒ vch a daye.
> He gef vus to be his homly hyne
> And precious perlez vnto his pay.

> > (Gordon's ed., 1201–1212)

---

[21] *Dan Michel's Aʒenbite of Inwyt*, ed. R. Morris, EETS, XXIII (1866), 110–113. An equally literal translation of this passage appears in the slightly later *Book of Vices and Virtues*, ed. W. N. Francis, EETS, CCXVII (1942), III.

The first line (1201), of course, repeats the wording of the initial line of the poem, in keeping with the tightly interlaced structure favored by that poet. The stanza as a whole may be broadly paraphrased as follows:

To please the prince or to be reconciled to him is made very simple for the good Christian. For I have found him day and night a God, a Lord, and a most noble friend. On this mound I was granted this lot [vision], lying prostrate in sorrow over my Pearl. Afterwards I commended my Pearl to God in the dear blessing and memory of Christ, Christ whom the priest shows us daily in the form of bread and wine. He granted that we may become his humble servants and precious pearls satisfying to him.

This formulation of the wisdom acquired by the Dreamer is a miracle of compression, yet it epitomizes the main argument of the entire poem. The "hyul" in line 1205 evokes the opening scene in the "erber grene" where the Dreamer first gives way to grief; and line 1207—"and afterwards I commended my Pearl to God"—recalls his wondering recognition that the celestial being before him is indeed his Pearl and that she dwells in heaven:

> "And þou in a lyf of lykyng lyȝte,
> In Paradys erde, of stryf vnstrayned." (247–248)
>
> [And you, arrived in an existence of delight,
> In the realm of Paradise, set free from turmoil.]

The account of the Mass in the concluding lines, however, would seem to represent a distinct break inasmuch as no certain reference to the consecrated elements or the Eucharist occurs at any earlier point. Most commentators suggest that the Eucharist is an appropriate note on which to close since it signifies the Sacrament by which "we have access in One Spirit to the Father"[22] and, by implication, a solacing access to the beatified Pearl who dwells with the Father. In all likelihood, these lines convey such a meaning to many readers.

---

[22] Eph. 2:18–19. Quoted in this context by Sister Mary Vincent Hillmann, p. 108.

A gain in unity and force results, however, if, in addition to the meaning just mentioned, one reads into the Eucharistic account an allusion to the penny of the vineyard and thus to the discourse which the Pearl-Maiden deduces from that parable. This argument, turning on the reward of heaven, is from many viewpoints the heart of the poem. The poet, of course, does not rely solely on his bare reference to wine and bread to remind his audience of the vineyard and of "þe peny þet he [God] yefþ to his workmen." Other and stronger clues are to be found in the echoing of key words and expressions, almost a compulsive stylistic device with the *Pearl*-poet. Thus, "homly hyne" (line 1211) and "pay" (line 1212) in the conclusion hark back to more than one phrase in the vineyard passage in the very middle of the poem. There, "hyne" occurs twice (lines 505 and 632) and nowhere else in the poem save the last stanza, whereas "pay," in the modern sense of 'remunerate' or 'remuneration,' is used four times (lines 584, 603, 632, and 635). Moreover, the two words flank each other in the line which, more than any other, describes the culminating event in the parable:

> "þe gentyle Lorde þenne payeȝ hys hyne." (Gordon's ed., 632)

> [The noble Lord then pays his servants.]

If one accepts these verbal parallels as significant, the Eucharistic passage may be seen to function more effectively both as a harmonious element in its own stanza and as the crowning summation of the central message of *Pearl*.

The suggestion about the poet's consciousness of the traditional association of the Host and the penny of the parable is not aimed at reviving R. M. Garrett's theory, long since discredited, to the effect that the poem is basically a Eucharistic vision.[23] Rather, it is hoped that the established position of both

---

[23] R. M. Garrett, *The Pearl, An Interpretation* (Seattle, Wash, 1918). See the review by C. Brown, *MLN*, XXIV (1919), 42–45. The present writer is also unable to read the first two lines of the poem —
> Perle, plesaunte to prynces paye
> To clanly clos in golde so clere —

the divine instructress and the multivalued penny of the parable in well-known treatises of popular Christianity, as opposed to the esoteric and far less accessible corpus of scriptural exegesis, may help place *Pearl* within the grasp of a relatively wide medieval audience instead of one composed of a few scholastically trained clerks.

> [Pearl, pleasing to a prince
> and fit to be set in gold so bright]

as a description of the consecrated wafer set in a gold monstrance, as suggested by F. E. Richardson, "*The Pearl:* A Poem and Its Audience," *Neoph.,* XXXVI (1962), 313.

11

THE MIDDLE ENGLISH *PEARL:*
ITS RELATION TO THE
ROMAN DE LA ROSE

Herbert Pilch

IN THE LITERARY CRITICISM OF THE MIDDLE ENGLISH *Pearl* THE following questions prevail: Elegy or allegory? Orthodox or heretical doctrine of grace? Poetry based on personal experience or literary convention? René Wellek has shown in one of his early studies[1] that at least the first two of these questions are misstated; today he would presumably say the same about the third.[2] Nevertheless, discussion of the poem has not left the beaten track. Although E. V. Gordon holds that, strictly speaking, the question of the poet's personal experience is irrelevant, he devotes seven pages to a discussion of this problem[3] and speaks in favor of an elegiac, rather than an allegorical, interpre-

Reprinted, by permission of the author and the Modern Language Society, from *Neuphilologische Mitteilungen*, LXV (1964), 427–446, where it appeared under the title "Das mittelenglische Perlengedicht: Sein Verhältnis zum Rosenroman." Translated by Heide Hyprath. Translations from Middle English are editorial. Throughout, the phrase *"Pearl* poet" refers simply to the author of the poem rather than to the hypothetical author of four poems of MS. Cotton Nero A. x, the so-called *Pearl*-poet.

[1] "The *Pearl,*" *Studies in English by Members of the English Seminar of Charles University, Prague,* IV (1933), 1–33.

[2] At that time René Wellek still spoke with certainty of the poet's "personal loss."

[3] Ed. *Pearl* (Oxford, 1953), pp. xiii–xix. We quote from Gordon's text but omit some of his emendations.

tation.[4] An allegorical interpretation, however, is given in the introduction and in the commentary of the latest edition of the poem.[5] A. C. Spearing[6] was the first to assert that allegorical interpretation according to the four levels of meaning is superfluous; he interprets the pearl as a multilayered symbol, the meaning of which is disclosed only gradually, whereas in allegory the meaning is supplied at the start.

Concerning the classification of *Pearl* in literary history, its editors list numerous quotations and paraphrases from the Bible. The classical model for the frame of the narrator's dream-vision is the Old French *Roman de la Rose* [*Romance of the Rose*]. As *Pearl* exemplifies, a reciprocal vocabulary of courtly and religious love characterizes broad areas of medieval literature.[7] W. H. Schofield refers to parallels between *Pearl* and Boccaccio's *Olympia*;[8] E. V. Gordon, however, thinks that these are accidental.[9] Charles G. Osgood and Dorothy Everett see similarities of presentation between *Pearl* and the *Divina Commedia*.[10] Moreover, the motif of the heavenly vision is also known to us from numerous legends of the saints such as the

[4] *Ibid.*, pp. xi–xiii.

[5] Sister Mary V. Hillmann, ed., *The Pearl* (University of Notre Dame Press, 1967). Recently Stanton Hoffman has also argued for a consistently allegorical interpretation, "The *Pearl*: Notes for an Interpretation," *Modern Philology*, LVIII (1960), 73–80.

[6] "Symbolic and Dramatic Development in *Pearl*," *Modern Philology*, LX (1962), 1–12.

[7] Cf., e.g., the terms "grace," "merci" [mercy], "pechiez" [sins], "comandemenz" [commandments], "penitence," "repentance," "sermon," "saintuaire" [sanctuary] in the dialogue between the narrator and Amor (*Roman de la Rose*, ll. 1955–2764). I quote the *Roman de la Rose* (abbr. *RR*) from the edition of E. Langlois, *Le Roman de la Rose* by Guillaume de Lorris and Jean de Meun, 5 vols. (Paris, I, 1914; II, 1920; III, 1921; IV, 1922; V, 1924), *SATF*.

[8] "The Nature and Fabric of *The Pearl*," *PMLA*, XIX (1904), 154–215.

[9] *Op. cit.*, p. xxxv.

[10] Dorothy Everett, *Essays on Middle English Literature*, ed. Patricia Kean (Oxford, 1955), p. 95; Charles G. Osgood, ed., *The Pearl* (Boston, Mass., 1906), pp. xxvi–xxviii, The Belles Lettres Series.

Vision of St. Paul, St. Patrick's Purgatory, and the *Vision of Tundale.*[11] As a dispute between father and daughter, *Pearl* can be further classified as a poetic example of a medieval genre, debate.[12]

Gordon[13] cites lines 749–752 as a literal allusion to the *Roman de la Rose;* neither nature nor art, we are told, can create such a beautiful pearl:

> Þy beauté com neuer of nature;
> Pymalyon paynted neuer þy vys,
> Ne Arystotel nawþer by hys lettrure
> Of carped þe kynde þese properteȝ.

> [Your beauty never came from nature;
> Pygmalion never painted your face,
> nor did Aristotle speak in his writings
> of the nature of these properties.]

Her creator is rather the spotless lamb Jesus Christ (765). In referring to the *Roman de la Rose,* 16013 f., in connection with this statement, Gordon was obviously mistaken.[14] In the wider context of this passage Jean de Meun speaks of the superiority of nature to art, i.e., to man's creation. Art kneels before Nature and begs for instruction. But art can imitate nature at best only like an ape; she cannot, like nature, create living beings. A little later, it is true, the names Aristotle and Pygmalion appear,[15] as

[11] Cf. the survey in John Edwin Wells, *A Manual of the Writings in Middle English 1050–1400* (New Haven, Conn., 1916), pp. 331–337, and the bibliography in Osgood, *op. cit.,* p. xxxvii, footnote 1.

[12] Cf. the survey of this genre in Wells, *op. cit.,* chap. 9, and W. Iser's observations, *Deutsche Vierteljahrsschrift,* XXXIII (1959), 316 f.

[13] *Op. cit.,* pp. xxxii, 72.

[14] Lines 16013–16014 of the *Roman de la Rose* read
> Quant autre conseil n'i peut metre,
> Si taille empreintes de tel letre.

> [When she can put no better idea to work,
> she imprints in such terms (style).]
The subject of the sentence is Nature, who tries to forestall death and decay.

[15] *RR,* 16170, 16177.

they do in *Pearl,* but they are mentioned simply as two names among many others and occur in a different context. The poet believes himself unable to describe Nature in her singular beauty—something, in fact, that not even the most famous writers, sculptors, and painters have managed to do. God is the only exception: "Nus fors Deus ne le pourrait faire" [Nobody but God could do this] (*RR,* 16210). In later English literature this "topos" [conventional (traditional) argument or motif] appears several times in this form: only Alanus de Insulis, but not the poet of the poem in question, could do justice to Nature:

> So hard it is for any liuing wight,
> All her array and vestiments to tell,
> That old Dan Geffrey (in whose gentle spright
> The pure well head of Poesie did dwell)
> In his Foules parley durst not with it mel
> But it transferd to Alane, who he thought
> Had in his Plaint of kindes describ'd it well.[16]

> [So hard it is for any living person
> to describe all her attire
> that old Master Chaucer (in whose noble soul
> the spring of poetry did dwell)
> dared not do so in his *Parliament of Fowls*
> but turned to Alanus, who in his *Complaint of Nature,*
> Chaucer thought, had described it well.]

Jean de Meun, who clearly alludes to *De planctu naturae* [Complaint of Nature] in the passage quoted, where he describes Nature as tired and weeping, does not except even Alanus from the universal inadequacy of human art.

If the poet of *Pearl,* in the passage in question, alludes to the *Roman de la Rose* at all, he does so rather with respect to the image of Raison [Reason], who is so well proportioned that not

---

[16] E. Spenser, *The Faerie Queen* VII, 7, 9, ed. E. Greenlaw, Charles G. Osgood, F. M. Padelford, and Ray Heffner (Baltimore, 1938). The lines referred to in Chaucer's *Parliament of Fowls* are 316–318; for the reference to Alanus de Insulis, *De Planctu Naturae,* see *Patrologia Latina,* ed. J. P. Migne, CCX, 432–439.

even Nature could have created her. God Himself created her in His image:

> Car Nature ne seüst pas
> Uevre faire de tel compas.
> Sachiez, se la lettre ne ment,
> Que Deus la fist demainement,
> A sa semblance e a s'image. (*RR*, 2987–2991)

> [For Nature could not
> create a work of that scale.
> Know that, if Scripture does not lie,
> God Himself made her
> in His own image and likeness.]

The *Pearl* poet combines this statement with the widespread "topos" of the superiority of nature to art[17] and arrives at a new argument. He does not contrast nature with art, but shows, rather, the inferiority of both to God. The poet's tendency to change the value of the ideas of traditional "topoi" and to confront them with the true world of God already becomes apparent.

A much more apparent allusion to the *Roman de la Rose* can also be found in the exordium of *Pearl*. The poem starts with an apostrophe to the matchless pearl. At first the word *pearl* is used in its literal meaning. The pearl in question is worthy of being mounted in gold for a prince.[18] Even in the Orient one would not find a pearl like this.[19] When it disappears into the grass, he suffers from his loss.

> I dewyne, fordolked of luf-daungere
> Of þat pryuy perle wythouten spot. (11–12)

---

[17] This "topos" is also used in Chaucer's *Physician's Tale*, lines 9–29, among other places. Further parallels are collected by Osgood in his edition of *The Pearl*. Cf. also E. R. Curtius, *Europäische Literatur und lateinisches Mittelalter*, 2nd ed. (Bern, 1954), pp. 522 f.

[18] I think that "to clanly clos" (line 2) is a split infinitive (cf. Gordon's note).

[19] A "topos." In the literature of that time especially exceptional pearls come from the Orient; cf. Chaucer, *Legend of Good Women*, 221 (text F). The diadem of Nature in Alanus comes "ab oriente" (*PL*, CCX, 443).

167

> [I languish, grievously wounded by the love-dominion
> of that pearl of my own without spot.]

Here it becomes apparent for the first time that the pearl has a symbolic meaning and represents a beloved human being, the maid who, adorned with pearls, appears later in the dialogue. Further allusions in the text indicate that she is the narrator's daughter, who died at the age of two.[20] Her death is figuratively expressed as a wound caused by Luf-daungere [Power of love].

In the *Roman de la Rose,* Dangiers [Danger; see below] is the allegorical guardian of the rose garden who hinders visitors from picking flowers.

> Por ceus espier e sorprendre
> Qu'il voit as roses la main tendre.   (*RR*, 2831–2832)
>
> [To spy out and to surprise
> those whom he sees reaching out for the roses.]

When Amant [the Lover] desires the bud, Dangiers chases him from the garden and plunges him into a life of torture:

> Si voi que livrez est mes cors
> A duel, a poine e a martire.   (*RR*, 2956–2957)
>
> [And I saw that my body
> was given up to suffering, pain, and martyrdom.]

Dangiers, as C. S. Lewis has shown,[21] here symbolizes the lady's refusal and hauteur. In this sense the term is frequently used in Chaucer, for example. Thus he says to the unbending beauty, who knows neither grace nor pity, and who is unmoved to see her lover die: "For Daunger halt your mercy in his cheyne"[22] [For Danger holds your mercy in his chain].

In the *Roman de la Rose* Amant must try to appease Dangiers and still approach the rose once more. In *Pearl* the rose as a

---

[20] Gordon, *op. cit.*, p. xiii, quotes the lines in question.

[21] *The Allegory of Love* (London, 1936), pp. 123 f., 364–366.

[22] "Merciles Beaute," l. 16. For numerous similar examples see J.S.P. Tatlock and A. G. Kennedy, *A Concordance to the Works of Geoffrey Chaucer* (Washington, D.C., 1927).

terrestrial being is lost irrevocably. Here Luf-daungere encounters the morally imperfect human being whose terrestrial desire prevents him from accepting the will of God and spiritual comfort:

> Þaȝ kynde of Kryst me comfort kenned,
> My wreched wylle[23] in wo ay wraȝte. (*Pearl*, 55–56)

> [Although the nature of Christ would have
>   taught me comfort,
> My wretched will in woe ever worked.]

From this state the narrator ascends to a morally complete devotion to the will of God, a devotion that has overcome earthly mourning and is now open to heavenly consolation:

> I do me ay in hys myserecorde. (*Pearl*, 366)

> [I put me ever in his mercy.]

> Bot kyþeȝ me kyndely your coumforde. (*Pearl*, 369)

> [But assuage me kindly with your comfort.]

He entrusts his pearl purposely to God. Dangiers can no longer harm him.

> Ouer þis hyul þis lote I laȝte,
> For pyty of my perle enclyin, (*Pearl*, 1205–1206)

> [Over this hill this lot I grasped,
> prostrate for pity of my pearl.]

the narrator says in retrospect,

> And syþen to God I hit bytaȝte
> In Krysteȝ dere blessyng and myn. (*Pearl*, 1207–1208)

> [And then to God I committed it
> in Christ's dear blessing and mine.]

---

[23] Here "wylle" means not only the willfulness of man in general but specifically lust. In the *Parliament of Fowls* Chaucer has "wille" represent the daughter of Cupid (versus 214 f.; cf. F. N. Robinson, ed., *The Works of Geoffrey Chaucer*, 2nd ed. [Boston, Mass., 1957], 794 a).

In *Pearl* the rose, the central symbol of the French romance, also connotes earthly desire. In the *Roman de la Rose* the rose is symbolic of the adored woman:

> Cele por cui je l'ai empris;
> c'est cele qui tant a de pris
> E tant est dine d'estre amee
> Qu'el doit estre Rose clamee.   (*RR*, 41–44)

> [The one for whom I have undertaken it (i.e., *RR*),
> it is she who has so much value
> and who is so worthy to be loved
> that she must be acclaimed Rose.]

All aspirations of Amant are centered on the rosebud. The bud stands for the supreme value in the world of the romance:

> Entre ces boutons en eslui
> Un si trés bel qu'envers celui
> Nul des autres rien ne prisai.   (*RR*, 1655–1657)

> [Among these buds I saw one
> so beautiful that in comparison to her,
> I did not prize any of the others a bit.]

The *Pearl* poet confronts the symbol of the rose with the symbol of the pearl. The rose designates the secularly adored lady; the pearl symbolizes the celestially transfigured virgin. When the narrator's daughter died, he did not lose a pearl as he first thought, but only a rose. Only her death glorified the girl and transformed her from a terrestrial to a celestial being. Figuratively, the coffin ennobles the rose and makes it a precious pearl:

> For þat þou lesteȝ watȝ bot a rose
> Þat flowred and fayled as kynde hyt gef.
> Now þurȝ kynde of þe kyste þat hyt con close
> To a perle of prys hit is put in pref.   (*Pearl*, 269–272)

> [For what you lost was but a rose
> that flowered and failed according to nature.
> Now through the nature of the chest that does enclose it,
> a pearl of price it has proved to be.]

In her life the rose was a creation of nature. The pearl is not only a symbol of the divinely glorified daughter of the narrator but signifies at the same time the kingdom of God—as an image of the pearl of great price:[24]

> I rede þe forsake þe worlde wode
> And porchace þy perle maskelles.   (*Pearl*, 743–744)
>
> [I advise you to forsake the mad world
> And purchase your spotless pearl.]

Once again in the dialogue the narrator calls his daughter a rose:

> I am bot mokke and mul among,
> And þou so ryche a reken rose.   (*Pearl*, 905–906)
>
> [I am but muck and dust together,
> And you so rich and splendid a rose.]

This address occurs at a moment when the narrator still lacks the knowledge of typological correspondences.[25] Just as he confuses the symbols of the rose (earthly daughter) and of the pearl (glorified daughter), so he also confuses the earthly Jerusalem and the New Jerusalem. Jerusalem, he objects in astonishment, is not situated here, where his vision takes place, but far away in Palestine (921 f.). His daughter must inform him first that there is another, eternal Jerusalem and that she spoke of the latter (949–960).

The description of the meadow in May full of gay flowers and with singing birds at the river bank is taken from the *Roman de la Rose* and belongs to the fixed usage of "topoi" concerning the dream exordium in the English literature of the fourteenth century.[26] The *Pearl* poet keeps the conventional framework of

---

[24] The comparison will be repeated in lines 729–744 of the poem.

[25] For typological biblical exegesis cf. Erich Auerbach, *Typologische Motive in der mittelalterlichen Literatur, Schriften und Vorträge des Petrarcainstituts,* 2nd ed. (Cologne, Krefeld, 1953).

[26] For instance, in the so-called minor works of Chaucer, in the prologue of *Piers Plowman,* in the *Parlement of Three Ages* (ed. M. Y. Offord, EETS 246 [1959], 1–101). E. R. Curtius, *op. cit.,* chap. 10, deals with the history of the "locus amoenus" [lovely place].

the dream-vision but makes significant changes. Instead of a holiday in May he chooses a holiday in August: "In Auguste in hyȝ seysoun . . ." [on a feast day] (*Pearl,* 39)—presumably the Assumption of Mary.[27] The traditional attributes—flowers and birds—are only hinted at: "þat floury flaȝt" [that flowery turf] (*Pearl,* 57); "Fowleȝ þer flowen . . . Þay songen wyth a swete asent" [Birds there flew . . . They sang with a sweet harmony] (*Pearl,* 89, 94). The grave is the center of the garden, its flora dominated by fragrant spices, the scent of which is finer than their appearance:

> Gilofre, gyngure and gromylyoun,
> And pyonys powdered ay bytwene.
> Ȝif hit watȝ semly on to sene,
> A fayr reflayr ȝet fro hit flot.   (*Pearl,* 43–46)

> [Gillyflower, ginger, and gromwell,
> and peonies powdered ever at intervals.
> If it was fair to look upon,
> A fair fragrance also floated from it.]

The spices have a symbolic meaning: the glorified daughter herself is called "that special spice"[28]; there must be ("nedes") a relation between herself and the spices that spring forth from her mound.

> Þat spot of spyseȝ mot nedeȝ sprede,
> Þer such rycheȝ to rot is runne.   (*Pearl,* 25–26)

> [That spot with spices must needs be overspread,
> where such riches to rot have run.]

With this she fulfills the simile of the kernel of wheat that dies in the earth and brings forth much fruit (John 12:24):

> Flor and fryte may not be fede
> Þer hit doun drof in moldeȝ dunne.   (*Pearl,* 29–30)

---

[27] According to Osgood, *op. cit.,* p. xvi. W. J. Knightley, "*Pearl*: The 'hyȝ seysoun,'" *Modern Language Notes,* LXXVI (1961), 97–102, thinks that this is an allusion to Christ's transfiguration. In the opinion of most other critics the harvest festival on August 1 is meant here.

[28] "Þat special spyce" (235), "Þat specyal spyce" (938).

[Flour and fruit may not be withered
where it sank down into dark earth.]

The metaphorical use of *spice* for a girl is traditional. Manuscript Harley 2253, written in the early fourteenth century, says of the desired "wild woman": Hire speche as spices spredes.[29] [Her speech as spices spreads]. In the second half of the thirteenth century Thomas de Hales calls the unsullied maiden "swetture þan eny spis"[30] [sweeter than any spice]. Here the passage from the Song of Solomon, in which the bride is represented as a garden with spices springing forth, was presumably an influential example (4:12–16):

> Hortus conclusus soror mea, sponsa, hortus
> conclusus, fons signatus . . . Surge, aquilo;
> et veni, auster; perfla hortum meum, et fluant
> aromata illius.[31]

> [My sister, my spouse, is a garden enclosed,
> a garden enclosed, a fountain sealed up . . .
> Arise, north wind, and come, south wind;
> blow through my garden, and let the aromatic
> spices thereof flow.]

According to the typological interpretation customary in the Middle Ages, the bride of the Song of Solomon is the Church of Christ and the redeemed soul of each believer.[32] In *Pearl* this interpretation is distinctly alluded to when Christ calls the glorified daughter with the words of the bridegroom in the Song of Solomon:

> "Cum hyder to me, my lemman swete,
> For mote ne spot is non in þe."   (*Pearl*, 763–764)

[29] *The Harley Lyrics*, ed. G. L. Brook, 2nd ed. (Manchester, 1956), No. 7,30.

[30] "Love Ron," ed. Carleton Brown, *English Lyrics of the 13th Century* (Oxford, 1932), pp. 68–74, l. 168.

[31] *Biblia sacra iuxta vulgatam clementinam*, ed. A. Colunga and L. Torrade (Madrid, 1959).

[32] Cf. F. Ohly, *Hoheliedstudien* (Wiesbaden, 1958), in particular pp. 66–70.

> [Come hither to me, my sweet beloved,
> For neither stain nor spot is in you.]

Cf. Tota pulchra es, amica mea, et macula non est in te.
Veni de Libano, sponsa mea, veni de Libano, veni.
(Song of Solomon 4:7–8)[33]

> [You are all beautiful, my beloved, and there is no spot in thee.
> Come from Lebanon, my spouse, come from Lebanon, come.]

On the other hand, the details of the garden of spices are depicted quite independently of the Song of Solomon. Again the individual spices remind us, rather, of the orchard of Deduiz [Pleasure] in the *Roman de la Rose:*

> Ou vergier mainte bone espice:
> Clos de girofle e ricalice,
> Graine de parevis novele,
> Citoal, gingembre e canele, (*RR*, 1341–1344, MSS.C,L)

> [In the garden many good spices,
> cloves and liquorice,
> grains of paradise,
> seeds of fresh pomegranates,
> zedoary, ginger, and cinnamon.]

The dying seed that brings forth many fruits is taken from the Bible[34]; the eternal leaves and blossoms of the miraculous garden are taken from a far-spread legend. In the garden of Deduiz the flowers are in bloom throughout the whole year:

> . . . il i avoit de flors plenté
> Toz jorz e iver e este.   (*RR*, 1401–1402)

> [. . . there was an abundance of flowers
> every day both in winter and in summer.]

In Chaucer, Cupid reposes at a fountain, "There grene and lusty May shal evere endure" [Where green and vigorous May

---

[33] Dante and Boccaccio (cf. Osgood, *op. cit.*, p. 84 f.) also use the quotation in question in a way similar to that of the *Pearl* poet.
[34] John 12:24.

shall always last] where one is tormented neither by cold nor heat, illness nor age.[35] Brendan lands at an equally favored island.

> Þis weder is euere murie her.
> & siknesse nis þer non.[36]
>
> [The weather is always fine here,
> and there is no sickness.]

With the transformation of the conventional dream exordium the *Pearl* poet effects a meaningful link between the introduction and the body of his poem. The grave and the spices that necessarily grow there symbolize the earthly, decaying maid and the glorified maid whom the Lord called to His kingdom as His bride. The powerful fragrance of the blossoms causes the narrator to fall asleep and thus motivates his dream. The motif of the virgin who is chosen by the Lord is also influential in the author's decision to choose August as the temporal setting. When he speaks of a festival day in August, the poet also refers to the Mariological interpretation of the Song of Solomon which considers the bride to be the Virgin Mary.[37] Even more obviously the symbolism of the spices of the "hortus conclusus"[38] puts *Pearl* in the literary neighborhood of the Song of Solomon. Though with all these changes the poet departs from the tradition of the *Roman de la Rose,* the form of the dream-vision experienced in the *hortus conclusus* by the narrator is

---

[35] *Parliament of Fowls*, lines 130, 204–207.

[36] "Saint Brendan," in *The South English Legendary*, ed. Charlotte D'Evelyn and Anna J. Mill, EETS 235 (1956), 302. Concerning the eternally blooming garden in Greek poetry cf. E. R. Curtius, *op. cit.*, pp. 193 f. A Cymric parallel can be found in a poem by Taliessin (*Llyfr Taliesin*, 33 f.)

[37] Cf. Ohly, *op. cit.*, pp. 125 f.

[38] In *Pearl* there is only a hint of the seclusion of the garden: "I entred in þat erber grene" [I entered into that garden green"] (38). The pearl stands apart from all the other jewels: "I sette hyr sengeley in synglure" [I accounted her unique] (8). The frequent use of the stem "syngl" in this connection reminds us of the apocalyptic pearls (Rev. 21:21).

fundamentally retained. But place, time, and landscape of the vision change the value of the secular ideals of this literary genre and confront it by pure virginity in the full Christian sense.

We can further follow up this radical transformation in the way the poet deals with Cortoisie [Courtesy], a central value in the courtly allegory of love. In the *Roman de la Rose* Cortoisie is one of the dancers in the garden. She incorporates not only social politeness but also the balance between body and soul:

> El ne fu ne nice n'ombrage,
> Mais sage e entre, senz outrage.   (*RR*, 1235–1236)
>
> [She was not stupid nor moody,
> but wise and temperate, without offense.]

At the allegorical court of Deduiz [Pleasure], Cortoisie is honored as a high ideal:

> . . . Cortoisie,
> Qui mout estoit de toz proisie.   (*RR*, 1229–1230)
>
> [. . . Courtesy,
> Who was much praised by all.]

The hospitality with which Cortoisie immediately welcomes the stranger (i.e., the narrator) to the society is referred to by Guillaume de Lorris with the religious expression "merci," "grace" [*RR*, 1233).

It is true that the vision of the *Pearl* poet is also directed to the court of a sovereign, not to the court of the god of love or the personified Deduiz [Pleasure], but to the court of the highest sovereign, to the realm of God with its 144,000 apocalyptic virgins ("the court of þe kyndom" [the court of the kingdom] [*Pearl*, 445]). Here, too, one of the central values is called "cortaysye." But "cortaysye" is represented not as a person but rather as a concept, something quite different from what it means in the *Roman de la Rose*. In *Pearl* "cortaysye" is mentioned, not together with earthly "Amors," but with divine (and also unpersonified) "charyté":

> "Cortaysé," quod I, "I leue,
> And charyté grete, be yow among."   (*Pearl*, 469–470)

> ["Courtesy," I said, "I do believe
> And great charity are among you."]

The *Pearl* poet translates the Latin "spiritualia" by "cortaysye" and understands it as spiritual gifts.[39] Because of "cortaysye," we are enabled to be members of the body of Christ:

> Of courtaysye, as saytʒ Saynt Poule,
> Al arn we membreʒ of Jesu Kryst . . .   (*Pearl*, 457–458)

> [Through courtesy, as says Saint Paul,
> we all are members of Jesus Christ.]

Here the body of Christ symbolizes not only the relation of Christ to his Church but also, simultaneously, the hierarchy of the heavenly society. Every glorified soul reigns by virtue of divine grace ("by cortaysye" [*Pearl*, 468]) as king or queen over the entire court of God:

> 'The court of þe kyndom of God alyue
> Hatʒ a property in hytself beyng:
> Alle þat may þerinne aryue
> Of alle þe reme is quen oþer kyng.'   (*Pearl*, 445–448)

> [The court of the kingdom of God alive
> has a property of its own being:
> all that may thither arrive
> of all the realm is queen or king.]

Above them stands the queen of heaven, Mary, as "Quen of cortaysye" [Queen of courtesy] (*Pearl*, 444):

> 'Bot my Lady of quom Jesu con spryng,
> Ho haldeʒ þe empyre ouer vus ful hyʒe.'   (*Pearl*, 453–454)

[39] Cf. I Cor. 12.

> [But my Lady, from whom Jesus did spring,
> she holds the imperial rule over us full high.]

Without envy they all accept the fact that many kings and queens reign side by side and that they are all subject to Mary:

> And þat dyspleseʒ non of oure gyng.　　(*Pearl*, 455)

> [And that displeases none of our company.]

All are oriented to courtesy, divine grace, as the central value of their life in society:

> 'So fare we alle wyth luf and lyste
> To kyng and quene by cortaysye.'　　(*Pearl*, 467–468)

> [So fare we all with love and joy
> as king and queen by courtesy.]

The different meanings of "cortaysye" as the ideal of the courtly or the heavenly society are played off against each other in the Middle English romance *Sir Gawain and the Green Knight* (abbr. *GGK*), probably also written by the *Pearl* poet.[40] Gawain is the knight of "clannes" [sinlessness] and "cortaysye" (*GGK*, 653). The challenge of the Green Knight is directed against the "cortaysye" of King Arthur's court; he puts this "cortaysye" on trial:

> And here is kydde cortaysye, as I haf herd carp,
> And þat hatʒ wayned me hider, iwyis, at þis time.
> 　　　　　　　　　　　　　　　　(*GGK*, 263–264)

> [And here is courtesy shown as I have heard say,
> and that has brought me hither, indeed, at this time.]

Gawain is the only one who dares to undergo the trial. All the others have already fallen victim to their pride, "surquidré." The Green Knight mocks Arthur's court: "Where is now your sourqudrye?" (*GGK*, 311). In order to expose this "surquidré,"

---

[40] The Gawain problem, recently dealt with by D. F. Hills, "Gawain's Fault," *Review of English Studies*, XIV (1963), 124–131, can probably be solved because of the double meaning of "cortaysye."

Morgan le Fay has sent the Green Knight to King Arthur (*GGK,* 2457).

To Gawain "cortaysye" means moral perfection. When, in a situation with no way out, he takes refuge in a white lie that is justified by society, he himself feels that this is a moral fault, a reversion to greed and cowardice:

> "Corsed worth cowarddyse and couetyse þoþe!
> In yow is vylany and vyse þat vertue disstryeȝ."
>
> (*GGK*, 2374–2375)
>
> [Cursed be cowardice and covetousness both!
> In you is villainy and vice that destroys virtue.]

When the temptress tries to win Gawain over, she thinks, however, of the conventional, courtly meaning of the concept "cortaysye." She wants him to kiss her because "cortaysye," courtly etiquette, demands this of him:

> "Þat bicumes vche a knyȝt þat cortaysy vses." (*GGK,* 1491)[41]
>
> [That becomes every knight that courtesy practices.]

Finally she forces Gawain to choose between two kinds of "cortaysye": he either must reject her openly and impolitely or commit a sin in the eyes of the lord of the house:

> He cared for his cortaysye, lest craþayn he were,
> And more for his meschef, ȝif he schulde make synne.
>
> (*GGK,* 1773–1774)
>
> [He cared for his courtesy lest he seem boorish,
> and more for harm to himself if he should commit sin.]

Gawain decides to compromise. Here is his only, though slight, moral fault, as the Green Knight tells him reproachfully:

> Bot here yow lakked a lyttel, sir, and lewté yow wonted.
>
> (*GGK,* 2366)
>
> [But here you lacked a little, sir, in loyalty.]

---

[41] Cf. *GGK,* 1297–1301.

179

In this context the pearl as a distinctive sign of moral perfection, and thus the central symbol of the poem, reappears:

> I sende hir to asey þe, and sothly me þynkkeʒ
> On þe fautlest freke þat euer on fote ʒede;
> As perle bi þe quite pese is of prys more,
> So is Gawayn, in god fayth, bi oþer gay knyʒteʒ. (*GGK*, 2362–2365)

> [I sent her to test you, and truly you seem to me
> the most faultless man that ever went on foot;
> as a pearl compared with a white pea is of more value,
> so is Gawain, in good faith, compared to other fine knights.]

If I were not loath to exaggerate, I should call *Pearl* an anti-*Roman de la Rose*. The *Pearl* poet adapts himself on principle to the literary genre of the dream-vision and keeps a few central motifs and symbols of the *Roman de la Rose*. He puts them, however, into a new context, interprets them differently, and thus *opposes* them to the *Roman de la Rose*. At the beginning of *Pearl* the narrator still belongs to the earthly world of the *Roman de la Rose,* of the lost rose, and of Luf-daungere. Instead of the gay May garden of the love allegory, however, we already have the spice garden of the Song of Solomon with its religious symbolism. In the course of the action the narrator recognizes that his previous worldly thinking was wrong. The rose for which he wept personified a false value. In its place he now finds the precious pearl, a symbol of multiple meaning. True "cortaysye" reveals itself to him as divine grace and not as what a worldly society takes it to be. The jewels of the *Roman de la Rose* decorate the allegorical figure "Richece" [Riches] (*RR,* 1087–1108); the jewels in *Pearl* form the foundation walls of the apocalyptic New Jerusalem.[42] In spite of his new knowledge the narrator cannot yet entirely master his "wreched wylle." A new madness again overcomes his better judgment: he tries to

---

[42] *Pearl*, 997–1020, according to Revelation 21:18–21. Catalogs of jewels are conventional in the literature of that time; cf., e.g., the twelve precious stones in the diadem of Nature in Alanus (*PL*, ccx, 433–435).

seize his pearl. This attempt motivates the awakening of the dreamer.

The designation anti-*Roman de la Rose* for *Pearl* is exaggerated to the extent that it covers only partial aspects both of *Pearl* and of the *Roman de la Rose*. *Pearl* is not carried through as a consistent allegory. Of the numerous allegorical characters of the *Roman de la Rose,* the *Pearl* poet selects only Dangiers, Cortoisie, and the rose itself, but without representing it as a personified being. Cortoisie, in the *Roman de la Rose,* dances among Amors, Biautez, Richece, Largece, Franchise, Oieuse, Jonece [Love, Beauty, Riches, Largess, Nobility of Soul (as well as Independence and Frankness), Idleness, and Youth] and other "franches genz e bien enseignies" [frank and genteel persons] (1282). Dangiers guards the rose garden, together with his comrades Male Bouche, Honte, and Peor [Gossip, Shame, and Fear], against Bel Acueil [Fair Welcome], who is friendly toward strangers.

Just as he did with the motifs already cited from the *Roman de la Rose,* so the *Pearl* poet uses other symbols and "topoi" from the literature of his time. The rose ("mundi rosa") [rose of the world or earthly rose] as a symbol of transitoriness appears in a poem that has been attributed to Hildebert of Le Mans (1056–1133).[43] There, however, the rose is confronted, not by a pearl, but by an eternal "rosa sancta . . . fine carens" [holy rose . . . without end], and the luxuriantly blooming garden itself perishes like the rose. Among other things, spices are also a feature of the garden: "Spirat ibi nardus, nascuntur aromata, nectar conficitur, sudant balsama" [There nard emits fragrance, perfumes are engendered, nectar is produced, balsams exude]. The idea of the rose as a creature of Nature may come

---

[43] *PL*, CLXXI, 1235–1238. This poem is mentioned in another context by E. R. Curtius, *op. cit.*, p. 205. He attributes it to Peter Riga, but M. Manitius in his *Geschichte der lateinischen Literatur des Mittelalters,* III (Munich, 1931), p. 856 f., thinks that Hildebert of Le Mans is the author.

from Alanus, who has depicted it (together with other flowers) on the shoes of Nature.[44] The man clad in black in Chaucer's *Book of the Duchess* is shattered because Fortune takes away his queen in the allegorical game of chess. The narrator of *Pearl* is reprimanded for his belief in Fortune. Fortune kills the flesh, but God awakens man and gives him new life (305 f.). On the whole, the elegiac theme of *Pearl* comes closer to the *Book of the Duchess* than to the *Roman de la Rose*.[45] But the theological discussion on the celestial rank of innocent little children, which is of central importance in *Pearl,* stands far removed from the allegory of love in the literature of that time. The form of the stanzas in *Pearl,* with their repetition of the first line in the last line and their anadiplotic connection of two consequent stanzas, reminds us of Cymric examples.[46]

Therefore I agree in principle with E. V. Gordon, who in his chapter "Sources, Analogues, and Traditions" stresses that ". . . the direct influence of the *Roman* is neither so clear nor so extensive as has sometimes been claimed."[47] Here Gordon objects to the mere singling out of isolated words, such as "gladness," "myrþes" [joy], "resoun" in *Pearl* and the similarly called allegorical characters in the *Roman de la Rose*. The attempts of both narrators to seize the adored thing (the rosebud or the pearl) correspond only superficially. In *Pearl* this passage leads up to what is absolutely necessary for the genre, the awakening of the narrator from his dream. In the *Roman*

---

[44] *PL*, CCX, 439.

[45] Osgood, *op. cit.*, p. xxi, compares the characterization of Mary as "Fenyx of Arraby" [Phoenix of Arabia] (*Pearl,* 430) to the similar characterization of Blanche in Chaucer (*Book of the Duchess,* 982).

[46] Cf. P. L. Henry, "A Celtic-English Prosodic Feature," *Zeitschrift für celtische Philologie,* XXIX (1962), 91–99. Anadiplosis (which is called "cyrch-gymeriad" in the Cymric poetic) is also very frequently used in the older Cymric poetry as a means of connecting stanzas in places where the end-rhyme changes (cf. John Morris Jones, *Cerdd Dafod* [Oxford, 1925], pp. 104, 508).

[47] *Op. cit.*, p. xxxii.

de la Rose the awakening is a stage within the allegorical courtship.

On the whole, then, sources and influences, those classical categories of research in literary history, characterize the relationship of the *Roman de la Rose* and *Pearl* only imperfectly. It is not very important to know whether the *Pearl* poet borrows this or that detail from the *Roman de la Rose*. But the place of *Pearl* within the literary genre that originates from the *Roman de la Rose* is an important question. To what extent does the poet keep within the bounds of the given genre and to what extent does his work extend these bounds? How does the poet incorporate into the structure of his own poem the elements taken from literary tradition? Though the *Pearl* poet uses the conventional dream-vision of the allegorical court of a sovereign, he intentionally makes a distinction between his poem and the conventional content of this genre. He reinterprets its values and symbols, and places them within the bounds of a theological poem of consolation.[48]

Whether *Pearl* goes back directly to precourtly allegory before the *Roman de la Rose*[49] is an urgent question at this point. H. R. Jauss[50] has recently discussed allegory within the tradition of the *Psychomachia*. Prudentius, as Jauss shows, places an allegorical "bellum intestinum" [civil war] within the bounds of the divine plan of salvation and supports his point by means of the typological exegesis of the Bible. "Guillaume de Lorris has separated his new *Psychomachia* completely from the life and suffering of Christ or from the mythology on which it was based in the case of his predecessors. Behind the purely courtly personifications of his virtues and vices are no longer any exem-

---

[48] Cf. V. E. Watt. *"Pearl* as a *Consolatio,"* *Medium Aevum,* XXXII (1963), 34–36.

[49] This question was pointed out to me by W. Iser, to whom I am also greatly indebted for several other critical remarks.

[50] "Form und Auffassung der Allegorie in der Tradition der Psychomachia," *Medium Aevum Vivum* (*Festschrift Walter Bulst*), (Heidelberg, 1960), pp. 179–206.

plary figures who can give historical depth to their representation. His allegorical world appears for the first time as a purely romantic fiction that stands by itself" (p. 195). In Prudentius the virtues and vices fight, not for the soul of a certain person, but for the general fate of all Christendom. The allegorical characters and the action of the *Roman de la Rose,* however, are centered in the participating "I" of the narrator. This person undergoes a development: he changes from a mere narrator into an acting Amant.

There is also a narrator in the center of *Pearl,* who experiences the action, but at the same time biblical exegesis, typological and anagogical, plays a decisive part in the action. The pearl is prefigured in the bride of the Song of Solomon, in Jesus' blessing of the children,[51] in the workmen who arrive late in the vineyard (501–588), and in the pearl of great price. In the poem these prefigurations fulfill themselves in a particular, personal fate with one exception: the dreamer himself does not play his role of the "jueler" (i.e., the merchant of pearls) to the end, but he awakens. The pearl is *one* of the 144,000 apocalyptic virgins. She does not represent them collectively. Now in the Middle Ages this type of biblical exegesis was not restricted to allegorical poetry; therefore the *Pearl* poet need not have taken these ideas solely from the tradition of Prudentius. Yet the material presented here shows that the *Pearl* poet, to a great extent, uses conventional motifs and "topoi" that do not belong to the tradition of the *Roman de la Rose.* We must also recognize that the literary dream did not come into being with the courtly allegory of love and the allegorical pilgrimage of Raoul de Houdenc, but already existed in the prophetic poetry of the Welsh (*Myrddin*) and in the Old English *Dream of the Rood.* A more detailed study of medieval Latin and Celtic material will lead to further findings.

[51] 721–728; cf. Luke 18:16 f.

12

PEARL: IMMORTAL FLOWERS AND
THE PEARL'S DECAY

Edward Vasta

AMONG THE OPENING STANZAS OF THE MIDDLE ENGLISH *Pearl,*
the third has proved very important, in some studies even crucial, to the understanding of the poem; it has yielded rich meanings, and for some scholars has figured in defining the work's
perspective.[1] The stanza reads:

> Þat spot of spyseȝ mot nedeȝ sprede,
> Þer such rycheȝ to rot is runne;
> Blomeȝ blayke and blwe and rede
> Þer schyneȝ ful schyr agayn þe sunne.
> Flor and fryte may not be fede
> Þer hit doun drof in moldeȝ dunne;
> For vch gresse mot grow of grayneȝ dede;
> No whete were elleȝ to woneȝ wonne.
> Of goud vche goude is ay bygonne;
> So semly a sede moȝt fayly not,
> Þat spryngande spyceȝ vp ne sponne
> Of þat precios perle wythouten spotte.   (25–36)

> [That spot with spices must needs be spread,
> Where such riches to rot is run;

Reprinted, by permission of the author and of the University of Illinois
Press, from the *Journal of English and Germanic Philology,* **LXVI**
(1967), 519–531. Footnote ten contains new material. Translations have
been supplied by the author.

[1] The text used here is *Pearl,* ed. E. V. Gordon (Oxford, 1953).

Blooms yellow and blue and red
There shine very bright against the sun.
Flower and fruit may not be faded
Where it sank down into the dark earth;
For each plant must grow from dead grains;
No wheat would else to dwellings come.
From good each good is always begun;
So seemly a seed must not fail,
That growing spices might not spring up
From that precious pearl without spot.]

The interpretation now generally accepted, as gathered from the scholarship of this century (from Schofield to the present), finds two fundamental ideas in this stanza: that lovely flowers draw life from the decayed Pearl, and that flowers springing from the lost Pearl cannot wither or decay and are thus immortal. The first idea comes from all three sentences of the stanza: the first sentence (25–28) says the decay of the Pearl has produced lovely flowers; the second (29–32) says this process is natural, for all plants grow from dead seeds; the third (33–36) expresses the hope that the Pearl might not fail in this process by not producing spices. The idea of the Pearl's decay producing new life is given moral and religious implications by the middle lines of the stanza (29–33), specifically by the statement that each plant must grow from dead seeds or else no wheat may be gathered into barns. This statement alludes to I Corinthians 15:36 ("Senseless man, what thou thyself sowest is not brought to life, unless it dies") and to John 12:24 ("Amen, amen, I say to you, unless the grain of wheat falls into the ground and dies, it remains alone. But if it dies, it brings forth much fruit"). The Pearl is therefore involved in both the natural process of corruption-generation and the spiritual process of death-resurrection.

The second idea in the current interpretation, that of immortal flowers, comes from the word *fede* in line 29. The accepted sense of the stanza has required that *fede* be glossed 'faded,' 'withered,' 'decayed,' or the equivalent, and that the statement say: Flower and fruit may not be withered, or decayed, where the Pearl lies. Such flowers, then, are immortal. The five translations[2] and five editions[3] I have been able to examine all gloss or translate *fede* in this way, and I have found no disagreement in the scholarship on the poem. Indeed for scholars interested in the poem's allegorical possibilities, the idea of immortal flowers, in conjunction with the motif of death-resurrection, has great importance.

The current interpretation, however, poses difficulties. While the Pearl is clearly depicted as having "run to rot" and become involved in the process of corruption-generation, the way in which the Pearl is so involved is not clear. Has it already decayed and already yielded new life in the form of flowers now spreading at the spot? Or has the Pearl not yet decayed, but will, and will produce flowers soon, but not those already there? The first four lines of the stanza clearly state that yellow, blue, and red blossoms do presently shine against the sun at the spot where the Pearl lies; and we have read these lines as saying that these flowers have grown from the decay of the Pearl. The last three lines of the stanza, however, as we have read them, express the hope that the Pearl might not fail to produce growing spices. Since the narrator could not hope for what has already happened, nor the Pearl fall short of a goal already reached, these lines imply that corruption-generation has not taken place.

The scholarship on this stanza reflects the confusion. W. H.

---

[2] *Pearl*, trans. G. G. Coulton (London, 1921); trans. Stanley P. Chase (New York, 1932); trans. Sophie Jewett, in Loomis and Willard, *Medieval English Verse and Prose* (New York, 1948), pp. 220–238; trans. Sister Mary Vincent Hillmann (Convent Station, N.J., 1961); and trans. John Gardner, in *The Complete Works of the Gawain Poet* (Chicago, 1965), pp. 93–145.

[3] *Pearl*, ed. Charles G. Osgood (Boston, 1906); ed. Members of the Chaucer Course in Bowdoin College (Boston, 1932); ed. E. V. Gordon (Oxford, 1953); ed. Sister Mary Vincent Hillmann (Convent Station, N.J., 1961); ed. A. C. Cawley (New York, 1962).

Schofield[4] and G. G. Coulton,[5] for example, while disagreeing in their interpretations, agree that the Pearl has already decayed and produced the lovely flowers. Sister Madaleva[6] and Marie Padgett Hamilton,[7] on the other hand, take the Pearl as already decayed, but the flowers that spring from it as still to appear. Charles Moorman, to cite one last example, first discusses the process of corruption-generation as still to happen, but then, on the same page, as having already happened.[8] Either way, his main point about this stanza is not affected: that it introduces the paradoxical relationship between beauty and death and looks forward to the larger theme of the apparently dual nature of divine justice. The confusion about the Pearl's decay, however, lies before us explicitly on his pages.

The second part of the current interpretation also involves difficulties. The gloss of *fede* as 'faded' is based on no sound linguistic evidence. Two possible derivations have been suggested, OFr. *fade* and ON *feyja;* but there is apparently no certain way of deriving ME *fede* from either source. In his edition of *Pearl,* Professor Gordon sums up the situation when he says, "The sense agrees with that of the adjective *fade* (OFr. *fade*) 'faded,' 'having lost colour,' but the vowel *e* is obscure. Gollancz suggests derivation from ON. *feyja* 'decay,' but the form is then equally difficult, and the sense less satisfactory."[9] Professor Gordon also cites the only other text in Middle English offered thus far where *fede* may have the meaning 'faded.' It is line 2474 of *Sir Tristram.* But even here the translation 'faded' is uncertain, as Gordon indicates when he says, and the emphasis is mine,

[4] W. H. Schofield, "Symbolism, Allegory, and Autobiography in *The Pearl*," *PMLA*, XXIV (1909), 617–618.

[5] G. G. Coulton, "In Defence of *Pearl*," *MLR*, II (1906), 41–42.

[6] Sister Madaleva, *Pearl: A Study in Spiritual Dryness* (New York, 1925), pp. 100–109.

[7] Marie Padgett Hamilton, "The Meaning of the Middle English *Pearl*," *PMLA*, LXX (1955), 812–813.

[8] Charles Moorman, "The Role of the Narrator in *Pearl*," *MP*, LIII (1955), 75 [page 106 above].

[9] *Pearl,* ed. Gordon, p. 47 n.

"PRESUMABLY the same word as *fede* in *Sir Tristram* 2474, where *forest fede* is PROBABLY equivalent to *hor wode* 'grey wood.'" Aware of these linguistic difficulties, C. G. Osgood and the Bowdoin editors, in their respective editions of *Pearl,* include question marks in their glosses of *fede*. The University of Michigan's *Middle English Dictionary,* which suggests derivation from OIcel. *feyja,* also includes a question mark in its entry to indicate difficulties. There is no sure linguistic basis for taking *fede* to mean 'faded' or 'decayed,' therefore, and consequently for taking the flowers as immortal.

Nor does the sense of the stanza provide a sound basis for taking *fede* to mean 'faded' or the equivalent. No other line besides the one in which *fede* occurs suggests the notion of immortal flowers, although an idea so important, and startling, demands elaboration. The Pearl is said to be capable of engendering in plants new life and, being good, goodness; but nowhere else in this stanza, or in the entire poem, is it said to be capable of endowing plants with immortality. The specific sentence in which *fede* appears, furthermore, is made by the current gloss to express a *non sequitur*. The sentence, again, is:

> Flor and fryte may not be fede
> Þer hit doun drof in moldeȝ dunne;
> For vch gresse mot grow of grayneȝ dede;
> No whete were elleȝ to woneȝ wonne.

This sentence has two parts: the first makes a statement, the second explains why this statement is made. "Flower and fruit may not be *fede* where the Pearl has sunk into the dark earth," the sentence says, "for each plant of grass must grow from dead seeds, or else no wheat would be gathered into barns." It does not follow, however, that because a plant grows from dead seeds the Pearl's flower and fruit are therefore incapable of withering. If not totally illogical, such a statement at least requires explanation. As it stands, the sentence is obscured when *fede* is translated by a word implying immortality; the reason the sentence gives for the statement it makes has no logical connection with the statement itself.

The current interpretation as a whole, to indicate one last difficulty, implies in the narrator a previsionary state of mind that is inconsistent with the narrator's explicit depiction of his mental state. According to the current interpretation, the narrator is revealed in the third stanza as enjoying a harmony between what his reason knows and what his will desires: he knows the Pearl is subject to becoming nourishment for plants, and he desires this end for it. The narrator is also, in the current interpretation, at peace with the order of nature: he hopes his Pearl will successfully participate in the ordained process of corruption-generation. In the fifth stanza, however, he describes himself as in precisely the opposite state:

> Bifore þat spot my honde I spenned
> For care ful colde þat to me caȝt;
> A deuely dele in my hert denned,
> Þaȝ resoun sette myseluen saȝt.
> I playned my perle þat þer watȝ spenned
> Wyth fyrce skylleȝ þat faste faȝt,
> Þaȝ kynde of Kryst me comfort kenned,
> My wreched wylle in wo ay wraȝte.   (49–56)

> [Before that spot my hands I wrung
> For the sorrow full cold that seized on me;
> A desolating grief in my heart lay deep,
> Even though reason set me at peace.
> I complained of my pearl that there was lodged
> With rash arguments that firmly fought,
> Though the nature of Christ taught me comfort,
> My wretched will in woe ever grieved.]

Here he describes himself as tormented by an interior conflict between reason and will: although reason strove to set him at peace, he says, a desolating grief nevertheless lurked in his heart; despite the fervent urging of vehement argument, he lamented the loss of his imprisoned Pearl. He adds, furthermore, that though "kynde of Kryst" taught him comfort, his will is wretched and in pain. "Kynde of Kryst" implies the totality of divine governance in the universe, since to Christ is traditionally appropriated the divine act of creation,[10] as well as redemption and salvation. Unmistakably, therefore, the narrator at this point knows the ultimate blessings of corruption-generation and death-resurrection, but his will takes no comfort from his knowledge. Contrary to what the current interpretation implies about his previsionary mental state, the narrator suffers an interior disharmony and is in conflict with the "laws" of life.

Difficulties in the current interpretation of the third stanza, therefore, invite us to reconsider what the stanza says. To insure that an alternate interpretation rests on solid linguistic grounds, we should first take *fede* to mean 'fed,' the past participle of ME *feden* 'to feed' from OE *fedan*. This is the normal, expected derivation and involves no difficulties. It might be objected that deriving from OE *fedan, fede* [feːdə] is not an exact rhyme with *sprede* [spræːdə], *rede* [ræːdə], and *dede* [dæːdə]; but neither would the rhyme be perfect if *fede* derived from OFr. *fade* or ON *feyja*. Besides, imperfect rhymes are not unusual in *Pearl*. Professor Gordon notes that imperfect rhymes involving *ē*, as in *fede,* occur in several places.[11] If we adhere strictly to the manuscript, furthermore, in which is written *runnen* instead of *runne,* we find a still more imperfect rhyme in this stanza; *runnen* rhymes with *sunne* and *dunne*. According to the

---

[10] The scriptural basis for this appropriation comes from the opening passage of the Gospel of St. John, in which it is said of the Word, "All things were made through him, and without him was made nothing that has been made" (John 1:3). The appropriation of the essential attributes to the Persons of the Trinity is a theological intricacy requiring precise language, but to risk a simple statement: the power to create is appropriated to the Father, the wisdom and art of creating is appropriated to the Son, and the quickening and governing of creation is appropriated to the Holy Spirit. On the validity of appropriating the essential attributes to the Persons of the Trinity see Thomas Aquinas, *Summa Theologica,* I, q. 39, a. 7–8; for the appropriation of the various aspects of creative causality, see *ibid.,* I, q. 45, a. 6.

[11] Gordon, "Introduction," pp. xlvii–xlviii.

linguistic evidence, then, the first line in the middle sentence of the stanza says flower and fruit may not be fed where the Pearl lies—may not feed on the Pearl's decay.

The word *may* in the same line must now be taken in a sense different from that taken heretofore. As long as we accepted *fede* as meaning 'faded,' we could accept *may* as expressing ability: the flower and fruit have not the ability to fade. But taking *fede* as 'fed,' it makes no sense to say that plants have no ability to feed on the Pearl's decay. By the laws of life, they have the ability—and the necessity. So the poet tells us in this very sentence: that each plant must grow from dead seeds, or else no wheat would be gathered into barns. The word *may*, then, must be taken as expressing permission rather than ability. Such a use of *may*, from OE *magan*, is common in the Middle Ages, as today. The *NED* lists six examples from Old and Middle English texts in which forms of *magan* express permission; and we all remember Chaucer's admonition, in the General Prologue to the *Canterbury Tales*, that anyone telling a tale "after a man" must repeat every word faithfully:

> He may nat spare, althogh he were his brother;
> He moot as wel seye o word as another.[12]

In the middle passage of the third stanza, then, the narrator expresses his desire that flower and fruit may not be permitted to feed on his Pearl.

The *non sequitur* is now removed. The first part of this middle sentence expresses the hope that plants may not feed on the lost Pearl; the second part explains why such a wish enters the narrator's mind: he knows that nothing in nature lives unless something first dies, that no plant grows that does not grow from a dead seed, that whatever in nature dies becomes nourishment for new life. In the intensity of his grief, the narrator does not want his Pearl to suffer the fate of ordinary seeds. The implica-

---

[12] *The Works of Geoffrey Chaucer*, ed. F. N. Robinson (2nd ed., Boston, 1957), I(A): 737–738.

tion is that he thinks of the Pearl as in a way still possessible lying in the earth—beyond his keeping but identifiable. When it decays and becomes transmuted into other things, as he knows it surely will, nothing will remain of the Pearl for him to possess; his loss will then be total. Thus he desires that the natural process of corruption-generation should suspend itself.

The inconsistency with the narrator's state of mind as described in the fifth stanza is also removed. As we now read the middle part of the third stanza, with its allusions to St. Paul and St. John, the narrator is aware that morally and spiritually, as well as naturally, death is but the beginning of rebirth; yet in his grief he desires that further movement toward this end be held off. His will desires the entire universe to stop, the moral and spiritual orders by which good comes from good and life is gained by losing it, as well as the natural order by which new life depends on antecedent death. He wishes his Pearl to be lost to him no further than it is lost now; in a sense, he wishes his Pearl to remain forever only dead. The third stanza, in fact, is now consistent with developments in the poem as a whole, for the psychological, moral, and spiritual experience the narrator undergoes in *Pearl* involves bringing his will into correspondence with right reason, thus into correspondence with the "kynde of Kryst."

The proposed interpretation as thus far developed also implies that the Pearl is not yet decayed, but will be, and that the present flowers have not sprung from the Pearl but are present from some other cause. The first and last passages of the third stanza can be read in a way consistent with the proposed reading of the middle passage. The first four lines, again, are:

> Þat spot of spyseӡ mot nedeӡ sprede,
> Þer such rycheӡ to rot is runne;
> Blomeӡ blayke and blwe and rede
> Þer schyneӡ ful schyr agayn þe sunne.

These lines do not unequivocally say the Pearl has already decayed. "Rycheӡ to rot is runne" can mean that the Pearl has gone to become decay, not necessarily that it has already decayed. *Rot* is a noun, not a verb; the preposition *to,* in "to rot," can mean 'toward'; and the use of the present perfect, "is runne," can convey the idea that the Pearl has taken the way toward corruption rather than being already corrupted. The verb *runne* seems chosen primarily to indicate the precipitateness of the Pearl's loss, rather than its destination. It continues the image of the first stanza: "Þurȝ gresse to grounde hit fro me yot" (10), and the second stanza: "Syþen in þat spot hit fro me sprange" (13). The Pearl is depicted as having fallen (*yot*) from the narrator's hands, sprung away (*sprange*), and rolled (*runne*) toward decay, all unexpectedly. In the fourth stanza, the narrator speaks of the Pearl as having *trendeled doun* 'rolled down' (41), again emphasizing how swiftly the Pearl was lost. The first passage of the third stanza, then, can be read in a way consistent with the second, indicating that while the Pearl will inevitably decay, it has thus far only just begun to take the way toward corruption.

Similarly, these lines do not unequivocally say that the flowers already there have sprung from the Pearl. That such spices "mot nedeȝ" spread where such riches lie can mean that because the Pearl was so excellent, it is fitting and inevitable that its resting place should spread with beautiful flowers. The statement here has the same construction as a statement in the previous stanza in which the narrator says that many sweet songs welled up in his mind "To þenke hir color so clad in clot" [To think of her color so clad in clay] (19–22). Songs that were sweet obviously did not come from thinking about the Pearl as "clad in clot," but from thinking about the Pearl's color, which is now, he adds, "clad in clot." Similarly, in the third stanza, that spot may necessarily spread with flowers, not because of the Pearl's decay, but because of its riches. The notion is elegiac, that nature responds sympathetically to the poet's loss and provides flowers as final attendants whose richness of color bespeaks the splendor of the one they attend. Thus the presence and quality of the flowers can be accounted for by the Pearl's riches rather than by its having "run" to decay.

In certain respects, the proposed reading of the first four lines places them meaningfully within the context of the work as a whole. For one thing, in this poem the conspicuous and predominant imagery has to do with the Pearl's setting rather than the Pearl itself. This imagery develops in a continuous line, each development indicating a change in the Pearl's setting and, more important, a change in the narrator's understanding of "þat spot" where the Pearl is truly located. Taken as growing around the Pearl but not from it, the lovely flowers already present in the third stanza become part of this developing line of imagery. The narrator sets the Pearl, before its loss, in clear gold; after its loss, among lovely flowers. In his vision he locates the Pearl-Maiden first in a stunningly beautiful country; then, coming to understand the Pearl's true "spot," in the bejeweled and shining Heavenly City. Thus the major "setting images" of the poem increase progressively in size, complication, and beauty; and the flowers, according to the suggested interpretation, provide a logical link in this continuous line of imagery.

Second, the opening lines of this stanza, read as suggested, become meaningful in view of another aspect, besides that already discussed, of the narrator's psychological state before his vision. Not only are reason and will disharmonious in him, but his mood alternates between bitter grief and wistful sadness. He describes his mental and emotional alternations in the second stanza:

> Syþen in þat spote hit fro me sprange,
> Ofte haf I wayted, wyschande þat wele,
> Þat wont watȝ whyle deuoyde my wrange
> And heuen my happe and al my hele.
> Þat dotȝ bot þrych my hert þrange,
> My breste in bale bot bolne and bele;
> Ȝet þoȝt me neuer so swete a sange
> As stylle stounde let to me stele.

> For soþe þer fleten to me fele,
> To þenke hir color so clad in clot.
> O moul, þou marreȝ a myry iuele,
> My priuy perle wythouten spotte.　　　(13–24)

> [Since in that spot it from me sprang,
> Often have I watched, longing for that weal,
> Whose wont it was formerly to cancel my woe
> And exalt my good fortune and all my well-being.
> That does but afflict my heart grievously,
> My breast in sorrow only swells and burns;
> Yet came to mind never so sweet a song
> As quiet times let steal on me.
> In truth there came to me many,
> To think of her color so clad in clay.
> O earth, you mar a merry jewel,
> My own dear pearl without spot.]

Longing for the Jewel that gave him all happiness and well-being, he says, only oppressed his heart all the more; yet, he continues, he never imagined a sweeter song than stole on him during moments of quiet. Many welled up in his mind when he thought of the Pearl's color, now clad in clay. Then the fact that the Pearl's color is now clad in clay turns sweet sadness into bitter grief, and in the end he directs his bitterness at the earth itself: "Oh, earth, you mar a merry jewel." Similarly, at the beginning of the third stanza the narrator is in an elegiac mood, as it were, and imposes on the scene what is actually, as already suggested, an elegiac convention. He is struck by the beauty of the flowers overspreading that spot and thinks of them as appropriate attendants for the splendid Pearl: that is, he sees nature, in accordance with the whole elegiac tradition, as responding sympathetically to his loss. Then against this mood his reason asserts his sense of realism, and his romantic sadness is transformed into bitter grief; he remembers that by the real laws of nature his Pearl will disintegrate and be transmuted into other life. Irrationally, he desires that this natural process should be suspended. If his will had its way, the elegiac convention would become real; nature would truly react unnaturally.

These thoughts and emotions are rooted in the narrator's character, however, rather than merely in the elegiac convention. One of his dominant traits—indeed, the most conspicuous of his characteristics—is that he has an intensely responsive aesthetic sensibility. When he describes his Pearl, it is her beauty on which he dwells; when he tells us the Pearl was the cause of all his happiness and well-being, her beauty was the specific cause; if sweet songs came to mind at quiet moments, they came from thinking on the Pearl's color. In his vision he dwells, through stanza after stanza, on the beauty of the vision country. The more beauty that confronted him, the more he desired; and it is the beauty of the dream surroundings that finally destroyed all grief and filled him with bliss:

> The dubbement dere of doun and daleȝ,
> Of wod and water and wlonk playneȝ,
> Bylde in me blys, abated my baleȝ,
> Fordidden my stresse, dystryed my payneȝ.
> (121–124)

> [The glorious adornment of hill and dales,
> Of woods and water and lovely plains,
> Stirred in me bliss, quelled my sorrows,
> Abolished my distress, destroyed my pains.]

Reading the third stanza as saying that the Pearl's beauty, rather than decay, inevitably causes lovely flowers to surround that spot, and that the Pearl itself should not decay and produce flowers, gives us an insight into the narrator's aesthetic sensibility. He apparently considers beauty and life as inextricably related, and beauty as of such value that it deserves, of itself, to live. If it tragically dies, then other living forms of beauty should bear witness. If dead, it at least should not decay. In other words, the narrator grieves for the loss of beauty as well as life; and his desire that nature should suspend its normal processes and prevent plants from feeding on his Pearl springs not only from his anxiety to preserve his Pearl as much as possible, but also from his conviction that beauty ought not to be subject

to corruption. These anxieties and convictions are finally resolved in the narrator's vision, where the Heavenly City is a
place not only of everlasting life, but of manifold and enduring
beauty as well.

The last passage of the third stanza, finally, can be read in a
way consistent with the interpretation thus far developed. The
passage, again, is:

> So semly a sede moȝt fayly not,
> Þat spryngande spyceȝ vp ne sponne
> Of þat precios perle wythouten spotte.

The current view that this statement is hortatory, with *moȝt*
expressing permission rather than ability and *sponne* a past subjunctive,[13] is already consistent with my suggested interpretation.
It lends consistency, in fact, to my having taken the previous
sentence as also hortatory with *may* expressing permission. It
should be added that the use, in the last three lines, of the past
tense rather than the present causes no difficulty since the past
tense frequently expresses desire or propriety in the present.
Such usage appears later in *Pearl,* for example, in the lines

> Bot ay wolde man of happe more hente
> Þen moȝte by ryȝt vpon hem clyuen.   (1195–1196)

> [But ever would man more of good fortune seize
> Than might justly upon him be bestowed.]

The meaning of this sentence is ambiguous, however, because
of the ambiguity of *fayly* in the independent clause of the first
line, and also the ambiguity of the dependent clause. According
to the current interpretation, *fayly* means 'Falter, fall short of,'
and the dependent clause expresses an undesired result. So
taken, the sentence means: So beautiful a seed must not falter
or else spices might not spring from it. But *fayly* can mean 'deteriorate,' as when we speak of failing health, a common meaning

---

[13] Gordon, p. 112.

in Middle English, and a sense used later in this poem. The dream-lady, speaking of the lost Pearl, says to the narrator,

> For þat þou lesteȝ watz bot a rose
> Þat flowred and fayled as kynde hyt gef. (269–270)
>
> [For what you lost was but a rose
> That flowered and failed as nature ordained for it.]

The dependent clause can also express a desired, rather than undesired, result, so that the sentence means: So beautiful a seed must not deteriorate so that growing spices might not spring from that precious Pearl without spot. Thus, consistently with the suggested interpretation, the last three lines can be taken as expressing the narrator's hope that the Pearl might possibly be exempt from corruption and that spices might not be nourished by its decay.

The alternate reading of this passage is also consistent with what has been said about the narrator's character and state of mind. It gives the stanza a complete logical structure expressive of the conflict in the narrator between desire and reason, elegiac romanticism and stern realism. According to the suggested interpretation, the first four lines of the stanza express an elegiac fancy resulting from the narrator's imposing his desire on the natural scene before him: he interprets nature as sympathizing with his loss and sending lovely flowers as attendants for the lost pearl. The next five lines then express the contrary and reasoned awareness that nature will actually transmute the pearl into other life. The last three lines, read as suggested, now resolve this logical conflict by rejecting reason and realism and reasserting instead desire and elegiac fancy: nature must not allow the Pearl to deteriorate, the narrator says, spices must not grow from the lost Jewel. This resolution, furthermore, springs from the narrator's aesthetic sensibility—his feeling that beauty ought not to be subject to decay. The Pearl-Seed, he says, must not deteriorate because it is "so semly."

The interpretation I am proposing, then, is consistent within its parts, with the context in which it occurs, with the narrator's character and state of mind, and with linguistic facts. If acceptable, it would make it clear that the Pearl is not yet decayed. The central point of this stanza would be that the oncoming process of corruption-generation, or death-resurrection, should be suspended. It would also be clear that no flowers have yet sprung from the Pearl; hence, the flowers already there would not be the Pearl's progeny, although the Pearl would have progeny in the future. It would be clear, furthermore, that no flowers in the third stanza, present or to come, are immortal.

Several other implications follow if the proposed reading is accepted. It would require future editors and translators of *Pearl* to reconsider the traditional but shaky gloss of *fede,* and the glosses of *may* and *fayly* as well. The entry for *fede* in the new *Middle English Dictionary* would also have to be reconsidered. The only texts cited for the meaning 'decayed, withered' are, of course, these very lines from *Pearl* and the possible line from *Sir Tristram* suggested by Professor Gordon.

Our understanding of the scene in the opening section of the poem would also require correction. The scene within the "erbere" would be given detail by two facts: one, that yellow, blue, and red blossoms do presently grow at "þat spot"; the other, that since flower and fruit are forbidden to feed on the Pearl, and growing spices forbidden to spring from it, nothing would be growing directly over the Pearl itself. The Pearl's hill must then be smaller than the area signified by *spot; spot* must refer to both the hill under which the Pearl lies and the area surrounding it. That the Pearl's hill is a small mound is supported by later passages:

> Pen wakned I in þat erber wlonk;
> My hede upon þat hylle watȝ layde
> Per as my perle to grounde strayd.   (1171–1173)

> [Then wakened I in that lovely garden;
> My head upon that hill was laid
> Where my pearl to the ground had strayed.]

> Ouer þis hyul þis lote I laȝte,
> For pyty of my perle enclyin.   (1205–1206)

> [Above this hill this fate I received,
> Out of sorrow for my pearl cast down.]

The spices already present must grow around the hill rather than on it. Named in the fourth stanza, the plants are gillyflower, ginger, gromwell, and peony. These normally grow to a height of several feet.[14] Thus they must rise around the Pearl's hill and shadow it against the sun. Such is the implication, in the third stanza, of the lines

> Blomeȝ blayke and blwe and rede
> Þer schyneȝ ful schyr agayn þe sunne.

That the spices shade the hill is, in fact, made explicit in the fourth stanza:

> On huyle þer perle hit trendeled doun
> Schadowed þis worteȝ ful schyre and schene,
> Gilofre, gyngure and gromylyoun,
> And pyonys powdered ay bytwene.   (41–44)

> [On the hill where the pearl rolled down
> Fell shadows of these plants full bright and fair,
> Gillyflower, ginger and gromwell,
> And peonies scattered everywhere between.]

The narrator, who in the fifth stanza "felle upon þat floury flaȝt" [fell upon the flowery turf] (57), must fall on the turf beside the hill, not on the hill itself. He falls asleep, his spirit "arises after a time," and he experiences his lovely vision. The manuscript illustration, as reproduced in Professor Gollancz's facsimile edition, depicts the scene in exactly this way. It is difficult to determine if the illustration has flowers growing directly from

---

[14] According to several standard reference works: for gillyflower and gromwell, A. R. Clapham, T. G. Tutin, and F. F. Warburg, *Flora of the British Isles* (Cambridge, 1962), pp. 391, 663; for ginger, L. H. Bailey, *Standard Cyclopedia of Horticulture* (New York, 1941), p. 3543; for peony, *Encyclopedia Americana*, XXI (New York, 1956), 559.

the Pearl's hill or from its margin; but the hill is much darker than the surrounding area and consequently has the appearance of fresh earth.

Since the Pearl would be lost but not decayed, finally, its loss would be recent—so recent that its hill is yet bare of growth. These details would make the Pearl seem very much a metaphor for a person who died within a matter of days, and its hill, now bare but soon to be grown over, very much an artificial mound; a grave. Physical death, a fresh burial, the expectation of decay that will nourish new biological life, these would reassert the literal basis on which an interpretation of the poem must rest. The Pearl must be either a lost child or, as has been recently suggested,[15] a beloved woman. Such details would not mean that *Pearl* is not a religious poem rich in symbolism. It is quite centrally a religious poem in which the narrator becomes more than reconciled with the loss of a loved one. He becomes reconciled with himself, reestablishing the interior harmony of his soul's faculties. He becomes reconciled with the laws of the physical universe. He becomes reconciled with the mortality of earthly beauty, coming to see that the changeless beauty of Heaven is far more splendid. He becomes reconciled, finally, with the "kynde of Kryst": that is, with the moral and spiritual orders of reality in which one good must give way to a higher good and one life must be lost that a higher life may be gained.

[15] Mother Angela Carson, "Aspects of Elegy in the Middle English *Pearl*," *SP*, LXII (1965), 17–27.

13

PEARL: THE LINK-WORDS AND THE THEMATIC STRUCTURE

O. D. Macrae-Gibson

IN E. V. GORDON'S EDITION OF *Pearl*, AN ACCOUNT OF THE "stanza-linking by echo and refrain" which forms so notable a feature of the structure of the poem appears under the general heading of "verse-form," and the discussion suggests that the poet found it a difficulty in the way of expressing his meaning, one even that sometimes defeated him, although the possibility of deliberate verbal wit in the various senses given to some of the link-words is allowed.[1] This still represents, I suppose, a quite usual view of the importance of the linking scheme; discussion of the thematic structure has concentrated on the significance of the pearl-symbol, the nature of the theological argument, the importance of the elegy-convention, and so on. Even Gordon, however, gives the link-words a place in the thematic structure: "the refrain in each stanza-group underlines the particular stage of thought with which that group is primarily concerned,"[2] and

Reprinted, by permission of the author and of the editors, from *Neophilologus*, LII (1968), 54–64. Translations have been supplied by the author, along with minor revisions.

[1] *Pearl*, ed. E. V. Gordon (Oxford, 1953), xxxvi–xxxix. The text of this edition is the basis of all quotations from the poem in the present article; all numerical references in parentheses are to this text, cited by line.

[2] *Ibid.*, xl.

Dorothy Everett puts the same idea more strongly. Emphasising that the link-words are *significant* words, she says: "the emphasis which certain words receive from so much repetition is rarely misplaced; indeed, most of the reiterated words and phrases are so essential to the poem as a whole that, taken in order, they almost form a key to its contents."[3] Curiously, this suggestion as to the thematic importance of the link-words does not seem to have been systematically developed[4]; it is the purpose of the present article to develop it. I shall use the term "refrain-line" for the last line of the stanza, even though it is by no means always a true refrain with the whole line maintained unaltered through a stanza-group, "refrain-word(s)" for the word(s) which are so maintained in the refrain-line, and "link-word" for the refrain-word which ends the refrain-line and which, from the emphasis its rhyming position gives it and from its use (or the use of a close variant) in the "echo" in the following line, forms the major verbal link within a stanza-group—it also, of course, provides the link between groups.

In the first stanza-group the refrain-line refers to the "perle wythouten spot" (the "pearl" is first presented as though a physical jewel, pleasing to a physical prince, but one of its significances, as representing a child, is almost at once apparent, although at this stage the great importance later to be attached to the idea that this child was without spot of sin is not evident; we would suppose the father[5] thinking only of the child's physi-

---

[3] *Essays on Middle English Literature* (Oxford, 1955), 89.

[4] After the submission of the present article, however, there was published P. M. Kean's valuable *The Pearl, An Interpretation* (London, 1967), which gives much attention to certain of the link-words as fundamental to the structure of parts of the poem (see especially part III, ch. I, "less and more"). In some cases explanations which I offer almost duplicate Miss Kean's; in others they diverge more or less widely. To have eliminated the one type and/or argued the other fully would have badly disturbed the structure of my article; it seemed best therefore to leave it as it stood.

[5] The question whether the poet was literally the father of a dead child or whether this apparent state of affairs is a literary contrivance does not concern the present article.

cal beauty). In counterpoint to this, the echo-word "spot" refers to the specific, restricted area of earth, the "erber" [a delimited, often enclosed, part of a garden; a "pleasance"], in which the poet represents himself as having lost his "pearl" and which he is now revisiting. There is, no doubt, some simple verbal enjoyment in the play on contrasted senses of "spot," but the contrast is probably of more importance than that. If the pearl is "wythouten spot" there is a submerged implication that it cannot be to be found within a particular "spot." That which was lost, and remains, in the limited spot cannot have been the veritable "pearly" quality of the child (an idea which becomes explicit later, when in line 269 the glorified child explains that what was lost was not the pearl, but a rose only); if the pearl is to be rediscovered it must, then, be by leaving the spot to which the poet's human mourning would confine him. This is exactly what happens in the transition to the second stanza-group, the echo-word "spot" providing the vehicle of transition: "fro spot my spyryt þer sprang in space" [from that spot my spirit after a while rose up] (61). Thus the refrain- and echo-words of the first stanza-group lay the foundation for much of the later development of the poem.

The function of the link-word in the second stanza-group is simpler. This is a descriptive group, of a heavenly region contrasted with the earthly "erber" in two ways. First, whereas the "erber" was essentially an enclosed, limited place the heavenly region is everextending: "þe fyrre in þe fryth, þe feier con ryse / Þe playn, þe plontteʒ, þespyse, þe pereʒ" [the further (I went) in the woodland the more beautifully the sward, shrubs, spice-plants and pear-trees were growing] (103–104). Second, the rich beauty of the region is such that the very leaves and stones greatly surpass the simple flowers of the earthly "spot." There the flowers merely "schyneʒ ful schyr agayn þe sunne" [shine most brightly to meet the sun] (28); in the heavenly place sunbeams would appear "bot blo and blynde" [merely dark and dim] (83) compared with the cliffs, trees, and gravel (it is noteworthy, further, that the beauty is a "pearly" beauty

[82], hinting that this is a suitable place to discover the pearl, where the earthly spot was not). As the main force of the stanza-group is rich description, the link-word "addubbement" [adornment] (sometimes "dubbement" or "dubbed" in the echo) forms a straightforward reinforcement.

With the change of scene, a mortal and sinful man has been introduced into a heavenly environment. The fundamental imperfection of his reaction to it, the one which will in the end cause his expulsion, is at once hinted at by the link in the third stanza-group, on the word "more." Disharmony is not yet strongly evident, yet the dreamer's first comment on the increasing joy he finds as he advances is one on the ways of fortune, who heaps more and more on those she favours (129–132)—there is a touch of human envy here, perhaps; then as he realises that even greater beauty lies beyond the water (147–148) his desire to come to it increases restlessly at his heart, even though the joy he has at hand is ten times more than an earthly heart could reach to (135–136). The refrain-words "more and more" and the echo "more" suggest that the calm beauty of the previous stanza-group is not being responded to with corresponding calm joy by the dreamer; the beginnings of conflict are present. It does not yet develop, however; for the present the vision progresses. "More" the dreamer has indeed been granted, and more yet he receives in the vision of the child which closes the group.

It is the appearance of the glorified child which occupies the fourth stanza-group, especially the pearly quality of her array and appearance, and which supplies the refrain-lines. One point about the description which is noteworthy is that nowhere in the group is she called "pearl" herself, though the description in lines 189–190 is clearly meant to echo that applied by the dreamer to the pearl-child in the first stanza of the poem and so to lead on to his enquiry in line 242 whether she is indeed *his* pearl. Instead, the emphasis is on the fact that she was *arrayed* in pearls, with a perfect pearl *set* on her breast; the importance of the word "pyȝt," which is used for both these ideas, is stressed by its use as the link-word of the group. As a variant, her complexion is *as fine as* the pearls she wears (215–216). The implication would seem to be that the child was not, in her original person, "pearl," but has *become* "pearly"—another glance at the idea hinted at in the first stanza-group and to be developed later.

The dreamer, however, views things with simple, mortal eyes. His pearl was lost; he hails the child as "perle" straightforwardly, treating the fact that she is "in perles pyȝt" as relatively unimportant (241). This makes the transition to the fifth stanza-group, where the inadequacy of his thought to cope with heavenly fact is for the first time clearly brought out. The linking of "jueler" and "juel" is a key to this. He calls himself "jeweller," emphasising his feeling that the child now revealed is *his,* as a physical pearl may be the property of a jeweller. The child takes up the image, but corrects his thought. Her mortal person, which could be considered to be the property of her father, was no pearl; only the immortal parts (including the glorified body, after the corruptible body has passed through death—implied, I take it, by the "kyste" of line 271, though the word also picks up the "cofer" and "forser" of lines 259 and 263, signifying the heavenly setting in which the pearl has been revealed[6]) are capable of being "pearl." It follows, then, that the father's claim to be a "jeweller" can imply no rights of possession over this jewel, which as is explicitly stated later (418) belongs wholly to Christ (the child's use of the phrase "your perle" in line 258 is simply quoting the father's thought); if he is indeed to be reckoned a jeweller, a worthy one who loves his craft, he ought to rejoice over such a supreme example of it as is here revealed, with the pearl not only set in a perfect casket but itself brought to being out of nothing (274).

Not surprisingly, such subtleties are not understood by the

---

[6] All three words can be used of various boxes, especially for valuables; the first two can also signify "coffin."

dreamer; though he thinks he has accepted what the child has said (277 ff.) he can get no further than the idea that he has recovered "his" pearl and can repossess it (282 ff.). The sixth stanza-group then shifts ground slightly (the transition between groups is not very good here, the echo-word "iueler" in line 301 being equivalent simply to "man"). If the dreamer cannot understand, he must at least accept, and the group is concerned with a fundamental principle which if he rejects he rejects the whole of heaven; that judgement belongs to the Lord, and it is man's part to abide this judgement. The essentiality of this concept is emphasised by the link-word "deme" [judge], used of God in lines 324, 348, and 360. Man is not forbidden to use his reason (313), but he must not rely on his judgement to understand divine things (312), or assume that he can judge what will be his own fate (336, 337), let alone presume to judge God (349). Nor is it the child who adjudges his fate to him (325), but God only. Only subject to this understanding can the dreamer use his own rational faculty, and talk sensibly to the child—the use of "demed" as the echo-word in the transition to the seventh stanza-group (361) is probably an exact one, with the sense "spoke judiciously," not, as normally rendered, merely "spoke." His acceptance (for the present at any rate) of the judgement of God enables him to return to harmony with the child, accepting the joy of heaven on its proper terms: he rejoices at her fair fortune (393–396), under Christ's mercy (383–384), and she rejoices at his humility, since this is beloved of Christ, in whom her joy resides (400–407, 419–420). The key ideas of the seventh group, joy and its proper bases, are reflected in the link-word "blysse," coupled in the refrain-lines with "grounde."

The heavenly characteristic that joy cannot belong to selfish possession but is mutual between those who rejoice in each other's joy is developed further in the eighth stanza-group. Mutuality is of the essence of the heavenly land, hence its characteristic that each of its denizens is sovereign over the whole, yet without trespassing on the equal sovereignty of each of the others. To denote this state of affairs the poet raises to heavenly status a word which on earth implies a proper and harmonious relationship between men, and the link-word is "cortaysye" (in the echo "cortayse" appears in line 433, and "court" for the realm which exemplifies this "cortaysye" in 445). This does not, of course, according to normal theological thought, prevent degrees of bliss within heaven according as the capacity to experience it differs, nor similarly does it prevent the acknowledged and rejoiced-in primacy of Mary, a fact emphasised by the use of her title "Quen of cortaysye" thrice in the refrain-lines and of a similar phrase once in the echo (433).

Though the dreamer had accepted his joy vis-à-vis his own child as being properly rooted only in her joyful state, this total extension of the same principle is quite beyond his grasp. The transition to the ninth stanza-group makes this evident when he uses the echo-word "cortaysé" with a qualification which had he understood the idea he would have seen as absolutely foreign to its nature: he calls it *too* generous ("to fre," 481). There ought to be a limit to it, he feels, a "date," and this notion of the limit, universally applicable on earth but perfectly inapplicable to heaven, is the basis of the dispute which occupies this ninth group and of its link-word "date." On earth, circumstances constantly impose limits. There is an appropriate time for cultivation, and if it is not taken it is lost. The day has a beginning and an end, and outside these limits no man can work. One's honour is limited by one's social status. It is a fundamental human idea, and the dreamer tries to impose it on his vision of heaven—but with God, he is told, no such concept is appropriate (493). This same theme, of the contrast between the limited nature of earth and the limitless nature of heaven, continues into the tenth stanza-group, the human feeling for the limit being expressed in terms of the labourers in the vineyard. Their work, which was earthly, was subject to "date"; but their reward is to be heavenly and is not so subject. Where there is no imposed limit the concept of a demand for "more" is irrelevant, and the stanza-group, linked on the word "more," presents again the impossibility of understanding heaven in terms of a concept appropriate to earth. The link-word reminds us of the third stanza-group, where the unheavenly wish to seek more was hinted at as a disharmonious characteristic of the dreamer. In the present group this hint is confirmed when the dreamer in effect associates himself with the labourers' complaint (589–600)—his use of the link-word at the beginning of the speech, "then more I meled" [then I spoke further] (589), even though not in the offending sense, serves emotionally to confirm his association with the demand for more.

The eleventh stanza-group is concerned to refute this false concept. In comparison with earth the term "more" can be used of heaven, since God's mercy and the rewards it brings are more than anyone on earth could deserve (576, 577 ff.), but within heaven itself the term has no meaning, as the transition-line 601 makes clear. The appropriate concept, instead, is "enough." From the "infinite treasury of grace" there is always enough to be drawn for any purpose—to save the innocent (625, 636), to save sinners (612, 624), to redeem the world (648, 660). This heavenly "enough" is no stinting measure, but the perfect supply for any purpose; that the word is used in this generous sense is, we may feel, emphasised by its use in the clear sense "certainly, completely" in line 637, "inoȝe is knawen" [it is well known]. The link-word is "innoghe"[7], and the particular application here is stressed by, for once, a complete refrain-line repeated almost

---

[7] Replaced in line 613 by "now," as the MS. stands. This is accepted by Gordon (he points out that "the syllable -nogh- was equivalent in sound to now"), as "showing that the poet in linking his stanzas aimed primarily at an echo of sound" (edition, note ad loc.), but in sense it makes a very weak link. We should probably read "bot inoghe þou moteȝ . . ." [you've been arguing at excessive length], contrasting a human use of the word applied to the dreamer with the divine one which is the key to the group. Miscopying from "inow" at some stage of transmission easily explains the error (this suggestion, in the form of an emendation to inow, was put forward by O. F. Emerson, "More Notes on Pearl," PMLA, XLII (1927), 824).

unaltered throughout the group, "for the grace of God is gret innoghe."

The transition to the twelfth stanza-group simply repeats the ruling concept of the eleventh (661); the group itself is concerned with the conditions which man must fulfil to be able to receive the infinite grace which is offered to him. This is an essential complement to the doctrine of all-sufficient grace, but it involves a difficult set of concepts, and it is not surprising that the twelfth group offers some difficulties of understanding. On the face of it, the refrain-line asserts four times that innocence has a right to salvation (672, 684, 696, 720), but on the fifth occasion contradicts this by contrasting salvation through innocence and salvation "by ryȝte" (708). The link-word "ryȝt" should be a key to the group, but what exact sense are we to give it? Gordon's gloss in his edition gives it its usual senses of "justice," "what is just," "justifiable title" and so on in all occurrences in *Pearl* except those in the first four refrain-lines mentioned above, where it is glossed "justification (by grace)," or (as adjective) "justified, sanctified by divine grace," and this interpretation in those lines is accepted by Cawley.[8] Now a specific contrast, using the word "bot" [but], has already been drawn between the penitent sinner, who can take to himself the offered grace only by repentance and penance, and the innocent,[9] to whose salvation no such conditions attach, since reason (or perhaps "resoun of ryȝt"—"natural justice" a modern lawyer might say) absolutely requires it (661–666), and the second term of this contrast has been further explained in lines 667–668. Surely when the stanza is closed by two lines restating the first term of the contrast (669–670), opposed with the same word "bot" to two final lines linking "inoscente," "saf" and

[8] *Pearl and Sir Gawain and the Green Knight*, ed. A. C. Cawley (Everyman's Library no. 346, London, 1962), text *ad. loc.*

[9] That is to say, of course, the *baptised* innocent (cf. lines 626–627); the poet does not discuss the fate of the infant unpurified by baptism from the sin of Adam.

"ryȝte," the natural assumption is that these final two lines restate the second term of the contrast, not that they introduce a new and special sense of "ryȝte." The matter is unfortunately complicated by what is generally agreed to be a faulty MS. reading in line 672, "at inoscente is saf & ryȝte." It seems to me that the most satisfactory emendation might be to interchange "at" and "&," taking "at ryȝte" as a simple variant on the "by ryȝt(e)" of the other refrain-lines. Then the contrast twice stated in this first stanza of the group is straightforwardly expanded in the next two, a contrast between the "harmleȝ haþel" [innocent man] who has never offended, and who is automatically saved (676–684), and the "ryȝtwys man" [righteous man], who shall also be saved—but not automatically, since his righteousness cannot be perfect so as to justify him before God and give him a right to salvation; only after his own efforts, "if he be wyȝte" [if he be strong], to make himself capable of receiving the divine grace (in the light of the argument elsewhere we shall have to interpret the "harmleȝ haþel . . . þat dyt not ille" as a child, for no adult can avoid "doing ill"). These two stanzas (the second and third of the group) are closed by lines (695–696) closely echoing those which closed the first stanza (671–672), the fact of the contrast being again stated by the use of "bot." The structure is less satisfactory if "and ryȝte" is retained in line 672 (whatever is done with "at inoscente"), and some rather unusual use of "ryȝte" must be supposed; I suggest that it might be taken as an adverb, ". . . is saved, and rightly so," and the general structure of the three stanzas suggested above is then little disturbed.

The fact that the sinner must make efforts towards his salvation does not, of course, imply that the efforts themselves procure the salvation. That remains the free gift of God's grace, which acts by restoring the innocence forfeited by sin, the sin being "washed away in Christ's blood" (to which doctrine a reference is implied, I take it, in line 705). This, I suggest, is the force of line 708. The innocent, who never offended, *could* in principle claim a right to salvation (though in fact, of course, the innocent of guilt would be equally innocent of knowledge of any such right[10]). One who has lost this state, who is aware of such a concept as "just claim," dare not make any claim; for him innocence (which by God's free grace may be restored to him) stands in contrast to any notion of a right springing from his own deserving. By restoration of innocence he becomes as a child again; we are reminded in the last stanza of the twelfth group and the first of the thirteenth that it is only children to whom saving innocence naturally belongs.

The contrast between the ways of salvation of the innocent and the penitent which occupied the twelfth group is looked at again, symbolically this time, in the thirteenth.[11] The state of innocence is now represented by the spotlessness of the perfect pearl, and the link-word, stressing this concept, is "mascelleȝ," in all but one of its occurrences associated with "perle." The spiritual interpretation of the phrase "wythouten spot," which was only implicit when this appeared in the first refrain-lines of the poem, is now made explicit. The child, saved by her innocence never spotted, has the spotless pearl set in her breast by the Lamb of God; the sinner, however, must procure the capacity to receive it by abandoning the things of this world which have stained his innocence, even as the jeweller of the parable sold all his goods to buy his perfect pearl (730–732). The word "jueler," of course, looks back to the link-word of the fifth

[10] It is possible that this idea is explicitly stated in lines 665–666, which can be rendered "but reason will always save the innocent who is incapable of talking foolishly about a just claim." This requires a rather awkward word-order, however, and I do not press the suggestion.

[11] As the MS. stands the echo-link is absent in the transition to the thirteenth group. The poet probably provided one; as Gordon points out, "the keyword *ryȝt* is one easy to work with." The original may well have had something like the "he ryȝt con calle" [he duly called], which Gordon suggests (edition, pp. 88–89), though it would be a sadly mechanical link. A more satisfactory one could be created, but only at the cost of considerable rewriting; the sense one would like would be to the effect: "Jesus said to his disciples, and justly, that no man . . . ."

stanza-group, and at once establishes that the parable of the purchase of the pearl of price is being applied to the father, before the specific exhortation to him of lines 743–744 confirms it. He must forsake the world, and "the world" for him must include that attachment to a merely mortal relationship with his daughter which he falsely interprets as possession of "his pearl." The fact that attachment to such a relationship is among the "goods" with which he is encumbered is perhaps implied by the choice of "wolen and lynne" ["wool and linen"] to represent the goods sold by the jeweller to purchase his pearl (731), since the mortal parts are as the clothing of the immortal soul. The father hears, but we are reminded once more of how imperfect is his understanding of the heavenly mysteries which are being revealed to him by way of a play on the words "mascelleȝ" and "makelleȝ"—the latter replaces the former as the echo-word in lines 733 and 757 and appears with it in the refrain-line 780. The Great Pearl, representing the perfect totality of heaven, is indeed peerless as well as spotless (732, 733), as the Lamb of God is also (757), but the father, lacking understanding, puts the two epithets together inappropriately when applying them to the glorified child (780); he has fallen into the same error as regards her bridehood of Christ which he made earlier as regards her queenship of heaven and the correction of which he never really understood: he is applying the concepts of earth, where the essentially limited nature of life allows but one queen of a realm and but one bride of a groom, to the circumstances of heaven, where no such limits apply. He never, in fact, does reach an understanding of this, though his false use of "makeleȝ" is duly corrected by the child in the transition to the fourteenth stanza-group (781 ff.), and the point is left for the time being, the fourteenth group being concerned to remind us that the possibility of glorified innocence in the heavenly Jerusalem was won by the sacrifice of the supreme Innocent in the earthly Jerusalem, an idea straightforwardly reinforced by the link-word "Jerusalem." It is returned to in the fifteenth group, however, and the heavenly fact that no honour or joy can there be lessened, whatever else be added, forms the key-thought of the group, as the key-word is "lesse," always in a negated phrase. The group thus forms a contrast with the tenth group: there human error sought to impose the inappropriate concept "more" upon heavenly things; here we are reminded that "never less" is, however, an essential of heaven. A subsidiary aspect of the principle that none of the glories of heaven reduce any other continues the fifteenth group: the glorious song of the spotless company of maidens is in no way impaired by the other glorious sounds as of waters and thunder (877–884), nor their glory by that of the four beasts and the elders about the Throne (885–888); their peculiar glory and song belongs to them and to no other (889–892). The use of the echo-word, in the form "nowþelese" (889) to emphasise this negative[12] may seem to strike a slightly jarring note in the presentation of heaven, but it has been led up to by the usage at 877, which is intermediate in sense, and it allows an easy transition to the dreamer's use of the link-word. A full understanding of the heavenly condition, and so a use of the link-word in its full implications, is beyond him, but he shows again the humility which he attained to in the seventh stanza-group, using the link in a simple way in craving to know more of the child's condition *although* his earthiness and foolishness make him unworthy to speak; thus far he has advanced into harmony with heaven, and so he can fairly be allowed the further vision he seeks, of the City itself.

This further vision is introduced by the account of the City contained in the sixteenth stanza-group. This group looks back to the fourteenth in that it repeats the figure of the two Jerusalems (937 ff.), but now the main emphasis is on the spotlessness of the City, an emphasis given largely by the play on the two

[12] One would gloss the word "nevertheless," but in context the implication is that the other denizens of heaven, despite their skill in praise, were *none the more* able to sing that song.

senses of the link-word "mote" [stain, city]. The group may be compared with the first group, which plays on two senses of "spot" very similar to the present two senses of "mote," but the applications of the plays are very different. In the earlier case the earthly "spot" was contrasted with the spotlessness of the pearl, implying that the pearl could not be found there; here the nature of the heavenly place shares the spotlessness of its Lord the Lamb (in line 945), of his company (947), and of the vision-child in particular (stressed by the application to her of the echo-word in the form. "moteleʒ" in line 961), so that this place appears as her natural home. By contrast, in the last refrain-line of the group (972) we are reminded that the dreamer is *not* "clene wythouten mote"; he cannot belong in the City.

There is little to say about the seventeenth group; the description is an accepted one and the link-word duly credits it to St. John.[13] In the eighteenth group, however, the poet stresses an aspect of the description of importance to his overall structure, the fact that the City needs neither sun nor moon, being brighter than either. This is the basis of the linking in the first half of the group, but in the second half the word "sunne" drops from the linking and the remaining "mone" is used in a very different way, reminding us forcibly of the imperfections of our own sublunary abode, and the impossibility that the dreamer, who shares them, could dwell in the heavenly place— he beholds it only by special grace, and that he can hardly bear. The use of "mone" in line 1080 is an exception, of course. Here the poet has briefly returned to pure description of the heavenly glory, but the appearance of the word, in a sense importing earthly time, gives a more ephemeral tone to the description than was present earlier. In itself this might give a hint that the vision is approaching its close; further suggestions of this come from a subsidiary emphasis on the "spotty" nature of the moon and the

---

[13] On significant modifications which the poet makes, however, in adapting the descriptions of the Apocalypse, see P. M. Kean, *op. cit.*, pp. 212–217.

sublunary world in lines 1068 and 1070, with a faint echo of the link-word of the first stanza-group (we may perhaps see an anticipation of this as far back as line 923, where the unexpected phrase "maskeleʒ *vnder mone*"[14] which the father is made to apply to the child reminds us of the existence of a spotty, sublunary world), from the reappearance in lines 1076 ff. of the image of the heavenly trees brighter than the sun which in lines 75 ff. formed part of the mechanism of transition from earth to heaven and so here will remind us again of earth, and—most forcibly—from the restressing of the point made at the end of the sixteenth stanza-group that the dreamer himself does not properly belong in heaven.

These uneasy implications, foreshadowing the end of the vision, continue in the transition to the nineteenth group, where the procession of perfect virgins is compared to the risen moon (1093 ff.). Gordon has pointed out[15] the subtle appropriateness of the image of the moon becoming visible in the evening for the procession appearing "wythouten sommoun" [without summons]; and the visual comparison of the full moon with a pearl, and the traditional feeling for the femininity and chastity of the moon, form further and straightforward parts of the basis for the image.[16] Yet when the moon was so recently described as "spotty, of body grym" [. . . ugly in body] (1070) a submerged disharmony is certainly created by the present comparison, a disharmony probably intended by the poet and meant to hint forward to the disharmony between the human imperfections of the dreamer and the perfection of heaven which will so soon expel him from his vision. For the moment, however, we seem to be returning to the harmonious mood of the seventh

[14] Possibly to be rendered "lacking any sublunary spot" (cf. 1068); more probably "wholly spotless," but with associations inappropriate to heaven since the sense "wholly" is derived from "even in comparison with the whole race of men *on earth* ('under the moon')."

[15] Edition, note *ad loc.*

[16] See P. M. Kean, *op. cit.*, pp. 143–147 on traditional symbolic associations of the moon, the pearl, and the Virgin.

group, with its mutual "blysse" here repeated in the synonymous link-word "delyt," a delight which the dreamer shares in his adoration of the Lamb (1128, 1129); but it is only a brief lightening before all the hints are fulfilled, serving to create a shock when the dreamer's sight of his "own" child among the glorious company brings to the fore his human inability to accept the wholly unselfish terms of heavenly joy. He falsely claims "delyt" in a possessive "luf-longyng" for the child (1152), and this emotion is not one of heavenly harmony but a driving, maddening force. This final explosion of incompatibility between his "maneȝ mynde" [human mind] and the heavenly condition forms the transition to the last stanza-group (1153 ff.), and it suddenly ends the vision.

The vision has not brought the dreamer to a full understanding of the heavenly mystery, and even the lesser attainment, acceptance of the fact that a man must submit to God's ways even if he does not understand them, which seemed to have been arrived at in the sixth stanza-group, has required the sharp lesson of a violent expulsion to be established firmly. But established it is; he does now accept that man must take his satisfaction in what pleases God, not in his own selfish desires, and in his own case he can now take settled content in the blissful state of the glorified child. This theme is emphasised straightforwardly by the link-word "paye," used of God's displeasure when men oppose His will (1164, 1165), and of the consequences, displeasing to man, of such opposition (1177), but chiefly, and crowningly, simply of the pleasure of God, which it should be man's part, prayer, and joy to incline himself to. The poem thus closes on the spiritual theme which was implicit in its very first line.

From the promise of this first line, then, we have followed the theme, guided by the link-words, from the earthly spot where the earthly "pearl" was lost to the heavenly region with its rich and pearly *addubbement,* and on to the eternal Jerusalem described by St. John, the *moteles mote* where the true pearl, *pyȝt* in pearls in token of perfect purity, has her home. The new relationship of father and daughter, the jeweller and the jewel, has been explored, and the child, speaking with the authority of her glorified state, has revealed the mystery of heavenly courtesy, in which the grace of God is enough to provide all with more than they could need, in which joy is essentially mutual, so that no one's felicity can be made less because of that gained by another. She has reminded us, too, that only childlike innocence can enter this state; *mascelles* innocence has indeed a right to do so where mere righteousness has none. But these mysteries of the luminous heaven which needs neither sun nor moon the father's sublunary understanding cannot penetrate to. He keeps trying to impose on his view of heaven the limited, *date*-laden concepts of earth, where we seek our restless satisfaction in craving more than we have been granted or more than another seems to possess, finding a false delight in selfish possession, and so in the end he is flung from the heavenly places. Still, he has achieved much: within the vision a rational appreciation of the need to accept whatever dooms God may deem and a real though insufficiently firm willingness to take his content in the blissful state of the child; after the shock which his failure in this brings, a more settled content in the child's felicity, and a hope only that himself, and all mankind, may become as acceptable to God's *paye* as she is.

Miss Everett's suggestion that the link-words can form a key to the whole structure is sound; it does not need the qualification of her "almost."

14

THE THEOLOGICAL STRUCTURE OF *PEARL*

Louis Blenkner, O.S.B.

LIKE THE UNDERGRADUATE WHO READ *Macbeth* TWICE IN HIGH school—"once for the truth and once for the beauty"—modern scholars seem content to restrict their reading of *Pearl* to an isolated consideration of either its artistry and appeal to emotion or its theology and appeal to the intellect, in spite of impressive efforts of Professors Fletcher and Wellek to resolve the elegy-allegory dispute.[1] Even the poem's most recent editors betray their partisanship: E. V. Gordon, who repeatedly refers to the narrator-dreamer as "the father," maintains that "Without the elegiac basis and the sense of great personal loss which pervades it, *Pearl* would indeed be the mere theological treatise on a special point, which some critics have called it"[2]; and Sister Mary Vincent Hillmann, in a veiled though determined effort to defend Sister Madeleva's view that *Pearl* is not a mere pathetic elegy, as some critics have implied, offers a disarmingly literal

Reprinted, by permission of the author and of the Fordham University Press, from *Traditio*, XXIV (1968), 43–75. Translations have been supplied by the author except as indicated.
[1] Jefferson B. Fletcher, "The Allegory of the Pearl," *JEGP*, 20 (1921), 1–21, and R. Wellek, "The Pearl: An Interpretation of the Middle English Poem," *Studies in English by Members of the English Seminar of the Charles University, Prague*, 4 (1933), 1–33.
[2] *Pearl* (Oxford, 1953), xviii; all quotations from *Pearl* are from this edition.

interpretation—asserting, rightly I believe, that *Pearl* is "an homiletic poem teaching that the soul must not be attached to earthly treasure if it is to attain the Kingdom of God."[3] We have returned to the position of Sir Robert Cotton's librarian, who, out of touch with the sensibilities of late nineteenth-century scholars, characterized the first poem in MS. Cotton Nero A. x. as "Vetus poema Anglicanum, in quo sub insomnii figmento multa ad religionem et mores spectantia explicantur" [An old English poem in which, under the figure of a dream, many things concerning religion and morals are explained]. I will attempt to show that the poet's treatment of "many things concerning religion and morals" is, like Dante's *Comedy* (never to my knowledge categorized as either a mere theological treatise or a mere elegy for Beatrice), a carefully structured poetic account of a spiritual itinerary culminating in an ecstasy of mystical contemplation.

My search for the unifying concept underlying *Pearl* rests on two basic assumptions: first, that the poet was an unusually deliberate and careful artist, and no detail of the poem is therefore gratuitous; and second, that the psychic change wrought in the dreamer is of central importance, and thus *Pearl* is truly an "interior drama." The deliberate artistry (evident in the refrains, frequently involving subtle variation and meaningful word-play, and in the complex stanza form with its rigid rhyme scheme and profuse, though not systematic, alliteration) is especially attested by the cyclical nature of the poem, ending with an echo of the opening line, and the very symmetry of the governing plan. The "erber" [garden] frame consists precisely of the initial and final stanza-groups. The dream proper, equally symmetrical, contains

---

[3] *The Pearl, Medieval Text with a Literal Translation and Interpretation.* (University of Notre Dame Press, 1967), viii; although Sister Madeleva's interpretation—equating the pearl-maiden to the dreamer's soul—in *Pearl: a Study in Spiritual Dryness* (New York, 1925) has not been generally accepted, the focusing of attention on the narrator and her characterization of the poem as a "spiritual autobiography" or "interior drama" underlies much modern criticism of the poem.

three divisions: the long central dialogue—the didactic heart of *Pearl* (stanza-groups 5–16)—is encased between two descriptive passages of equal length, the *visio* [vision] of the land "þer meruayleʒ meuen" [where marvels occur] (stanza-groups 2–6) and the *visio* of the heavenly City (stanza-groups 17–19).

I. DREAM-VISION CONVENTIONS

Pearl exhibits similarities to a variety of types of medieval dream-visions, and each major division of the poem relies heavily on a distinct set of literary conventions.[4] The effect of the poet's shifting from one set of conventions to another (from those of patently fictional, secular love visions to those of religious visions considered unquestionably authentic in the Middle Ages)[5] can be most readily seen by contrasting the moods of the opening and closing scenes of the "erber" frame.

The initial stanza-group follows the conventions of courtly-love visions such as *The Romance of the Rose:* the summer's date, the detailed description of the beautiful garden setting, and the symbolic presentation of the beloved. Some idea of the extent to which literary tradition influences the reader's interpretation of *Pearl* can be seen in the way the description of the singular "pryuy perle"[6] [my own pearl] and the phrase "for-

---

[4] The relation of *Pearl* to other vision literature is treated in detail in Charles Louis Blenkner, "*Pearl* as Spiritual Itinerary" (Unpubl. diss., Chapel Hill, 1964), 8–42.

[5] A rough estimate of the progressively religious emphasis within the dream proper may be made by looking at Gordon's table of "Biblical Quotations and Allusions" (165–167): for the land "þer meruayleʒ meuen" [where marvels occur] (61–240) he cites four passages—an average of one every 45 lines; for the dialogue (241–976), fifty-five—one every 13 lines; for the New Jerusalem (977–1152), thirty-seven—one every 5 lines.

[6] The lines on the lost pearl's superiority to other pearls—"Ne proued I neuer her precios pere" [I never found its precious equal] (4) and "I sette hyr sengeley in synglere" [I set it apart alone in its uniqueness] (8) —evoke another symbol for a beloved, the bud superior to all the other roses in Mirth's garden in *The Romaunt of the Rose:* "Among the knop-

dolked of luf-daungere" [deprived by love's power] (11) suggest that the poem may be about the tribulations of a soulful
courtly lover; however the recurrent images of decay—"clot,"
"moul," and "rot" [clay . . . mold . . . rot]—lead one to suspect he may be reading an elegy using the conventions of the
love vision. Nothing in the opening section suggests that the lost
pearl is anything other than an object of the narrator's love.
Although Sister Mary Vincent would deny that the object of
love is a person,[7] a strong tradition of symbolically presented
maidens in medieval love visions prompts the reader, *cherchez
la femme,* early in the opening section. The allusion, appropriate
in an elegy, to St. Paul's discussion of the resurrection of the
dead in I Corinthians 15:35–55,

> For vch gresse mot grow of grayneȝ dede;
> No whete were elleȝ to woneȝ wonne   (31–32)
>
> [For every blade of grass must spring from dead seeds
> or else no wheat would be brought home]

and the reference to the "kynde of Kryst" [Christ's nature]
(55) are the only explicitly religious elements in the entire initial
stanza-group.

On the other hand, a reader encountering the concluding
stanza-group as a displaced fragment would be hard pressed to
connect it with secular poetry. Its tone is distinctly religious.
The "erber" with its decorative details has become simply "þat
erber wlonk" [that noble garden] (1171), "þat hylle . . . þer
as my perle to grounde strayd" [that hill . . . where my pearl
strayed to the ground] (1172–1173), even "þys doel-doungoun"

---

pes I ches oon / So fair, that of the remenaunt noon / Ne preise I half so
well as it, / Whanne I avise it in my wit" [Among the buds I chose one
so fair that I prize none of the rest half so much as it when I consider
them] (1691–1694). Significantly the maiden later tells the dreamer
"þat þou lesteȝ watȝ bot a rose / Þat flowred and fayled as kynde hyt
gef" [What you lost was only a rose that bloomed and faded according
to its nature] (269–270).

[7] Hillmann, xi.

[this dungeon of sorrow] (1187). The central symbolic pearl is itself downgraded, and the dreamer's chief lament is not for the lost gem but for the loss of "þis veray avysyoun" [this true vision] (1184). The refrain "Prynceȝ paye" [Prince's pleasure] here clearly refers to the Divine Prince, and in addition to the refrain, the final forty-eight lines contain numerous other references to the Diety—"Goddeȝ present" [God's presence] (1193), "Lorde" (1199), "A God, a Lorde, a frende ful fyin" [A God, a Lord, a most noble friend] (1204), "Krysteȝ dere blessyng" [Christ's precious blessing] (1208), and ten pronouns with divine antecedents—as well as mention of the Eucharistic sacrament,

> Þat in þe forme of bred and wyn
> Þe preste vus scheweȝ vch a daye.   (1209–1210)
>
> [that the priest shows to us every day
> in the form of bread and wine.]

The dreamer, "fordolked of luf-daungere" [deprived by love's power], slid into his "slepyng-slaȝte" [sleeping-fit] in an "erber" suitable to a love vision. He awakes in that same "erber" oblivious to its traditional beauties (at least he does not reenumerate them), exhibiting the traditional characteristics of a contemplative returning from mystical rapture—sighing, bodily faintness, sorrowful longing after the vanished vision, and humble submission to the will of God:[8]

> I raxled, and fel in gret affray,
> And, sykyng, to myself I sayd,
> 'Now al be to þat Prynceȝ paye.'
> Me payed ful ille to be outfleme
> So sodenly of þat fayre regioun,
> Fro alle þo syȝteȝ so quyke and queme.
> A longeyng heuy me strok in swone,
> And rewfully þenne I con to reme.   (1174–1181)
>
> [I stretched and fell into great dismay,
> and sighing, said to myself,

---

[8] See Madeleva, *op. cit.* (see n. 3 *supra*), 112–125.

"Now all be to that Prince's pleasure."
It ill pleased me to be cast out
so suddenly from that fair country,
from all those sights so vivid and pleasant.
A heavy longing struck me into a faint,
and then I sorrowfully began to lament.]

His switch from a secular to a religiously oriented point of view reveals a profound psychic change brought about by a dream which, we are told explicitly, was a gift of grace. "My goste is gon in Godeʒ grace / In auenture þer meruayleʒ meuen" [My spirit, in God's grace, has gone on an adventure where marvels occur] (63–64). This progress from grief and confusion—"A deuely dele in my hert denned, / Þaʒ resoun sette myseluen saʒt" [An evil grief dwelt in my heart, even though reason would set me at peace] (51–52)—to peace suggests the progress of the contemplative as set forth by Hugh of St. Victor in *De arca Noe morali*. Hugh's brethren, marveling at "the unstableness and disquiet of the human heart," would be shown "the cause of such whirlings of thought":

It was my plan to show first whence arise such violent changes in man's heart, and then how the mind may be led to keep itself in stable peace. And although I had no doubt that this is the proper work of grace, rather than of human labour, nevertheless I know that God wishes us to co-operate . . . [Man] was driven from the face of the Lord, since for his sin he was struck with the blindness of ignorance, and passed from that intimate light of contemplation. . . . [his] heart which had [before the fall] been kept secure by divine love, and one by loving one, afterwards began to flow here and there through earthly desires. For the mind which knows not to love its true good, is never stable and never rests. Hence restlessness and ceaseless labour, and disquiet, until the man turns and adheres to Him. The sick heart wavers and quivers; the cause of its disease is love of the world; the remedy, the love of God.[9]

[9] Henry Osborn Taylor, *The Medieval Mind* (Cambridge, Mass., 1949), 2, 396; *PL*, 176, 617–620: Primo igitur demonstrandum est, unde tanta in corde hominis vicissitudo oriatur, ac deinceps quomodo ad pacem stabilem mens humana reduci, qualiterque in eadem stabilitate sua conservari possit insinuandum. Et licet hoc proprium divinae gratiae opus esse non dubitem, et non tam humana industria, quam divino munere,

The progress in *Pearl,* like that presented by Hugh, begins in "restlessness" and "whirlings of thought"—"Wyth fyrce skylleȝ þat faste faȝt . . . My wreched wylle in wo ay wraȝte" [with violent thoughts that obstinately contented . . . my wretched will labored ever in woe] (54–56)—and is "led to keep itself in stable peace"—"To pay þe Prince oþer sete saȝte / Hit is ful eþe to þe god Krystyin" [To please the Prince or be set at peace is quite easy for the good Christian] (1201–1202). Such a progress to the contemplation of God should, as Hugh suggests, be made "in Godeȝ grace." The cause of the heart's disease is, according to Hugh, "love of the world": in *Pearl* the grieving narrator is "fordolked of luf-daungere / Of þat pryuy perle" [deprived by love's power of my own pearl] (11–12); the remedy, says Hugh, is "love of God": in *Pearl* the final *visio* so moves the dreamer that he tries to join the company adoring the Lamb, "For luf-longyng in gret delyt" [For love-longing in great delight] (1152).

The writings of contemplatives not only provide conventions for the final "erber" scene but also suggest a traditional source for the poem's schematic structure—the progression from the secular and human to the religious and divine. As the opening and closing stanza-groups each show striking parallels to distinct types of dream-visions, so too do the major divisions of the dream itself: the initial *visio,* the highly original description of a marvelous land, has marked affinities to visions of the other

---

et sancti Spiritus inspiratione possideri; scio tamen quod cooperari nobis vult Deus. . . . Sed projectus est [homo] a facie Domini quoniam propter peccatum caecitate ignorantiae percussus ab intima contemplationis illius luce foras venit. . . . Cor ergo hominis, quod prius divino amori affixum stabile praestitit, et unum amando unum permansit, postquam per desideria terrena diffluere coepit; quasi in tot divisum est, quod ea sunt quae concupiscit. Sicque fit, ut mens quae verum bonum amare nescit, numquam valeat esse stabilis . . . hinc igitur nascitur motus sine stabilitate, labor sine requie, cursus sine perventione, ita ut semper sit inquietum cor nostrum, donec illi adhaerere coeperit. . . . Ecce ostendimus morbum cor fluctuans, cor instabile, cor inquietum. Et causam morbi, amorem videlicet mundi, et remedium morbi amorem Dei.

world and descriptions of the earthly Paradise[10]; the central dialogue setting forth the theological argument has been compared to dialogues or *consolationes* of the type of Boethius' *Consolation of Philosophy*[11]; and the final *visio*, a straightforward presentation of a traditional symbol of beatitude, is lifted almost verbatim from the Apocalypse of St. John, the archetypal Christian revelation. In general the elegists have noted the resemblance of the initial "erber" scene to secular visions, and allegorists have commented on the dialogue's indebtedness to theological and philosophical writings and pointed out similarities of the final "erber" scene to the accounts of mystics, but no one has demonstrated how the literary affinites of *Pearl* imply a consistent progression from secular to religious paralleling the narrator's advance from limited human knowledge to divinely inspired wisdom according to a pattern well established in medieval theology.

Not only do the three divisions of the dream proper manifest the increasingly religious nature of the poem, but each is apprehended by the dreamer according to a separate mode of cognition. Hugh of St. Victor writes:

Three are the modes of cognition (visiones) belonging to the rational soul: cogitation, meditation, contemplation. It is cogitation when the mind is touched with the idea of things, and the thing itself is by its image presented suddenly, either entering the mind through sense or rising from memory. Meditation is the assiduous and sagacious revision of cogitation, and strives to explain the involved, and penetrate the hidden. Contemplation is the mind's perspicacious and free attention, diffused everywhere throughout the range of whatever may be explored. . . . Meditation always is occupied with some one matter to be investigated; contemplation spreads abroad for the comprehending of many things, even the universe. Thus meditation is a certain inquisitive power of the mind, sagaciously striving to look into the obscure and unravel the perplexed. Contemplation is that acumen of intelligence which, keep-

[10] See Howard Rollin Patch, *The Other World According to Descriptions in Medieval Literature* (Cambridge, Mass., 1950), 134–137; 190.
[11] John Conley, "*Pearl* and a Lost Tradition," *JEGP*, 54 (1955), 332–347.

ing all things open to view, comprehends all with clear vision. Thus contemplation has what meditation seeks.[12]

The dreamer perceives the land "þer meruayleȝ meuen" [where marvels occur] "by its image . . . through sense or rising from memory." With the help of the maiden's discourse he "strives to explain the involved and penetrate the hidden." Contemplating the heavenly Jerusalem he "comprehends all [even the universe] with clear vision."

II. SPIRITUAL GEOGRAPHY

The dream in *Pearl* is an adventure into the realm of the spirit, "Fro spot my spyryt þer sprang in space; / My body on balke þer bod in sweuen" [From that spot my spirit sprang for a time; my body remained there on the bank in a dream] (61–62). The three stages of that adventure correspond to the Augustinian division of the rational soul into three faculties— memory, understanding, and will—which furnish the basis for the theologians' traditional threefold division of the soul's ascent to God through "the triple substance in Christ, Who is our ladder, namely, the corporeal, the spiritual, and the divine."[13]

---

[12] Taylor, 2, 388–389; *PL*, 175, 116–117: Tres sunt animae rationalis visiones, cogitatio, meditatio, contemplatio. Cogitatio est, cum mens notione rerum transitorie tangitur cum ipsa res, sua imagine animo subito praesentatur, vel per sensum ingrediens, vel a memoria exsurgens. Meditatio est assidua et sagax retractatio cogitationis, aliquid, vel involutum explicare nitens, vel scrutans penetrare occultum. Contemplatio est perspicax, et liber animi contuitus in res perspiciendas usquequaque diffusus. . . . Et quod meditatio semper circa unum aliquid rimandum occupatur; contemplatio ad multa, vel etiam ad universa comprehendenda diffunditur. Meditatio itaque est quaedam vis mentis curiosa; et sagax nitens obscura investigare, et perplexa evolvere. Contemplatio est vivacitas illa intelligentiae quae cuncta in palam habens, manifesta visione comprehendit. Et ita quodammodo id quod meditatio quaerit, contemplatio possidet.

[13] Saint Bonaventura, *The Mind's Road to God*, trans. George Boas (New York, 1953), 8; *Opera Omnia* (Quaracchi, 1882–1902), 5, 297: haec etiam respicit triplicem substantiam in Christo, qui est scala nostra, scilicet corporalem, spiritualem et divinam.

Christ, explains St. Bonaventure, teaches "the knowledge of the truth according to the triple mode of theology—that is, the symbolic, the literal, and the mystical—so that by the symbolic we may make proper use of sensible things, by the literal we may properly use the intelligible, and by the mystical we may be carried aloft to supernatural levels."[14]

The three divisions of the dream in *Pearl,* apprehended in the three modes of cognition, are presented "according to the triple mode of theology." The dreamer's "goste" [spirit], having "gon in Godeʒ grace / In auenture þer meruayleʒ meuen" [gone; in God's grace, on an adventure where marvels occur] (63–64), receives the initial *visio* of the marvelous land, presented in terms of sensible things, "through sense or rising from memory" (*cogitation*). The *visio* is *symbolic* in that symbols or images are described though not at this time explained; the images themselves, not their meaning, comfort the grieving dreamer:

> The dubbement dere of doun and daleʒ,
> Of wod and water and wlonk płayneʒ,
> Bylde in me blys, abated my baleʒ.   (121–123)

> [The precious ornament of down and dale,
> of wood and water and noble plain,
> built bliss in me, lessened my sorrow.]

But the beauties of the land "þer meruayleʒ meuen" do not suffice, for the dreamer is aware of a greater beauty:

> More and more, and ʒet wel mare,
> My lyste to se þe broke byʒonde;
> For if hit watʒ fayr þer I con fare,
> Wel loueloker watʒ þe fyrre londe.   (145–148)

> [More and more, and still even more,
> I desired to be beyond the brook;

[14] *Mind's Road,* 10; *Opera Omnia,* 5, 298: *scientiam veritatis* edocuit secundum triplicem modum theologiae, scilicet *symbolicae, propriae* et *mysticae,* ut per *symbolicam* recte utamur sensibilibus, per *propriam* recte utamur intelligibilibus, per *mysticam* rapiamur ad supermentales excessus.

> for if it was fair where I went,
> even lovelier was the farther shore.]

As he seeks "To fynde a forþe" [To find a ford] (150), he encounters the heavenly maiden across the stream, who, properly using the intelligible to console him, appeals ultimately to the "inquisitive power of the mind, sagaciously striving to look into the obscure and unravel the perplexed":

> A juel to me þen watȝ þys geste,
> And iueleȝ wern hyr gentyl saweȝ.
> 'Iwyse,' quod I, 'my blysfol beste,
> My grete dystresse þou al todraweȝ.' (277–280)

> [A jewel to me then was this guest,
> and jewels were her gentle words.
> "Indeed," I said, "my blissful and best one,
> you draw away all my great distress."]

Her discourse which follows is much more than a collection of "gentyl saweȝ" [gentle words], for she brusquely chides the dreamer—"Wy borde ȝe men? So madde ȝe be!" [Why do you men jest? You are so mad!] (290)—to jolt him into making an "assiduous and sagacious revision of cogitation" in an effort "to explain the involved and penetrate the hidden" in the manner of *meditation*. The central dialogue is *literal* in that it is discourse, and although imagery, such as in the parable of the vineyard, is used, the images are presented directly to the dreamer's intellect as words of the maiden, not as things to be apprehended by the senses. In the process of instructing the dreamer the maiden shows him the spiritual sins within his own soul—pride (301–310), anger (341–360), and envy (613–616)[15]

---

[15] In the common classification of the seven deadly sins, Pride, Wrath, and Envy are sins of the Devil or spiritual sins, appropriate to the world *within*. In the "erber" the dreamer exhibited the sin of the World, Cupidity, in his too great attachment to the lost pearl; of the sins of the Flesh, also appropriate to the "erber" where his "body on balke þer bod" [body remained there on the bank], only the first, Sloth (manifested as *tristitia*) is evident; perhaps Lust and Gluttony are omitted because, according to Augustinian psychology, the sinner succumbs to these sins after he has descended by stages from Pride to Despair, and the dreamer, through grace, begins his regeneration before reaching the bottom of the ladder.

—and at last directs him to a hill from which he may see the New Jerusalem in *contemplation,* which "comprehends all with clear vision" and "has what meditation seeks":

> And [I] blusched on þe burghe, as I forth dreued,
> Byʒonde þe brok fro me warde keued,
> Þat schyrrer þen sunne wyth schafteʒ schon. (980–982)

> [And as I hurried along, on the other side of the brook
> from me I saw lowered down the city
> that shone with gleams brighter than the sun.]

The final *visio* carries the dreamer aloft to supernatural levels, and although the scene is presented in visual images it is *mystical* in that it presents things divine, hidden and beyond the measure of the mortal mind,

> Delyt me drof in yʒe and ere,
> My maneʒ mynde to maddyng malte   (1153–1154)

> [Delight assailed me through my eyes and ears,
> my man's mind melted into madness]

its effect, beyond sense and beyond intellect, is ravishment—"So watʒ I rauyste wyth glymme pure" [Thus I was ravished by the pure radiance] (1088).

As long as the soul contemplates the ultimate reality, figured by the heavenly City, it shuns the intellectual and sensual modes of cognition. In effect, it accepts the maiden's primary advice, "I rede þe forsake þe worlde wode / And porchace þy perle maskelles" [I counsel you to forsake the mad world and purchase your spotless (and matchless) pearl] (743–744)—the usual condition for the contemplative life. In the words of Richard Rolle, "A man or woman þat is ordaynd til contemplatife lyfe, first god enspires þam to forsake þis worlde, and al þe vanite & þe couayties and þe vile luste þarof"[16] [A man or woman who is called to a contemplative life, God first inspires to forsake this

---

[16] C. Horstman, ed., *Yorkshire Writers: Richard Rolle of Hampole, an English Father of the Church, and His Followers* (New York, 1895), 1, 48.

world and all its vanity and covetousness and vile desires]. The Pseudo-Dionysius exhorts the would-be contemplative:

loke þou forsake with a strong & a sleiʒ & a listi contricyon boþe þi bodely wittes (as heryng, seyng, smelling, taastyng, & touching), and also þi goostly wittes, þe whiche ben clepid þin vnderstondable worchinges; and alle þoo þinges, þe whiche mowe be knowen wiþ any of þy fyue bodely wittes without-forþe; and all þoo þinges, þe whiche mow be knowen by þi goostly wittes wiþinne-forþ. . . . And, as it is possible to me for to speke & to þee to vnderstonde, loke þat þou rise wiþ me in þis grace, in a maner þat is þou woste neuer how, to be onid with hym þat is abouen alle substaunces and al maner knowyng.[17]

[see that you forsake, with a strong and careful and vigorous contrition, both your bodily senses (as hearing, sight, smell, taste, and touch) and also your spiritual senses which are called the workings of reason; and all those things which may be known with your bodily senses without, and all those things which may be known by your spiritual senses within. . . . And, as it is possible for me to speak and for you to understand, see that you rise along with me in this grace (in what manner, you know not) to be united with him who is above all substance and all manner of knowing.]

The references to "bodely wittes without-forþe" [bodily senses without], "goostly wittes wiþinne-forþ" [spiritual senses within], and "hym þat is abouen" [him who is above] suggest a traditional classification for the stages of contemplation as the threefold ascent from *without* to *within* to *above*.[18] Although

---

[17] *Deonise Hid Diuinite,* ed. Phyllis Hodgson, *EETS,* no. 231 (London, 1955), 3.

[18] Cf. St. Augustine on Psalm 41, *CCL,* 38, 465–466: Quaero ego Deum meum in omni corpore, siue terrestri, siue caelesti, et non inuenio; quaero substantiam eius in anima mea et non inuenio; meditatus sum tamen inquisitionem Dei mei, et per ea quae facta sunt, inuisiblia Dei mei cupiens intellecta conspicere, *effudi super me animam meam*; et non iam restat quem tangam, nisi Deum meum. [Dom Cuthbert Butler, *Western Mysticism: The Teaching · of S.S. Augustine, Gregory, and Bernard on Contemplation and the Contemplative Life* (2nd ed.; London, 1926), 22: I seek my God in every corporeal nature, terrestrial or celestial, and find Him not: I seek His substance in my own soul, and I find it not; yet still have I thought on these things, and wishing to see *the invisible things of my God, being understood by the things made,* I have poured forth my soul above myself, and there remains no longer any being for me to attain to, save my God.]

the three faculties are all within the soul, the memory receives its sense impressions from the corporeal world without, and the will, when properly oriented, longs for union with Him that is above. Thus the three stages of the dream in *Pearl* are contained within the second division of a larger triad which underlies the partition of the poem's *locus operandi* [setting] into three distinct realms: the corporeal world—perceived sensibly, and entirely *without* the dreamer—is the "erber" where he lost his earthly pearl and where his "body on balke þer bod in sweuen" [body remained there on the bank in a dream] (62); the spiritual world—comprehended intelligently, and contained *within* the dreamer's mind—is the marvelous land where his "goste is gon in Godeʒ grace" (63) and where he remains throughout the entire dream until he awakes attempting to cross the stream; and the divine world—apprehended mystically, and entirely *above* the dreamer—is the heavenly Jerusalem, which sinks down to facilitate his viewing, but which he does not enter.

The order of the presentation of these three worlds is determined by the narrative structure of the mystical experience. The narrator progresses from the temporal, corporeal world without to the spiritual world within, and thence contemplates the eternal, divine world above; and since the contemplative cannot enter that celestial world in this life,[19] he must return to the "erber." Each realm of this spiritual geography has a principal affinity for one person of the Blessed Trinity, and each reflects the workings of the other two persons. Before the three realms are examined in detail to establish the significance of their relationship to the Trinity, it is helpful to recall that the special province of the Father as Creator is the sensible world, that of the Son as Word or Wisdom is the intelligible, and that of the Holy Ghost as Love is the mystical,[20] and to keep in mind the

[19] This, at any rate, is the doctrine asserted by the poet and held by St. Gregory and St. Bernard, though not by St. Augustine or St. Thomas.
[20] Bonaventure, *Opera Omnia*, 5, 305: Si igitur Deus perfectus est spiritus, habet *memoriam, intelligentiam* et *voluntatem,* habet et *Verbum* genitum et *Amorem* spiratum qui necessario distinguuntur, cum unus ab altero producatur, non *essentialiter,* non *accidentaliter,* ergo *personaliter.*

Neoplatonic concept of reality as held by the late medieval Augustinians: the ultimate reality is God, man is made in His image, and in creation we can see the traces of His handiwork. This concept is the basis for the theory of ascent from without to within to above:

That we may arrive at an understanding of the First Principle, which is most spiritual and eternal and above us, we ought to proceed through the traces which are corporeal and temporal and outside us [extra nos]; and this is to be led into the way of God. We ought next to enter into our minds, which are the eternal image of God, spiritual and internal [intra nos]; and this is to walk in the truth of God. We ought finally to pass over into that which is eternal, most spiritual, and above us [supra nos], looking to the First Principle; and this is to rejoice in the knowledge of God and in the reverence of His majesty.[21]

The contemplative's ascent to God figures the three stages of fallen mankind's return to the Father through the Law of Nature, the Law of Scripture, and the Law of Grace, which contain the shadow of truth, the image of truth, and the body of truth, respectively.[22] Fallen man

---

Dum igitur mens se ipsam considerat, per se tanquam per speculum consurgit ad speculandam Trinitatem beatam, Patris, Verbi et Amoris. [*Mind's Road*, 26: If then God is perfect spirit, He has memory, intelligence, and will; and He has both the begotten Word and spirated Love. These are necessarily distinguished, since one is produced from the other —distinguished, not essentially or accidentally, but personally. When therefore the mind considers itself, it rises through itself as though a mirror to the contemplation of the Blessed Trinity—Father, Word, and Love].

[21] Bonaventura, *Mind's Road*, 8; *Opera Omnia*, 5, 297: quod perveniamus ad primum principium considerandum, quod est *spiritualissimum* et *aeternum* et *supra nos*, oportet nos *transire* per *vestigium*, quod est *corporale* et *temporale* et *extra nos*, et hoc est *deduci in via Dei;* oportet, nos *intrare* ad mentem nostram, quae est *imago* Dei *aeviterna, spiritualis* et *intra nos,* et hoc est *ingredi in veritate Dei;* oportet, nos *transcendere* ad *aeternum, spiritualissimum,* et *supra nos,* aspiciendo ad primum principium, et hoc est *laetari in Dei notitia et reverentia maiestatis.*

[22] *Hugh of Saint Victor on the Sacraments of the Christian Faith* (*De Sacramentis*), trans. Roy J. Deferrari (Cambridge, Mass., 1951), 185–186; *PL*, 176, 346: Videntur ergo prima illa sacramenta quae sub naturali

was placed in this world in a place of repentance, since a time for repenting was granted that he might correct his evils, restore his goods, so that finally coming to judgment corrected he might receive not punishment for guilt but the glory prepared for him for justice. It remains, therefore, that while there is time he seek counsel and ask help for his correction and liberation. But, since he is found sufficient of himself for neither, it is necessary that He, who by His grace postpones judgment, by the same grace meanwhile show counsel for escaping, and after counsel bring help. . . . For such a reason, therefore, in the time of the natural law man was left entirely to himself, afterwards in the time of the written law counsel was given to him when he realized his ignorance, finally in the time of grace help was furnished him when he confessed his lack.[23]

Alone in the "erber" the narrator, like man in the time of the natural law, a time of sorrow and repentance, is left entirely to himself, unable to overcome his "deuely dele" [evil grief] (51), until "He, who by his grace postpones judgment, by the same grace meanwhile show counsel for escaping." When the dreamer's "goste is gon in Godeʒ grace / In auenture þer meruayleʒ meuen" [spirit has gone, in God's grace, on an adventure where marvels occur] (63–64), he, like man in the time of the written

---

lege praecesserunt, quasi quaedam umbra veritatis; illa vero quae postea sub scripta lege secuta sunt, quasi quaedam imago vel figura veritatis; ista autem quae sub gratia novissime consequuntur non jam umbra vel imago, sed corpus veritatis. [Therefore, those first sacraments which preceded under the law seem as it were a kind of shadow of the truth; those indeed which followed afterwards under the written law seem, as it were, a kind of image or figure of the truth, but these which follow last under grace not indeed a shadow or image but a body of truth.]

[23] Hugh of St. Victor, *On the Sacraments*, 143; *PL*, 76, 307: Positus est ergo homo in mundo isto in loco poenitentiae, spatio paenitendi indulto, ut mala corrigeret, bona repararet, ut tandem correctus ad judicium veniens; non pro culpa poenam, sed pro justitia gloriam sibi praeparatam acciperet. Restat ergo ut dum tempus est consilium exquirat et auxilium requirat correctionis et liberationis suae. Sed quia ipse per se ad neutrum sufficiens invenitur, necesse est ut ille qui per gratiam suam differt judicium, interim per eamdem gratiam ostendat evadendi consilium; et post consilium conferat auxilium. . . . Tali igitur ratione in tempore naturalis legis totus homo dimissus est sibi; postea in tempore scriptae legis cognoscenti ignorantiam suam datum est consilium; postremo in tempore gratiae confitenti defectum suum praestitum est auxilium.

law, must "seek counsel and ask help for his correction and liberation" from the heavenly maiden. Finally, when, like man in the time of grace, he has "confessed his lack"—"I am bot mokke and mul among" [I am only muck and mold mingled] (905)— help, in the form of the *visio* of the New Jerusalem, is furnished by that same grace through the Redeemer:

> Bot of þe Lombe I haue þe aquylde
> For a syȝt þerof þurȝ gret fauor.   (967–968)

> [But I have obtained for you from the Lamb
> a vision of it through His great kindness.]

III. The Realm Without

The "erber" is the created sensible, transitory world of man under the natural law. It is described as a real medieval garden; there is nothing in it that is not earthly: the "gresse" [grass] (10) and the "Blomeȝ blayke and blwe and rede" [yellow, blue, and red blossoms] (27) and "Gilofre, gyngure and gromylyoun, / And pyonys powdered ay bytwene" [gillyflower, ginger, and gromwell, and peonies sprinkled all between] (43–44) are all indigenous to this terrestrial globe. The details are all from "the world of growing things," which supplies one of the two main groups of imagery in the poem and is "associated with the dust of the earth."[24] The narrator overemphatically asserts that "Flor and fryte may not be fede" [Flower and fruit may not be faded] (29), but this in the season "Quen corne is coruen wyth crokeȝ kene" [When grain is cut with sharp sickles] (40), and in the teeth of an accumulation of words denoting corruptibility and decay—*clot, moul, rot, moldeȝ, dede,* and *fayly* [*clay, mold, rot, molds, dead* and *fail*]. There is beauty, but there is also decay. This world is, according to Hugh of St.

---

[24] Wendell Stacy Johnson, "The Imagery and Diction of *The Pearl*: Toward an Interpretation," *ELH*, 20 (September, 1953), · 165 [page 32 above].

Victor, the only place where there are both good and evil.[25] Above all the "erber" is a place of sorrow although the narrator has known happiness there: his pearl "wont watʒ whyle deuoyde my wrange / And heuen my happe and al my hele" [once used to ease my ills and lift my fortune and my spirits] (15–16).

The "erber," though essentially the created world of the Father, also contains intimations of the worlds of the Son within and of the Holy Ghost above. The second stanza records unrelieved grief, tempered only by the mysterious sweet song, the first inkling of immortality perceived by the narrator—"ʒet þotʒ me neuer so swete a sange / As stylle stounde let to me stele" [yet it seemed to me that there never was such a sweet song as that quiet hour brought me] (19–20). Since no physical, earthly source is mentioned, the song, it would seem, must come from within or above. The reader may be reminded of the

---

[25] *On the Sacraments*, 142; of the five places discussed—heaven, paradise, the world, purgatory, and hell—only the higher three are represented in *Pearl*: *PL*, 176, 306–307: Quinque sunt loca. Unus in quo est solum bonum et summum bonum. Unus in quo est solum malum et summum malum. Post haec alia duo. Alter sub summo in quo est solum bonum, sed non summum. Alter supra imum in quo est solum malum, sed non summum, in medio unus, in quo est et bonum et malum, neutrum summum. In coelo est solum bonum et summum; in inferno est solum malum et summum; in paradiso est solum bonum sed non summum; in igne purgatorio solum malum, sed non summum; in mundo est bonum et malum, neutrum summum. Paradisus est locus inchoantium et in melius proficientium; et ideo ibi solum esse bonum debuit, quia creatura a malo initiandi non fuit. Non tamen summum esse debuit, quia si summum ibi esset bonum illic positis profectus non esset. Coelum locus est confirmatorum bonorum et per disciplinam ad summum profectum pertingentium. Unum solum summumque bonum in eo collocatum est. . . . Mundus est locus errantium et reparandorum; et ideo simul bonum et malum in eo ordinatum est, ut per bonum quidem consolationem accipiant; per malum vero correctionem. Non tamen summum bonum aut summum malum ibi est, ut sit quo et persistentes in malo deficere, et recedentes a malo proficere possint. [*On the Sacraments*, 142; There are five places: one in which there is only good and the highest good; one in which there is only evil and the highest evil; after these two others, one below the highest in which there is only good but not the highest, the other above the lowest in which there is only evil but not the highest; in the middle a

music of the spheres or of angel song.[26] But the poet does not defy explicit augury; and if my theory of the poem's didactic structure is correct, the song presages a detail of both the marvelous land *within* and the heavenly City *above*. There is in the land "þer meruaylez meuen" [where marvels occur] the song of the birds

---

place in which there are both good and evil, neither the highest. In heaven there is only good and the highest; in hell there is only evil and the highest; in paradise there is only good but not the highest; in the fire of purgatory, evil only but not the highest; in the world there are good and evil, neither the highest. Paradise is the place of those beginning and progressing into better, and there must have been only good there, since creature must not have had its beginning from evil. Yet it must not have been the highest, since if the highest were there those placed there would have no progress. Heaven is the place of the confirmed good and of those who through discipline attain to the highest progress. One good alone and the highest was placed there. . . . The world is the place of the erring and of those who are to be restored, and so good and evil simultaneously were ordered in it, that though good indeed they might receive consolation, but through evil correction. Yet the highest good or the highest evil is not there, that there may be a place where those who persist in evil can regress, and those who recede from evil can progress.]

[26] Walter Hilton, "Of Angels' Song," Horstman, *op. cit.* (see n. 16 *supra*), 1, 177–178: "oure lorde confortes a saule be aungels sange. Qwat þat sange is, it may nouʒt be discried be na bodily lykenesse, for it is gastly and abouen almaner of ymagynacion & reson. It may be felid & perceyued in a saule, bot it may not be schewed. Neuyr-þe-latter I speke þerof to þe as me thynke. Qwen a saule is purified be lufe of god, illumyned by wysdome, stablid be þe myʒte of god, þan is þe eyghe of þe saule opynde to behalde gastly thyngys, as vertuse & aungels & haly saulys [cf. *Pearl*, 1121–1126], & heuenly thyngys." [Our Lord comforts a soul with angels' song. What that song is may not be discovered by any bodily likeness, for it is spiritual and above all manner of imagination and reason. It may be felt and perceived in a soul, but it may not be demonstrated. Nevertheless I tell you how it seems to me. When a soul is purified by the love of God, illumined by wisdom, given stability by the power of God, then the eye of the soul is opened to behold spiritual things such as Virtues and angels and holy souls and heavenly things.]

See also St. Augustine on Psalm 41, *CCL*, 38, 467: quamdam dulcedinem sequendo, interiorem nescio quam et occultam uoluptatem, tamquam de domo Dei sonaret suauiter aliquod organum: et cum ille ambularet in tabernaculo, audito quodam interiore sono, ductus dulcedine, sequens quod sonabat, abstrahens se ab omni strepitu carnis et

Of flaumbande hweʒ, boþe smale and grete;
Bot sytole-stryng and gyternere
Her reken myrþe moʒt not retrete.　　　(90–92)

[of flaming hues, both small and large;
but citole-string and cittern player
cannot recreate its fresh joy.]

In the dialogue the maiden, giving a preview of the heavenly
City, describes its music "As harporeʒ harpen in her harpe"
[so harpers play on their harps] (881), which clearly puts it
a cut above the cittern-and-guitar-like song of the birds. Lest
there be any doubt whether such music could be heard in the
"erber," the dreamer answers an explicit yes, when he describes
the music heard while contemplating the New Jerusalem:

Þen glory and gle watʒ nwe abroched;
Al songe to loue þat gay iuelle.
Þe steuen moʒt stryke þurʒ þe vrþe to helle
Þat þe Vertues of heuen of ioye endyte.
　　　　　　　　　　(1123–1126)

---

sanguinis, peruenit usque ad domum Dei. Nam uiam suam et ductum
suum sic ipse commemorat, quasi diceremus ei: Miraris tabernaculum in
hac terra; quomodo peruenisti ad secretum domus Dei? *In uoce*, inquit,
exultationis et confessionis, soni festiuitatem celebrantis. . . . In domo
Dei festiuitas sempiterna est. . . . Festum sempiternum, chorus angel-
orum: uultus praesens Dei, laetitia sine defectu. . . . De illa aeterna et
perpetua festiuitate sonat nescio quid canorum et dulce auribus cordis;
sed si non perstrepat mundus. [Butler, 23: by following the leading of a
certain delight, an inward mysterious and hidden pleasure, as if from the
house of God there sounded sweetly some instrument; and he, whilst
walking in the tabernacle, hearing a certain inward sound, led on by its
sweetness, and following the guidance of the sound, withdrawing himself
from all noise of flesh and blood, made his way on even to the house of
God. For he tells us of his progress and of his guidance thither; as if he
had been saying, "You are admiring the tabernacle here on earth; how
came you to the sanctuary of the house of God?" and he says, "In the
voice of joy and praise, the sound of keeping holiday." In the house of
God there is a never-ending festival; the angelic choir makes an eternal
holiday, the presence of God's face, joy that never fails. From that everlasting, perpetual festivity there sounds in the ears of the heart a
mysterious strain, melodious and sweet, provided only the world does not
drown the sounds.]

239

[then glory and glee were newly sounded;
all sang for love of that bright jewel.
The sound that the Virtues of heaven sing for joy
might pierce through the earth into hell.]

A reference to the Word may be detected in the biblical allusion
—"graynez dede" [dead seeds] (31). Less vague are the allusions
to the higher faculties, intelligence and will, in the final stanza
of the section, which shows the effect of sorrow on the intellect
and the will, and relates these faculties in turn to the Son and
the Holy Ghost:

À deuely dele in my hert denned,
Þaȝ resoun sette myseluen saȝt.   (51–52)

[an evil grief dwelt in my heart,
even though reason would set me at peace.]

The dreamer's grief clearly runs counter to the intellect, whose
promptings, if followed, would bring peace. His resistance to
the counsel of "resoun" may account for the adjective "deuely,"
which Sister Mary Vincent glosses "wicked."[27] The following
three lines equate the counsel to the lesson taught by the incarnate Word:

I playned my perle þat þer watȝ spenned
Wyth fyrce skylleȝ þat faste faȝt,
Þaȝ kynde of Kryst me comfort kenned.   (53–55)[28]

[I lamented my pearl that was imprisoned there
with violent thoughts that obstinately contended
even though Christ's nature would teach me comfort.]

It is especially fitting that it is the nature of Christ, "the virtue

---

[27] "Some Debatable Words in *Pearl* and Its Theme," *MLN*, 60 (April,
1945), 242 [page 10 above]; Gordon glosses *deuely*, "desolating, dreary,"
but in a note to line 54 (p. 49), he assumes a degree of wickedness in
the narrator's persistence in remaining in that grief: "the nature of Christ
gave him grounds for comfort, but his self-will made him suffer in the
pain of his sorrow."
[28] For lines 54–58, I follow the punctuation of the Hillmann edition.

and wisdom of God, the Word incarnate"[29]—whose resurrection is figured by the *nudum granum* [bare grain] of I Corinthians—that teaches in the "erber." Although the narrator is not able to accept that teaching here, it is essentially the same as the counsel given later in the maiden's discourse. In his present situation, the narrator, alone and unaided, cannot act upon the advice of reason:

> My wreched wylle in wo ay wraȝte;
> I fell vpon þat floury flaȝt.   (56–57)

> [My wretched will labored ever in woe,
> I fell upon that flowery plot.]

The inability of the will to function—to yield either to the "deuely dele" [evil grief] or to the counsel of "resoun"—is explained in the concluding lines of the initial "erber" scene:

> Suche odour to my herneȝ schot,
> I slode vpon a slepyng-slaȝte
> On þat precios perle wythouten spot.   (58–60)

> [Such an odor rose to my brain,
> I fell into a sleeping-fit
> on that precious pearl without spot.]

That the sleeping-fit is directly induced by the odors that rise to the dreamer's brain—the "fayr reflayr" [fair fragrance] that floated from the "erber"—suggests that the temporary arresting of the will is due to the intervention of the Holy Ghost, conventionally designated by the epithet *pneuma*—air, wind, breath, etc.[30] In the following stanza, the explicit statement, "My goste

[29] Bonaventura, *Mind's Road,* 10; *Opera Omnia,* 5, 298: Quod totum fit per Iesum Christum. . . . . Qui cum sit Dei *virtus* et Dei *sapientia,* sit Verbum incarnatum. [All of which is done through Jesus Christ, Who of God is made unto us wisdom and justice and sanctification. . . . He is the virtue and wisdom of God, the Word incarnate.]

[30] This association is supported by Robert of Tombelaine's commentary on Canticles 4:16; *Supra Cantica Canticorum Expositio* (attributed to Gregory the Great by Migne); *PL,* 79, 516: Per Austrum vero calidum scilicet ventum, Spiritus sanctus figuratur: qui dum mentes electorum

is gon in Godeȝ grace," confirms that the "slepyng-slaȝte" [sleeping-fit] is the work of the Holy Ghost. The necessity for divine aid if man is to ascend from this world of sorrow is confirmed by St. Bonaventure in the first chapter of his *Itinerarium mentis in Deum:*

> Blessed is the man whose help is from Thee. In his heart he hath disposed to ascend by steps, in the vale of tears, in the place which he hath set [Ps. 83:6]. Since beatitude is nothing else than the fruition of the highest good, and the highest good is above us, none can be made blessed unless he ascend above himself, not by the ascent of his body but by that of his heart. But we cannot be raised above ourselves except by a higher power raising us up. For howsoever the interior steps are disposed, nothing is accomplished unless it is accompanied by divine aid. Divine help, however, comes to those who seek it from their hearts humbly and devoutly; and this means to sigh for it in this vale of tears, aided only by fervent prayer.[31]

The opening stanza-group of *Pearl* provides a setting eminently suited not only to an elegy or an allegory of fallen mankind's return to God but also to an account of the contemplative experience patterned along the lines of the *Itinerarium*. The "erber"

---

tangit, ab omni torpore relaxat, et ferventes facit, ut bona quaeque desideranter operentur. . . . Surgat ergo Aquilo, et veniat Auster, et perflet hortum Sponsi, et fluant aromata illius: ut videlicet spiritus malignus ab Ecclesia vel ab unaquaque anima discedat, et Spiritus sanctus adveniat. [Through the Southwind, namely the warm wind, the Holy Spirit is figured: which when it touches the minds of the elect, relaxes their torpor, and makes them fervent, so that they work the good things which are desired. . . . The Northwind surges, and the Southwind comes and flows through the garden of the bridegroom, and the aromas thereof flow forth; so that the evil spirit is driven from either the Church or the individual soul, and the Holy Spirit comes.]

[31] *Mind's Road*, 7; *Opera Omnia*, 5, 296–297: *Beatus vir, cuius est auxilium abs te, ascensiones in corde suo disposuit in valle lacrymarum, in loco, quem posuit.* Cum beatitudo nihil aliud sit, quam summi boni fruitio; et summum bonum sit supra nos: nullus potest effici beatus, nisi supra semetipsum ascendat, non ascensu corporali, sed cordiali. Sed supra nos levari non possumus nisi per virtutem superiorem nos elevantem. Quantumcumque enim gradus interiores disponantur, nihil fit, nisi divinum auxilium comitetur. Divinum autem auxilium comitatur eos qui petunt ex corde humiliter et devote; et hoc est ad ipsum suspirare in hac *lacrymarum valle*, quod fit per ferventem orationem.

is verily a vale of tears; it contains no detail that is not appropriate to the corruptible, temporal world of fallen man: the central imagery is traditionally associated with the transitory—"Omnis caro foenum, et omnis gloria ejus quasi flos agri" [All flesh is grass, and all the glory thereof as the flower of the field] (Isaias 40:6). It is a place of both good and evil, beauty and decay, light and shade—"Schadowed þis worteʒ ful schyre and schene" [Shaded by these plants full bright and fair] (42). It is a place of repentance, where man is found sufficient of himself for neither correction nor liberation. In the final stanza of group 1, the sorrowful narrator, lamenting his lost pearl, is given counsel and help, and the nature of these is presented most systematically, albeit poetically: (1) the reason offers counsel (51–52); (2) the source of that counsel is the incarnate Word (52–54); (3) the will is unable to act according to that counsel (56–57); (4) so the Holy Ghost, the dispenser of grace, brings help.

IV. THE REALM WITHIN

The land "þer meruayleʒ meuen" [where marvels occur] is the intelligible, spiritual world of man under the written law, a realm midway between earth and heaven. It is a land of gems as well as of plants: gems, which provide an appropriate imagery for the eternal and incorruptible, comprise almost exclusively the adornment of the heavenly City; plants, which provide the only adornment for the corruptible earthly "erber," are in the marvelous land notably unearthly—trees with "bolleʒ as blwe as ble of Ynde" [trunks as blue as the dye of India] (76) and leaves shimmering "As bornyst syluer" [as burnished silver] (77). There is only beauty here, no hint of decay, and the only suggestion of possible evil is that which the dreamer brings with him from his earthly experience of having loved a transitory good too well:

> But woþeʒ mo iwysse þer ware,
> Þe fyrre I stalked by þe stronde.

> And euer me þo3t I schulde not wonde
> For wo þer wele3 so wynne wore.   (151–154)

> [But more perils, indeed, were there,
> the farther I walked along the strand.
> And it ever seemed to me that I should not go
> where such delightful riches were for fear of woe.

Among the *quinque loca* [five places] of Hugh of St. Victor is one where "there is only good but not the highest. . . . Paradise is the place of those beginning and progressing into better, and there must have been only good there, since creature must not have had its beginning from evil. Yet it must not have been the highest, since if the highest were there those placed there would have no progress."[32] The marvelous land is certainly a place of progress for the dreamer, who tentatively identifies it as "Paradyse" (137)—understood by theologians to be either an actual place or a stage of the spiritual life.[33]

Although the dreamer is somewhat hesitant to state outright that the land "þer meruayle3 meuen" is the earthly Paradise, he shows no reticence when it comes to asserting its superiority to the "erber" or its inferiority to the maiden's side of the stream, the heavenly Paradise, which as yet he cannot enter—"Þy corse in clot mot calder keue" [your body must sink colder into the clay] (320). The landscape has such a powerful effect on the narrator that not once before he encounters the maiden is the

---

[32] *On the Sacraments*, 142; see *supra* n. 25.

[33] Patch, 143 ff., discusses the three general opinions as to the nature of Paradise: "One by which its physical reality is understood and accepted; one by which it is taken in a spiritual and so figurative way; and a third by which at times it is understood as a material fact and at times interpreted spiritually. The third view is the one which he [St. Augustine] himself favors; so for him Paradise undoubtedly signifies the place in which man was first created. . . . But he recognizes also the spiritual paradise not only in derivative meaning but as an actual region—in fact, every place wherein it is well with the soul or where blessed souls are." Patch cites the opinions of, among others, Isidore of Seville, Rabanus Maurus, Peter Lombard, St. Thomas Aquinas, and St. Bonaventure, all of whom agree with the double interpretation.

lost pearl mentioned, and grief is alluded to only in a negative way: "The adubbemente of þo downeȝ dere / Garten my goste al greffe forȝete" [the adornment of those precious downs caused my spirit to forget all grief] (85–86). His "deuely dele" [evil grief] is, in fact, so effectively subdued that even the sight of pearls does not revive it when the dreamer, all of whose "hele" [well-being] in the "erber" had been a single small pearl so fine that "Oute of oryent" he never "proued . . . her precios pere" [from the orient . . . found its precious equal] (3–4), is confronted by the meanest adornment of this paradise—"þe grauayl þat on grounde con grynde / Wern precious perleȝ of oryente" [the gravel that crunched on the ground was precious orient pearls] (81–82).

Having grown accustomed to the wonders about him and having become aware of degrees of the wonderful, desire (a movement of the will) becomes again operative and he seeks a means of attaining the farther shore: "Abowte me con I stote and stare; / To fynde a forþe faste con I fonde" [I stopped and stared around me; I tried diligently to find a ford] (149–150). With the revival of will he becomes again aware of the "daungere" [danger of loss] inherent in the felicity of earthlings—of "wo þer weleȝ so wynne wore" [woe where such delightful riches were]. At this moment he sees on the far shore "A mayden of menske, ful debonere" [a maiden of dignity, of high estate] (162), whom he identifies with his lost pearl. As the "adubbemente" [adornment] of the earthly Paradise caused him to forget his grief for the lost earthly pearl associated with "luf-daungere" [love's power to withhold] (11), the sight of the pearl-maiden associated with "luf-longyny" [love-longing] (1152), by reminding him of his earthly desire, reintroduces the concept of loss, an awareness of the potential "daungere" [danger of loss] in desire:

> More þen me lyste my drede aros.
> I stod ful stylle and dorste not calle;

Wyth yȝen open and mouth ful clos
I stod as hende as hawk in halle.   (181–184)

[More than my desire my dread arose.
I stood absolutely still and dared not call;
with eyes wide open and mouth shut tight,
I stood as quiet and alert as a hawk in the hall.

The dreamer is once again reduced to a state of inaction; the forces of desire and dread are in balance. In the "erber" reason offered counsel which his "wreched wylle" rejected. He is now in a somewhat better position to accept reason's counsel when it is offered by the maiden; the *visio* of the marvelous land with all its brilliance has enabled the soul, in the words of Hugh of St. Victor, "to distinguish light from darkness, that is virtues from vices, so that it may dispose itself to order and conform to truth."[34] The dreamer, if not clearly able to distinguish vices

---

[34] *On the Sacraments*, 16–17. The significance of the dazzling brilliance of the marvelous land—where the "rych rokkeȝ" [precious stones] are so bright "þe lyȝt of hem myȝt no man leuen, / Þe glemande glory þat of hem glent" [no man can believe their light—the gleaming glory that shines from them] (69–70)—appropriate to the dreamer's enlightenment (cf. the Lamb-lamp pun—945), is suggested by Hugh's explanation of why light was created before the sun; *PL*, 176, 195: Ego puto magnum hic aliquod sacramentum commendari; quia omnis anima quandiu in peccato est, quasi in tenebris est quibusdam et confusione. Sed non potest evadere confusionem suam et ad ordinem justitiae formamquae disponi, nisi illuminetur primum videre mala sua, et discernere lucem a tenebris, hoc est virtutes a vitiis, ut se disponat ad ordinem et conformet veritati. Hoc igitur anima in confusione jacens sine luce facere non potest; et propterea necesse est primum ut lux fiat, ut videat semetipsam, et agnoscat horrorem et turpitudinem confusionis suae, et explicet se atque coaptet ad illam rationabilem dispositionem et ordinem veritatis. [*On the Sacraments*, 16–17: I think that here a great sacrament is commended, because every soul, as long as it is in sin, is in a kind of darkness and confusion. But it can not emerge from its confusion and be disposed to the order and form of justice, unless it be first illumined to see its evils, and to distinguish light from darkness, that is, virtues from vices, so that it may dispose itself to order and conform to truth. Thus, therefore, a soul lying in confusion can not do without light, and on this account it is necessary first that light be made, that the soul may see itself, and recognize the horror and shamefulness of its confusion, and extricate itself, and fit itself to that rational disposition and order of truth.]

from virtues, is at least able to distinguish the good of the near side of the stream from the higher good of the far side, and while remembrance of the transitory earthly pearl revives dread, thoughts of a higher, spiritual good bring hope:[35]

> I hoped þat gostly watȝ þat porpose;
> I dred onende quat schulde byfalle,
> Lest ho me eschaped þat I þer chos.   (185–187)

> [I hoped that the purpose was spiritual;
> I dreaded concerning what was to happen
> lest she whom I beheld there escape from me.]

His hope and dread arise from his present limited knowledge of the two pearls—hope from the sight of the heavenly maiden, dread from the memory of the lost earthly gem. As the dreamer awaits what shall befall, he not only retains the present appearance of the maiden but also recalls his lost pearl and looks to a possible future good. The initial *visio*, through description, presents the realm *within* as it exists in the memory, whose operation is "retention and representation, not only of things present, corporeal, and temporal, but also of past and future things, simple and eternal. For memory retains the past by recalling it, the present by receiving it, the future by foreseeing it."[36]

Dread does not now outweigh hope as it did in the "erber,"

---

[35] "Hope" as a verb in *Pearl* frequently has the meaning "think" or "believe," but in this passage it is contrasted to "drede," which Gordon glosses "was afraid" though it can also mean "doubted." That the contrast "hope-dread" rather than "belief-doubt" takes precedence here is suggested by "Lest ho me eschaped" [Lest she escaped from me], which recalls that the lamented earthly pearl "fro me yot" [went from me] (10); similarly, in "I hoped þe water were a deuyse" [I hoped (believed) the water was a device] (139), and "I hoped þat mote merked wore" [I hoped (believed) that city was situated] (142), there is some ambiguity, especially in view of the poet's fondness for word-play—e.g. "mote" in line 142 which is played upon in stanza-group 17.

[36] Bonaventura, *Mind's Road*, 22; *Opera Omnia*, 5, 303: *Operatio* autem *memoriae* est retentio et repraesentatio non solum *praesentium, corporalium* et *temporalium,* verum etiam *succedentium, simplicium* et *sempiternalium.*—Retinet namque memoria *praeterita* per recordationem, *praesentia* per susceptionem, *futura* per praevisionem.

and when the maiden hails him, the dreamer's eagerness to answer suggests that he is ready to receive her instruction—that counsel of "resoun" rejected earlier:

> Wel watʒ me þat euer I watʒ bore
> To sware þat swete in perleʒ pyʒte!   (239–240)
>
> [It was good for me that I was born
> to answer that sweet one adorned in pearls!]

The foregoing analysis of the dreamer's side of the marvelous land, which I have identified with the *paradisus terrestris* [earthly paradise], locates it between the earthly and heavenly realms. The identification of the maiden's side with the *paradisus coelestis* [heavenly paradise] is somewhat tenuous but seems borne out by the fact that in the final section of the poem the maiden clearly enjoys the beatific vision and the dreamer cannot cross the stream without first suffering death. What is important is the identification of the marvelous land with the spiritual state, the realm *within,* the realm of the faculties of the soul—memory, intelligence, and will. The dream proper, entirely an adventure of the dreamer's "goste" [spirit] and as such belonging to the *within* realm of the contemplative, has as its *locus operandi* [setting] the earthly Paradise. The realm described in the initial *visio* in terms which relate to the world *without* through sense images is retained and represented in the *memory;* the heavenly maiden in the central dialogue, which constitutes the major portion of the dream, instructs the *intellect;* and in the final *visio,* the will, the affective faculty, relates to the world *above* through desire. Thus the dream is threefold according to the faculties, but the dreamer's spirit remains in the *within* realm. The primacy of the intelligible and spiritual is confirmed by the central position of the dialogue, whose unquestionably intellectual character is pointed out by Gordon: "Dramatically the debate represents a long process of thought and mental struggle, an experience as real as the first blind grief of bereavement. In his first mood, even if he had been granted a vision of the blessed in Heaven, the dreamer would have received it incredulously or rebelliously."[37]

He would, that is, have received it in precisely the manner in which he first receives the instruction of his celestial mentor, who must warn him "anger gayneȝ þe not a cresse. / Who nedeȝ schal þole, be not so þro" [Anger will get you nothing. Whoever has to, will suffer, be not so stubborn.] (344–345). The debate corresponds to Hugh of St. Victor's meditative mode of cognition, in which "there is a wrestling of ignorance with knowledge."[38] Ultimately knowledge and reason prevail, and the dreamer, purged of his pride, asks one last boon, a sight of the maiden's dwelling. She then directs him to the "borneȝ heued" [stream's head] (974) where he comes to a hill from which he can contemplate the heavenly City as it sinks to within his range.

V. The Realm Above

The heavenly City—" 'ceté of God,' oþer 'syȝt of pes' " ["city of God" or "vision of peace"] (952), where there "is noȝt bot pes to glene / Þat ay schal laste wythouten reles" [is nothing to harvest except peace that shall last forever without end] (955–956)—is a traditional symbol of the mystical, divine world perceived under the law of grace. Its superiority to the other realms is both explicit and implied in the imagery. It must sink down in order to be viewed, and the refrain of stanza-group 18, "sunne ne mone," emphasizes its position above the corruptible sublunary realm. The marvelous land dazzled with its brilliant "adubbemente" [adornment], but here is a realm of "glymme pure" [pure radiance] (1088), where the Lamb is "her lantyrne"

---

[37] Gordon, xix.

[38] Taylor, 2, 389; *PL*, 175, 117: In meditatione quasi quaedam lucta est ignorantiae cum scientia, et lumen veritatis quodammodo in media caligine erroris emicat. [Taylor, 2, 389: In meditation there is a wrestling of ignorance with knowledge; and the light of truth gleams as in a fog of error.]

[their lantern] (1047) and "Þe planeteȝ arn in to pouer a plyȝt, / And þe self sunne ful fer to dym" [the planets are in too poor a condition and the sun itself is far too dim] (1075–1076). It is primarily the land of enduring precious gems, not only brilliant but also "sotyle cler" [transparent and clear] (1050), and the only plants "arn tres ful schym / Þat twelue fryteȝ of lyf con bere ful sone" [are bright trees that quickly bear the twelve fruits of life] (1077–1078).

The dreamer does not enter the third, highest and brightest realm but only contemplates it because, as the maiden informs him,

> . . . þat God wyl schylde;
> Þou may not enter wythinne hys tor,
> Bot of þe Lombe I haue þe aquylde
> For a syȝt þerof þurȝ gret fauor.
> Vtwyth to se þat clene cloystor
> Þou may, bot inwyth not a fote;
> To strech in þe strete þou hatȝ no vygour,
> Bot þou were clene wythouten mote.   (965–972)

[. . . that God will prevent;
you may not enter within his castle,
but I have obtained for you from the Lamb
a vision of it through His great kindness.
From outside you may see that pure cloister,
but from within not so much as a square foot;
to walk in its street you have not the power
unless you were pure without spot.]

This preface to the final *visio* appropriately contains an allusion to the Blessed Trinity based on the distinction of the persons according to power, wisdom, and goodness, who operate, dispose, and will:[39] God the Father, "who by His grace postpones

---

[39] Hugh of St. Victor, *On the Sacraments*, 34–35; *PL*, 176, 211: Et vidit [rationalis creatura] Creatoris potentiam et sapientiam et bonitatem a semetipsa, per ea quae foris apparuerunt in agnitionem excitata. Et haec erant quasi admonitio et recordatio prima trinum esse Deum; . . . sed praedicabatur Trinitas ex istis, non significabatur in istis; et tamen haec tria aeterna erant, et causa omnium erant et per haec facta sunt

judgment,"[40] shields in justice; the Lamb disposes in mercy; and "þurʒ gret fauor" (grace), the Holy Ghost wills in love.[41] It also emphasizes the fact that man's return to the Father, "to Whom no one can enter properly save through the Crucified,"[42] must be the gift of grace, which after counsel brings help.

If my theory is tenable that the triple division of the dream proper is based on the division of the soul into three faculties— memory, intelligence, and will—the ascendency of the will over the other two should be demonstrable in this final vision. To determine this ascendency it is necessary first to review the func-

---

omnia, et ipsa non sunt facta; et assignavimus bonitati voluntatem, et sapientiae dispositionem; et postestati operationem. [And it (the rational creature) saw the power and wisdom and goodness of the Creator by itself, on being moved to perceive them through these things which appeared externally. These things were, so to speak, the first admonition and recollection that God is threefold . . . but the Trinity was predicated from these, not signified in these. Yet these three things were eternal and were the cause of all things; through these all were made, and they themselves were not made. We have to goodness will, and to wisdom disposition, and to power operation.]

[40] See *supra* n. 23.

[41] For a discussion of will and the Holy Ghost see E. Talbot Donaldson, *Piers Plowman: the C-Text and Its Poet* (New Haven, 1949), 188– 192. In *Piers Plowman* the three props of the tree of charity are listed in the C-text (Passus xix): (1) "*Potencia-dei-patris*" [Power-of-god-the-father] (line 34), (2) "*Sapiencia-dei-patris*, The which is the passion and penaunce and the parfytnesse of Iesus" [Wisdom-of-god-the-father, which is the passion and penance and the perfection of Jesus] (lines 40–41), and (3) "*Spiritus-sanctus* [Holy Spirit]. . . . And that is grace of the Holy Gost" (lines 51–52); in the corresponding section of the B-text (Passus xvi), the first two props are similarly named (lines 30; 36–37), and the third, though not named, is wielded by "Liberum-Arbitrium" [Free Choice] (line 50).

[42] Bonaventura, *Mind's Road*, 4; *Opera Omnia*, 5, 295: Effigies igitur sex alarum seraphicarum insinuat sex illuminationes scalares, quae a creaturis incipiunt et perducunt usque ad Deum, ad quem nemo intrat recte nisi per Crucifixum. [For by those six wings are rightly to be understood the six stages of illumination by which the soul, as if by steps or progressive movements, was disposed to pass into peace by ecstatic elevations of Christian wisdom. The way, however, is only through the most burning love of the Crucified.]

tion of the will in the "erber" and in the marvelous land. According to St. Bonaventure, there are three aspects of an act of the will:

The operation of the power of choice is found in deliberation, judgment, and desire. Deliberation is found in inquiring what is better, this or that. But the better has no meaning except by its proximity to the best. But such proximity is measured by degrees of likeness. No one, therefore, can know whether this is better than that unless he knows that this is closer to the best. . . . Therefore the idea of the good must be involved in every deliberation about the highest good.

Certain judgment of the objects of deliberation comes about through some law. But none can judge with certainty through law unless he be certain that that law is right and that he ought not to judge it. But the mind judges itself. Since, then, it cannot judge the law it employs in judging, that law is higher than our minds; and through this higher law one makes judgments according to the degree with which it is impressed upon it. But there is nothing higher than the human mind except Him Who made it. Therefore our deliberative faculty in judging reaches upward to divine laws if it solves its problems completely.

Now desire is of that which especially moves one. But that especially moves one which is especially loved. But happiness is loved above all. But happiness does not come about except through the best and ultimate end. Human desire, therefore, seeks nothing unless it be the highest good or something which leads to it or something which has some resemblance to it. So great is the force of the highest good that nothing can be loved except through desire for it by a creature which errs and is deceived when it takes truth's image and likeness for the truth.[43]

[43] Bonaventura, *Mind's Road*, 25–26; *Opera Omnia*, 5, 304–305: *Operatio* autem virtutis *electivae* attenditur in *consilio, judicio* et *desiderio*. —*Consilium* autem est in inquirendo, quid sit melius, hoc an illud. Sed melius non dicitur nisi per accessum ad optimum; accessus autem est secundum maiorem assimilationem: nullus ergo scit, utrum hoc sit illo melius, nisi sciat, illud optimo magis assimilari. . . . omni igitur *consilianti* necessario est impressa notio summi boni.

Iudicium autem certum de consiliabilibus est per aliquam legem. Nullus autem certitudinaliter iudicat legem, nisi certus sit, quod illa lex recta est, et quod ipsam iudicare non debet; sed mens nostra iudicat de se ipsa: cum igitur non possit iudicare de lege, per quam iudicat; lex illa superior est mente nostra, et per hanc iudicat, secundum quod sibi impressa est. Nihil autem est superius mente humana, nisi solus ille qui fecit eam: igitur in iudicando *deliberativa* nostra pertingit ad divinas leges, si *plena resolutione* dissolvat.

Desiderium autem principaliter est illius quod maxime ipsum movet.

In the final stanza of the opening section the dreamer's "wreched wylle" (56) has been deceived and taken truth's image and likeness (the earthly pearl) for the truth, and has also been unable to accept reason's counsel as to what was better; as a result the will has been rendered inoperative, and the narrator "slode vpon a slepyng-slaȝte" [fell into a sleeping-fit] (59)—the initial gift of grace. In the marvelous land the dreamer exhibits certain functions of the will; perceiving the degrees of goodness evident on the two sides of the stream, he desires to cross over to the "loueloker" [lovelier] land and seeks "To fynde a forþe" [to find a ford] (150), but the sight of the maiden halts his purpose. It is as if he cannot judge between the maiden before him (something which leads to the highest good) and the lost pearl held in his memory (something which bears the resemblance to it) until he is informed by that law which is higher than our minds. His will once more is temporarily stayed:

> I stod ful stylle and dorste not calle;
> Wyth yȝen open and mouth ful clos
> I stod as hende as hawk in halle.   (182–184)

> [I stood absolutely still and dared not call;
> with eyes wide open and mouth shut tight,
> I stood as alert and quiet as a hawk in the hall.]

The dialogue which follows is in part an impressing of this higher law upon his mind so that he may properly make judgment (note especially the use of "deme" [consider, allow, judge] as refrain for stanza-group 6) according to the higher reason. He is at last ready to receive the final *visio* neither

---

Maxime autem movet quod maxime amatur; maxime autem amatur esse beatum; beatum autem esse non habetur nisi per optimum et finem ultimum: nihil igitur appetit humanum *desiderium* nisi quia summum bonum, vel quia est ad illud, vel quia habet aliquam effigiem illius. Tanta est vis summi boni, ut nihil nisi per illius desiderium a creatura possit amari, quae tunc fallitur et errat, cum effigiem et simulacrum pro veritate acceptat.

incredulously nor rebelliously, and the heavenly City descends. It is described almost precisely as it was seen by the Apostle in an earlier and more famous "gostly drem" [spiritual dream] (790), and its effect on the dreamer is recorded in terms which insist on comparison to the initial effect of the *visio* of the marvelous land:

> An-vnder mone so great merwayle
> No fleschly hert ne myʒt endeure   (1081–1082)
>
> [No fleshly heart beneath the sphere of the moon
> could endure so great a marvel.]

The adornments of the marvelous land were such that

> . . . vrþely herte myʒt not suffyse
> To þe tenþe dole of þo gladneʒ glade.   (135–136)
>
> [. . . earthly heart might not contain
> a tenth part of those glad joys.]

Even more striking is the use of the bird figure recalling the earlier "hawk in halle":

> I stod as stylle as dased quayle
> For ferly of þat frelich fygure,
> Þat felde I nawþer reste ne trauayle,
> So watʒ I rauyste wyth glymme pure.   (1085–1088)
>
> [I stood as still as a stunned quail,
> in amazement at that noble figure,
> so that I felt no bodily sensations
> I was so ravished by that pure radiance.]

The similarity of the figures used to depict wonder—the hawk and the quail—further emphasizes that as "þo downeʒ dere" [those precious downs] surpass the "erber," and as the pearl-maiden surpasses the earthly Paradise, so the heavenly City surpasses the maiden amid the beauties of the heavenly Paradise. The effect portrayed is that recorded by the contemplatives. In the commentary on Psalm 41, St. Augustine describes the effect of arriving at the house of God (the throne, "Þe hyʒe Godeʒ self hit set vpone" [the high God himself sat upon it] [1054], is seen in the heavenly City): "when I come to *the house of God,* I am even struck dumb with astonishment."[44] St. Bonaventure, in the *Itinerarium,* says of contemplation of the eternal light, "The irradiation and consideration of this light holds the wise suspended in wonder."[45] The earlier simile of wonder, "as hende as hawk in halle" [as alert and quiet as a hawk in the hall], hints of the dreamer's disposition to receive the instruction necessary to judge the forces of desire and dread: the simile here, "as stylle as dased quayle," suggests not discipline but astonishment, as does "ferly" [amazement] of lines 1084 and 1086. In this instance there are no conflicting stimuli; the dreamer feels "nawþer reste ne trauayle" [neither rest nor toil, i.e., no bodily sensations] (1087). The inaction is not a weakening of the will, but the necessary reaction of a mortal creature—appropriately figured by an animal[46]—when confronted by the highest good; it is but a prelude to ravishment, which is a violent movement of will and the ultimate effect of intense desire.

The dreamer's will at this point contemplates the highest good itself, not something that leads to it or something which has some resemblance to it; it sees truth, not "truth's image and

---

[44] Butler, 23; *CCL*, 38, 466: stupeo cum peruenio usque ad domum Dei.

[45] *Mind's Road,* 27; *Opera Omnia,* 5, 305–306: Et ideo mens nostra tantis splendoribus irradiata et superfusa, nisi sit caeca, manuduci potest per semetipsam ad contemplandam illam lucem aeternam. Huius autem lucis irradiatio et consideratio sapientes suspendit in admirationem et econtra insipientes, qui non credunt, ut intelligant, ducit in perturbationem. [And thus our minds, illumined and suffused by such great radiance, unless they be blind, can be led through themselves alone to the contemplation of that eternal light. This irradiation and consideration of this light holds the wise suspended in wonder; and, on the other hand, it leads into confusion the foolish, who do not believe that they may understand.]

[46] The infrequent animal images in *Pearl* appear to be used to figure the soul joined to the flesh in its earthly existence. The hawk and quail similes serve to remind the reader that the dreamer's soul, only temporarily released from his body by the dream, is still subject to certain limitations of the earthly condition, and the doe image (line 345) likewise suggests the soul's confinement.

likeness." The cause of his ravishment is the essence of the heavenly City, the "glymme pure" [pure radiance], an intensity of light which traditionally figures the essential, hidden, divine reality in the writings of contemplatives.

In his *Confessions,* St. Augustine describes the ascent to light in a passage containing a remarkable number of parallels to the marvelous adventure in *Pearl:*

Step by step was I led upwards, from bodies to the soul which perceives by means of the bodily senses; and thence to the soul's inward faculty to which the bodily senses report external things, which is the limit of the intelligence of animals; and thence again to the reasoning faculty, to whose judgment is referred the knowledge received by the bodily senses. And when this power also within me found itself changeable, it lifted itself up to its own intelligence, and withdrew its thoughts from experience, abstracting itself from the contradictory throng of sense images, that it might find what that light was wherein it was bathed when it cried out that beyond all doubt the unchangeable is to be preferred to the changeable; whence also it knew That Unchangeable: and thus with the flash of one trembling glance it arrived at THAT WHICH IS. And then at last I saw Thy "invisible things understood by the things that are made:" but I could not sustain my gaze, and my weakness being struck back, I was relegated to my ordinary experience, bearing with me but a loving memory and a longing for what I had, as it were, perceived the odour of, but was not yet able to feed upon.[47]

The ultimate truth symbolized by the "glymme pure" is also fig-

---

[47] Butler, 31–32; *PL,* 32, 745: Atque ita gradatim a corporibus ad sentientem per corpus animam; atque inde ad ejus interiorem vim, cui sensus corporis exteriora annuntiaret; et quosque possunt bestiae: atque inde rursus ad ratiocinantem potentiam ad quam refertur judicandum quod sumitur a sensibus corporis. Quae se quoque in me comperiens mutabilem, erexit se ad intelligentiam suam; et abduxit cogitationem a consuetudine, subtrahens se contradicentibus turbis phantasmatum, ut inveniret quo lumine aspergeretur, cum sine ulla dubitatione clamaret incommutabile praeferendum esse mutabili; unde nosset ipsum incommutabile, quod nisi aliquo modo nosset, nullo modo illud mutabili certo praeponeret. Et pervenit ad id quod est, in ictu trepidantis aspectus. Tunc vero invisibilia tua, per ea quae facta sunt, intellecta conspexi; sed aciem figere non evalui: et repercussa infirmitate redditus solitis, non mecum ferebam nisi amantem memoriam, et quasi olfacta desiderantem quae comedere nondum possem.

ured in *Pearl* by the heavenly City, presented in a set of images as detailed as those of the earthly Paradise. I suggest that the poet adheres strictly to the details of the Apocalypse precisely because the contemplatives tend to shun all corporeal images except those authenticated by Sacred Scripture.

St. Bernard of Clairvaux, noted for his use of the love imagery of Canticles to depict contemplative union, offers a theory of visual imagery in his commentary on Canticles 1:10 which helps explain the use of such imagery in the final *visio* of *Pearl,* which I assert appeals not to the memory but to the will:

"Pendants of gold and studs of silver." This means, I think, nothing else than to weave certain spiritual likenesses, and to bring the most pure meanings of divine wisdom into the sight of the mind which is contemplating, in order that it may perceive, at least by a mirror and in an enigma, what it cannot at all as yet look upon face to face. What I speak of are things divine, and wholly unknown but to those who have experienced them, how, that is, in this mortal body, while yet the state of faith endures and the substance of the clear Light is not yet made manifest, the contemplation of pure truth can yet anticipate its action in us, at least in part; so that some, even among us, to whom this has been granted from above, can employ the Apostle's word, "Now I know in part," and again, "We know in part, and we prophesy in part." For when something from God (divinitus) has momentarily and, as it were, with the swiftness of a flash of light, shed its ray upon the mind in ecstasy of spirit, whether for the tempering of this too great radiance, or for the sake of imparting it to others, forthwith there present themselves, when I know not, certain imaginary likenesses of lower things, suited to the meanings which have been infused from above, by means of which that most pure and brilliant ray of truth is in a manner shaded, and becomes both more bearable to the soul itself, and more capable of being communicated to whomsoever the latter wishes.[48]

[48] Butler, 105; *PL*, 183, 986: Quod ego non puto esse aliud, quam texere spirituales quasdam similitudines, et in ipsis purissima divinae sapientiae sensa animae contemplantis conspectibus importare, ut videat, saltem per speculum et in aenigmate, quod nondum facie ad faciem valet ullatenus intueri. Divina sunt, et nisi expertis prorsus incognita quae effamur; quomodo videlicet in hoc mortali corpore, fide adhuc habente statum, et necdum propalata perspicui substantia luminis, jam tamen [*alias,* interim] purae interdum contemplatio veritatis partes suas agere

The highest good, the "glymme pure," "that most pure and brilliant ray of truth," is expanded into a detailed visual image so that it may be "more bearable to the soul itself, and more capable of being communicated." The initial *visio* was received by the memory as a set of images which in themselves had the power to enchant, to draw the dreamer from thoughts of his earthly pearl, itself an image which bears but a likeness to good. The final *visio* is apprehended as truth itself, and the images which make it bearable and communicable are all authenticated by "þe apostel John." The images of sense with which the light that "holds the wise suspended in wonder" is veiled, are seen by St. Bonaventure to be a renewal of the *inner* senses:

For it [contemplation] occurs in affective experience rather than in rational consideration. On this level, when the inner senses are renewed in order to perceive the highest beauty, to hear the highest harmony, smell the highest fragrance, taste the highest delicacy, apprehend the highest delights, the soul is disposed to mental elevation through devotion, wonder, and exultation. . . . When this is accomplished, our spirit is made hierarchical to mount upward through its conformity to the heavenly Jerusalem, into which no one enters unless through grace it has descended into his heart, as John saw in his Apocalypse.[49]

---

intra nos vel ex parte praesumit; ita ut liceat usurpare etiam alicui nostrum, cui hoc datum desuper fuerit, illud Apostoli: *Nunc cognosco ex parte*: item, *Ex parte cognoscimus, et ex parte prophetamus* (I Cor. 13:12–9). Cum autem divinius aliquid raptim et veluti in velocitate corusci luminis interluxerit menti spiritu excedenti, sive ad temperamentum nimii splendoris, sive ad doctrinae usum, continuo, nescio unde, adsunt imaginatoriae quaedam rerum inferiorum similitudines, infusis divinitus sensibus convenienter accommodatae, quibus quodam modo adumbratus purissimus ille ac splendidissimus veritatis radius, et ipsi animae tolerabilior fiat, et quibus communicare illum voluerit.

[49] *Mind's Road*, 29–30; *Opera Omnia*, 5, 306–307: quia magis est in experientia affectuali quam in consideratione rationali. In hoc namque gradu, reparatis sensibus interioribus ad sentiendum summe pulcrum, audiendum summe harmonicum, odorandum summe odoriferum, degustandum summe suave, apprehendendum summe delectabile, disponitur anima ad mentales excessus, silicet per *devotionem, admirationem* et *exsultationem*. . . . Quibus adeptis, efficitur spiritus noster *hierarchicus* ad conscendendum sursum secundum conformitatem ad illam Ierusalem supernam, in quam nemo intrat, nisi prius per gratiam ipsa in cor descendat, sicut vidit Ioannes in Apocalypsi sua.

It is the heavenly Jerusalem, "Byȝonde þe brok fro me warde keued" [sunk down on the other side of the brook from me] (980) that ravishes the dreamer, and that city is presented in images as "In þe Apokalypce is þe fasoun preued" [the manner is shown in the Apocalypse] (983). As the dreamer contemplates he becomes suddenly "war of a prosessyoun" [aware of a procession] (1096) and great rejoicing and adoration of the Lamb, and he is moved to love:

> To loue þe Lombe his meyny in melle
> Iwysse I laȝt a gret delyt.   (1127–1128)

> [To love the Lamb among his company,
> I indeed took a great delight.]

This love builds in the dreamer and reaches its climax when he sees his "lyttel quene"—a rank he enviously refused her at the beginning of the dialogue—among her peers:

> Lorde, much of mirþe watȝ þat ho made
> Among her fereȝ þat watȝ so quyt!
> Þat syȝt me gart to þenk to wade
> For luf-longyng in gret delyt.   (1149–1152)

> [Lord, great was the mirth she made
> among her companions that were so white!
> That vision caused me to decide to wade
> the stream for love-longing in great delight.]

A slight difficulty in interpreting *Pearl* stems from improper identification of the antecedent of "Þat syȝt" [that vision]. The supporters of the "tender elegy" school accept the sight of the maiden as the sole object of "luf-longyng" [love-longing]. Since the whole dialogue instructs the dreamer in identifying the proper object of desire from among three pearls—the earthly gem, the pearl-maiden, and the "wonder perle wythouten wemme / Inmyddeȝ hyr breste" [wondrous pearl without flaw set in her breast] (221–222) that is "commune to alle þat ryȝtwys were" [common to all who were righteous] (739)—to assert that the sole object of his desire is the pearl-maiden is a bit like saying that the Mystical Rose in Dante's *Paradiso*

(Canto 3) moves the pilgrim merely because it contains Beatrice. Clearly the pearl which "Is lyke þe reme of heuenesse clere" [Is like the realm of heaven clear] (735) and was set in her breast "in token of pes" [as a token of peace] (742) is the proper object of his desire. It is, in fact, a traditional scriptural symbol of the heavenly City, which holds the throne of God, the Lamb, and the maiden and all her "fereȝ" [companions]. "Þat syȝt" [that vision] refers not to the maiden but to the final *visio* in its entirety. The maiden counselled the dreamer,

> I rede þe forsake þe worlde wode
> And porchace þy perle maskelles   (743–744)
>
> [I counsel you to forsake the mad world
> and purchase your spotless (and matchless) pearl],

not, "come live with me and be my love." Her presence among the rejoicing multitude is the final confirmation of her teaching. Her participation in eternal bliss demonstrates the efficacy of the "Ryche blod [that] ran on rode so roghe" [precious blood that ran on the cross so cruel] (646), which insured the right of both maiden *and* dreamer to purchase the matchless pearl.

The dreamer's act of will is an act of "luf-longyng" for eternal beatitude, symbolized by the heavenly City of the final *visio;* the inclusion of the pearl-maiden among the many adoring the Lamb—"Lorde, much of mirþe watȝ þat ho made" [Lord, great was the mirth she made] (1149)—confirms not only her salvation but also the dreamer's potential for salvation. The elements of the culminating *visio* cannot be separated; there is no choice to be made between City, Lamb, or maiden; there is only desire to be a part of that unity now that his potential beatitude has been demonstrated; sense is battered, intelligence annihilated, and only will, "luf-longyng," remains:

> Delyt me drof in yȝe and ere,
> My maneȝ mynde to maddyny malte;
> Quen I seȝ my frely, I wolde be þere. (1153–1155)

[Delight assailed me through my eyes and ears,
my man's mind melted into madness;
when I saw my fair one, I would be there.]

There is no "luf-daungere" [love's power to cause grief], no
dread; he is determined "To swymme þe remnaunt, þaȝ I þer
swalte" [to swim the remainder of the stream even though I
would die] (1160). He cannot pass by that water in his earthly
condition and so does not attain his goal.

His first words on awaking are not a lament for the loss of his
pearl nor for the loss of the heavenly vision, but a statement that
his will is now completely reconciled to the divine Will; the
maiden has not instructed in vain:

'Now al be to þat Prynceȝ paye.'   (1176)

[Now all be to that Prince's pleasure.]

VI. THE REALM WITHOUT REVISITED

In the final section of *Pearl* the dreamer returns to the
"erber," the *valle lacrymarum* [vale of tears] of the 83rd Psalm,
no longer troubled "Wyth fyrce skylleȝ þat faste faȝt" [with violent thoughts that obstinately contended] (54), but "sete saȝte"
[set at peace] (1201) for he has progressed from love of the
transitory earthly pearl to longing for eternal bliss: "For the
mind which knows not to love its true good is never stable and
never rests. Hence restlessness, and ceaseless labour, and disquiet, until the man turns and adheres to Him. The sick heart
wavers and quivers; the cause of its disease is love of the world;
the remedy, the love of God."[50] He is no longer conscious of
the beauties of the "erber" which is as nought in comparison to
those "kytheȝ þat lasteȝ aye" [regions that last forever] (1198)
which he has just visited; he is no longer "a creature which errs
and is deceived when it takes truth's image and likeness for the

[50] See above, p. 225.

truth."[51] Having perceived the three realms, he can set them in order and realize that the "erber" for all its beauty is truly "þis doel-doungoun" [this dungeon of sorrow]—"the place of the erring and those to be restored."[52] It appears different because before his dream he was as one living under the law of Nature, but now though not in the realm of grace, he is as one living under the law of Grace and he longs for his restoration:

> And rewfully þenne I con to reme:
> 'O Perle,' quod I, 'of rych renoun,
> So watȝ hit me dere þat þou con deme
> In þis veray avysyoun!'　　　　(1181–1184)

> [And then I sorrowfully began to lament:
> "O Pearl," I said, "of rich renown,
> so very precious to me was that which you revealed
> in this true vision!"]

The dreamer's vision of the New Jerusalem, his "syȝt of pes" [vision of peace] (952), obtained at the request of the maiden, we are explicitly told is a true vision, as was implied by the insistent comparisons to the vision which the Apostle "segh in gostly drem" [saw in a spiritual dream] (790). If the maiden has been granted a place in that scene through grace, the dreamer can hope to be granted a similar place also through grace:

> If hit be ueray and soth sermoun
> Þat þou so stykeȝ in garlande gay,
> So wel is me in þys doel-doungoun
> Þat þou art to þat Prynseȝ paye.　　(1185–1188)

> [If it is a true and real account
> that you are thus set in a fair garland,
> then it is well for me in this dungeon of sorrow
> that you are to that Prince's pleasure.]

In the next stanza the dreamer considers his expulsion from the dreamland. Having "ȝerned" [yearned] for "more þen

---

[51] See above, pages 251–252.
[52] Hugh of St. Victor, *On the Sacraments*, 142 (see n. 25 *supra*).

watʒ me gyuen" [more than was granted to me] (1190) and desired more than "moʒte by ryʒt" [might by right] be his portion at that time (1195–1196), he was awakened. His rashness, while not opposing the divine Will, was not in complete accord with it. His penalty completed his lesson in humility:

> Lorde, made hit arn þat agayn þe stryuen,
> Oþer proferen þe oʒt agayn þy paye.   (1199–1200)

> [Lord, they are mad that strive against you
> or offer you aught against your pleasure.]

In the final stanza the dreamer acknowledges the goodness which God has shown him:

> For I haf founden hym, boþe day and naʒte,
> A God, a Lorde, a frende ful fyin.   (1203–1204)

> [For I have found him, both day and night,
> a God, a Lord, a most noble friend.]

In his sorrow, God granted him a marvelous adventure, and afterwards the narrator, no longer coveting his pearl, committed it to God in the blessing of Christ:

> Ouer þis hyul þis lote I laʒte,
> For pyty of my perle enclyin,
> And syþen to God I hit bytaʒte
> In Krysteʒ dere blessyng and myn.   (1205–1208)

> [Upon this mound, bowed down with sorrow for my pearl,
> I received this gift of fortune,
> and afterwards I committed it to God
> with Christ's blessing and my own.]

It is through Christ, the Lamb of God, that we advance to the heavenly City, and attain to St. Bonaventure's highest level of contemplation:

during the first six days in which the mind has to be exercised that it may finally arrive at the Sabbath of rest after it has beheld God *outside* itself through His traces and in His traces, *within* itself by His image and in His image, *above* itself by the likeness of the divine light shining down upon us and in that light, insofar as is possible in this life and the exercise of our mind—when, finally, on the sixth level [St. Bonaventure divides each realm into two steps] we have come to the point of beholding in the first and highest principle and the Mediator of God and men, Jesus Christ, those things of which the likeness cannot in any wise be found in creatures and which exceed all the insight of the human intellect, there remains that by looking upon these things it [the mind] rise on high and pass beyond not only this *sensible world* but *itself* also. In this passage Christ is the way and the door, Christ is the stairway and the vehicle.[53]

The dreamer committed his pearl to God in Christ's blessing, and it is through Christ's blessing that he hopes for his own salvation. "The triple substance in Christ, Who is our ladder, namely, the corporeal, the spiritual, and the divine,"[54] remains with us, even in this vale of tears, as the sacrament of the altar, the ever-renewed sacrificial Lamb. *Pearl* appropriately concludes with a reference to the corporeal presence, in "þys doel-doungoun" [this dungeon of sorrow] of the Lamb,

> Þat in þe forme of bred and wyn
> Þe preste vus scheweȝ vch a daye.   (1209–1210)
>
> [that the priest shows to us every day
> in the form of bread and wine.]

It is through the Eucharist that the triple substance is present here—that the three realms, corporeal, spiritual, and divine, are before us as "visible appearance, truth of body, and virtue of spiritual grace":

---

[53] *Mind's Road*, 43, my italics; *Opera Omnia*, 5, 312: *sex diebus primus, in quibus mens exercitari habet, ut tandem perveniat ad sabbatum quietis; postquam mens nostra contuita est Deum extra se per vestigia et in vestigiis, intra se per imaginem et in imagine, supra se per divinae lucis similitudinem super nos relucentem et in ipsa luce, secundum quod possibile est secundum statum viae et exercitium mentis nostrae; cum tandem in sexto gradu ad hoc pervenerit, ut speculetur in principio primo et summo et mediatore Dei et hominum, Iesu Christo ea quorum similia in creaturis nullatenus reperiri possunt, et quae omnem perspicacitatem humani intellectus excedunt: restat, ut haec speculando transcendat et transeat non solum mundum istum sensibilem, verum etiam semetipsam; in quo transitu Christus est via et ostium. Christus est scala et vehiculum.*

[54] See *supra* n. 13.

For although the sacrament is one, three distinct things are set forth there, namely, visible appearance, truth of body, and virtue of spiritual grace. For the visible species which is perceived visibly is one thing, the truth of body and blood which under visible appearance is believed invisibly another thing, and the spiritual grace which with the body and blood is received invisibly and spiritually another. . . . Therefore, what is seen according to appearance is the sacrament and the image of that which is believed according to the truth of the body, and what is believed according to the truth of the body is the sacrament of that which is perceived according to spiritual grace. . . . So the most divine Eucharist, which is treated visibly and corporally [sic] on the Altar, according to the appearance of bread and wine and according to the truth of the body and blood of Christ, is a sacrament and a sign and an image of the invisible and spiritual participation with Jesus, which is being accomplished within the heart through faith and love.[55]

Through the Sacrament of the Altar, Christ's "homly hyne" [household servants] may participate in the adoration of "þe Lombe his meyny in melle" [the Lamb among his company] (1127) by worshiping the Apocalyptic Lamb under the appearance of bread and wine, which was figured under the Written Law by the flesh and blood of the paschal lamb:

the paschal lamb, whose flesh was eaten by the people and by whose blood the posts of the houses were marked, preceded in the figure of the sacrament of the body of Christ. . . . Finally we eat the flesh of the

---

[55] Hugh of St. Victor, *On the Sacraments*, 308–309; *PL*, 176, 466–467; *Tria esse in sacramento altaris: panis et vini speciem, corporis Christi veritatem, gratiam spiritualem.* Nam cum unum sit sacramentum, tria ibi discreta proponuntur: species videlicet visibilis, et veritas corporis, et virtus gratiae spiritualis. Aliud est enim visibilis species quae visibiliter cernitur; aliud est veritas corporis et sanguinis quae sub visibili specie invisibiliter creditur, atque aliud gratia spiritualis quae cum corpore et sanguine invisibiliter et spiritualiter percipitur. . . . Quod ergo videtur secundum speciem sacramentum est, et imago illius quod creditur secundum corporis veritatem; et quod creditur secundum corporis veritatem, sacramentum est illius quod percipitur secundum gratiam spiritualem. . . . Ergo divinissima Eucharistia quae in altari et secundum panis et vini speciem et secundum corporis et sanguinis Christi veritatem visibiliter et corporaliter tractatur, sacramentum est et signum; et imago invisibilis et spiritualis participationis Jesu, quae intus in corde per fidem et dilectionem perficitur.

lamb when by taking His true body in the sacrament we are incorporated with Christ through faith and love.[56]

The concluding reference to the Eucharist is not merely a final allusion to Christ as Lamb, nor a gratuitous reminder that the only way to the realm *above* is through Christ; the Sacrament of the Altar reasserts the relationship of the sensible, intelligible, and mystical realms—the "erber," the marvelous land, and the heavenly City—and it demonstrates not only their unity but their presence to man here and now under the Law of Grace. The priest shows us, in the sensible form of bread and wine, the intelligible body and blood of the Lamb, by which we are mystically incorporated with the Divine Trinity. In the presence of the Holy Eucharist, man may know

> To pay þe Prince oþer sete saȝte
> Hit is ful eþe to þe god Krystyin.   (1201–1202)

> [To please the Prince or be set at peace is
> quite easy for the good Christian.]

VIII. CONCLUSIONS

The narrative structure of *Pearl* consists of an "erber" frame (stanza-groups 1 and 20), which records the spiritual change wrought in the dreamer, and a three-part dream—a ghostly adventure composed of a vision of the earthly Paradise (stanza-groups 2–4), a theological dialogue in which a celestial mentor instructs the dreamer (stanza-groups 5–16), and a vision of the heavenly City (stanza-groups 17–19). The triple division of the dream corresponds to the theologian's traditional division of the soul's ascent to God into three stages (from *without* to *within*

---

[56] Hugh of St. Victor, *On the Sacraments*, 307; *PL*, 176, 465: *Quod agnus paschalis figura corporis Christi fuit. . . .* ita agnus paschalis cujus carnes a populo edebantur, et sanguine postes domorum signabantur, in figura sacramenti corporis Christi praecessit. . . . Denique carnes agni comedimus, quando in sacramento verum corpus ejus sumendo, per fidem et dilectionem Christo incorporamur.

to *above*), which may be roughly equated to man's three sources of knowledge (sense, intellect, and inspiration); or, to use Hugh of St. Victor's classification, the three modes of cognition: cogitation, meditation, contemplation. The relationship of the divisions of the dream to the modes of cognition is suggested by the manner of presentation of each. The initial *visio* of the marvelous land, itself an extended image, is perceived and described by the dreamer in terms of sense impressions but is not explained except for the solitary hint,

> Forþy I þoȝt þat Paradyse
> Watȝ þer ouer gayn þo bonkeȝ brade.   (137–138)
>
> [And so I thought that Paradise
> was over there opposite those broad banks.]

The dialogue, the discursive heart of the poem, consists essentially of the heavenly maiden's informing the intellect of the dreamer so that he may ultimately understand the reasonableness of the divine Will. The final *visio* of the heavenly City—mystical contemplation *per se*—is presented wholly in terms of inspired revelation, and is a remarkably close paraphrase of the vision of "þe apostel John" recorded in the Apocalypse.

The contemplative experience asserts the possibility of man's attaining to the eternal word of God, however momentarily, even while remaining in this transitory world of the flesh; it is the soul's ascent from the things that are made, to the Creator. Such an ascent is suggested by the parallels between *Pearl* and other medieval works using the same major forms, and it accounts for the juxtaposition of secular and theological elements in the poem. The narrator's experience is presented in terms which reveal a markedly consistent progression from the worldly to the religious point of view. In the dream proper, the details of the initial *visio* suggest details from the lands of both secular courtly-love poetry and accounts of the earthly Paradise; the chief affinities of the dialogue are with overtly didactic literature, especially the "vertical" debate in which one of the participants has supernatural superiority[57]; and the final *visio* has as its sole source the Apocalypse and scriptural commentary. The progressively religious character of the dream is borne out by the poet's use of biblical allusions, which reveal a progressive increase with each successive section of the dream proper. Even more striking is the nature of the literary parallels found in the "erber" frame. The opening scene, with its panegyric on the lost pearl and its description of the garden, clearly belongs to the tradition of the love vision as exemplified by *The Romance of the Rose;* the closing scene, recording the spirit's return to the body, offers a remarkable number of parallels to the writings of contemplatives. The opening scene presents the worldly view of a lost transitory good, the earthly pearl-rose, in the terms of secular poetry; the closing scene presents the religious view of an anticipated eternal good, the pearl of great price which is the bliss of heaven, in the terms of a religious treatise.

Finally, I should like to point out the import of this interpretation of *Pearl* as an account of a contemplative experience, in relation to the opposing theories that it is either an elegy or an allegory—an opposition not entirely laid to rest, as the commentary of the poem's two most recent editors attests. My interpretation assumes the death of a child beloved by the dreamer as the starting point of the narrative; that the poet suffered a personal loss similar to that of the dreamer I neither affirm nor deny, but I do maintain that there is a natural relationship between personal grief and the search for God. It is just possible that the poet, confronted by the death of a beloved infant "nerre þen aunte or nece" [nearer than aunt or niece] (233), in seeking consolation sought confirmation of the child's salvation and in so doing turned to God and was reassured of his own potential salvation. It is equally possible that the poet, considering the composition of a theological poem on the advantage (indeed, the necessity) of pursuing heavenly in preference to earthly

[57] See Stephan Gilman, *The Art of La Celestina* (Madison, 1956), 159.

goals, of abandoning the madness of worldings for the wisdom of contemplatives, hit upon the happy device of depicting the consequences of attachment to earthly goods in terms of personal bereavement. The *memento mori* prompts active goodness ideally not through fear of hell but through desire for heaven, and deaths of infants (as theologians have noted) may prompt doting parents to turn to God. In discussing the possibility of a child's earning merit, Saint Augustine remarks upon the effect of the child's suffering on his elders and associates him with the Holy Innocents:

Often, by the bodily pain of the child, God works the betterment of elders when their dear ones are so tormented by pain or death. Elders thus begin to live better, or turn from earthly to heavenly things. Often their harshness is softened, their faith is exercised, their pity proved. Who knows what compensation God keeps for these little ones who brought about such goods by their sufferings? So not even in vain did the Holy Innocents die since they have a place in the honor the Church pays to martyrs.[58]

[58] Sister Mary Melchior Beyenka, *Consolation in Saint Augustine*, The Catholic University of America Patristic Studies 83 (Washington, 1950), 47–48; St. Augustine, *De libero arbitrio, CSEL*, 74, 145–146: Cum autem boni aliquid operatur deus in emendatione maiorum, cum parvulorum suorum qui eis cari sunt doloribus ac mortibus flagellantur, cur ista non fiant, quando cum transierint, pro non factis erunt in quibus facta sunt, propter quos autem facta sunt, aut meliores erunt, si temporalibus incommodis emendati, rectius elegerint vivere, aut excusationem in futuri judicii supplicio non habebunt, si vitae huius angoribus ad aeternam vitam desiderium convertere noluerunt? 231. Quis autem novit quid parvulis, de quorum cruciatibus duritia maiorum contunditur aut exercetur fides, aut misericordia probatur, quis ergo novit quid ipsis parvulis in secreto judiciorum suorum bonae compensationis reservet deus, quoniam, quamquam nihil recte fecerint, tamen nec peccantes aliquid ista perpessi sunt? Non enim frustra etiam infantes illos, qui, cum Dominus Iesus Christus necandus ab Herode quaereretur, occisi sunt, in honore martyrum receptos commendat ecclesia. See also the tale "De versutia diaboli et quomodo Dei judicia sunt occulta," in the *Gesta Romanorum*, the popular fourteenth-century collection probably written in England (reprinted in *A Primer of Medieval Latin: an Anthology of Prose and Poetry*, ed. Charles H. Beeson [Chicago, 1925], 60–61): a good angel explains why he strangled the son of a knight who had received him with honor: Demum filium illius militis de nocte strangulavi qui nobis bonum hospi-

If *Pearl* records the consolation for the death of an actual child, it is indeed convenient that the lost little girl was of an age with the Holy Innocents, "þou lyfed not two ȝer in oure þede" [you did not live two years in our land] (483), for this fact enables the poet to relate the doctrine of grace—a doctrine not suited solely to the convenience of the righteous, as the parable of the vineyard implies—to all the children of Adam. As my interpretation does not deny an elegiac element in *Pearl* but rather insists on one, so it does not deny an elaborate allegorical interpretation but rather suggests one, for the admonition of the contemplative to forsake the world and purchase the pearl of great price is an admonition to all men. The contemplative's spiritual itinerary may be an apt figure for fallen mankind's return to God, who gave us to be His servants "Ande precious perleȝ vnto His pay" [And precious pearls to His pleasure] (1212).

It is even possible that further study may be able to demonstrate the presence in *Pearl* of all four levels of allegory, dear to the hearts of medieval scriptural commentators and twentieth-century medievalists. Sister Mary Vincent recounts the literal level of the narrative in her edition of the poem: the narrator is a jeweler, the lost pearl is a pearl, the heavenly maiden is a dream-figure reminiscent of the lost pearl, and the "erber" is an "erber." An interpretation suitable to the allegorical level is provided by the elegists: the narrator is a bereaved father, the lost pearl is a dead child, the pearl-maiden is her heavenly soul,

---

tium dedit. Scias quod antequam puer ille natus erat, miles optimus elemosinarius erat et multa opera misericordiae fecit sed postquam natus est puer factus est parcus, cupidus et omnia collegit ut puerum divitem faciat, sic quod erat causa perditionis eius, et ideo puerum occidi et iam, sicut prius, miles factus est bonus christianus. [Then in the night he strangled the son of this knight who received us hospitably. Know that before that boy was born, the knight was the best of almsgivers and did many works of mercy, but after the boy was born he became frugal and covetous and he kept everything so that the boy would be rich; thus that was the cause of his perdition, and because of this I killed the boy, and now, just as before, the knight has become a good Christian.]

and the "erber" is her flowered grave. The tropological level may be represented by my interpretation: the narrator is a contemplative, the lost pearl is a worldly attachment, the pearl-maiden is a soul who has forsaken the world, and the "erber" is the created world.[59] A possible anagogical interpetation records fallen man's return to God the Father through the Law of Nature, of Scripture, and of Grace:[60] the narrator is Everyman, the lost pearl is his lost innocence, the pearl-maiden represents that portion of mankind who have already been restored, and the "erber" is Eden, where man's innocence was lost and to which he spiritually returns when he is in a state of grace, exemplified by his contrite longing to return to God—his sorrowful desire to regain his lost innocence. Whether or not *Pearl* contains so elaborate an allegorical interpretation is beyond the scope of this study, but I hope I have demonstrated that the poet is an artist with the deftness and subtlety necessary for weaving contemporary literary and theological conventions into so complex a web.

[59] It is on this level that the protean pearl symbol is unified: the lost pearl is the shadow of Truth, the pearl-maiden is the image of Truth, and "þe perle of prys" (line 746) is the body of Truth (see *supra* nn. 21–22).

[60] See Marie Padgett Hamilton, "The Meaning of the Middle English *Pearl*," *PMLA*, 70 (September, 1955), 805–824.

15

SOME CONSOLATORY
STRATEGIES IN *PEARL*

Richard Tristman

IN THE FOLLOWING ESSAY I ACCEPT AS PROVED THAT *Pearl* IS neither simple elegy nor simple allegory, but consolation in a formal and thematic sense.[1] I propose, then, to sketch an analysis of the poem on the basis of this conclusion.

On the face of it, a Christian should no more need consoling than he should need to be tragic. He is "a new creation," who "no longer knows men according to the flesh" and for whom "all things are made new" (II Corinthians 5:16–17). He is "in Christ" and expands, so to speak, to fill that container; the sort of affliction that in an outdated and merely human scale of values would be calamitous should not overwhelm him. In fact,

---

Translations have been supplied by the author.

[1] This is most thoroughly argued by John Conley, "*Pearl* and a Lost Tradition," *Journal of English and Germanic Philology*, LIV (1955), 332–347. Conley compares our poem thematically, and, to a degree, structurally, with Boethius's *Consolation*. Further, he attempts to use scholastic categories in his interpretation of the Middle English poem, observing that our narrator would appear to theologians as an exemplar of folly (*stultitia*) because he mistakes a mutable, albeit spiritual, good for an immutable one (343 ff.) [pages 65 ff. above].

Another useful discussion of *Pearl's* place in the consolatory tradition is V. E. Watt's brief article "*Pearl* as a *Consolatio*," *Medium Aevum*, XXXII (1963), 34–36. Schofield long ago observed the analogy between the poem and Boethius's work, but made little use of it; see his "The Nature and Fabric of *The Pearl*," *PMLA*, XIX (1904), 154–215.

as long as he can be sure that the Kingdom is at hand, he may
regard his imminent salvation as in itself a consolation—and
he may read his own suffering at least as a sign that the Kingdom *is* at hand: "as ye are partakers of the sufferings, so shall
ye be also of the consolation" (II Corinthians 1:7).

With the defeat of the early Christian's hope for the Kingdom's quick coming, he is obliged to reach an accommodation
—but not a compromise—with the world. Christianity must
hereafter learn to use—though not to enjoy[2]—secular and historical goods; on the pastoral level it must bring the "new creation" who is a Christian into some sort of accord with his
lingering humanity; and, ultimately, it must evolve from a form
of life, embodied in sacramental acts and utterances, into a dogmatic system as well. Further, this evolution does not subvert
the immediacy of early Christianity but, on the contrary, assures
the faithful one that *all* things are renovated by his faith.

Watts observes[3] that the pagan "*consolatio* was traditionally
divided into two sections, the first devoted to the afflicted person, the second to the cause of the affliction," but that Christian
writers gradually deviated from this form and, even in the early
centuries of Christianity, "there are . . . indications of the
adoption by Christian writers of the *consolatio* as a vehicle of
instruction" rather than of old-fashioned consolation. This formulation ignores, of course, the systematic renovation of the
world which is the strongest motive of Christianity. We should
do better to suppose that Christian writers reappraised the
pagan form, not to subvert its purposes but to adapt them—to
suppose, in short, that Christian grief is not pagan grief but
something new, requiring a new process of consolation. Nor is
it hard to see why doctrine should be so important a force in
such consolation. For Christian doctrine means to be something
more principled than ordinary speculation; it means to be the

---

[2] This is, of course, Augustine's fundamental distinction, *De doctrina
christiana,* 2.40.60.
[3] *Op. cit.,* 35.

Christian's air of life, in which his most private or idiosyncratic actions resonate and which, obversely, determines the quality and even the kind of his actions. In this way the well-schooled Christian, while he awaits the Kingdom, is made to see the ways in which he is already in Christ, a member of His body.

Grief is, of course, no idiosyncratic behavior, but a virtually universal blight of mankind; accordingly, it refers us to a fundamental tenet of doctrine—that "every sin consists in the desire for some mutable good . . . the possession of which gives . . . inordinate pleasure."[4] In this life all grief must, however, turn about the loss of goods whose very loss proves their mutability; and the fact itself that we grieve is an expression of our rational imperfection. In these terms it would be hard to conceive of a good Christian consoler who did not resort to doctrine in order to fulfill his charge. Grief is error; its alleviation correction. Thus, where it is sometimes possible to bring consolation about by meliorative utterances—by, for instance, discovering whatever good there is in the afflicted one's misfortune—this can never be more than an intermediate step in a Christian consolation, and not even that unless the discovered good is of the spirit and helps turn the sufferer from the mutable good which he misses to the immutable one for which he should yearn. Thus the Christian *consolatio* must have two abstract purposes: first, to soothe the mere humanity and—ideally by virtue of the first—second, to awaken the spirituality of the afflicted.

The whole process which I have been describing in a general way is concisely illustrated in a consolation-in-little which Augustine provides himself in the ninth book of his *Confessions.* Since it is less problematic than *Pearl,* let me use it as a perspective. Augustine here recalls the death of his friend Nebridius:

Not long after our conversion and regeneration by Your baptism, You took him from this life, by then a baptized Catholic and serving You in

---

[4] Aquinas, *Summa Theologica*, I-II, q. 72, a. 2. Quoted by Conley, *op. cit.*, 343 [page 66 above], whose interpretation I assume.

Africa in perfect chastity among his own people, for he had made his whole family Christian. And now he lives in Abraham's bosom. Whatever is meant by that bosom, there my Nebridius lives, my most beloved friend, Your son by adoption and no longer a freedman only. There he lives. For what other place is there for such a soul? There he lives, in the place of which he asked me, an ignorant poor creature, so many questions. He no longer puts his bodily ear to my lips, but the lips of his spirit to Your fountain, drinking his fill of wisdom, all that his thirst requires, happy without end. Nor do I think he is so intoxicated with the draught of that wisdom as to forget me, since You, O Lord, of whom he drinks are mindful of us.[5]

We note at once the tension between Augustine's bereaved humanity and his counterpoised spirituality. The one is prone to expressions like "there my Nebridius lives, my most beloved friend," "He no longer puts his bodily ear to my lips," "Nor do I think he is so intoxicated . . . as to forget me"; the other to expressions like "[he puts] the lips of his spirit to Your fountain . . . happy without end," "You, O Lord, . . . are mindful of us." But what, we want to know, makes this tension visible, what do we actually see between its poles? First, there is Augustine's sense that his friend's purposes in life have not been defeated by death, but really better satisfied: "There he lives, in the place of which he asked me," now he puts "the lips of his spirit to Your fountain, drinking his fill of wisdom, . . . happy without end." Second, Augustine's recognition that, in order to affirm the previous point, he must resort to metaphors and other such rhetorical shape-shiftings whereby heaven may be spoken of as a kind of earth: "the lips of his spirit," the draught of wisdom, "Whatever is meant by that bosom," "Your son by adoption and no longer a freedman only," and the like. Last, Augustine's discovery that in the highest sense he and Nebridius are united still, as on earth they were united through baptism in God and therefore through a shared conception of the Christian form of life—"perfect chastity"[6]: he does not

---

[5] Book nine, chapter three. Trans. F. G. Sheed (New York, 1942), pp. 153–154.

[6] The phrase suggests here a Christian disposition to life in general, and not simply sensual continence.

now forget me *because* "You, O Lord, of whom he drinks are mindful of us."

Reflection should show that no other structure of consolation is so effectively Christian as the one we have just anatomized. And the structure of *Pearl* is fundamentally the same, though less attenuated than Augustine's, for the narrator of the poem is "in a mad porpose" and so needs the long chastisement of doctrine, while Augustine is doctrinally sane and goes through his self-consolation formulaically.

Since the function of consolation is to mediate between natural human dispositions and the exigencies of the spirit, it is at least appropriate that the *Pearl*-narrator's first comfort, though spiritually quite inadequate, should be his reunion itself with his lost gem:

> I trawed my perle don out of dawe3.
> Now haf I fonde hyt, I schal ma feste,
> And wony wyth hyt in schyr wod-schawe3,
> And loue my Lorde and al his lawe3
> That hat3 me bro3t thys blys ner.   (282–286)[7]

> [I'd thought my pearl beyond my grasp.
> Now that I've found it I shall rejoice
> and live with it in the glowing groves,
> and love my Lord and all his laws,
> for He has brought me to this bliss.]

But though the Pearl-maiden calls him "madde" in the following stanza and convicts his words of exceeding his understanding—"Thy worde byfore thy wytte con [does] fle" (294)—we would do well to observe the ways in which the narrator's schooling in spiritual goods has already begun. First, then, he recognizes that, whatever he might call bliss, a Lord has brought him to it and deserves love and deference in consequence. This is easy enough to see. But in this section of the poem (lines 241–300) the concatenated word is "juel" or "jueler," and we

[7] I use Gordon's standard edition of the poem (Oxford, 1953) but modernize the Middle English thorn as "th."

are, presumably, expected to take it seriously and to recall, accordingly, the premises with which the poem *literaliter* begins: a jeweler has lost, in the ground of an arbor, a pearl more precious than those of India. But now in a vision he finds himself in a landscape which, unlike his own "erbere," not only does not mar "a myry iuele" (23) but is really overrun with such gems and made brilliant by them:

> Dubbed wern alle tho downeʒ sydeʒ
> Wyth crystal klyffes so cler of kynde.
> Holtewodeʒ bryʒt aboute hem bydeʒ
> Of bolleʒ as blwe a ble of Ynde;
> As bornyst syluer the lef on slydeʒ,
> That thike con trylle on vch a tynde.
> Quen glem of glodeʒ agaynʒ hem glydeʒ,
> Wyth schymeryng schene ful schrylle thay schynde.
> The grauayl that on grounde con grynde
> Wern precious perleʒ of oryente:
> The sunnebemeʒ bot blo and blynde
> In respecte of that adubbement.   (73–84)

> [Those hill-sides were all adorned
> with crystal cliffs, by nature clear.
> Woods were bright and set around them
> whose boles were blue as indigo.
> Like burnished silver the leaves spread out
> that grew thick and quivered on each branch.
> When clear patches of sky let the light strike them
> they shone brilliantly, shimmering.
> The gravel that one tread upon
> was made of precious Orient-pearls.
> The sunbeams were but dark and dim
> compared with all that splendor.]

It is, of course, a sight to enchant a jeweler, to convince him that—professionally speaking—his hard loss has resulted in a windfall. When, ultimately, he discovers his own lost pearl among these rough treasures, his professional bliss is, understandably, restored—the more so because she wears herself (to maintain the convention of the poem) in a crown of that gold which the first stanza called her proper setting; indeed, she wears herself many times over (cf. lines 192–228), thus giving her jeweler a further sense of his own enrichment.

Whether this degree of consolation has waked the narrator's spirit seems doubtful, but when his jeweler's sensuality (even venality) has duly expressed itself and has duly vexed the doctrinally superior maiden, it is indeed to a jeweler that she addresses her lesson first:

> I halde that jueler lyttel to prayse
> That leueʒ wel that he seʒ wyth yʒe,
> And much to blame and vncortayse
> That leueʒ oure Lorde wolde make a lyʒe. . . .
>
> (301–304)

> [I think that jeweler worth little praise
> who believes firmly what his eyes see,
> and blameworthy and ungracious
> who thinks our Lord would make a lie. . . .]

The doctrinal point is, of course, clear: the narrator suffers from spiritual blindness.[8] But, then, if the maiden means to keep to the conventions of the poem, should she not condemn the jeweler's profession outright for its easy love of brilliancy? As she states it, her criterion for measuring a jeweler's competence seems a bit queer. Yet she has already criticized *this* jeweler's eye at an earlier point, playing there upon his own sense of the vegetable-mineral antagonism which has recently excited him and which earlier grieved him: the earth never really marred his "myry juele" because

> . . . that thou lesteʒ watʒ bot a rose
> That flowred and fayled as kynde hyt gef.
> Now thurʒ kynde of the kyste that hyt con close
> To a perle of prys hit is put in pref.   (269–272)

> [. . . what you lost was but a rose
> that flowered and wilted as nature decided.
> Now, by virtue of the chest which encloses it,
> it has indeed been proved a pearl of price.]

---

[8] Cf. Conley, *op. cit.*, 347 [page 72 above].

In this light we discover, too, how faulty our jeweler's vision had been at the start of the poem. For in every important sense he there regards his lost gem as a thing apart. He isolates her name—*Perle*—from the grammatical body of the stanza, as though he were making an entry in a lapidary.[9] He imagines her enclosed in a gold setting; he judges her peerless and sets her metaphorically "sengeley in synglere" [alone in a class apart]. By the poem's end, of course, he will recognize what a bad judge he has been, will learn that his pearl of price has 144,000 peers, all of them well set. (This lesson has, in a sense, begun, but only that—for how else are we to read his wonderment at the gravel on which he stands?) But the maiden's insult to his competence recalls, I think, yet another isolation into which the first stanza puts the gem, and this the most foolish of all:

> I dewyne, fordolked of luf-daunger
> Of that *pryuy perle* wythouten spot.
>
> (11–12—my italics)
>
> [I pine, wounded by the strength of love
> for my privy pearl without a spot.]

For to place this pearl in a state of privity is to take it off the market or at least to place it on a seller's market—either case a way of keeping it from the "prynces paye" [Prince's pleasure] for which it is meant. From this point we may also see in that troublesome expression "luf-daunger" a dramatically ironic connotation which its abstract meaning lacks: it becomes, that is, a term, not for the narrator's own strong love, but for the more powerful love who is Christ.[10]

---

[9] Schofield notes the similarity of the first stanza of the poem to the style of lapidaries in "Symbolism, Allegory and Autobiography in *The Pearl*," *PMLA*, XXIV (1909), 593–600.

[10] This reading is not only plausible but, I think, inevitable, given the etymological overtones of the word "daunger." For even in the fourteenth century it easily bears its original meaning, "lordship." Cf., for instance, Chaucer's characterization of Absolon in *The Miller's Tale* (l. 3338), as being "of speche daungerous" [arrogant or lordly in his speech].

But if the maiden's implication in the stanza which begins with line 301 is to convict the jeweler of premature possessiveness because he is governed by gemological considerations only, and not by questions of property, she is nevertheless obliged to subordinate this point to the consolatory purpose of the poem, which is to convince the narrator that he should submit himself to the "prynces paye," and no longer regard the "pearl of price" as an object of speculation. One motive, then, of the lines

> ꝫe setten hys wordeꝫ ful westernays
> That leueꝫ nothynk bot ꝫe hit syꝫe   (307–308)
>
> [You make nonsense of His words
> if you believe only what you see.]

must be simply to stir the jeweler's professional appetite still more—to tease him with anticipation. And if we accept the principles of the first stanza (and our own common sense, too) —that gems are enforced in value by being well and richly set —we understand the suasive effect upon the jeweler of his later vision:

> If hit be ueray and soth sermoun
> That thou so stykeꝫ in garlande gay,
> So wel is me in thys doel-doungoun
> That thou art to that Prynseꝫ paye.   (1185–1188)
>
> [If it is a true and proved account
> that says you're set in a bright garland,
> I'm well enough in this dungeon of sorrow,
> knowing the pleasure you give that Prince.]

This metaphoric elaboration of words like "stykeꝫ" and "garlande" began, really, a long time ago, in the jeweler's first doctrinal concession to the maiden, wherein he shifts his ground from the pearly gravel which had earlier given him delight to another ground more eternal:

> Thaꝫ cortaysly ꝫe carp con,
> I am bot mol and manereꝫ mysse.

> Bot Crystes mersy and Mary and Jon,
> Thise arn the grounde of alle my blisse. (381-384)

[Though you may argue courteously,
I am but dust and ill-mannered.
But Christ's mercy, and Mary's and John's—
these are the ground of all my bliss.]

Functionally these shifts from literal to allegorical usages are quite like Augustine's smoother one: "He no longer puts his bodily ear to my lips, but the lips of his spirit to Your fountain."

Now the movements which we have been observing on the level of fiction complete themselves on the level of doctrine. For instance, the maiden's warning against premature possessiveness finds universal significance in her advice that

> Forthy to corte quen thou schal com
> Ther alle oure causeȝ schal be tryed,
> Alegge the ryȝt, thou may be innome,
> By thys ilke spech I haue asspyed;
> Bot he on rode that blody dyed,
> Delfully thurȝ hondeȝ thryȝt,
> Gyue the to passe, when thou arte tryed,
> By innocens and not by ryȝte.   (701–708)

[Therefore, when you come to court
where all our cases shall be tried,
if you claim your right, you may be convicted
by those same words which I have cited.
But He who died bloody on the cross,
pierced there grievously through the hands,
may let you by, when you are tried,
because of your innocence and not your right.]

In similar fashion, and prior even to this last counsel, the maiden's hint—that the treasures prepared by God for men (if they would but die to this life [cf. line 320]) outdo in splendor and value the "dere adubbemente" [opulent splendor] with which the narrator's dream first confronts him—this hint is fulfilled doctrinally in her report that

> Of more and lasse in Godeȝ ryche
> . . . lys no joparde, . . .

> For the grace of God is gret inoghe.
>
> (601, 602, 612)

> [Of more and less in God's kingdom
> there is no question, . . .
> For the grace of God is great enough.]

It is a lesson with the important immediate effect of subverting the scarcity-economics which has been the basis of all the jeweler's judgments so far.

When these lessons are done, the maiden is in a position simply to exhort her jeweler:

> I rede the forsake the worlde wode
> And porchace thy perle maskelles. (743–744)

> [I urge you to abandon the mad world
> and purchase your unblemished pearl.]

And he, dazed as it seems by the air of life which he has just begun to breathe, inquires about the jeweler who fashions that saving stone:

> 'O maskeleʒ perle in perleʒ pure,
> That bereʒ,' quod I, 'the perle of prys,
> Quo formed the thy fayre fygure?' (745–747)

> ["O spotless pearl decked in pure pearls,
> who bears," I said, "the pearl of price,
> who formed your fair shape for you?"]

But the line of questioning which begins here does not mean to invite doctrinal elaboration—it points more in a formal than in an informative direction. It affords the maiden an opportunity to bring her consolatory lesson home to all of us, to suggest a universal counterpart to her own and her narrator's private history—as Augustine does when he speaks of Nebridius's "regeneration" and "perfect chastity" in life and of the fact that the Lord of whom his friend now "drinks" is "mindful of us."

Unlike Augustine, who may summon what rhetorical figures he cares to to enact his consolation, the Pearl-maiden is bound by the fictional premises of the poem to effect the transition from private significance to public—as the poem has effected all transitions hitherto—by elaborating the fundamental image of the pearl yet further.Thus, in answer to the jeweler's question "Quo formed the thy fayre fygure?" and its implications, she relates first the history of Christ's innocent mission in the historical Jerusalem and tells of His humiliation and suffering there, and with this story as a basis she then enforces an analogy between this "Jerusalem Lombe" and a spotless pearl:

> Thys Jerusalem Lombe had neuer pechche
> Of other huee bot quyt jolyf
> That mot ne masklle moȝt on streche,
> For wolle quyte so ronk and ryf.   (841–844)
>
> [This Jerusalem Lamb had not a spot
> of any color but fair white,
> which neither mar nor stain could spoil
> because that fleece was rich and thick.]

And this analogy itself would seem the basis of the high salvation of the pearl-like innocents, their wedlock with the Lamb:

> *Forthy* vche saule that hade neuer teche
> Is to that Lombe a worthyly wyf. . . .
>   (845–846—my emphasis)
>
> [Therefore, each soul that has stayed unstained
> is a deserving wife for that Lamb. . . .]

Once we are persuaded that all jewels attain their value and significance by their subordination to the "dere juelle" (795) who is Christ, we are in a position to recognize the formal importance in the poem of the narrator's vision of the heavenly Jerusalem. For that city is not simply a scriptural commonplace of great convenience for a poem about gems; but, conversely, it is itself a justification (though not the only one) for our poem's being about gems. For we can hardly help noticing that the heavenly Jerusalem is none other than the artificially reorganized—and scripturally publicized—equivalent of that rough mineral landscape which began the narrator's vision and which he had then mistaken for his own private windfall. And here he learns that Christ is the gem under whose influence all gems assume value and, even more, that He is the source of that brilliancy which is the virtue *sine qua non* of gems and, in that sense, their constitution:

> Of sunne ne mone had thay no nede;
> The self God watȝ her lombe-lyȝt,
> The Lombe her lantyrne, wythouten drede;
> Thurȝ hym blysned the borȝ al bryȝt.   (1045–1048)

> [They had no need of sun or moon;
> God Himself was their lamplight,
> The lamb was, in truth, their lantern;
> Through Him the city shone bright.]

In this way, which fully satisfies at least the fictional premises of the poem, the lesson that our delights and benefits are without exception manifestations of God and so expressions of His grace is concluded.

But, though our poet has persuaded us of this last point on the fictional or symbolic level, I think that he has failed to do so on the theological level. For, despite the view of most students of this poem that it is essentially an anti-Pelagian work in the spirit of Augustine and Bradwardine (the poet's contemporary), it is difficult to understand how any argument which dwells with Augustine's singularity upon the *mystery* of grace can be linked to the kind of preachments which pervade *Pearl*. Where, for instance, the poet accepts the justification of the infant as an issue of "resoun" [reason] (665), Augustine enlists it as a certain proof of God's secrecy:

Men, however, may suppose that there are certain good deserts which they think are precedent to justification through God's grace; all the while failing to see, when they express such an opinion, that they do nothing else than deny grace. But . . . let them suppose what they like respecting the case of adults, in the case of infants, the Pelagians find no means of answering the difficulty. For these in receiving grace have no will, from the influence of which they can pretend to any merit. We see, moreover, how they cry and struggle when they are baptized, and feel the divine sacraments. Such conduct would, of course, be charged against them as a great impiety, if they already had free will in use. . . . But most certainly there is no prevenient merit, otherwise grace would no longer be grace. Sometimes, too, this grace is bestowed upon children of unbelievers . . . but, on the other hand, the children of believers fail to obtain grace, some hindrance occurring to prevent the approach of help. . . . These things, no doubt, happen through the secret providence of God, whose judgments are unsearchable, and His ways past finding out. . . .[11]

In the light of this passage, how righteous must the maiden's own account appear, with its odd implication that infants will their own baptism and descend into the font on their own:

> Bot innoghe of grace hatȝ innocent.
> As sone as thay arn borne, by lyne
> In the water of babtem thay dyssente:
> Then arne thay boroȝt into the vyne.
> Anon the day, wyth derk endente,
> The niyȝt of deth dotȝ to enclyne:
> That wroȝt neuer wrang er thenne thay wente,
> The gentyle Lorde thenne payeȝ hys hyne.
> Thay dyden hys heste, thay wern thereine;
> Why schulde he not her labour alow,
> Ȝys, and pay hem at the fyrst fyne?
> For the grace of God is gret innoghe.[12] (625–636)

---

[11] "On Grace and Free Will," trans. by P. Holmes, from *Basic Writings of St. Augustine*, ed. Whitney Oates (New York, 1948), p. 503.

[12] Contrast, too, Augustine's interpretation of Matthew 19:13–14—"Let the children come to me," etc—with that provided in *Pearl*, 11. 721 ff. The Saint finds children so unspiritual that he concludes, in *Confessions* I, 19, for instance, that the Lord must have been speaking figuratively.

An even more bizarre misreading of Scripture on the part of our poet than the present one of the parable of the vineyard occurs in *Cleanness*, where he considers the significance of Mary's virginity:

> For, loke, fro fyrst that he lyȝt wyth-inne the lel mayden,
> By how comly a kest he watȝ clos there,
> When venkkyst watȝ no vergynyte, no vyolence maked,
> Bot much clener watȝ hir corse, God kynned therinne.

[But the innocent have sufficient grace.
As soon as they are born, in succession
they descend into the waters of baptism.
Then they are brought to the vineyard.
At length the day, overcast with darkness,
inclines toward the night of death.
They did no wrong before they parted,
so the gentle Lord pays his laborers.
They did his bidding, they had entered the vineyard;
why should he not accept their labor—
yes, and pay them fully?
The grace of God is great enough.]

The innocence which the maiden recommends to the narrator as a surer justification than any claim of right would thus itself seem the basis of just such a claim. So it is that, in the poem's last stanza, having duly conjoined his will and Christ's, the narrator takes his leave of us with the thought that being a Christian is fundamentally a kind of earnest, fellow-well-met servitude:

Ouer this hyul this lote I laȝte,
For pyty of my perle enclyin,
And sythen to God I hit bytaȝte
In Krysteȝ dere blessyng and myn,
That in the forme of bred and wyn
The preste vus scheweȝ vch a daye.
He gef vus to be his homly hyne
Ande precious perleȝ vnto his pay.   (1205–1212)

[On this hill I had this experience,
having languished in sorrow over my pearl.
And then I commended it to God,
in Christ's dear name and my own—
He who in the form of bread and wine

[For, see how from the first moment that He lay within the untouched maiden
by what a comely chest he was enclosed.
When virginity remained unvanquished, unviolated,
when her body was utterly clean, God lodged in it.]
From Israel Gollancz's edition (London, 1921), p. 41 (ll. 1069 ff.).

is shown us daily by the priest.
He allows us to be His household help
and precious pearls for His good pleasure.]

The brilliancy of this poem's symbolic surface does not, finally, manage to conceal the dullness of spirit within. And, in matters of salvation, poetic brightness may actually be a detriment because of the blindness which it induces.

PART III

16

THE "HERESY" OF *THE PEARL*

D. W. Robertson, Jr.

THE CHARGE THAT *The Pearl* IS HERETICAL IS A VERY GRAVE one. Heresy was not something to be taken lightly in the fourteenth century; moreover, heretical doctrine seems especially strange in a work which emphasizes the importance of purity of spirit with evident sincerity. It has been said that the poet's interpretation of the Parable of the Vineyard includes the "heresy of Jovinian," to the effect that there is no differentiation in status in the celestial Jerusalem. Further evidence is available, however, in support of the view of J. B. Fletcher, R. Wellek, and others to the effect that there is no heresy in the poem.[1]

St. Augustine explains the parable at length in one of his sermons.[2] The general agricultural image is treated first. We cultivate God, and He cultivates us: "Colimus enim eum ado-

---

Reprinted, by permission of the author and of The Johns Hopkins Press, from *Modern Language Notes*, LXV (1950), 152–155. Translations of Latin passages, with a few minor exceptions, have been supplied by the author.

[1] Fletcher's article, "The Allegory of *The Pearl*," *JEGP*, XX (1921), 1–21, is still one of the most fruitful studies of the poem. On heresy, see especially pp. 17–18. Although Wellek denies the existence of heresy in the poem, *Studies in English by Members of the English Seminar of the Charles University* (Prague, 1933), pp. 20–26, he seems to find some self-contradiction in the doctrine.

[2] Sermo LXXXVII, *PL,* 38, 530–539.

rando, non arando. Ille autem colit nos tanquam agricola agrum"[3] [For we cultivate Him by worshipping, not by plowing. But He cultivates us as a farmer a field]. In His labor of cultivation, God extirpates the seeds of evil from us and opens our hearts as with a plow in order to plant the seeds of the precepts, whose fruit is piety. Since God is in this sense a farmer, he planted a vineyard and called workers into it. The workers called at various times throughout the day are interpreted in two ways in the sermon. The second interpretation is relevant to *The Pearl:*

Tanquam prima hora vocantur, qui recentes ab utero matris incipiunt esse christiani; quasi tertia, pueri; quasi sexta, juvenes, quasi nona, vergentes in senium; quasi undecima, omnino decrepiti: unum tamen vitae aeternum denarium omnes accepturi.[4]

[Those who begin to be Christians soon after emerging from their mother's womb are those called as if at the first hour; those who become Christians as children are called as if at the third hour; those who become Christians as youths are called as if at the sixth hour; those who become Christians when growing old are as if called at the ninth hour; those who become Christians when they are altogether decrepit are as if called at the eleventh hour. But all will receive the same penny of eternal life.]

Those who are called first are baptized infants; those called at the third hour are children, and so on. The fact that the Pearl is said in the poem to have died in infancy has made this interpretation seem irrelevant, since she says that she went to the vineyard "in euentyde"[5] [at eventide]. In other words, she could not have gone into the vineyard in old age if she died in infancy.

In medieval exegesis it was not unusual for early interpretations of Scriptural passages to become elaborated with the passage of time. A comment of a few lines in Augustine or

[3] Col. 530.
[4] Col. 533. The first interpretation involves the ages of mankind rather than the ages of man.
[5] Osgood's text, l. 582. See his note, p. 75.

Bede may fill a column by the twelfth century. In the process, the basic meaning or *sentence* remained with very little change, but there were frequently changes in detail. Let us compare the interpretation of Augustine just quoted with that of Bruno Astensis in the twelfth century:

Regnum coelorum, Ecclesia est; paterfamilias, Christus Dominus noster: ejus namque familia, et angeli et homines sunt: magna quidem est familia, quia magnus est et paterfamilias. Venit autem iste paterfamilias ut conduceret operarios in vineam suam. Vinea enim Domini Saboath, domus Israel est: vinea, Dei Ecclesia est: extra quam qui laborat, mercedem non recipit: in qua qui laborat, denarium suscipit. Ille enim denarius, remuneratio est aeternae beatitudinis: ideo unus denarius omnibus datur: unus primis, et unus novissimis. Et alii quidem primo mane laborare incipiunt: alii vero circa horam tertiam: alii autem circa sextam, et nonam horam: alii quoque circa horam undecimam. . . . Primo namque mane in vinea Dei laborare incipiunt, qui a primaeva aetate, id est a pueritia in Ecclesia Dei Domino serviunt: illi autem circa horam tertiam laborare veniunt, qui in adolescentia servire incipiunt: veniunt autem et illi circa sextam et nonam horam, qui vel in juventute, vel in senectute, ad poenitentiam convertuntur. Undecima vero hora illa est, quae in qualibet aetate fini appropinquat et morti proxima est. Hanc enim horam non solum juvenes et senes, verum etiam pueri habent.[6]

[The Kingdom of Heaven is the Church. The Householder is Christ Our Lord, whose family is made up of both angels and men. It is a great family, for the Householder is great also. That Householder went to hire workers in his vineyard. The vineyard of the Lord of Hosts is the House of Israel, and the vineyard of God is the Church. He who labors outside it receives no reward, but he who labors within it receives a penny. And that penny is the reward of eternal beatitude. Thus a single penny is given to all, one for the first and one for the last. Some indeed begin to labor early in the morning; others about the third hour, others about the sixth and the ninth hour, others also about the eleventh hour. . . . Those who serve from the earliest age, or from childhood, in the Church of the Lord are those who begin to labor in the vineyard of God at the first hour of the morning. Those who begin to serve in adolescence are those who come to labor about the third hour. Those who are converted to penance in youth or age are those who come at about the sixth and the ninth hours. But the eleventh hour is the hour at which one of

---

[6] *PL*, 165, 237.

whatever age begins to serve when he approaches his end and is near death. Not only the youthful and the aged, but also even children have this hour.]

The general pattern and the basic meaning of the two interpretations are the same; but Bruno makes the eleventh hour, "in euentyde," an hour which can apply to persons of any age. Those who begin to labor in the church in the eleventh hour are those who go shortly before death. That this interpretation was widely accepted is attested by the fact that it survives as an English idiom, *at the eleventh hour*.[7] When the Pearl says that she went "in euentyde," therefore, she is simply stressing the fact that she did not labor in the vineyard of the church. That is, she was baptized only shortly before death.

The poet's general interpretation of the parable is thus not an "inversion" of St. Augustine's. Nor are his remarks concerning heavenly reward contrary to St. Augustine's. In his sermon, St. Augustine emphasizes the fact that in the reward which they receive for their labors, the workers in the vineyard are all equal, "unum tamen vitae aeternum denarium omnes accepturi" [but all will receive the same penny of eternal life]. It is this doctrine which has been mistaken in *The Pearl* for the "heresy of Jovinian":

Erimus ergo in illa mercede omnes aequales, tanquam primi novissimi, et novissimi primi: quia denarius ille vita aeterna est, et in vita aeterna omnes aequales erunt. Quamvis enim meritorum diversitate fulgebunt, alius magis, alius minus: quod tamen ad vitam aeternam pertinet, aequalis erit omnibus. Non enim alteri erit longius, alteri brevius, quod pariter sempiternum est: quod non habet finem, nec tibi habebit, nec mihi. Alio modo ibi erit castitas conjugalis, alio modo ibi erit integritas virginalis: alio modo ibi erit fructus boni operis, alio modo corona passionis. Illud alio modo: illud alio modo: tamen quantum pertinet ad vivere in aeternum, nec ille plus vivet illo, nec ille plus illo. Pariter enim sine fine vivunt, cum in suis quisque claritatibus vivat: et ille denarius vita aeterna est. Non murmuret ergo qui post multum tempus accepit,

[7] *NED. s. v. eleventh.*

contra eum qui post modicum tempus accepit. Illi redditur, illi donatur; utrisque tamen una res donatur.[8]

[We shall all be equal in that reward, the last like the first, and the first like the last. For that penny is eternal life, and all will be equal in eternal life. Although they will be radiant with a diversity of merits, one more, one less, that which pertains to eternal life will be equal to all. For that which is eternal to all will not be longer to one and shorter to another, for since it has no end, it will have none either for you or for me. Conjugal chastity will be there in one way, and virginal purity in another. The fruit of good works will be there in one way, and the crown of martyrdom in another. This one will be there in one way, that one in another; but insofar as living in eternity is concerned, this one will live no longer than that, nor that one than this. They live equally without end, although each lives in his own splendor. And that penny is eternal life. Let him who has received the reward after a long time not murmur against him who has received it after a short time. It is rendered to one, it is given to another; yet to both one thing is given.]

In answer to the "murmuring" of the dreamer, who is astonished to find the Pearl among the blessed after little or no labor, she expresses precisely this doctrine:

> Of more & lasse in Godeʒ ryche
> Þat gentyl sayde, lys no joparde,
> For þer is vch mon payed inlyche,
> Wheþer lyttel oþer much be hys rewarde.[9]

> ["Of more and less in God's kingdom,"
> that gentle one said, "no uncertainty exists,
> for there each one is paid alike,
> whether little or much be his reward."]

In other words, "in vita aeterna omnes aequales erunt" [in life eternal all will be equal], whether the reward is "lyttel oþer much"; or "quamvis enim meritorum diversitate fulgebunt . . . aequalis erit omnibus"[10] [for although they will be radiant

---

[8] Col. 533.

[9] 601–604.

[10] Cf. the doctrine which Fletcher, op. cit., 17–18, found in St. Thomas: "Just as one man can get more good out of a penny than another, so one spirit in the presence of God can realize him more fully than another."

with a diversity of merits . . . eternal life will be equal to all]. There is certainly no heresy here.[11] Just as St. Augustine and Bruno use the parable as a basis for warnings against despair and vain hope,[12] the author of *The Pearl* uses it to show that anyone, no matter what he has done in the past, may through repentance regain sufficient purity of spirit to achieve his reward.[13] The phrase "in euentyde" simply emphasizes the fact that the Pearl, who died in infancy, had been baptized only at the eleventh hour. A reexamination of the evidence has shown that the interpretation and use of the Parable of the Vineyard in *The Pearl* are consistent with medieval exegetical tradition.

[11] In stanza 38 it is said that in the celestial city everyone is "quen oþer kyng" [queen or king]. This is not heresy either, but a reference to the symbolism of the denarius. Rabanus comments, *PL*, 107, 1028–1029, "Denarius figuram regis habet. Recipisti ergo mercedem quam tibi promiseram imaginem et similitudinem meam" [The penny has the image of the king. You have received the reward I had promised you, namely, my image and likeness]. In the celestial city where the distorting forces of cupidity do not operate, the human soul is the true image of God, the King.

[12] *Loc. cit.*

[13] See stanza 56 and the final stanza of the poem.

17

PEARL: SYMBOLISM IN A GARDEN SETTING

C. A. Luttrell

IN AN ATTEMPT TO CONTRIBUTE TOWARDS THE UNDERSTANDING and appreciation of *Pearl,* a particular aspect of the opening— a section that employs a procedure no longer familiar to the reader—has been chosen for study within the context of the life and literature of the period. Two important and interlocking pieces in the mechanism that sets *Pearl* on its course are the *erber* and its *huyle,* on which the narrator came to lie and dream, and the aim of this enquiry is first to establish what they actually were like, and then to bring out their function and effect in the poem.

Much of the subject is traversed by R. W. V. Elliott, who, in *"Pearl* and the Medieval Garden: Convention or Originality?" Les Langues Modernes,* XLV, 85 ff. (1951), sets out to determine the distinctive features of the medieval garden and the *erber,* and proceeds to relate his findings to the description of the sleeper's garden in *Pearl.* But the present writer disagrees both in details and fundamentally with Elliott's treatment, and by rebuttal intends to clear the way for different conclusions.

Reprinted, by permission of the author and the editors, from *Neophilologus,* **XLIX** (1965), 160–176; also by permission of the Indiana University Press and Robert J. Blanch. Translations have been supplied by the author, along with minor revisions.

From illustrations, Elliott judges vines, arbours, and galleries to be common in medieval gardens, and asserts that *erber,* originally designating a herb-garden, gradually acquired the kind of sense we now associate with "arbour," being applied to an inner enclosure in the garden, turfed and planted with trees, in which more elaborate structures of laths with vine or roses trained thereon were in use from the thirteenth century. For its characteristics he cites Chaucer, *Legend of Good Women,* Prologue, G. 97 f., whose *erber* was *Ybenched newe with turves, fresshe ygrave* [with seats newly covered with slabs of freshly cut turf], and *Kingis Quair,* 211 ff., in which he finds "its agreeable cool shade suggested by" line 224, *The bewis spred the herber all about* [the boughs spread all around the *erber*], as well as *Flower and the Leaf,* 49 ff., where it is described as being like a pretty parlour, *roofe and all.* A similar conception of the *erber* is held by D. A. Pearsall, *The Floure and the Leafe* (1962), who believes that it was a shady bower tucked away in a corner of a garden, an arbour without which no fifteenth-century garden was complete. Yet in *Pearl,* explains Elliott, the pleasant features of the typical arbour are markedly absent, which leads to the following inference:

> The omission is undoubtedly a deliberate one, and instead of describing an arbour of the kind mentioned by Chaucer or King James, the *Pearl* poet uses the word as a convenient synonym for garden.

For much of his information Elliott leans heavily on Sir Frank Crisp's *Mediæval Gardens* (1924), going so far as to make use of his translation of a French report of the Latin text of Albertus Magnus, instead of the original, and he does not check the sense attached to *erber,* by a survey of contexts where the term appears, nor examine with any care the sleeper's garden portrayed on folio 37 of the manuscript of *Pearl* itself. The present account springs from consideration of these and other kinds of evidence; including Crisp's rich collection of pictures—which illustrate gardens of many types, and range from the fifteenth to the seventeenth centuries and from England to Persia—when the validity for the purpose is testified by correspondence with details found in texts.

The word is from OFr *erbier,* which means "greensward; herbage"; as well as "kitchen-garden," a sense it shares with MedLat *herbarium.*[1] *Erber* is equated by the fifteenth-century *Promptorium Parvulorum* with *herbarium* (defined by *Hortus Vocabulorum* as "an erber, *ubi crescunt herbe, vel ubi habundant* [where herbage grows, or shoots up with great luxuriance], or a gardyn"), with *viridale* (compare *viretum,* in *Medulla Grammatice* explained as *"locus pascualis virens,* a gres-ȝerd, or an herber" [a verdant mead, a herb garden]), and with *viridarium,* a pleasure-garden, the same as Medieval French *vergier,* in which there was *erbier.*[2] Contexts confirm that *erber* ranged in application from "kitchen-garden" and "cottage-garden" to "grass-plot" and "pleasure-garden," and it seems that "orchard," one of the usages given by the *NED,* s.v. *arbour,* really should be "kitchen-garden, etc., with one or more fruit-trees." Eventually *erber* acquired the meaning "arbour," but it did not lose its former connotations for some time, and the coexistence of the two branches, the old and the new, sometimes led to an attempt to distinguish them, in the middle of the sixteenth century, by taking spelling variants such as *herboure* and *arboure* to represent different words, as in Levins, *Manipulus Verborum,* who defines them as respectively (i) *herbaretum, viretum,* and (ii) *arboretum* [(i) a place grown with herbage, (ii) a place grown with trees]. Clearly, the sense-development that *erber* underwent could not be a gradual passage of the type A→B. It must be A→A + B→B, with the word in *Promptorium Parvulorum* showing no sign of the second stage, which it reached by the time of Levins. The rift A + B would be due to the use of *arbour* for something which, though grown

---

[1] See Tobler-Lommatsch, s. v. *erbier.*
[2] Cf. Froissart, *La Prison Amoureuse,* 1391.

out of its other applications, had so extended the arboreous quality that there arose semantic overload of the kind that produced pairs such as flower/flour, metal/mettle, and person/parson.

In contexts, there are instances of the *erber* right up to the sixteenth century, as will be seen below, which are identifiable with plesaunces in Crisp's pictures that are no more like arbours than are modern gardens with trees, and the first example of an *erber* resembling an arbour is that in *Flower and the Leaf.* In spite of the ascription of early citations by the *NED* to "espaliers, etc." and "a bower or shady retreat with sides and roof, etc.," none earlier than this poem, which Pearsall dates to the late fifteenth century, can be accepted as illustrating the B-branch of the word's meaning.

One kind of *erber* has a spring or fountain, by which people sit, and from which water flows to the rest of the garden, park, or chase. A man on horseback rides into such a place early in Sir Gilbert Hay's *Buke of the Ordre of Knychthede* (1456), there is one in Metham (*fl.* 1448), *Amoryus and Cleopes,* 1612 ff., and Hawes, *Pastime of Pleasure* (1509), describes another, which is square, in the middle of a garden. This type of plesaunce is very familiar indeed. For instance, Machaut, *Remede de Fortune,* in a park, and a *praiel* (Latin *pratellum* "little mead") of a *vergier* in his *Le Dit dou Lyon.* Such a part of a larger garden is treated romantically in the *Roman de la Rose,* whose *vergier* contains many springs from which water passes in conduits through velvet grass, where lovers can lie under trees forming a protective screen against the sun. A late fifteenth-century manuscript of the *Roman,* B. M. Harl. 4425, has a detailed and full-page illustration (in Crisp as fig. lxxv) on folio vi verso that shows a walled garden of which two parts, separated from each other by a latticework fence with a high gateway, occupy all but the background. In the centre of the left-hand section, which is a square lawn with trees along one side only, the back, closed by a rose hedge grown on palings—the remaining two sides are the walls—there is a fountain with people sitting near it and a runnel that flows down a channel in the turf. From this type of garden is descended that described in the sixteenth century by Estienne and Liebault, *Maison Rustique,* in a passage whose *preau* (= *praiel*) is rendered by *arbour* in the seventeenth-century English version:

Il y a trois sortes de vergers, l'un que l'on appelle autrement le preau, & ne contient autre cas qu'herbe verte, & la fontaine au milieu[3] [there are three kinds of *verger,* of which one is otherwise called a *preau,* and has nothing but green grass, and a fountain in the middle].

Where no spring with water-course is mentioned, as with the *praiel* [little mead] of a castle-garden in *Les Voeux du Paon,* 2682 ff., on which carpets for sitting are spread under a branching tree, for this *The Avowis of Alexander* (1438), 3687 ff., uses *erber*. Similarly in the English *La Belle Dame sans Mercy,* 191, for *preau* of Chartier's line 164. People sit *on,* not in, the *erber* of a castle in *Sir Ferumbras,* 1773, that is, on the grass plot so characteristic of the small *vergier,* and a typical description of one with plants in the turf, giving the pattern of a flowery mead, is that in Lydgate's *Siege of Thebes,* 2279 ff., where a knight rides into the grounds of a castle, finds an *erber* which is *Soote and fressh lich a paradys, Verray heuenly of inspeccioun* [sweet and fresh like a paradise, really heavenly to see], dismounts and lets his horse loose to pasture on the grass, and lies down *Vpon the herbes grene, whit and red* [on the green, white, and red herbage]. A green *erber,* with a holly in it, occupied the fireplace in summer,[4] imitating the plan, seen in many contexts, and in Crisp's pictures, of a tree in the middle of a lawn. There the juniper stands in *Kingis Quair,* whose noble garden shows some familiar details. In each corner an *erber* was *with wandis long and small Railit about* [railed off with tall and thin stakes]: a fenced-off and grassed

[3] C. Estienne and J. Liebault (1572), p. 116; English version by R. Surflet (1616), p. 333.

[4] *The Boke of Curtasye,* 399 ff.

area, as often seen in Crisp. *All the place* was knit with hedges and set about with trees that shaded the alleys, and those walking past could hardly see within: the hedges and the trees were related to each *erber* after the fashion illustrated in B. M. Harl. 4425, so that it was screened from alleys running across the garden. The juniper in the turf-plot, growing so well that, *as it semyt to a lyf without* [as it would seem to anyone outside it], its boughs extended all about the *erber,* is of a slow-growing species with little spread, at best six feet, hardly a shady tree, and the poet, who stresses flourishing green growth throughout this passage, conveys that its head looked impressive from the other side of the hedge.

A description which particularly recalls that of many a *vergier* occurs in *Siege of Thebes,* 3024 ff., where Greeks scour a parched land and come across an *erber:*

> With trees shadowed for the sonne shene,
> Ful of floures and of herbes grene,
> Wonder hoolsom both of syyt and ayr;
> Ther-inne a lady which passingly was fayr,
> Sittyng as tho vnder a laurer tre.

> [Shaded from the bright sun by trees,
> full of flowers and green herbage,
> exceedingly pleasant of both sight and odour;
> and in it a lady who was very beautiful,
> sitting just then under a laurel-tree.]

The flowers need not just spangle the turf, but, as in Froissart, *Le Paradys d'Amours,* whose *praiel*—in a wood, like several instances of the *erber*—is enclosed by lilies and columbines, may go round the grass as a border. For the layout of a small garden of this type, we can refer to the prescription for a *viridarium* that is found in Albertus Magnus, *De Vegetabilibus,* Lib. VII, tract. I, c. xiv, and was imitated by Petrus de Crescentiis for a chapter on the *viridarium herbarum parvum* [small pleasure garden grown with herbage] in his *Opus Ruralium Commodorum,* Lib. VIII, c. i. There are borders about a square lawn for all kinds of flowers and medicinal and aromatic herbs, which not only please by the odour of their scent but, by the variety of flower, refresh the sight. Elliott maintains that plants were cultivated in medieval gardens primarily for utilitarian purposes, the element of pleasure being incidental though beauty and aroma were not unappreciated, but Albertus insists that it is considerations of usefulness which are secondary here and must give way to those of delight: *delectatio enim quaeritur in viridario, et non fructus* [for one seeks delight in a pleasure garden, and not produce]. In the turf, as a screen against the sun, trees are to be planted, or alternatively vines trained. The centre of the lawn should be clear of trees, so that pure air can play freely over the grass plot—superfluous shade breeds impurities—and if possible there should be a spring flowing into a stone receptacle. A garden answering this description appears in the early fifteenth-century picture given by Crisp in fig. xlvi: it is square or rectangular, and by the planted border illustrated there is a tree, and in the grass a springhead in the form of a trough.

The evidence shows that for the *erber* in *Pearl* we should expect to find a *praiel,* small *vergier,* or *viridarium parvum,* and this is indeed what there is in the manuscript illustration, which portrays, it will be observed, the kind of garden that has just been described. Along the foreground, plants for one border; two rows of plants and one or two trees marking off other borders, and converging towards the background from left and right, to indicate, by their recession, the shape as a square or a rectangle; a curve, by a form of perspective, defining the limits of the *erber*—and beyond it trees in the distance.

The feature of this garden called a *huyle* is also spelt *hyul* and *hylle,* the first two forms showing it is not "hill," for which a West Midland type of spelling would be *hull(e),* while *uy* is recognisable as the representative in this region of OE $\bar{y}$ or lengthened y. The proposed identification with Rochdale dialect *hile,* and some cases of *hylle* in *Catholicon Anglicum,* meaning "mound; clump of plants," must be accepted. This is a place-name element in Lancashire and Cheshire, which form part of the dialectal area to which the language of *Pearl* belongs. It may go back to an OE **hygel* "hillock," and such a sense need not convey any idea of specific size, which allows Sister Mary Vincent Hillmann, a recent editor of *Pearl,* to take the *huyle* as large enough to have the *erber* on it, and understand line 41, *On huyle þer perle hit trendeled doun* [on the *huyle* where the pearl rolled down], to mean that the pearl was lost when it rolled away from its owner down the incline. Elliott also sees in the wording a suggestion that the ground sloped. Yet it may indicate no more than the revolving motion of a round object as it slipped and fell from someone's grasp, and down *þurȝ gresse to grounde* [through the grass to the ground] (10).

If one follows Hillmann's view, the poet becomes remarkably persistent in bringing before his readers the situation of the *erber*. There is the passage that has been quoted, then the narrator slept on a *balke,* which she says was the bank or slope of the hillside, woke up with his head lying on that *hylle* (1172), and refers to the dream as having taken place while he was prostrate *ouer þis hyul* (1205). After the pearl's loss what would be the point of emphasising that the *erber* was on a hillock? To suggest actuality? But if the *huyle* was inside it, the position is quite different. The garden was nowhere in particular. Conversely, with the hillock carrying the *erber,* there is vagueness as to the exact spot within it where the pearl was lost. As Hillmann has it: "One day, on the hillock down which his pearl had rolled away from him, he sees a lovely growth of spice-blooms . . . [and] he falls prostrate upon the flower-grown hill." But the other way round there is some definite place in the garden where everything happened. One choice makes for intriguing topography of the *erber* and vague location of the loss; the other, a garden setting around a particular spot where the events took place. It will now be shown that the text, the manuscript illustration, and the setout of this type of garden, all indicate that the *huyle* was inside the *erber,* and point to its identification with a feature to be expected there.

At the end of the lawn, between it and the plants, Albertus and Petrus prescribe a raised piece of turf, square, flowery and pleasant, and suitable as a seat, for mental refreshment and delightful repose:

Inter quas herbas et caespitem [planum] in extremitate caespitis per quadrum elevatior sit caespis florens et amoenus et quasi per medium (*or* modum) sedilium aptatus, cum quo reficiendi sunt sensus, et homines insideant ad delectabiliter quiescendum [between these plants and the lower stretch of turf, at the end of this, there should be a raised piece of turf, square, flowery, and pleasant, suitable as a sort of seat, for re-freshment of the senses, and for people to sit on for delightful repose].

For these turfed mounds, see Crisp, chapter 11. Several of his illustrations have people sitting on them, and herbs and flowers planted on the tops. A good example is portrayed in the picture cited above for the *viridarium herbarum parvum,* fig. xlvi, where it is square or rectangular, with high-standing flowers, and at the end of the lawn. Crisp's volumes show that these mounds came to have plank supports, or even brick sides, and that continuous seating of this form, backed by a staked rose hedge or a wall, could go along the borders of the lawn, and so it does in the *praiel* of B. M. Harl. 4425; but the free-standing mound still remained as an alternative. As late as the seventeenth century, the English version of *Maison Rustique* specifies that some of the sweet herbs and flowers which are cited for nosegays should be set upon seats, and on these *The Country Housewifes Garden* puts daisies and violets, and herbs whose scent is released by touch—pennyroyal and camomile.[5] In our own day there may be no raised seat of this kind, but R. Genders, *Perfume in the Garden* (1955), p. 112, advises that a delightful addition would be a scented corner where:

[5] Surflet, p. 235; W. Lawson, *The Country Housewifes Garden* (1618), p. 18.

the refreshing fragrance of the plants will only be appreciated to the utmost if one has time to take out a cushion on which to rest one's head and then to lie flat over the carpet of fragrant herbs. Pennyroyal and the trailing evening primrose, camomile and semi-prostrate thyme, can all be used but like all herbs they are only richly fragrant if they are given a dry, sunny position where they can be warmed by the summer sun. Then let this warmth penetrate through one's clothes, so that upon rising you smell like a packet of fragrant herbs which will keep fresh and aromatic the whole day through.

The Middle English term for the turf-mound is *bench* (*MED*, sense 4), and on one, planted with camomile, the sleeper lay and dreamed in the fifteenth-century poem, *Why I can't be a Nun.*[6] A lady was torn by mental conflict, went into the *erber* section of a garden, prayed, and committed her cause to God. Upon her saying, *"Now do to me aftyr thy wylle"* (111 ff.):

> at that worde for-feynte I fylle
> Among the herbes fresche and fyne;
> Vnto a benche of camomylle
> My wofulle hede I dyd inclyne.

> [on these words I fell
> among the fresh and choice herbs;
> on a bench of camomile
> I leaned my woeful head.]

Thus the turfed bench is a normal feature of an *erber,* and a seat on which one could lie, and dream. As in *Pearl,* 42 ff., on it there would be herbs casting their shadow in the summer sun, it would be seemly to look at, from it would float delicious scent, and as one lay across it the fragrance could be powerful. Planted as it would be with herbs and flowers, this would fittingly be called a *huyle.* In the manuscript illustration of *Pearl,* the curved sweep from the sleeper's legs to his side indicates its existence: his feet are on the ground, his trunk on the *huyle,* and he is leaning on his right arm. The head is outlined against the background halfway up a tree as well as far up the garden,

---

[6] *Phil. Soc. Trans.* 1858.

and so is not lying on the mound, as it was when he woke up, but the posture is meant to show his visionary condition. Between him and the border plants in the foreground there are flowers, on a dark blue and sinuous patch, which will be the shadow cast by them in a strong sun, and dips down the side of the *huyle* to the ground. The situation is like that described in *Why I can't be a Nun,* and the sleeper looks as if he has fallen to lie on his side after sitting on the *huyle,* turned towards the flowers at this place where, *Syþen in þat spote hit fro me sprange, Ofte haf I wayted* [since it dropped from me in that spot, I have often lingered] (13 f.), and, on this occasion, *Bifore þat spot* (49) clenched his hand.

He lay on a *balke* (62), the usual sense of which is an "unploughed ridge dividing furlongs," and between this and a turfed mound there were resemblances: both were pieces of raised ground with grass, plants, and flowers, across a lower surface. *Balke* never meant a hill, nor the bank or slope of a hill; it was a ridge or bank which ran across and divided or was an obstacle. So Hillman's treatment of this word involves a slip from the latter to the former "bank," and *balke,* on her interpretation of *huyle,* can only give a disturbing complex of rises, a mound on a hillock.

It was *þat floury flaȝt* (57) on which he fell, to sleep, and *flaȝt,* so it is assumed, refers to a stretch of turf, the greensward. But this is not a usage known for the word, which normally means "a piece of turf cut from the ground," and sometimes "a snowflake," in MScots "a flash." The basis is "a stripped-off piece, a detached fragment like a flake," the noun (probably on OE Angl. **flæht*) being related to the verb *flay.* Taking *flaȝt* in its usual sense, the phrase will refer to a flowery slab of turf, and this is a suitable and imaginative appellation for a turfed bench, which looked like some gigantic cut sod, with flowers, dropped on the lawn. Elliott's identification of the *floury flaȝt* with a flowery mead is therefore rejected.

But he also sees reference to a flowery mead elsewhere, and

even a possible suggestion of fruit on trees. This is in the third
stanza, which is read:

> Þat spot of spyseʒ mot nedeʒ sprede,
> Þer such rycheʒ to rot is runne;
> Blomeʒ blayke and blwe and rede
> Þer *schyneʒ* ful schyr agayn þe sunne.
> Flor and fryte may not be fede
> Þer hit doun drof in moldeʒ dunne;
> For vch gresse mot grow of grayneʒ dede;
> No whete were elleʒ to woneʒ wonne.
> Of goud vche goude is ay bygonne;
> So semly a sede moʒt fayly not,
> Þat spryngande spyceʒ vp ne sponne
> Of þat precios perle wythouten spotte.   (25–36)

> [That spot, where such riches have run to rot,
> must surely spread with spices,
> and yellow, blue, and red flowers
> shine there brightly in the sun (*passage as here emended*).
> Flower and fruit cannot be without vigour
> where it fell down into the dark soil;
> for every plant must grow from dead seed;
> otherwise no wheat would be gathered into the barn.
> Everything good always takes its origin from what is good;
> so excellent a seed cannot then fail
> to have rising spices springing up from it,
> that precious pearl without a spot.]

Yet if *schyneʒ* were *schyne,* infinitive, dependent like *sprede*
on *mot,* and a comma, instead of a semicolon, supplied after
the second line, the stanza would be argument from beginning
to end, with the narrator saying that spices, flowers, and fruit
ought to spring from the pearl. It is in the following lines that
he mentions the occasion when he entered the *erber* and found
spices flowering at the site of the loss. With this simple emendation there comes a unity to the whole stanza—no longer
does he suddenly shunt to a description of the *erber* and back
again to the main track of his thoughts—a balance between the
first two pairs of lines, and a smooth operation of the foursome,
as a complete piece in the pattern, that carries its own convic-

tion. Now we have only an expectancy of spices and their blooms and ripening seeds somewhere sunny in the *erber,* and in the ensuing stanza this idea can only be connected with the *huyle,* that *floury flaʒt,* and its herbs. There is no suggestion of trees with fruit, and Elliott's flowery mead is completely dispelled, so that, apart from the turf-bench and its plants, the only detail given about the *erber* is that it was green.

Elliott comments on the comparative absence of description of the garden, and his observation is even truer now that the discussion has denuded the *erber* of some features he sees there. Instead it has been found that to all intents and purposes the poet gives nothing in it except a feature that is not apparent to Elliott, and this by itself leads to results that differ from his, to begin with, on the question of convention or originality.

The details of the garden given by the author of *Pearl* are strictly conventional, Elliott says, because "the poet adorns his garden with the customary flowers and fragrant herbs whose powerful aroma pervades the scene," and the ground is "decked with flowers: the familiar pattern of the flowery mead." But this is not so. The plants are not, in the usual manner, vaguely arrayed about the *erber,* but only on the *huyle,* the sole source of that powerful aroma. And yet, on the other hand, "convention gives place to a deliberate and truly admirable artistic originality" because "plants and flowers grow, not in neat raised beds or pots, but in apparently indiscriminate profusion," without the conventional touch of "severe uniformity." But to think so is to confuse the pictorial and literary arts, for any English or French poem of Chaucer's day speaking of flowers and plants in neat raised beds or pots would be refreshing, and, if the author of *Pearl* had his plants in indiscriminate profusion about the *erber,* no reader of the literature of this period, in which, with garden after garden, writers do just this, would find any artistic originality. Thus, in having the herbs so definitely located, on a turfed mound, the poet is unconventional, and draws on reality.

Then Elliott argues that, as a garden was a playground of joy and happiness, "clearly no suitable setting for sorrow," somehow in *Pearl* it had to be reconciled with the mood, and so the poet is careful to omit those features felt to be most expressive of joy and delight. Therefore, since it would conflict with the elegiac and mournful effect that the author intends, spring is avoided, in deliberate rejection of an accepted poetic tradition, since customarily the medieval plesaunce is almost instinctively associated with this season. Claiming that the poet practises, in a manner reminiscent of the Anglo-Saxons, the art of making Nature share a person's mood, Elliott extends himself on the topic of the natural background in the garden being "one with the heart of man, while it reflects the thoughts and passions that agitate the latter." But how and why this is so, it will emerge, differs from what he supposes, and, as will now be shown, his arguments have no foundation.

The effect of melancholy is anything but spoilt by a contrast between an unhappy person's condition and the blissfulness of Nature, and in fact it is used by medieval poets as a conventional method of emphasising mournfulness. In *Why I can't be a Nun* the writer goes into joyous detail of the *erber,* and has birds singing away merrily on every spray:

> But my longyng and my dolowrys
> For alle thys sport wolde not away.
>
> [But my melancholy and my sorrows
> would not depart, in spite of all this diversion.]

Which is typical. As for *Pearl's* choice of season, first of all why should August, which is *a seson mery & glad,* according to Lydgate, *Debate of the Hors,* 134, and the time of harvest, so joyous in the seasonal headpiece of *King Alisaunder,* 5745 ff., make a garden suit sadness? More fitting would be a setting somewhat later, in the fall, as in *The Assembly of Ladies,* Hoccleve's *Complaint,* and various French poems. Second, is there such a seasonal contrast between the garden scenery of *Pearl* and that of other medieval literature, when in half of the poems set in a plesaunce by Machaut, the most influential poet of this period, there is no mention of spring, but an impression given of only a summerish part of the year, and our author does not show an August in the *erber* at all? There it is just a time when spices flower. The season of harvest and ripe fruit is not in the garden, but in the atmosphere, harmonising the date of the dream with the subject which is to be treated, an example of a technique of which illustrations are readily available both in English and in French medieval poetry. There is a harvesttime and August opening in the dream-vision poem of *La Panthere d'Amors,* and from R. Tuve's *Seasons and Months: Studies in a Tradition of Middle English Poetry* (1933) one can conclude that in using the seasonal motif of the kind found in *Pearl,* 40, *Quen corne is coruen wyth croke3 kene* [when the grain is cut with sharp sickles], the poet adopts a convention.[7] Chaucer drew on both the Middle English tradition and the French model of a plesaunce. Clearly, in placing the dream in August, and shunning a picture of the garden in the manner of French literature, the author of *Pearl* is not rejecting any poetic tradition, but taking only what is to his purpose. And this is not to avoid description because it would not go with elegiac impression, nor, blending external setting with thought and inward sentiment as the Anglo-Saxons did, to make the *erber* reflect the narrator's mood, for mournful associations are not conveyed by it as a garden. Beautiful flowers are not sad things, though flowers connected with sad things are.

To lay the foundation for an understanding of the *Pearl* poet's use of the garden it has to be related to the practices of his period. He was on the same cultural level as Chaucer, and, as with the one it has been found useful to scan contemporary French literature, so it would seem likely that light can be thrown on the work of the other from there, too, and especially

---

[7] On the seasonal headpiece, see also G. V. Smithers, *King Alisaunder,* II (*EETS,* 237), pp. 35 ff.

by the prime fourteenth-century exponent of such scenes in gardens, that is, Machaut. In a characteristic poem of his, *Le Dit dou Vergier,* the narrator goes into a garden which appears to be virtually a terrestrial paradise as he looks around it, savouring its delights. In this setting he has throes of conflicting thoughts concerning a lady, until a visionary state supervenes that settles his heart. The same type of situation occurs in *Remede de Fortune,* and also *Le Dit de l'Alerion,* where there is no vision proper, but the narrator has a transport of rapture, the mental change setting in after realisation of the *vergier's* fragrance and beauty. Particularly from the last it can be seen that, while in medieval poems a forest is often a place in which an alteration of mood is associated with a change of scenery, with the garden is implied rest till the therapy of the surroundings, by sight and smell, exerts its effect. For a modern reader the impression which a medieval garden made is lost chiefly with respect to the perfume, which, right up to much later times, is repeatedly said to comfort and revive the spirits. The location of a mental conflict there, one gathers, suggests that there will be a cure.

Unlike Machaut, the poet of *Pearl* does not mention trees, flowers in profusion on the ground, birds singing, etc., but the same implication is stamped on the *erber,* because of its aromatic herbs of strong impact:

> On huyle þer perle hit trendeled doun
> Schadowed þis worteȝ ful schyre and schene,
> Gilofre, gyngure and gromylyoun,
> And pyonys powdered ay bytwene.
> Ȝif hit watȝ semly on to sene,
> A fayr reflayr ȝet fro hit flot.   (41–46)

[On the turf-mound where the pearl rolled down,
shadows were cast by very bright and beautiful plants,
clove, ginger, and gromwell,
and peonies scattered at regular intervals.
If it was beautiful to look upon,
an even lovelier scent came floating from it.]

Yet one must enquire why all attention is concentrated on no other feature of the garden but a *huyle,* and no other source of delight but spices on it—and of strange nature. The peony should not, in August, cause odour to float from it, its month being May. If *gilofre* were the clove-pink, as is assumed, then this is a July flower, but is it necessary to consider the native plant when there is ginger here, and in *Wars of Alexander,* 5426, strange snakes of the East browse on ginger and *gyloffre,* the clove-spice? The collection is divorced from season and geography, and has no place in physical dimensions, even if gromwell does flower at this time of the year. With the effect of a mosaic the plants were disposed as they would be in decorative art, like a charge on a field of green—*powdered* was a heraldic term. Or, to place beside other contexts with *bitwene* "here and there," like an ornamental pattern, as on embroidered stuff, upon which in *Sir Gawain,* 611, appear *papiayeʒ paynted pernyng bitwene* [preening parrots painted here and there]; or on the apparelled and painted walls of a hall, which have *dyamountis full dantely dentit betwene* [diamonds very elegantly set at intervals] in *Rauf Coilʒear,* 665.[8] And *gyngyure* alliterates with *gylofre,* in the same context as *gromyl,* along with nutmeg, cinnamon, etc., in a stanza of *Annot and John* (B. M. Harl. 2253) which employs them in an extended metaphor of the curative powers of a lady. To the same sphere belonged peony seeds. The mound in the *erber* bore plants that appear to be really dried spices, springing from the pearl, and flowering, with neither their medicinal nor spicing qualities

---

[8] With the wording in *Pearl* compare *Sir Gawain,* 167, *þe golde ay inmyddes,* of plaiting where gold thread takes part in some regular pattern of alternation along with the coloured hair. Of interest, as supplying some kind of analogue to the *Pearl* passage, is Milton's *Paradise Lost,* IV, 699 ff.:

> each beauteous flow'r,
> *Iris* all hues, Roses and Jessamin
> Rear'd high thir flourisht heads between, and wrought
> Mosaic.

brought out by the poem, but beauty and aroma, which if not synaesthetic, as if the narrator was seeing and smelling things by his sense of taste, are metaphoric, of healing properties. The mention of a tropical plant such as ginger, according to Elliott, here exemplifies the conventional element in medieval plant lists, and "its inclusion may simply be an alliterative device or a straight borrowing from the *gingere* of the English *Romaunt.*" Against this prosaic view of a piece of imaginative poetry can be cited the *Roman de la Rose* itself, in which the presence of ginger, there with *clowe-gelofre* and other spices *To eten whan men rise fro table* [to eat when men rise from the table] (*Romaunt,* 1372), is bound up with the nature of the dream-garden. The plants in the *erber* must correspond in some way to the pearl, from which the previous stanza has led one to expect the rise of appropriate spices, and they put the *huyle* on the level of the contents of the garden of the *Roman de la Rose*—imagery.

This is not the only occasion when an *erber* in late four-teenth-century poetry contains a symbol. The Tree that bears the fruit of Charity in *Piers Plowman,* B. xvi. 4 ff., grows from the root of Mercy in the *erber* of Man's Heart. The figure of being rooted in the heart is a common one, illustrated, for instance, by the Medieval French usage, with *cuer,* of the verb *enter* "to implant," or in Augustine's writings, as when he speaks of *duae radices, charitas et cupiditas* [two roots, love and greed], each of which might be planted in the heart. A homily by Hugh of St. Victor, like *Piers Plowman,* has an allegorical Tree in the *cordis hortus* [garden of the heart]. The conception of a parallel between inmost processes and those of horticulture is imbedded in Christian writing, and derived from such New Testament passages as the sowing parables and John 15:1, *Pater agricola est* [the Father is the husbandman]. We also have the idea of the *mentis hortus* [garden of the mind], therefore, as in a lyric by Philip the Chancellor; the heart being the seat of what goes on in the *animus,* the soul as thinking, feeling, willing, a relation exists between it and the mind. Because there is many a metaphor resting on the response of Man to Nature—such as Hugh of St. Victor's interpretation of *flores apparuerunt in terra nostra* [flowers appeared in our land], in which the flowers are *aeterna gaudia* [eternal joys] and the land *intus, in nobis*[9] [within, inside us]—and the private garden was a place where one often stayed in reflection, or even prayer, as contexts often show, such a locality is a fitting symbol for the heart, or the mind, on which its workings are projected. If the garden well renders these, then the going into it is suitable for an occasion when a process takes place within them. In the allegory of a lyric, by the fifteenth-century poet Charles d'Orleans, one enters alone, with the heart, into a garden of Thought:

> Dedans mon jardin de Pensée
> Avecques mon cueur, seul entray.[10]

> [Inside my garden of Thought,
> together with my heart, I entered alone.]

Imagery of this nature is also to be found in Machaut. A simple type is used in the lyric that treats a lady as truly like the spring, clothing the heart with verdure by turning misery into delightful thought:

> Tout resjoit, tout ranature
> Cuer secrement en verdure,
> Et fait de tristece obscure
> Joieuse pensée.[11]

---

[9] For the examples from Hugh of St. Victor, *see Sermones Centum*, VI (Migne, *Patrologia Latina*, CLXXVII, 914), and *Sermo de Assumptione B. Mariae* (*ibid.*, 1218 ff.). Phillip's lyric is in *The Oxford Book of Medieval Latin Verse*, no. 253.

[10] Charles d'Orléans, *Poésies*, edited by P. Champion (1923), Rondeaux, CCLVII, 4 f.

[11] Machaut, *Poésies Lyriques*, edited by V. F. Chichmaref (1909), Les Chansons Baladées, XIX, 19 ff.

> [All delights, all transforms
> my heart secretly with verdure,
> and turns dark sorrow
> into happy thought.]

And, for a case of full deployment, expressing the conception of the garden setting illustrated from Charles d'Orleans, we return to *Le Dit de l'Alerion,* which proves to be a poem of importance for our purpose.

It is an allegory drawn from hawking, and tells of hunting birds that passed through the narrator's hands, in representation of a series of love affairs. The breakup of the last relationship left him very unhappy. He wandered till he entered a garden, sat down, and was tossed between pleasurable and grievous thoughts, until his heart prayed to Amours for deliverance, and he emerged from his brown study to smell the delicious fragrance, see the verdure and the colourful flowers, and to realise what a beautiful spot he was in, a veritable paradise. He was led to have a *dous souvenir* [sweet memory] of the *alerion,* a hunting-bird of his past, and then it appeared and perched on his wrist, and he was enraptured. When true lovers part, he explains, they should preserve the memory of their love through thick and thin and any further affairs, and in times of depression have recourse to Amours, who will send them to the *vergier amoureus* [garden of love], that is, call their hearts to sweet remembrance of love; and where they will find fragrant plants—sweet thoughts—which give hearts peace. And so on. This garden is interpreted in a passage that begins in lines 4691 ff.:

> Cils vergiers dont je ci raconte,
> Par quoy je ne faille a mon compte,
> C'est Amours especiaument
> Qui cuers rapelle doucement . . .
> Après, les herbes odorans,
> Qui tient cuers en pais demourans,
> Ce sont les trés douces pensées
> Selonc l'art d'Amours apensées.

[This garden of which I tell here,
without failing in my account,
it is Love in particular
that the heart sweetly remembers . . .
Next, the scented herbs,
which the heart keeps resting in peace,
these are the very sweet thoughts
called up according to the art of Love.]

That the symbolism of *les herbes odorans* is not coined by
Machaut for the occasion can be seen from his *Le Lay Mortel,*
191 ff., where perfume surpassing that of scented plants comes
through thought of a lady:

Rose, lis, mente, cerfueil
Tant douce oudeur à mon vueil
N'ont com celle que je cueil,
Quant parfondement
Pense bien à son acueil.

[Rose, lily, mint, chervil
have no such sweet scent to please me
as that I receive
when I think
deeply of her welcome.]

Romaunt, 1025 ff., has the conception not only that sweet
thoughts have perfume, but also that it is perceived in the
heart, as with the scent of symbolic roses in lines 1661 ff.

In *Le Dit de l 'Alerion,* then, we have an allegory which at
first is related to events which are physical, of people coming
together and going apart. But in its further development, the
scene in the garden, it is taken to refer to an occasion, no
matter where, when these experiences are thought over. The
allegory now pertains to the mental. Seeing the garden with
fresh eyes, and appreciating its fragrance and beauty, is coming to remembrance of affection and attachment, having Sweet
Thought that, in the *Roman de la Rose:*

makith lovers to have remembraunce
Of comfort, and of high pleasaunce . . .

> For Thought anoon thanne shall bygynne,
> As fer, God wot, as he can fynde,
> To make a myrrour of his mynde.
>
> [causes lovers to remember
> delight and great pleasure . . .,
> for Thought at once then will begin,
> as far, God knows, as he can manage,
> to make a mirror of his mind.]

And the arrival of the *alerion* stands for this calling to mind of the loved lady. When the bird remains forever after with the narrator, it is because a picture of the beloved is kept in the heart:

> de ceste douce figure
> Que Douce Pensée en toy figure,
> S'en dois en ton cuer une ymage
> Faire.[12]
>
> [of this sweet form,
> which Sweet Thought imagines within you,
> you should make a picture in your heart.]

That is, to apply the phraseology of a lyric by Machaut—and come full circle—in the place where she had planted memories and thoughts like a gardener's slips:

> elle ente
> Un dous penser et souvenir parfait
> Dedens mon cuer.[13]
>
> [she implants
> a sweet thought and perfect memory
> within my heart.]

As in *Le Dit de l' Alerion* the narrator of *Pearl* entered a garden, from nowhere. How the *erber* reflects thought and inward sentiment bears no relation to practices in Anglo-Saxon, but can be understood against the background of French liter-

---

[12] *Romaunt of the Rose,* 2801 ff.; Machaut, *Le Confort d'Ami,* 2187 ff.
[13] Chichmaref, *op. cit.,* La Loange des Dames, CXIV, 9 ff.

ature of the poet's day. The marvellous Fountain of the dream-garden of the *Roman de la Rose* appears in garden settings for persons who fall asleep and dream, for example in Machaut's *La Fonteinne Amoureuse;* so in the *erber* there was an expressive object, a *huyle* that is more than a blend of *les herbes odorans,* in *Le Dit de l' Alerion,* and, in the same author's *Le Lay de Plour,* 17 ff., the surviving root of a tree torn out of the ground—a dead lover—producing green growth, flower, and fruit, which are *souvenir.* With the mournfulness of the flourishing root's symbolism it lay within a setting often used by Machaut for a scene of mental turmoil, while its fragrant and beautiful spice plants hold his other image's promise of relief, and also point to significance. And in *Pearl* as in *Le Dit de l'Alerion* the scene is a further development of an initial allegory about a past that was responsible for what happened in the garden. One can interpret the narrator's entry into the allegorical garden as his thinking deeply, and the plants on the *huyle* as memories and thoughts concerning what lay in it, and:

> Þat wont watȝ whyle deuoyde my wrange
> And heuen my happe and al my hele.   (15–16)
>
> [that once used to dispel my sorrow
> and cause my happiness and well-being.]

There were lovely and richly scented herbs on the *huyle,* i.e. he thought of what it stood for, and memories crowded upon him; he remained grief stricken before the spot where the *worteȝ* [plants] were, i.e. these thoughts caused an onset of great sorrow; grief and reason strove in his confused mind, till the odour of the herbs shot to his brain and overcame him, i.e. he had a mental crisis; and he slid into sleep on the *huyle* and its plants, and his spirit left the *erber,* i.e. he was rapt out of his senses while intent on nothing but the matter represented by the *huyle* that so stirred him because there he had lost the pearl:

> I felle vpon þat floury flaȝt,
> Such odour to my herneȝ schot;
> I slode vpon a slepyng-slaȝte
> On þat precios perle wythouten spot.   (57–60)

> [I fell upon that flowery sod,
> for such a perfume went straight to my head;
> I slipped into a sleep that struck me down,
> to lie on that precious pearl without a spot.]

Because *Pearl* shares here basic structural elements with *Le Dit de L'Alerion,* there is cogency in the use of the *Dit,* not only to shed light on the methods of the English poem, but also to throw into relief the distinctive handling of fundamental ingredients in its opening. The *Pearl* poet takes the conventional garden setting for a dreamer and makes it the foundation of an initial allegory. The scene before the dream is further anticipated both by the preliminary visits to the site and by a stanza of argument using a metaphor, to do with its nature as a place of herbs and flowers, that prepares one to find them growing where the pearl was lost. As with the *Dit,* a change in level is not explicit, and, in the passage from one to the other, allegory pertaining to the physical melts into what relates to the mental. So much so in *Pearl,* because the integration of the initial allegory and the scene in the garden telescopes the former into the latter, that the preparatory visits can figure either going to a place or thinking about a loss. Since this structure of superposition limits the narrator's concern to what is within the *erber,* and makes him react for its own sake, and not in relation to any thing, matter, or event outside, physical action is compatible with self-withdrawal, whereas in Machaut portrayal of a pensive is also that of a nonactive condition. In the garden, as the Frenchman makes parts of it into symbols, so the author of *Pearl* turns for an image, and an unconventional one, to a normal characteristic of an *erber,* the *caespis elevatior, florens et amoenus et quasi per medium sedilium aptatus.* With this choice the poet achieves great economy and fulfils many unities, for at one stroke he acquires the essential symbol and a feature which can be, on the one hand, the location of thought and act, at the very place where one would expect a person, engaged in reflection, to be in an *erber,* and, on the other, the dreamer's couch, not, as usual, devoid of implication, but charged with it—and he strips the garden of everything but this and the verdure.

Pearl differs from the *Dit,* obviously, for instance in the poet's restriction of both parts of the structure of the opening to a brief compass—his aim is to develop instead the dream—and in the lack of interpretation, which is replaced by an overt symbolism in the presence of those spices. But also, subtly, in the reliance on ambiguity. Machaut makes some use of simultaneous verbal reference to the literal and the allegorical, but he has nothing like the delicate play with connotations that the *Pearl* poet displays when describing the garden and what it contains. At first, the *erber* is a *praiel* or *viretum,* a place with a plot of turf. The pearl was lost in the grass. Later, in the *erber,* the features of a *viridarium herbarum parvum* are implied. Yet it is no more definitely a garden than the pearl is a pearl:

> So rounde, so reken in vche araye,
> So smal, so smoþe her sydeȝ . . .
>
> [so rounded, so fair in every form of adornment,
> so small in circumference, and so smooth her sides . . .]

Erber, supposed by Elliott to be merely a convenient synonym for "garden" in *Pearl,* proves to be so convenient that it is used three times and any alternative appellation is excluded. The usage is not only proper and precise, but deliberate, the *erber* remaining both a grassplot and a garden, and the poet exploiting this range of meaning, on the one hand to strengthen the application of the allegory, and to give, on the other, scope for garden imagery to follow. And the *huyle* that appears to be such a natural part of an *erber*—were it not for those herbs—

is never called a *benche,* nor is it explicitly a seat, but only a mound with plants, a transverse piece of raised ground overgrown with herbage, and a flowery sod.

But when the loss of the pearl is told, the narrator's attitude towards this is less in terms of a pearl than of what it signifies, as also during the distressing visits to the *erber,* so that it becomes a grass stretch with a particular implication. This is carried into the scene at the site of the loss, which now comes fully into focus. There he acted a little one-man play, clenching his hand before the place of the herbs, and performing his part as if concerned, in thought, more with a mound on turf in a locality of another kind than with a feature of a garden. A certain significance, to do with that other sort of grassy plot, is thus attached to the *huyle,* and yet, given what it would be in a garden, its purpose was to be sat on, and for him to lie there and dream, as in *Why I can't be a Nun,* was natural. But, if it were not for the transcendent whole of which part is the conception of this situation as a scene in a garden, he might as well have been anywhere, completely absorbed in thought, even lying where he grieved for Pearl, *Regretted by myn one on nyȝte* [grieved for as I lie alone at night] (243), that is, in bed, with head on pillow.

On one level, therefore, he was in a garden and on a turfed mound; on another, the mound was on the *erber* of the initial allegory; on a third, he was in a Garden of Remembrance. The aspects of the *erber* and the *huyle* are so related that if they stand, in terms of the initial allegory, for graveyard and grave, there is a shift to Garden of Remembrance and thoughts about one who has died. Between a grave and a turf bench, even if both were planted with herbs, there were indeed differences in use and appearance, but they did not exceed those between a graveyard and a pleasure garden, and the symbolic power of the *erber* and the *huyle* is made to rest partly on the symbolic power of language. Also, the narrator lay in a garden on a turfed seat, not on what it means except as a topic that engrossed him, for there is no free-for-all among the dimensions, and the bones of the structure are articulated thus:

> An Initial Allegory (about a sad Event), made up of the same kind of material as its further development, a Garden Scene [before a Dream], which functions as a Critical Occasion (somewhere) of Reflection and Remembrance (about the Event) that to a mind in torment brought repose [after the Dream].

No side of the *erber* and the *huyle* works by itself, and one can only arrive at a proper idea of the organism by synthesis. In addition, rather than definite and clearly defined interpretations leaping at one from the text, suggestions of their nature are apprehended, as with the comparable fantasies of Machaut and his disciple Froissart, in which the literal level exists very much in its own right, as a story shimmering with significance. This is even so when explanations are provided by the author, for in *Le Dit de l'Alerion* the garden stands not simply, but *especiaument* [particularly], for what it is taken to mean, and the *alerion* is not just one's lady, but *Ce puet estre sa douce dame* [it could be his sweet lady] (4723). So, too, in *Pearl,* as one begins to read, it should be felt that the garden and the turfed mound, in the context of the loss, *could* be a graveyard and a grave, and, on that dramatic occasion before the dream, they *could* be the mirror of thought and the thought about.

Also, the appeal, in image-making scenes of the French poems, is first not to the understanding but the imagination, and expressiveness lies in evocation by what in itself is already poetically evocative. Their luxuriance may be lacking in the treatment of this *erber,* but there is richness in the shifting symbolism, when the garden of the allegory becomes a garden of the heart, and here again the evocation not only of meaning is the poet's procedure. Primarily, his *huyle* impinges as a feature which fully partakes of an *erber's* attributes of beauty and perfume, and specially promotes the deep reflection and mental refreshment associated with it, a penetrating rich fragrance, enveloping and soothing, in the drowsy sunshine being exhaled from plants no less efficacious than the peppermint that is "valuable for fatigue as everyone knows who has gone off to sleep on a bank" of it (Genders, p. 109). And, dreamlike in the spices it bears and the grief directed upon it, the *huyle* where the pearl was dropped recalls a certain mound on its turf in a way that presents it as if preserved, without account of place or time, within a garden of the kind that was delightful, like a little paradise, and pleasantly green—the poet refers to this quality—a place of rest among the fresh and unwithered. So the dynamic flow of effect begins from the potential in the form, and the reader is led towards a dream in whose Paradise the narrator was made to understand wherein, for him who had lost such a Pearl, lay comfort and peace of mind.

18

A NOTE ON *PEARL*[1]

Norman Davis

> Ouer þis hyul þis lote I laȝte,
> For pyty of my perle enclyin,
> And syþen to God I hit bytaȝte
> In *Krysteȝ dere blessyng and myn.*   (1205–1208)
>
> [This was what befell me upon this mound,
> as I lay grieving for my pearl;
> and then I commended it to God,
> in Christ's precious blessing and mine.]

FORMULAS OF GREETING IN MEDIEVAL LETTERS NATURALLY differ according to the relation of the writer to the person addressed. Some years ago I noted that characteristic phrases were used by parents to their children, and that Dr. F. E. Harmer had found ancient occurrences of a formula which is

Reprinted, by permission of the author and of the Clarendon Press, Oxford, England, from the *Review of English Studies*, N. S., XVII (1966), 403–405. The appendix contains hitherto unpublished material. Translations have been supplied by the author.

[1] I owe to Professor J. R. R. Tolkien the suggestion for this footnote to my article "The *Litera Troili* and English Letters" (*R. E. S.*, N.S., XVI [1965], 233–244). I quote *Pearl* from E. V. Gordon's edition (Oxford, 1953).

evidently the ancestor of one of them.[2] It is reported of King Harold Harefoot (1037–1040): "Þa sende Harold king Ælfgar munuc agen to þam arcebiscope Eadsige and to eallon Cristes cyrcean munecan, and grette hig ealle *Godes gretincge and his*" [Then King Harold sent the monk Ælfgar back to Archbishop Eadsige and to all the monks of Christ Church, and greeted them all with God's greeting and his]; and the same greeting was used by Gilbert Crispin, abbot of Westminster (d. 1117) in writs to sheriffs: "G. abbod and alle tha brodera on Westmynstr' gretith N. schirerefan on Estsex' *Godes gretyng' and owr*"[3] [Abbot G. and all the brethren at Westminster greet N., sheriff of Essex, with God's greeting and ours]. A more elaborate form of similar sense occurs in a spurious papal privilege interpolated into the Peterborough Chronicle; it is under the year 675, but must have been written down about 1122: "Ic Agatho Papa of Rome grete wel seo wurðfulle Æþelred Myrcene kyning . . . and alle þa abbotes þa sindon on Englalande *Godes gretinge and minre bletsunge*"[4] [I Agatho, Pope of Rome, cordially greet Ethelred, honoured king of Mercia . . . and all the abbots in England, with God's greeting and my blessing].

After these early twelfth-century occurrences the formula seems to disappear from sight until soon after the middle of the fourteenth century. Then what must surely be its descendant appears, in a very different environment, in one of Thomas Sampson's model letters in C.U.L. MS. Ee. iv. 20, dated about 1365. A mother replies to a letter from her son at Oxford asking for money: "Salutz od le benisone Dieu et la meusmez [*sic*]" [Greetings, with the blessing of God, and mine]. A

---

[2] "The Language of the Pastons," *Proceedings of the British Academy*, xl (1955), 138, n. 2; F. E. Harmer, "The English Contribution to the Epistolary Usages of Early Scandinavian Kings," *Saga-Book of the Viking Society*, xiii (1950), 115–155, esp. p. 150.

[3] F. E. Harmer, *Anglo-Saxon Writs* (Manchester, 1952), pp. 62, 542; J. Armitage Robinson, *Gilbert Crispin* (Cambridge, 1911), p. 37.

[4] *The Peterborough Chronicle* 1070–1154, ed. C. Clark (Oxford, 1958), p. 103.

variant appears at the ends of some other model letters of about 1383 and 1385, both from father to son: "Et nostre Seignur vous doigne grace a ce faire, vous octroiant sa benisone, et je vous doigne la mesne" [And Our Lord give you grace to do this, granting you his blessing, and I give you mine]; "Et nostre Seignur vous esploit, vous donant sa benesone, et Jeo vous doigne la mesne"[5] [And Our Lord prosper you, giving you his blessing, and I give you mine].

In English the same pattern of words, but with "Christ's" instead of "God's," first reappears in the Lincoln's Inn manuscript of *Arthour and Merlin* (dated before 1425), line 880:

> Go now hom, douȝter myn,
> And haue Cristes blessyng and myn.[6]
>
> [Go home now, daughter,
> and have Christ's blessing and mine.]

From this time on "blessing" takes the place in the phrase of the earlier "greeting." (Both had appeared in the Peterborough privilege.)[7] In addition to this passage the *Middle English Dictionary* quotes a will made in 1444 by Sir Giles Daubeney of Somerset: "I wol that William my sone have ij salers gilt . . . and al myn armour and ij of my best horsse and goddis blessing and myn with a condicion that he lette not my last will"[8] [I wish my son William to have two gilt saltcellars . . . and all my armour and two of my best horses, and God's blessing and mine, on condition that he does not obstruct my last will]; and

---

[5] *Formularies which bear on the History of Oxford c. 1204–1420,* ed. H. E. Salter, W. A. Pantin, H. G. Richardson (Oxford Hist. Soc., 1942), ii. 375, 403, 407.

[6] Ed. E. Kölbing (Leipzig, 1890), p. 317. The Auchinleck text has "Go now hom, douhter min, And haue Crist in hert þin" (875–876).

[7] For the persistence of "greeting" in the sense of "blessing" cf. "In Godes greting mote heo go" in the Harley lyric "A wayle whyt ase whalles bon" (*Early Middle English Verse and Prose,* ed. J. A. W. Bennett and G. V. Smithers [Oxford, 1966], viii G. 49).

[8] *Somerset Medieval Wills (Second Series),* ed. F. W. Weaver (Somerset Record Soc. 19, 1903), p. 341.

a letter from Jane Stonor to her son William in 1475: "Sone, I send you Goddys blessyng and myne."[9]

The formula and variants of it are to be found in many other places in the fifteenth century. (Much the commonest form is "God's blessing"; "Christ's" is occasional.) Another Stonor letter slightly earlier than the one just quoted, from Thomas Stonor to his son (the same William) in 1468 or 1469, has the same words as his wife's with a few spelling differences.[10] The Pastons provide no fewer than 34 examples: 7 in letters written by Agnes over the years 1445 to 1453 (1 to Edmond Paston I, the others to John I), the remaining 27 by Margaret between 1463 and 1478 (16 to John II, the rest to John III). Most of them come at the beginning of the letter, after the opening greeting: "Soon, I grete ȝow wel wyth Goddys blyssyng and myn"; "I greet yow wel and send yow Goddys blyssyng and myn."[11] But a few, couched in slightly different terms, come at the end: "God make yow ryȝht a good man, and sende Goddis blessyng and myn"; "God kepe you and send you hes blyssyng wyth myn."[12] The following are examples of forms other than "God's blessing": "þe wyfe of Harman hathe þe name of Owre Lady, whos blyssyn ye haue and myn"; "Ryght welbelouyd son, I grete you well and send you Cristes blissyng and myne."[13]

The pattern persists well into the sixteenth century: so in Sir Thomas More's last letter to Margaret Roper, 5 July 1535: "I sende nowe vnto my goode dowghter Clemente her algorisme stone and I sende her and my goode sonne and all hers

[9] *The Stonor Letters and Papers*, ed. C. L. Kingsford (Camden Soc., 3rd series 29–30, 1919), i. 165.

[10] *Ibid.*, p. 102.

[11] Agnes to John I, not after 1449; Margaret to John II, 27 May 1478 (Gairdner's editions [1900, 1904], 70/93, 818/933).

[12] Agnes to Edmond I, 4 Feb. 1445; Margaret to John III, 23 Nov. 1472 (Gairdner 46/62, 707/816).

[13] Agnes to John I, probably 21 Nov. 1451; Margaret to John III, 23 May 1475 (Gairdner 162/196, 758/871).

Goddes blissinge and myne"; Sir Thomas Wyatt to his son, 1537: "I send you gods blessing and myne" (at the end); Sir William Plumpton to his son, between 1538 and 1547: "Son Robart Plompton, I hertely recommend me to you, and sending you and your brother God blesing and mine."[14]

Here then are more than forty cases of this pattern of blessing in English in the fifteenth and sixteenth centuries. The most striking feature of them is that every one without exception— unlike the eleventh- and twelfth-century forerunners—is used by a parent to a child. There can be little doubt that the pattern had come to be considered peculiarly appropriate to that relationship. *Pearl* is admittedly earlier than any of the surviving English examples except perhaps the one in *Arthour and Merlin;* but the usage is so well established in the fifteenth century that it must have had a considerable history, to which Sampson's French examples further testify. The use of the form at the end of the poem thus perfectly accords with the natural interpretation of line 233, "Ho watȝ me nerre þen aunte or nece" [She was closer to me than an aunt or niece]—the poet is speaking of his child.[15]

Appendix

Since this note was written I have come upon the same form of blessing in a number of other places, both in letters and in literature. The most important examples were printed in *R.E.S.,* N.S. xviii (1967), p. 294. The opportunity of the present publication has been taken to add to them, in this conflated statement, the rest of those I have so far found; no doubt a systematic search would turn up more, but the result would be unlikely to justify the labour.

[14] *The Correspondence of Sir Thomas More*, ed. E. F. Rogers (Princeton, 1947), p. 564; *Life and Letters of Sir Thomas Wyatt*, ed. K. Muir (Liverpool, 1963), p. 39; *Plumpton Correspondence*, ed. T. Stapleton (Camden Soc., 1839), pp. 234–235.

[15] End of original Note. [Ed.]

The use of the formula outside letters is not restricted without exception to a parent addressing a child. One example is entirely unconnected with this relationship, and I can suggest no special explanation of it. In *The Castle of Perseverance* Humanum Genus addresses Ira:

> Wrethe, for þi councel hende
> Haue þou Goddys blyssynge and myn.[16]
>
> [Wrath, for your kind advice
> may you receive God's blessing and mine.]

In other cases a parental relation exists, but spiritually, not physically. This is best seen in the letters of John Shillingford, mayor of Exeter, concerning a mission that he and some colleagues carried out in 1447–1448 on behalf of the city to the Chancellor in London. In three letters Shillingford himself reports that the Chancellor received him affably and said that "y sholde have Goddes blessyng and his"; and in another his representative William Spere writes that he delivered a letter from Shillingford to the Chancellor through the Recorder, who "putte hyt yn to my lordes blessed hond, and my lord with a gladde contynance receyved the letter and seid that the Maier and alle the comynes sholde have Cristis blessyng and his."[17] The Chancellor was John Kemp, Cardinal Archbishop of Canterbury. Shillingford's respectful conclusion to a draft letter to him eloquently expresses his view of the relation between them: "Please your gode and gracious lordship to have yn rem[em]brance that I and all the Comminalte of the seide Cite ben your gostly children and your men at your commaundement and ever shall be by Godds mercy, whiche preserve your gode and gracious lordship and your blessed faderhed yn

---

[16] *The Macro Plays*, ed. F. J. Furnivall and A. W. Pollard (E.E.T.S., E.S. 91, 1904), p. 110, l. 1105; ed. M. Eccles (E.E.T.S. 262, 1969), p. 35, l. 1102.

[17] *Letters and Papers of John Shillingford*, ed. S. A. Moore (Camden Soc., 1871), pp. 8, 15, 22, 63.

his high mercy."[18] The Chancellor's use of the blessing formula is probably to be seen as a continuation of the earlier use by ecclesiastical personages noticed in the opening paragraph of the note above. An example at a more modest level appears in *The Cloud of Unknowing,* at the end of which the author takes leave of the disciple to whom he has addressed the book: "Farewel, goostly freende, in Goddes blessing & myne ! & I beseche Almiȝti God þat trewe pees, hole counseil, & goostly coumforte in God wiþ habundaunce of grace, euirmore be wiþ þee & alle Goddes louers in eerþe"[19] [Farewell, kinsman in the spirit, in God's blessing and mine; and I beseech Almighty God that true peace, wholesome mind, and spiritual comfort in God with abundant grace may forever be with you and all on earth who love God].

Other examples of the formula are typically parental. In the *Paston Letters* it appears not only in the normal composition of letters as described above but also in a report by Edmond Paston II to his elder brother John III in a letter of 1471: "My modyre gretys ȝow wel and send ȝow Goddys blyssyng and heres," and another by John III to John II in 1475: "My modyr sendyth yow Godys blyssing and hyrs." A particularly instructive case is a draft by John III of two letters which he asks his mother to send in furtherance of his plans to marry Margery Brews—the letters to be written "of some other manys hand." The first, addressed to Dame Elizabeth Brews, opens with the conventional terms of polite society: "Ryght worchepfull and my verry good lady and cosyn, as hertly as I can I recomand me to yow"; but the second, destined for John himself, uses the "parental" form: "I gret yow well and send yow Godys blyssyng and myn."[20] Earlier in the Paston collection the letter written to his son by William de la Pole, Duke of

---

[18] *Ibid.*, p. 29.

[19] Ed. Phyllis Hodgson (E.E.T.S. 218, 1944), p. 133. I owe this reference to Mr. E. P. Wilson.

[20] Gairdner, LXXXV/789, 763/876, 801/915.

Suffolk, on going into exile—in fact to his death—on 30 April 1450 lays particular stress on the usual relationship: "And last of alle, as hertily and as lovyngly as ever fader blessed his child in erthe, I yeve [give] you þe blessyng of oure Lord and of me."[21] And in the Stonor collection a letter of 1478 to Dame Elizabeth Stonor from Thomas Betson reports that "yff my lady your modyr mete my cossen Anne, she will say no more but 'Godes blissynge have ye and myne,' and so goo hir waye forthe as thow she had no joye off hir"[22] [if my lady your mother meets my cousin Anne, she will say no more but "God's blessing have you and mine," and so go her way as though she were not pleased with her]. Since "my lady your modyr" was "my cossen Anne's" grandmother, this is effectively in the parental tradition.

The remaining examples are all literary. In the York play of *Noah* the closing lines, spoken by Noe to his sons, are

> And wende we hense [And go we hence] in haste
> In goddis blissyng & myne,

and in *Abraham's Sacrifice* Abraham, as he prepares to kill Isaac, says

> Fare-well, in goddis dere blissyng
> And myn, for euer and ay [forever and always].[23]

In the Brome play of *Abraham* the blessing is repeated in slightly differing terms:

> A ! Ysaac, my owyn son soo dere,
> Godes blyssyng I ȝyffe the, and myn

and

---

[21] *Ibid.*, 91/117.
[22] Kingsford, no. 224.
[23] *York Plays*, ed. L. Toulmin Smith (Oxford, 1885), IX.321–322, X.295–296.

Now, Ysaac, with all my breth
  My blyssyng I ȝeve þe upon thys lond,
And Godes also ther-to, i-wys.[24]

[Now, Isaac, I give you my blessing
  here as earnestly as I can,
  and God's also in addition, indeed.]

In the *Ludus Coventriae* version the formula is expanded:

Al-myghty god þat best may
his dere blyssyng he graunt þe
And my blyssyng þou haue all way
in what place þat evyr þou be[25]

and in the Chester play still further elaborated:

My blessing, deere sonne, give I the
and thy mothers with hart so free;
the blessing of the Trynitie,
my deare sonne, on the lighte ![26]

[Dear son, I give you my blessing,
and that of your mother noble in heart;
may the blessing of the Trinity,
my dear son, come down upon you!]

In the Towneley play of *Isaac,* Isaac blesses Jacob thus:

The blyssyng my fader gaf to me
god of heuen & I gif the.[27]

And Malory tells how Merlin asked the dying Uther Pendragon, "Syre, shall your sone Arthur be kyng after your dayes of this realme with all the appertenaunce?" Uther replied: "I gyve hym Gods blissyng and myne, and byd hym pray for my soule,

[24] *The Non-Cycle Mystery Plays,* ed. O. Waterhouse (E.E.T.S., E.S.104, 1909; revised ed. to be published 1970), Brome play ll. 114–115, 214–216.
[25] Ed. K. S. Block (E.E.T.S., E.S. 120, 1922), V.29–32.
[26] Ed. H. Deimling (E.E.T.S., E.S. 62, 1892), IV.333–336.
[27] Ed. G. England and A. W. Pollard (E.E.T.S., E.S. 71, 1897), V.7–8.

and righteuously and worshipfully that he clayme the croune upon forfeture of my blessyng."[28]

In comparison with all these other examples the use in *The Castle of Perseverance* remains puzzling. In spite of it there can be no doubt that the formula in lay use was overwhelmingly associated with a parent's blessing.

[28] *The Works of Sir Thomas Malory*, ed. E. Vinaver (2nd ed., Oxford, 1967), p. 12.

19

PEARL AND THE AUGUSTINIAN DOCTRINE OF CREATION

Alfred L. Kellogg

IN LINES 273–276 OF THE MIDDLE ENGLISH *Pearl*, THE PEARL-maiden, having doffed her crown in the joy of reunion, replaces it firmly and proceeds to lecture the dreamer upon his ill-advised comments. In his complaint over her death, he has recklessly impugned the justice of God:

> And þou hatȝ called þy wyrde a þef,
> Þat oȝt of noȝt hatȝ mad þe cler;
> Þou blameȝ þe bote of þy meschef,
> Þou art no kynde jueler.[1]

Reprinted, by permission of the author and of the editor, from *Traditio*, XII (1956), 406–407, where it appeared under the title "Note on Line 274 of the *Pearl*." Footnote 6 contains some new material. Translations have been supplied by the author.

[1] *Pearl*, ed. E. V. Gordon (Oxford, 1953), p. 10. The great difficulty in translating this passage is that the line in question contains a play on the words "something out of nothing," highly practicable in Middle English, but, because of shifts in connotation, hardly meaningful in modern English. Furthermore, the word "wyrde," having sinister connotations, both before and after the *Pearl* poet, is here used, not in terms of these connotations, but rather in the sense of a kindly Divine Providence, the significance of whose actions the Dreamer's mortal perceptions are completely incapable of apprehending. I should thus translate the four lines as follows: "And Divine Providence hast thou called 'Thief,' / That (same Providence) which out of the void brought thee into being (made something out of nothing). / For the evil befallen thee, thou blamest the Good. / Thou are no true jeweller."

The second of these lines, "þat oȝt of noȝt hatȝ mad þe cler," is a difficult one and has been the subject of varying interpretations,[2] the prevailing one being that followed in the latest edition of the *Pearl*. Thus Gordon translates, " 'that has clearly made for you something out of nothing,' i.e. has made an eternal pearl out of a short-lived rose."[3] However, what is not generally recognized in the translation of this line is that the language here used is not purely the product of the poet's mind, but is in fact a rather well-known allusion. A study of this allusion and its occurrence in other Middle English poets will, I think, yield a somewhat different translation.

Perhaps the center of Augustinian metaphysics is the conception of *creatio ex nihilo*. In the *Contra Fortunatum Manichaeum* St. Augustine states the principle very directly:

> I say that the soul was made by God, as were all other things made by God. . . . If, however, you seek to know whence God made the soul, recall that—in accord with you—I professed the belief that God is omnipotent. However, he is not omnipotent who seeks assistance in some material thing whence he may create what he wishes. From this it follows that, according to our faith, all that God made through His Word and His Wisdom, He created out of nothing.[4]

This conception of creation from nothingness the Middle English poet seems characteristically to have treated in the con-

---

[2] In his first edition of 1891 Gollancz felt that one could more easily understand the line by reversing the order to read "of noȝt oȝt," the sense being that the dreamer had not been robbed in the least. The influence of this interpretation is perhaps to be found in G. G. Coulton's version (1906): "which truly hath robbed thee of nought, I swear."

[3] *Pearl*, ed. Gordon, 57. With this reading compare Osgood (1906): "That hath clearly made for thee something out of nothing, a pearl from an ephemeral rose"; and Chase (1932): "Thy fate from nought made aught for thee."

[4] Animam dico factam a Deo, ut caetera omnia quae a Deo, facta sunt. . . . Si autem quaeris unde Deus animam fecit, memento confiteri me tecum, Deum esse omnipotentem. Omnipotens autem non est qui quaerit adjuvari aliqua materia unde faciat quod velit. Ex quo est consequens, ut secundum fidem nostram, omnia quae Deus fecit per Verbum et Sapientiam suam, de nihilo fecerit. *Contra Fortunatum* 1.13 (PL 42.117).

text of the praise of God, a context already established by St. Augustine and followed by the scriptural commentators.[5] Thus in *Piers Plowman,* Repentance exclaims:

"Now god," quod he, "that of thi goodnesse · gonne the worlde make,
And of nauȝte madest auȝte · and man moste liche to thi-selue. . . ."[6]

and in the Envoy to the ballad *Truth,* Chaucer advises Vache:

Crye him mercy, that of his hy goodnesse
Made thee of noght. . . .[7]

If one were to put together the above passages from Chaucer and Langland, he would get something like "Made the auȝte of nauȝte," a result reasonably close to the line in question. Hence I suggest as a possible translation: "that out of nothing has clearly made you something." In this interpretation the Pearl-maiden would not be saying that God has favored the Dreamer by making his mortal rose into an immortal pearl, but rather that the Dreamer, instead of complaining against God for a presumed injustice, should be praising God for his very existence.[8]

---

[5] See *Confessions,* XI, 5, and Nicholas of Lyra's comment on *Apoc.,* IV, 11: "Dignus es, Domine Deus noster, accipere gloriam, ac honorem et virtutem, quia tu creasti omnia." Nicholas interprets "Quia tu creasti omnia" (because Thou hast created all things) as "de *nihilo* producendo" (by producing [all things] from *nothing*) in *Glossa Ordinaria cum Postilla Nicolai Lyrani* (Lyons, 1589).

[6] "Now God," said he, "that of Thy goodness, did make the world,/ And out of nothing created something, and man most like unto Thyself" (B Text V, 488–489). See also Skeat's note to the passage, where he points out the connection of the following "O felix culpa" [O fortunate fault] with the Canticle "Exultet" (*Piers Plowman,* ed. W. W. Skeat [Oxford, 1886]). A recent allusion, very much in these terms, can be found in Joyce: "O foenix culprit! Ex nickylow malo comes michelmassed bonum" (*Finnegans Wake* [New York: Viking Press, 1939], p. 23).

[7] Lines 24–25, in *Works,* ed. F. N. Robinson (2nd ed., Boston, 1957), p. 536.

[8] Cf. *Everyman,* lines 56–57: "They thanke me not for þe pleasure that I to them ment,/ Nor yet for theyr beynge that I them haue lent" [They thank me not for the pleasure that I meant for them, nor for their being that I have lent them].

20

PEARL 609–611

F. T. Visser

THE FOLLOWING PASSAGE IN *Pearl* (XI, 609–611) APPEARS TO have puzzled the ingenuity of various philologists:

> Hys fraunchyse is large þat euer dard
> To Hym þat matȝ in synne rescoghe;
> No blysse betz fro hem reparde. . . .

One of the several rival interpretations is: "His [God's] generosity, which is always inscrutable [lit. lay hidden], is abundant to the man who recovers his soul from sin. From such men no happiness is withheld." This interpretation is objected to by E. V. Gordon (ed. 1953 of *Pearl,* Notes, p. 67), who, observing that this is a notoriously difficult passage, remarks *"þat euer dard* is an unnatural phrase to use of the inscrutability of God's grace, since it is in the past tense, and ME. *dare,* though it may mean 'lie hidden,' bears usually a connotation of fear; moreover, *Hym þat matȝ in synne rescoghe* 'him that makes rescue in sin' certainly seems more applicable to God than to a man who rescues his own soul, especially in a passage emphasizing the bounty of God's grace, not grace conferred according to merit."

Another interpretation is that proposed by C. G. Osgood

Reprinted, by permission of the author and of the editor, from *English Studies,* XXXIX (1958), 20–23.

and Sir I. Gollancz in their editions of *Pearl* (1906 & 1921 respectively): "That man's privilege is great who ever stood in awe of Him [God] who rescues sinners. From such men no happiness is withheld." To E. V. Gordon (*loc. cit.*) this interpretation "would seem preferable, and although no parallel use of *dare* with *to* can be adduced, it seems not unlikely that the poet, hard pressed for a rhyme-word (in a series of six), is using *dard* in the sense 'cowered to, shrank in fear before,' having in mind possibly such phrases as *bowed to, louted to.*" This interpretation, however, is opposed by R. Morris (*Academy* xxxix) and K. Sisam (*Fourteenth Century Verse and Prose,* p. 227), the latter observing that "it is difficult to believe that even a poet hard pressed would use *dard to Hym* to mean, 'feared Him.' "

It appears from this that it is especially the sense and construction of *dard* which has been the chief obstacle to a satisfactory solution.

One wonders why none of the above mentioned linguists should have proposed to take "dard to Hym" as meaning "dared to go to Him," "had the courage to turn to Him," since this would render the passage quite easily understandable. How strong a case can be made out for this interpretation appears from the following points:

In the first place there is the fact that in Middle English nearly all the other "auxiliaries" could be used with a connotation of motion in combination with an adjunct denoting direction, so that "I must to Oxford," "I shall to Oxford" stood for "I must go to O."; "I shall go to O." etc. The usage dates from the earliest Old English and was of Germanic origin; it was common in OHG and OS, and is still current in modern Dutch, German and the Scandinavian languages. To call this idiom elliptical, as OED does, is misleading, since it would suggest that the construction with the infinitive of a verb of motion (e.g. *go*) after the auxiliary should be the regular ("correct") one. A few Old and Middle English examples follow. (Later examples

339

—which certainly do occur—have not been adduced, since they are irrelevant in discussion of the language in *Pearl*.)

SHALL. Beowulf 2815, *Ic him, æfter sceal.* | Idem 1179, þonne þu *forþ scyle.* | Ælfric, Saints' Lives 33, 86, þin fæder *sceal* mid me *to mynstre.* | 12.. O.E. Homl. (Morris) ii, 183, for þine gulte i *shal* nu *to pine.* | c1200 Vices & V. (EETS) 25, 30, þo ðe euele habbeþ idon and naht ibett, he *sculen in to ðan eche fiere.* | c1300 Harrowing of Hell (Everym. ed.) p. 148, Who that ones commys helle within He *shalle* never *owte.* | 1297 R. Glouc., 7113, þe ssephurdes & þe ssep al so *ssolleþ to þe pine of helle.* | c1330 Why Werre (Wright, Polit. Songs of Engl.) 171, He *shal into the freitur* and ben i-mad ful glad. | 1350 Will of Palerne 2361, þe beres fel *schal* neuer *fro my bac.* | c1386 Chaucer, C. T. D1637, Thou *shalt* with me *to helle* to-night. | c1390 tr. Liber Catonis, in Minor Poems Vern. MS (EETS) 44, Whon þou *schalt to market,* A-tyre þe as þou can. | 1390 Gower, Conf. Am., (Morley 1889) IV p. 182, I wot never what I am, Ne *whider* I *shall,* ne whenne I cam. | c1450 Capgrave, Life St. Aug. xi, þe same man stand in study wheither he *schal to þe good wey* or nowt. | c1450 Cov. Myst. (Pollard) Mary Magd. 1183, *On xall* my westment and myn aray. | 1475–88 Cely Papers (Malden) no 98, as for Botterell he *shall owte of preson* and all that were ther yn for the same mater.

SHOULD. Ælfred, Oros. 6, 31, He nyste *hwær* he *ut sceolde.* | Idem 3, 5, hie . . . wiston *hwider* hie *sceoldon.* | Idem 86, 3, ic ær sæde þæt we *to helle sceoldon.* | Ælfric, Gen. XXII, 4, þa dune . . þær þær hig *to sceoldon* to ofsleanne Isaac. | c1275 Layamon 4729, Brenne . . flockede his cnihtes alse hii *solde to fihte.* | c1377 Piers Pl. XV, One . . tolde me *whyder I shulde.* | 1462 Marg. Paston, 18 May (in: Paston Lett.), sche seithe . . her frendes thynke that she *schulde up to London.*

WILL. Beowulf 318, Ic *to sæ wille.* | Leechdoms (Cockayne) ii, 134, 22, ær *him* se fefer *to wille.* | Paris Psalter (Krapp) 100, 1, Hwænne ðu *me wille to.* | Genesis 760, Nu *wille* ic eft ðam lige near. | 11.. O.E. Homl. (Morris) i, 35, þenne heo [sc. the soul] *wulle ut of þon licome.* | a1225 Ancr. R. 60 (MS T.), Hund *wil in* at open dure. | 1250 Fox & Wolf 244, *Weder wolt* þow? | 13.. Curs. M. 20356, now my ladi *wil me fro.* | c1330 Sir Orfeo 316, *þider ichill,* bi Godes name! | c1386 Chaucer C. T. B1766, Mordre *wol out.* | Idem D1387, Seyde this yeman, "*wiltow fer* to day?" | c1400 Gawain & Gr. Kn. 2132, Bot I *wyl to þe chapel,* for chance þat may falle. | c1400 Maundev. 19, 8, He may go be londe ʒif he *will to jerusalem.* | c1425 Lydgate, Siege Theb. (EETS) 4, 1862, For he *woll forth.* | c1440 Tale of Guiscardo & Ghism. (EETS) 35, 579, Youth *wol to youth.*

WOULD. O.E. Chron. an 1009, þa hi *to scipan woldon.* | Ælfric, Num.
XXI, 33, Hig gewendon þonne and *woldon to Basan.* | a1240 Sawles
Warde 9, þe þeof *walde to his hus.* | 1330 Sir Orfeo 71, Ac ever she held
in a cry And *wold up and away.* | Idem 378, He *wolt in* after, *ȝif he
miȝt.* | Idem 296, neuer he nist *whider þai wold* | c1350 Will. of Pal. 735,
a-way wold it neuer. | a1425 (c1400) Laud Bk. (EETS) 10862, He held
his horse & *wolde no ferre.* | c1485 Tale of Guiscardo & Ghism. (EETS)
335, She said *to her chamber* . . she *would* forth right.

MAY. O.E. Gospels, Mk. X 15, Swa hwylc swa Godes rice ne onfehð
swa lytling, ne *mæg* he *on pæt.* | Genesis 381, Ic . . ne *mæg of ðissum
lioðobendum.* | Crist & Satan 420, Nu ic þe halsige . . þæt ic *up heonon
mæge and mote* mid minre mægþe.[1] | Ælfric, Gen. VI, 21, of eallum
mettum, þe *to mete magon.* | c1290 Southern Leg., Mich. (Ld. EETS)
604, It ne *may no feor* for þe colde. | c1330 Arth. & Merl. (Kölbing)
7907, For we no *mow no whar oway.* |

MIGHT. Beowulf 754, No ðy ær *fram meahte.* | O.E. Chron. an. 1131
(MS E), þær man him held þæt he ne *mihte na east na west.* | O.E.
Chron. (Peterb.) an. 1137, þat he ne *myhte nowiderwardes.* | c1290
Southern Leg., Becket (Ld. MS; EETS) 1160, He sat adoun and ne *miȝte
no fer.* | a 1375 Will. of Palerne 2441, Meliors was al mat; sche ne *miȝt
no furþer.* | c1386 Chaucer. C.T. A4117, it was nyght and *forther myghte*
they noght. | c1400 Maundev. 99, 13, he was so wery, þat he *myghte no
ferthere.* | a1400 Lanfranc, Science of Cirurgie (EETS) 139, 10, He
myȝte forþ wiþ no word. | ?a1400 Wars Alex. (Skeat) 1369, þat he
feghys & fermes so fast to þe wall, So negh þat vnneth a nedyll *myght*
narowly *bytwene.*

MOTE. Crist & Satan 622, Wenaþ þæt heo *moten to þære mæran byrig
up to englum,* swa oðre dydon. | Idem 300, Us ongean cumað þusend
engla, gif [we] *þider moton.* | Idem 420, Nu ic þe halsige . . . þæt ic *up
heonon mæge and mote.* | O. E. Riddles (Krapp) 39, 20, Næfre hio . . .
to helle mot. | a1338 Mannyng, Chron. II, 308, *Ferrere mote* he nouht. |
c1374 Chaucer, Troil. III, 1475, Now fele I that myn herte *mot a-two.*

MUST. Ælfric, Saints' Lives 3, 328, He begeat leafe þæt he *of þam lande*

---

[1] Cf. what G. Ph. Krapp (ed. Junius MS 1931, Note, p. 240) says
about this passage: "Thorpe, Bouterwek assume a loss in the MS. after
mægðe. Ettmüller supplies *feran* after *mægðe* and assumes a loss after
feran. Graz, *Eng. Stud.* XXI, 21, would either read *fare* for *mægðe,* or
assume a loss in the MS. But the text may stand, with the verb of motion
omitted (my italics) after *mæge* and *mote.*"

moste. | (Idem 10, 221, þæt is þæt se sunu sceolde symle fon *to þam hade* . . æfter his fæder geendunge and non oðer ne *moste.*) | 1250 Fox & Wolf 85, *Adoun* he *moste.* | c1386 Chaucer C.T. B281, Allas! *unto the Barbre nacioun* I *mooste* anoon. | c1425 Cast. Persev. 3038 in Macro Plays 167, For, wrechyd sowle, þou muste to helle (OED). |

MUN. c1435 Torr. Portugal 1113, Sir, he said, I trow, she *mone To the prynce off Aragon.* | c1475 Rauf Coilȝear 425, Thow *mon to Paris* to the King (OED).[2]

Secondly there is the fact that the O.E. verbs *(ge)neþan* and *geþristian*, and the ME verb *adventure*, all of them synonyms or near-synonyms of *to dare* = "to have boldness or courage," "to be so bold as," are frequently used in combination with an adjunct of direction to express motion, e.g.:

Beowulf 508, git . . *on deop wæter* . . *neþdon.* | Idem 537, wit *on garsecg ut* . . *neðdon.* | Rune Poem (Dobbie) 64, gif hi sculun *neþan on nacan tealtum.* | Judith 277, He *in þæt burgeteld* neðde. | Juliana 302, *Neþde ic* . . *þær ic Neron besweac.* | Andreas 950, Nu ðu, Andreas, scealt . . *geneðan in gramra gripe.* | Alfred, Oros. (EETS) 77, 20, He *geneðde under anne elpend.* | Fates of the Apostles (Vercelli Bk, Krapp) 50, Thomas þriste *geneðde on Indea.*

Ancient Laws & Instit. of Engl. (Thorpe) Th. i, 324, 12, Gif morðwyrhtan . . *to þam geþristian* . .

c1340 Alisaunder (Skeat) 902, þe . . Atenieeins *auntred hym till.* | c1350 Gamelyn, in M.E. Metr. Romances (French & Hale) 666, I wil *auntre to þe dore.* | 1436 Libelle of Engl. Polycye (Warner) 324, They *aventure* ful gretly *unto the baye* For salte (MMED). |

Lastly—and this is perhaps the strongest point—the following quotations show that the verb *to dare* was actually used with a connotation of motion. Though the evidence is meagre —no Old English and only two Middle English examples having been found[3]—it at least proves that in this respect *to dare*

[2] With *can* I have only been able to find later instances, e.g. a1536 Tindale, Pathw. Holy Script., Wks I 27, "The more tangled art thou therein, and *canst nowhere through*"; c1620 Ben Jonson, "The Golden Age Restored" (in *Songs & Poems of B. J.*, 1924), p. 124, "And I *can not away.*"

[3] A later instance is 1697 Dryden, Virg. Past. VI, 6, "Apollo . . . bade me feed My fatning Flocks, nor *dare beyond the Reed*" (OED).

was not an exception among the auxiliaries. (It may by the way be observed that in Pres. D. Dutch the type "Hij durft niet naar school" [lit. "He dares not to school"] represents current idiom.)

c1380 Sir Ferumb. (EETS) 3726, *Ferrer* ne *draste* þay noȝt for fere.
c1385 Chaucer, L.G.W. 2215, For though so be that shyp or boot here come, *Home to my contree dar* I not for drede.

If what has been postulated above should be applicable to the construction "dard to Hym"in *Pearl* (and when *euer* is not taken in the sense "always," but in the sense "at any time"), the translation of the passage would run: "That man's privilege is great who (at a certain moment in his life) had the courage to go or turn to Him [God] who rescues sinners. From such men no happiness is withheld."

INDEX*

* The titles of literary studies have been excluded, and the names of contributors appear only as cited by other contributors.